PROCEDURES FOR THE PROFESSIONAL SECRETARY

Patsy J. Fulton, Ph.D., CPS

President
Brookhaven College
Farmers Branch, Texas

Joanna D. Hanks

Associate Professor and Director
Center for Office Development
J. Sargeant Reynolds Community College
Richmond, Virginia

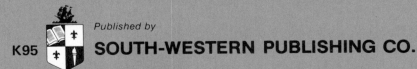

K95

Published by

SOUTH-WESTERN PUBLISHING CO.

CINCINNATI   WEST CHICAGO, IL   DALLAS   PELHAM MANOR, NY   PALO ALTO, CA

PREFACE

Being a professional secretary today is a great challenge. In developing this textbook we, the authors, have recognized the challenges facing the secretary. We have designed this textbook to prepare you for job responsibilities requiring a high level of skill, depth of understanding and knowledge, and a large degree of motivation and initiative. We have also encouraged you to take a realistic look at your abilities as well as your reasons for pursuing a secretarial career.

Procedures for the Professional Secretary has been organized into six parts. In Part 1, "The Secretarial World—What Is Your Role?" you examine the secretarial profession and what it takes to become part of this profession. You are given instructions on how to apply for a secretarial position. You are also provided with information about efficiently managing your work as a secretary. In Part 2, "Interpersonal Relations—How Do You Communicate?" you learn about the communication process, how good communication results in the achievement of effective office relationships, and the responsibilities of a secretary who supervises other employees. In Part 3, "Correspondence Responsibilities—What Skills Do You Need?" you study correspondence related activities from typewriting to dictating-transcribing and composing original documents to handling incoming-outgoing mail. In Part 4, "Administrative Support Responsibilities—When and How Do You Provide Assistance?" you are presented with procedures for using reference sources and preparing reports, assisting at meetings and conferences, handling financial records, and planning and making executive travel arrangements. In Part 5, "The Office Today and Tomorrow—Where Are We Headed?" you are acquainted with the technology prevalent in today's offices. Topics such as data and word processing, reprographics, and telecommunications are in this part. In Part 6, "Records Management—How Do You File and Find Information?" you are given the rules of filing. Filing systems are discussed with special emphasis given to automated methods for information storage and retrieval.

Each of the twenty-one chapters in this text includes aids to help you learn and remember the information presented. General Objectives are given at the beginning of each chapter. At the end of each chapter are Professional Pointers, For Your Review questions, a Case Problem, and Production Projects. The General Objectives enable you to know what you are expected to achieve in each chapter. The Professional Pointers are tips that can be used in your work as a secretary. The For Your Review questions help you recall the main points in a chapter. The Case Problem consists of an office problem for you to solve. It will help you become aware of ways to solve realistic problems that may occur in the office. The Production Projects give you an opportunity to assimilate the knowledge and skills that you have learned in the text. You are given assignments related to the objectives of the chapter. You complete each assignment as though you were working in an office situation. You are required to think through each assignment and to make sound decisions about the work that is to be done.

At the back of this text is a Reference Section. Covered in the Reference Section are topics relating to English fundamentals such as abbreviations, capitalization, numbers, often misused words and phrases, plurals and possessives, proofreaders' marks, punctuation, spelling, and word division. This material was designed to help you briefly review the language arts rules that you should know and be able to apply in your work as a secretary.

A *Supplies Inventory* accompanies your text. In the first part of the *Supplies Inventory*, you will find the forms needed to complete the Production Projects given in the text. Simulated office activities, called Office Applications, are also in the *Supplies Inventory*. In performing these simulated activities, you work as a supervising secretary for Ms. Eleanor Tennenbaum, sales manager for Jarrell Office Supplies Company. The last part of the *Supplies Inventory* contains a Language Skills Practice. The exercises in the Language Skills Practice correlate with the Reference Section of the text. By completing the language exercises, you will improve your familiarity with the Reference Section as well as strengthen your skills in grammar, punctuation, spelling, and word division.

Printed tests are available that measure your knowledge of the information within this text. Your instructor may use these tests to determine how well you have learned the material in each part of the text.

We wish you success and happiness as you prepare to enter the business world as a secretary. You are entering a profession in which there are many opportunities for fulfillment and rewards.

Patsy J. Fulton
Joanna D. Hanks

CONTENTS

Part 1 The Secretarial World—
What Is Your Role?

Chapter 1 Defining the Secretarial Position   2

Chapter 2 Applying for a Secretarial Position   20

Chapter 3 Managing Your Work Efficiently   44

Part 2 Interpersonal Relations—
How Do You Communicate?

Chapter 4 Communicating—The Process and the Product   74

Chapter 5 Developing the Office Team   100

Chapter 6 Responding to Office Callers   125

Chapter 7 Supervising Employees   147

Part 3 Correspondence Responsibilities—
What Skills Do You Need?

Chapter 8 Using Typewriting Equipment and Supplies   170

Chapter 9 Preparing Office Correspondence   191

Chapter 10 Utilizing Dictation and Transcription Skills   215

Chapter 11 Processing Mail and Using Shipping Services   239

Part 4 Administrative Support Responsibilities— When and How Do You Provide Assistance?

Chapter 12   Using Reference Sources and Preparing Reports   268

Chapter 13   Assisting in Meeting and Conference Preparation   302

Chapter 14   Providing Financial Assistance   325

Chapter 15   Making Travel Arrangements   361

Part 5 The Office Today and Tomorrow— Where Are We Headed?

Chapter 16   Exploring Data Processing   384

Chapter 17   Analyzing Word Processing   406

Chapter 18   Understanding Office Reprographics   426

Chapter 19   Knowing about Telecommunications   449

Part 6 Records Management— How Do You File and Find Information?

Chapter 20   Managing Records Effectively   470

Chapter 21   Understanding the Technology of Records Management   514

Reference Section   540

Index   563

PART 1
The Secretarial World— What Is Your Role?

Chapter 1   Defining the Secretarial Position

Chapter 2   Applying for a Secretarial Position

Chapter 3   Managing Your Work Efficiently

Chapter 1

DEFINING THE SECRETARIAL POSITION

The need for secretaries will never disappear. There are approximately 4 million secretaries employed in the United States today. Secretarial positions are expected to increase faster than the average for other occupations through the 1980s and into the 1990s. The United States Department of Labor predicts that more than 5.5 million secretaries will be needed by 1990. Literally hundreds of thousands of jobs will become available for secretaries as new businesses are created, existing corporations grow, and the amount of paperwork in most offices continues to increase.

Technology has had a great impact on secretarial work. The ways secretaries perform their duties are affected by technological changes. Much of the routine work that was done manually by secretaries in the past is now done by machines. Today secretaries have more administrative duties and more opportunities to work directly with their employers in company management.

As you discover in this book the advantages of a secretarial career, you will find that your success will depend on your determination to be among the best in your field. The successful secretary continually strives to improve basic skills and to learn the nature of changes in the office. Change has created new and challenging work for secretaries, and successful secretaries must be adaptable to change.

General Objectives

Your general objectives for Chapter 1 are to:

1. *Define the title of secretary*
2. *Explain the different titles used to describe secretarial work*
3. *Describe the personal qualities necessary to succeed in a secretarial position*
4. *List and explain the skills a secretary must have*
5. *Discuss the characteristics of a professional secretary*
6. *Discuss ways in which a secretary can grow professionally*

THE SECRETARIAL TITLE

What is a secretary? What does the title mean? The largest organization of secretaries in the world, Professional Secretaries International (PSI), defines a *secretary* as:

> ... an executive assistant who possesses a mastery of office skills, demonstrates the ability to assume responsibility without direction or supervision, exercises initiative and judgment, and makes decisions within the scope of assigned authority.

A *title* is the name given to a particular classification of work and usually reflects the nature of the work. You should always question the duties to be performed when applying for a secretarial position, because some positions are advertised as secretarial when in fact they are not. A summary of the duties frequently assigned to secretaries is listed in Illus. 1-1. This list is not all inclusive, but it should give you a good idea of the nature of secretarial tasks.

Some titles that describe secretarial positions with which you should be familiar are listed here.

Clerk stenographer
Receptionist-Secretary
Correspondence secretary
Word processing operator
Executive secretary/Administrative assistant
Administrative secretary
Office assistant
Educational secretary
Legal secretary
Medical secretary
Technical secretary
Bilingual secretary

Because of the multitude of titles used to describe secretarial work, you should take time to research a position before applying for it. It is wise to ask questions about the level of responsibility as well as the duties involved in the position for which you are applying. Some large organizations have several levels of responsibility associated with different secretarial positions. An entry level position, for example, may be as a stenographer. A top-level secretarial position may be as an executive secretary. Illus. 1-2 gives a comprehensive description of various secretarial positions as compiled by the Administrative Management Society. Secretaries who move up through the ranks to top secretarial positions, such as executive secretary, must possess the technical, administrative, and interpersonal skills to advance their careers and earn the recognition they deserve.

SUMMARY OF SECRETARIAL DUTIES

- Type letters in proper style and with correct punctuation.
- Take dictation by shorthand or machine.
- Take direct dictation at the typewriter.
- Transcribe from recorded dictation.
- Open, read, and sort incoming mail.
- Prepare outgoing mail.
- Handle incoming and outgoing telephone calls.
- Arrange appointments and keep a record of them.
- Meet callers at the office.
- Handle certain types of correspondence and communications without assistance.
- Compose letters and draft reports.
- Type from rough drafts. Organize data from rough drafts into finished reports.
- Gather material and assist in the preparation of written reports and speeches. Prepare copy for publication.
- Use reference books of various kinds.
- Take notes at meetings and prepare minutes.
- Keep company financial records including payroll records.
- Handle banking and other financial transactions of the company.
- Keep personal and financial records of the employer.
- Make travel reservations and prepare itineraries.
- Help with travel expense records of the employer.
- Perform mathematical computations.
- Maintain office files.
- Understand the use of as well as prepare office forms.
- Requisition and keep record of office supplies.
- Operate photocopy and other office machines.
- Organize office procedures.
- Supervise other workers.
- Serve as a buffer to relieve your employer of many details.

Illus. 1-1
Typical duties that describe a secretary's responsibilities.

Within this concept a secretary is a highly qualified person who has not only mastered the necessary office skills but has also developed a pleasing personality and good judgment in business deportment. A secretary must know the scope of authority given and must discharge the responsibilities that are within that sphere. For example, the secretary must judge correctly when to follow through independently and when to consult the employer. A secretary is a person capable of making decisions, of skillfully composing correspondence, and perhaps of supervising other office workers.

ADMINISTRATIVE MANAGEMENT SOCIETY (AMS) DESCRIPTIONS OF SECRETARIAL POSITIONS

Title	Description	Title	Description
Word Processing Trainee	Performs routine transcription and manipulation of information from various sources, such as dictation and handwritten copy. Proofreads work, and performs light secretarial duties.	Secretary A	Performs a wide range of secretarial duties for middle management personnel or several individuals. Takes and transcribes and/or composes correspondence that is complex and confidential. Applies a knowledge of company policies and procedures. Possesses above average secretarial and administrative skills.
Word Processing Operator	Uses word processing equipment to input, edit, and revise average to complex typed documents. Adheres to established quality and time standards. Proofreads work, and follows company practices. Uses equipment, such as microprocessor-based, standalone, or shared-logic word processing systems utilizing a CRT. Is familiar with departmental terminology, and performs some general secretarial duties.	Executive Secretary/ Administrative Assistant	Performs a full range of secretarial and administrative duties for a high-level executive. Often relieves the executive of routine tasks. Handles project-oriented duties and may be held accountable for the timely completion of such duties. Possesses an in-depth knowledge of company procedures and structure. Must maintain a high degree of technical skills.
Lead Word Processing Operator	Uses a wide range of equipment to produce and revise complicated documents. Obtains input from various sources including the retrieval of text and data. Directs the activities of lower level operators.	Legal Secretary	Performs a wide range of secretarial duties for one or more members of a firm. Takes and transcribes dictation with a high degree of speed and accuracy. Must understand specific legal terminology within certain areas of specialization. May use word processing equipment.
Secretary B	Performs a limited range of secretarial duties in a small company or for a supervisor in a large firm. Takes and transcribes machine dictation and may answer routine correspondence. Makes appointments and travel arrangements. Screens telephone calls. Maintains filing system.		

Illus. 1-2
Job titles and descriptions of various secretarial positions

IMPORTANT PERSONAL QUALITIES

Being successful in a secretarial position will mean that you must possess certain personal characteristics. Many books have been written and numerous studies made to determine which qualities are essential for success in the secretarial field. Too much emphasis cannot be placed on the need for developing the personal qualities that are discussed in the following paragraphs.

Trustworthiness

A Code of Ethics for the Professional Secretary was adopted by Professional Secretaries International in 1980. This code provides guidelines to govern the professional conduct of all secretaries. The Code of Ethics states that secretaries should "recognize that a position of trust imposes ethical obligations upon secretaries to act for the benefit of employers, clients, and the public . . . ."

A secretary must be a trustworthy individual—one on whom an employer can rely. A secretary is often responsible for handling confidential matters and frequently knows about changes in company policies or personnel before other employees. A secretary must use discretion in disclosing confidential information.

Pleasing Personality

Of utmost importance is a secretary's ability to get along well with people. A secretarial position often requires public contact. A secretary greets callers to the office and handles incoming and outgoing telephone calls. A secretary must maintain a good relationship with the public. In daily contacts with co-workers, the secretary is often the link between top management—the decision makers—and those who carry out the decisions of management. This responsibility requires flexibility, a sincere desire to be part of a team, and true consideration of others.

Dependability

Supervisors learn quickly which of their employees are dependable. Dependability may involve staying late or missing an occasional lunch to finish a rush job or accepting duties that are not a part of your regular work load. A dependable person maintains a good attendance record and strives to be punctual. All these elements of dependability are usually weighed heavily when your performance is evaluated. The secretary who is truly professional can be counted on to get the job done in any situation.

Positive Attitude

As a secretary, if you like your work and experience real job satisfaction, you should have an attitude that affects others positively. The way you think about your position and your employer has a very important bearing on how well you do your work. A good attitude is shown through the quality of your work, by your loyalty to the company, and by your concern for doing a good job. Every position contributes to the objectives of the company. Therefore, you will do a better job if you think your work makes an important contribution to the company.

Illus. 1-3
A good attitude affects others positively and is reflected in your work.

Initiative

Another important quality is initiative. *Initiative* means knowing what work can be done and what responsibilities you can assume without being told what to do. Employees are often criticized because they wait to be told when and how to do almost everything. Secretaries need to learn what work can be done without direct supervision. As you learn various secretarial duties, you will acquire the confidence and expertise you need to exercise the initiative that will make you an asset to the office.

Organizational Ability

A secretary needs to be able to handle a demanding job without showing irritation. Using your judgment in establishing priorities is basic to maintaining a well-organized workday. You may find it useful to make a list at the end of each day of things that must be done the next day. This procedure will ensure that the most important things will be done first. Deciding the order in which tasks should be accomplished will make your job easier. A wise secretary, however, does not schedule too tightly. Some gaps must be left in the day to allow for emergencies or for unexpected jobs that need immediate attention.

NEEDED SECRETARIAL SKILLS

The skills required to perform secretarial tasks are many. The secretary is expected to be proficient in the three *R*'s (reading, writing, and arithmetic) as well as in the ability to type, transcribe, file, and use the telephone. Today's professional secretary must have technical skills in addition to the personal qualities discussed previously.

Minimum standards of performance vary from one company to another. However, the better your overall skills, the greater are your chances of promotion. A beginning secretary plans and works at making his or her skills better than average!

Proficiency in Typewriting, Shorthand, and Transcription

Typewriting is still the major skill required for secretarial positions. The required typing rate varies from 40 to 80 words per minute, with 60 words per minute the average rate that is expected. To determine your typewriting skill businesses give you a five-minute straight copy test, accept your word about your typewriting ability, or check with your school for the grades you received in typewriting. The majority of businesses expect you to be able to type with no more than one error per minute on a five-minute straight copy test. Your goal should be to develop the best typewriting skills possible—in both speed and accuracy.

Although it has been predicted for many years that shorthand will become obsolete, many businesses still require secretaries to take shorthand. The shorthand dictation rate required by most businesses varies from 80 to 120 words per minute. Increasing numbers of secretarial positions, however, do not require shorthand because employers dictate to a recording machine. The secretary at a later time listens through a headset to transcribe the recorded dictation in mailable form.

Your transcription skill—that is, your ability to type correspondence quickly from your shorthand notes or from a transcribing machine—is also important. Most companies do not establish a transcription rate for their employees. A good rate to strive for while you are in school is 30 to 40 net words per minute. *Net words per minute* means that you correct all errors as you transcribe. Transcription skill requires an excellent background in grammar, spelling, and punctuation.

Effective English for Business Communication

A secretary must have good English skills. Enough cannot be said about having a good vocabulary; being able to spell; and knowing the rules of grammar, punctuation, and capitalization. Producing work that is error free involves proofreading, and proofreading involves recognizing all errors in written material. An employer often relies on the secretary to correct errors in English usage.

If you have good English skills, you should make a point of using correct grammar when you speak. Do not be lazy in your diction. Speak clearly, correctly, and courteously. As a representative of a company, you should make a favorable impression each time you speak.

Ability to Operate Office Equipment

As a secretary you should be acquainted with the automated equipment that aids in the processing of information. Secretaries must often prepare documents that will be processed by automated equipment. Automated office equipment and systems are discussed in detail in Part 5.

Knowledge of Office Procedures

The goals of the company are a concern of the professional secretary. An experienced secretary should make suggestions for improving office procedures. A secretary should, with the help of the employer, have the goal of working toward changes that ultimately benefit the entire organization. To recommend changes that benefit the organization, a secretary needs to have a good understanding of the organization's management policies and objectives. Information of this nature can be learned by reading company reports and policy manuals and through day-to-day on-the-job experiences.

YOUR PROFESSIONAL IMAGE

Your professional image is based on how you act and appear in the eyes of other people. People perceive you by your actions, your appearance, and your manners. As a secretary, you will project either a positive or negative image not only by your conversation but by your body language and your attitude.

Self-Confidence

How others perceive you has much to do with their impression of your personal effectiveness. First, you must believe in your ability to project a positive self-image. Second, you must stay on top of your work in order to perform your tasks in a knowledgeable manner. The professional secretary knows what to do and the best way to do it. A positive attitude about your abilities enhances your image in a company.

Eye contact is essential in projecting honesty and confidence. Direct eye contact is interpreted as a friendly overture to communication. No eye contact indicates lack of interest or personal dislike. Good eye contact is a powerful way to communicate self-confidence as well as understanding and acceptance.

Your posture when sitting or standing constitutes a set of potential signals about your self-confidence. When you sit, stand, and walk erectly, you communicate self-assurance. When you slump, you communicate a negative image, such as defeatism or even laziness.

Appearance

Dressing for today's office is really no different from what it has ever been. Do not think that any outfit is acceptable just because others wear something like it. All too often we are influenced by what others wear. The office is the place to dress conservatively. Outfits should be coordinated and comfortable. The basic suit complements any working person's wardrobe. The well-groomed, attractively dressed, and poised secretary represents the company; therefore, a competent secretary is aware of a responsibility to present a favorable image in public. After all, a company is made up of people, and their appearance influences its image in the community.

Illus. 1-4
Proper grooming and dress enhance your professional image.

Etiquette

Being knowledgeable about proper business etiquette is important. A secretary must know how to handle situations such as making introductions, greeting executives or dignitaries, announcing callers, and hosting meetings and luncheons. The efficient secretary learns and practices correct social behavior so as to be poised and at ease in every business situation.

ETIQUETTE SUGGESTIONS
FOR THE
PROFESSIONAL SECRETARY

Etiquette is defined as good manners and common courtesy. Good manners should be observed at all times—in business and in the social environment. Professional secretaries often find themselves in business situations that require social grace. Knowledge of the elementary rules of courtesy described below should put you at ease in a few of the more common situations that arise almost daily in the business world.

The Business Lunch

1. If you are a woman and are a guest of a man at lunch, be poised and professional. If you are a man and are a guest of a woman at lunch, extend her common courtesies and let her be your host. In either case, the host should see that reservations are made, if they are required.

2. When you are a guest at a business lunch, follow the host when ordering. Do not order food or beverages that can be a source of embarrassment later.

3. If you are the host, observe the current practice in leaving the appropriate gratuity (tip). Do not overtip, but do not leave a tip that is less than the standard percentage of the total check. If you pay by credit card, you may add the tip to the charge slip before you sign it. If you pay by cash, observe the custom of the restaurant in which you are dining: put the tip on the plate when the waiter returns your change or leave the tip alongside your plate before you leave the table.

4. If you smoke, do not be the first to light a cigarette. Even if you are in a smoking area of a restaurant, refrain from smoking until your host makes it known that it is permissible to smoke at the table. If no one at the table smokes, refrain from smoking. In any circumstance make certain that smoking will not offend anyone present. In all circumstances it is wise to refrain from smoking if no one else is smoking.

5. *Never* use a toothpick or dental floss in public. If you must remove something from your teeth, excuse yourself and go to the rest room.

The Introduction

1. When introducing people, present the younger *or* the individual of lesser position to the older or person of higher rank.

    For example, "This is Ann Vlocovich, our vice-president. Leann Davis." or "May I present Leann Davis."

2. When introducing a man and a woman of approximately the same age and status, the man is presented to the woman.

    For example, "Glenda Lyons, I would like you to meet Richard Kennedy."

3. Use an individual's title when making a business introduction: Doctor, Professor, Mayor.

4. The American business introduction calls for a firm handshake.

5. It is polite to stand for an introduction.

6. Give a cordial reply when introduced. It is a courteous gesture to use the name of the individual to whom you have been introduced.

    For example, "It is nice to meet you, Mr. Hiteman."

7. When you introduce two persons, look at one person as you state the *other* person's name.

PROFESSIONAL GROWTH

Most entry level secretarial positions require minimum standards for employment. You should not be satisfied, however, with meeting just the minimum requirements. Career advancement will require increased skill, additional knowledge, and a broader education than you now have. In order to continue to grow professionally, you should continue your education at every possible opportunity. Most community colleges and universities offer courses at night and on Saturdays. You may consider taking additional business courses that are directly related to your present position. You may choose to broaden your general education by taking courses in the humanities. Many companies provide workshops and seminars for their employees.

Illus. 1-5
Professional growth increases your knowledge and broadens your education.

In addition to formal education and training, there are other ways to achieve professional development. You can read business and secretarial magazines or participate in professional organizations. You should be familiar with the following list of recommended periodicals for a secretary.

Business Week (weekly)
McGraw-Hill, Inc.
1221 Avenue of the Americas
New York, NY 10020

Datamation (monthly)
Technical Publishing Company
875 Third Avenue
New York, NY 10022

From Nine to Five (semimonthly)
Dartnell Corporation
4660 Ravenswood Avenue
Chicago, IL 60640

Information Management
  (monthly)
PTN Publishing Corporation
101 Crossways Park West
Woodbury, NY 11797

Management World (monthly)
Administrative Management
  Society
Maryland Road
Willow Grove, PA 19090

Modern Office Technology
  (monthly)
Penton/IPC, Inc.
1111 Chester Avenue
Cleveland, OH 44114

The Office (monthly)
Office Publications, Inc.
1200 Summer Street
Stamford, CT 06904

*Office Administration and
  Automation* (monthly)
Geyer-McAllister Publications, Inc.
51 Madison Avenue
New York, NY 10010

P.S. for Professional Secretaries
  (semimonthly)
Bureau of Business Practice, Inc.
24 Rope Ferry Road
Waterford, CT 06385

The Secretary (nine times a year)
Professional Secretaries
  International
2440 Pershing Road
Crown Center G10
Kansas City, MO 64108-2560

*The Secretary's Improvement
  Program* (semimonthly)
Bureau of Business Practice, Inc.
24 Rope Ferry Road
Waterford, CT 06385

The Secretary's Workshop
  (monthly)
Bureau of Business Practice, Inc.
24 Rope Ferry Road
Waterford, CT 06385

The Word (monthly)
Word Processing Society, Inc.
P.O. Box 92553
Milwaukee, WI 53202

The largest organization of secretaries is Professional Secretaries International, which has chapters throughout the United States, Puerto Rico, and Canada as well as affiliate associations in 30 foreign countries. PSI administers, through its Institute for Certifying Secretaries, the only business-oriented certification program in the secretarial field. There are qualifications an individual must meet as a candidate for the certificate before taking the examination. CPS (Certified Professional Secretary) after a secretary's name is indicative of the achievement of the highest professional standard within the field.

CPS—WHAT, HOW, AND WHY?

WHAT: Certification is achieved by individuals who pass a written examination and have certain verified minimum secretarial experience. The certificate and CPS designation signify a standard of achievement, the accomplishment of a professional goal, and pride in one's profession.

HOW: To take the examination an application must be submitted to the Institute for Certifying Secretaries. Certain minimum requirements must be satisfied before taking the examination, and a fee is payable in advance.

The examination is given once a year at over 100 locations in the United States. It is administered on two consecutive days in the month of May. (The CPS examination is also administered in Canada, Puerto Rico, Jamaica, the Virgin Islands, and Malaysia.)

The CPS examination is comprised of six parts:

I. Behavioral Science in Business
II. Business Law
III. Economics and Management
IV. Accounting
V. Office Administration and Communication
VI. Office Technology

An educational review program at a local university is advised prior to taking the examination.

WHY: CPS holders often receive special consideration for promotions and salary increases. Many holders of the certificate have used it as a stepping-stone into supervisory and/or management positions.

Many colleges grant college credits to individuals with CPS certificates.

The CPS designation leads to opportunities for leadership positions within professional organizations oriented toward office and secretarial work.

THE SECRETARY IN TODAY'S OFFICE

As you have learned, secretarial duties and the titles representing secretarial positions are diverse. Secretarial salaries also vary and are influenced by many factors:

1. Geographical location (Salaries are generally higher in large cities than in rural areas.)
2. Size of the business or organization
3. Status or position of the person for whom the secretary works
4. Actual job responsibilities
5. An individual's education, work experience, skills, and overall level of proficiency in secretarial skills

The *1983-84 AMS Office Salaries Directory for the United States & Canada* gives the following salary information for the seven secretarial classifications described on page 5:

Secretarial Classification	Weekly Salary Levels for One Half of Employees Surveyed	Number of Employees Surveyed
Word Processing Trainee	$176–$235	2,739
Word Processing Operator	$216–$285	6,850
Lead Word Processing Operator	$236–$325	2,250
Secretary B	$216–$285	32,618
Secretary A	$246–$325	38,308
Executive Secretary/Administrative Assistant	$286–$400	18,824
Legal Secretary	$246–$350	3,735

The equipment used by secretaries may be limited or very complex. A little over half, or about 55 percent, of all businesses have some type of automated office equipment. There are, of course, some offices that have remained relatively unchanged in the last ten years or so. Many excellent opportunities are found with employers whose staffs are small and whose equipment is not the most up to date.

While some offices have not changed, many others have modernized. An attractive and efficient office environment has been recognized as important in helping secretaries working alone or in groups to accomplish their assigned objectives. Managers realize that office conditions affect employee morale, productivity, and safety. Office planning has resulted in some innovative approaches to the design of offices, such as the open landscape design.

The open landscape concept eliminates the use of inside walls for many private offices. Work groups are divided by panels, file cabinets, and the use of plants. Bright, vivid colors are used to enhance the overall appearance of the office. Office landscaping has been successful in fostering teamwork and in improving communications.

Whatever office you work in, make it your home during working hours. Take pride in making it as attractive, comfortable, and productive as you possibly can.

PROFESSIONAL POINTERS

Professional secretaries work continuously on sharpening their skills. Use the following helps to improve your spelling and to increase your word power.

1. Read as much as you can. Reading enlarges your vocabulary and enhances your ability to communicate orally and in writing.

2. When you see or hear unfamiliar words, look them up in a dictionary. Learn to pronounce them correctly, spell them correctly, and use them correctly in sentences.

3. Compile a list of spelling demons that torment you. Write those words frequently. Writing and seeing the correct spelling will be more beneficial than just reviewing the word mentally.

4. Memory triggers help you spell or use certain words correctly. For example, princip*le* is a ru*le* or a theory. Princip*al* is the spelling for *al*l the other meanings. Another helpful memory or mnemonic device is *i* before *e* except after *c* or as in *a* in the sound of *neighbor* and *weigh*.

FOR YOUR REVIEW

1. How does Professional Secretaries International (PSI) define the term *secretary*?

2. List five duties that are a part of most secretarial positions.

3. Name five titles that represent secretarial positions.

4. In order to be successful, secretaries must possess certain personal qualities. Name four of these qualities and explain why they are essential.

5. What are four skills required for most secretarial positions?

6. Name three factors that affect a secretary's professional image.

7. Name at least three ways that you can grow professionally.

CASE PROBLEM

Kendal Alvereze was graduated with an associate degree in applied science from the local community college last June. Kendal's program of study consisted of secretarial, data processing, and other business related courses. The degree actually reads AAS Degree in Business, Administrative Assistant.

Kendal has applied for positions throughout the city. In each case Kendal has requested an administrative assistant position. Three companies called Kendal in for an interview, but she was not offered a job.

Kendal makes a point of letting interviewers know that she is not interested in secretarial work. She says that she went to college in order to prepare herself for a top-level job. Kendal did maintain an extremely high grade point average, and she has the potential to be a valuable employee to an organization. In order to show her ability, however, she needs someone to give her a chance.

1. Why do you think Kendal is experiencing difficulty in obtaining a job?

2. How could Kendal change her attitude toward her first job?

3. If Kendal's college training prepared her to be an administrative assistant, should she expect to wait for a position with the same title? Why?

PRODUCTION PROJECTS

PP 1-1

(Objectives 1 and 2)

The descriptions of a secretary are diverse. Review the secretarial openings in your local newspaper. (The Sunday edition will yield the most opportunities.) Circle with a red pencil all the jobs that are referred to as secretarial. Titles may not read SECRETARY, and you may have to read the descriptions to determine whether they are actually secretarial positions. Bring your advertisements to class; and be prepared to give an oral report on the variety of positions listed, the various titles, salary ranges offered, and skills required.

PP 1-2

(Objectives 1 and 2)

Using the most recent edition of the *Occupational Outlook Handbook* in your school library, type a list of duties performed by an administrative secretary, a stenographer, and a technical secretary.

PP 1-3
(Objective 3)

Contact two secretaries in two different organizations, and question them as to which of the six personal qualities listed in Chapter 1 they consider most essential for success in the secretarial field. Write a short report including the names and companies of the persons you interviewed, their titles, how long they have worked as secretaries, and their comments regarding your questions.

PP 1-4
(Objective 3)

Complete the self-evaluation chart on personality and character traits in the Supplies Inventory.

PP 1-5
(Objective 4)

Assess your skills to determine how good they are at this point in your preparation for a job. Your instructor will give you a five-minute straight copy timed typing test and a dictation test to determine your shorthand rate. Proofread the letter in your Supplies Inventory to see how good you are in locating errors. Circle all errors that you find, and retype the letter making all necessary changes.

PP 1-6
(Objective 5)

Take a survey of your current wardrobe. Decide which clothes and accessories are appropriate for office wear. Determine which ones are inappropriate. Type a chart entitled *Office Attire*, and list at least five items in each of the two categories.

PP 1-7
(Objective 6)

No one can predict the future. Who could have predicted that self-correcting typewriters would virtually eliminate the need for typing erasers? Who would have believed 30 years ago that photocopying would make carbon copies almost obsolete? Compile a list of things that you can do now to grow professionally so that your skills as a secretary do not become obsolete in the future.

Chapter 2

APPLYING FOR A SECRETARIAL POSITION

Now that you are familiar with secretarial positions and the duties performed by most secretaries, you must familiarize yourself with the steps you will follow in seeking employment. If you work full-time, as do the majority of people, you will spend approximately 50 percent or more of your waking hours at your job. Make sure, then, that the job you select will be a rewarding one to which you can give your best effort.

Begin your job selection with an enthusiastic attitude. Enthusiasm is contagious, and it is obvious when you have it. Employers are impressed by an enthusiastic attitude, and they will want to have you on their team if you show enthusiasm for secretarial work during the interview.

General Objectives

Your general objectives for Chapter 2 are to:

1. *Identify your career goals*
2. *List sources of job information*
3. *Write a letter of application*
4. *Prepare a personal data sheet*
5. *Complete an employment application*
6. *Develop interview skills*
7. *Analyze your potential for promotion*

CAREER GOALS

Know what you want out of life and how hard you are willing to work for what you want. Make a master plan for your career! Every job you hold will be a critical step in developing your career plan. A career is a long-term commitment to reaching your professional potential.

A master plan consists of long-range goals and short-range or more immediate objectives. First, map out a long-range plan of action that is realistic for you. Next, develop immediate objectives that will help you achieve your long-range goal. Of course, few people really know what they can or will be doing at the peak of their career. You may never reach your peak, however, if you do not plan ahead by setting objectives.

Your master plan should contain options that allow for changes if necessary. You should periodically review and update your plan, but do not alter your commitment to reaching your long-term goals.

A master plan begins with a realistic self-assessment. You must take a personal inventory of your needs, wants, interests, and abilities. As you evaluate your career goals, ask yourself the following questions:

1. What are my strong points?
2. What are my weak points?
3. What are my achievements?
4. What is my motivation—money, job satisfaction, status?
5. What type and size company do I want to work for?
6. What kind of secretarial position will give me the most satisfaction?
7. Do I have strong ambitions? Do I want to be promoted to a higher level within the company?
8. How long do I plan to work?

Illus. 2-1
What is your job motivation—money, status, satisfaction?

SOURCES OF JOB INFORMATION

Knowledge of the traits and skills needed for secretarial work is only the first step in preparing yourself for employment as a secretary. You will need to become acquainted with sources of information about secretarial positions if you are to be successful in your job search.

A good initial source for exploring job openings is the *Occupational Outlook Handbook*. This handbook is distributed by the United States Department of Labor and contains information on about 250 occupations. It tells where jobs are to be found, what work is involved, and what training or other qualifications are needed. The handbook also lists sources of specific occupational information. Other common sources of job information include friends and relatives, school placement offices and instructors, newspaper advertisements, and employment agencies.

Friends and Relatives

You have been told that there is a critical shortage of qualified secretaries. How do you determine which companies have secretarial openings? One of the best ways is through people you know who are employed. Employees usually are informed about available positions through bulletin board announcements, memos, or company newsletters. Ask your friends and relatives if they know of possible secretarial openings. Seek the help of everyone you know. But, remember, getting the job you want is your responsibility; and you will have to work hard at finding it.

School Placement Offices and Instructors

Most schools and colleges have placement counselors that aid students in career planning. College placement offices offer the following services:

1. Printed materials about specific careers
2. Directories of private industries and governmental agencies
3. General occupational information
4. An opportunity to develop job-hunting skills
5. Announcements about available positions

Job information is frequently posted on bulletin boards in placement offices. Occasionally employers visit schools to recruit and interview students. Your instructors may also know of employment opportunities. Take advantage of these two sources, and begin your inquiries early in the year. As graduation nears, students flood the market searching for jobs.

Newspaper Advertisements

The classified section of newspapers is a major source of job openings. Two kinds of classified advertisements are listed in newspapers: signed and blind. A *signed advertisement* includes the name of the firm placing the advertisement. A *blind advertisement* does not show the firm's name. In many cases only a telephone number or a post office box number is given in a blind advertisement. Private employment agencies must place signed advertisements; they must give the name of the agency, an abbreviation for it, or its initials. Therefore, if an advertisement is blind, it cannot be from a private employment agency.

If an abbreviation or initials appear in an advertisement and you cannot determine the name of the company, you can call the telephone number listed and ask for the company's name and location. If no telephone number is given, look in your local telephone directory under the business section or in the Yellow Pages to see if you can learn the nature of the business. Illus. 2-2 gives examples of signed and blind advertisements.

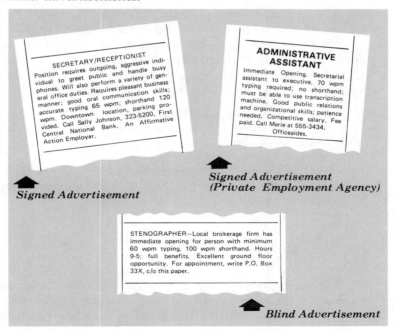

SECRETARY/RECEPTIONIST
Position requires outgoing, aggressive individual to greet public and handle busy phones. Will also perform a variety of general office duties. Requires pleasant business manner; good oral communication skills; accurate typing 65 wpm; shorthand 120 wpm. Downtown location, parking provided. Call Sally Johnson, 323-5200, First Central National Bank. An Affirmative Action Employer.

Signed Advertisement

ADMINISTRATIVE ASSISTANT
Immediate Opening. Secretarial assistant to executive. 70 wpm typing required; no shorthand; must be able to use transcription machine. Good public relations and organizational skills; patience needed. Competitive salary. Fee paid. Call Marie at 555-3434.
Officeaides.

Signed Advertisement
(Private Employment Agency)

STENOGRAPHER—Local brokerage firm has immediate opening for person with minimum 60 wpm typing. 100 wpm shorthand. Hours 9-5; full benefits. Excellent ground floor opportunity. For appointment, write P.O. Box 33X, c/o this paper.

Blind Advertisement

Illus. 2-2
Signed and blind job advertisements

Search thoroughly through your newspaper's classified advertisement section, reading especially the duties and job responsibilities given for each position. Not all secretarial positions will be listed as you might expect them to be.

Employment Agencies

There are two types of employment agencies: private and state operated. State operated employment agencies are supported by tax dollars. As a taxpaying citizen, you can take advantage of the services provided by your state operated agency free of charge.

Private employment agencies are in business to make money. A fee is charged for their services. Either you or the employing firm must pay for these services. If you are expected to pay the fee, it is usually stated as a percentage of your beginning salary. Generally you must sign a contract with private employment agencies when you make your initial visit. This contract may contain clauses that are legally binding. Read carefully any contract before signing it.

Many private employment agencies advertise jobs that are *fee paid*; that is, the fee is paid by the recruiting company to the employment agency when an applicant is hired. You should ask about the fee for all jobs referred to you by a private agency. Information regarding how the fee is determined, the amount, and how you are to be charged should be included in the contract you are asked to sign.

Whether private or state operated, the agency will screen applicants according to their qualifications for a particular job. You should be prepared to complete an application and take several tests. These tests will measure the following:

1. Typewriting speed and accuracy
2. Shorthand speed and transcription skills
3. Grammar, punctuation, and proofreading skills
4. Mathematical aptitude
5. Skill in operating office machines
6. Specific skills that you may have in areas of specialization, such as the legal or medical field

THE JOB APPLICATION PROCESS

You may possess excellent secretarial skills and may know of openings in the secretarial field; but, without proper preparation and know-how, your search for employment may not be successful. Some qualified applicants miss good job opportunities because they do not know the proper way to apply for a job. Preparation and confidence are the keys to rewarding experiences when seeking employment.

Company Information

Before you apply for a job with a particular company, find out all you can about the company. This information is needed for two major reasons. First, you need to know if you can meet your career goals by working for this company. Will the job allow you to work to the best of your ability and to achieve what you want? Will the company provide security for you? Second, you need to know as much about the company as possible in order to be prepared for the interview. One question often asked in the interview is, "Why do you want to work for this company?" Unless you know something about the company, you cannot satisfactorily answer this question.

How do you get information about a company? If you learn about a job through a friend, relative, employment agency, or placement office, seek information about the company from that source. Find out what the company does. If it is a manufacturing organization, find out what products it manufactures, the market for these products, and how many employees it has. If it is a service organization, find out what services it provides, whether it is a growing company, and how long the company has been in existence.

Illus. 2-3
Find out all you can about a company before the interview

It is more difficult to find out about a company if you are applying for a job through a newspaper advertisement. One way of getting information, however, is through the library. The major companies are listed in such publications as *Standard & Poor's Register of Corporations, Directors and Executives* and *Moody's Handbook of Common Stocks*. From these sources, you can find out what the company does, how large it is, what the growth history is, the names of the officers, and the like. Another way of getting information is to write directly to the company for a copy of its annual report. You may also seek company information through your chamber of commerce or the Better Business Bureau.

The Letter of Application

In most cases it will be necessary for you to write a letter of application when you apply for a job. Remember that this first contact makes the initial impression on an employer. You should write a letter of application in response to a newspaper advertisement (unless a telephone number only is given), to a company that has an opening that you learned of through a friend, or to those companies for which you would like to work but have no specific information about available positions.

When applying for a secretarial position, follow these tips for preparing an attractive letter of application:

1. Type the letter in proper form using an acceptable letter style.
2. Make absolutely sure that there are no spelling, punctuation, or capitalization errors.
3. Proofread carefully for typographical errors. If there are any corrections in the letter, make sure they are not noticeable. It is preferred that the letter be typed perfectly without any erasures.
4. Use a good grade of 8 1/2-by-11-inch white stationery. Personal or fancy stationery as well as erasable paper should not be used.
5. Type an original letter for each application. Never send carbon copies or photocopies of your letter of application.
6. Do not copy a letter of application from a book. Make your letter representative of your personality.
7. Be clear and concise.
8. Sign your letter of application with a black or blue ink pen.

Illus. 2-4 shows the format and style of a typical letter of application. Many other letter styles are acceptable, however.

A letter of application should be concise and to the point. It should be one page and contain three or four paragraphs. The first paragraph should include your purpose for writing the letter. If you know of a specific job opening, state that you are applying for it and how you learned about it.

2120 Accommodation Drive
Richmond, VA 23224-2037
June 25, 1984

Personnel Department
Abacus Corporation
475 Finley Avenue
Richmond, VA 23219-2001

Ladies and Gentlemen:

Please consider me an applicant for the position of secretary
which you advertised in the Sunday, June 24, 1984, Richmond
Dispatch. The advertisement states that the applicant should
have pleasant telephone manners, good typing skills, and the
ability to assume responsibility and take some shorthand. I
have these qualifications, and I believe that I am the right
person for the position.

My high school and college education have been in the field
of secretarial science. The courses that I have taken have
prepared me well for full-time work as a secretary. Courses
such as human relations and secretarial procedures have impressed upon me the need for building good working relationships and producing quality work.

You can see on my personal data sheet that I have received
scholarship awards for my achievements in school. These
awards have made it possible for me to further my education
and training so that I can reach my goal of becoming an
excellent secretary.

I would like to discuss my qualifications and my desire to
work for Abacus Corporation. May I come to your office for
an interview at your convenience? Please contact me at the
above address or by telephone at 782-1121 any afternoon after
3 p.m.

Sincerely,

Beverly K. Brooks

Beverly K. Brooks

Enclosure

Illus. 2-4
Letter of application

In the second paragraph, emphasize your qualifications. Do not list all your skills, but highlight those areas that will give you an advantage over other applicants. Create interest in your abilities and state your desire to work for that particular firm. You might also state your understanding of the position for which you are applying and why you think you are the right person for that position. If you are enclosing a personal data sheet, and in most cases you should, the details of your qualifications will be listed on it.

Request an interview in the third paragraph. Be clear as to when and where you can be reached. For example, state that you can only be reached at a certain telephone number before 5 p.m. Include other times when someone can contact you. Do not make it difficult for a prospective employer to get in touch with you. Of course, you will want to include your mailing address on the letter of application.

Personal Data Sheet

The *personal data sheet* or *résumé* is a concise statement of your background, education, skills, and experience. Illus. 2-5 shows the format and style of a typical résumé. In writing your personal data sheet, remember that it is one of the tools that should help you get a job. You should present your qualifications in the best light possible. In addition to personal information such as your name, address, and telephone number, other information includes your career objective, education, skills and abilities, work experience, achievements and accomplishments, and references. Your participation in organizations, school or community activities, and civic affairs may be pertinent to the job that you seek. If so, list these activities on your personal data sheet. Now is the time for you to show what abilities and expertise you can bring to a position. If you are applying for a secretarial position, you should highlight your secretarial skills, knowledge of office procedures and equipment, and personal attributes that will make you an asset to the company.

Additional tips for your personal data sheet include the following:

1. Include as educational qualifications the subjects taken in both high school and college that are pertinent to the position for which you are applying. Awards and achievements in school are good to list. A perfect attendance award is a real plus.
2. Give a complete work experience history. Begin by listing your most recent work experience. Include part-time jobs as well as full-time employment with beginning and ending dates of employment, each employer's name, and type of position held. If you have not had any work experience for which you were paid, list volunteer jobs including those while in school. Never list a category for work experience and put none. Think of something you have done for someone that proves you are a responsible person.

```
                         PERSONAL DATA SHEET

                           Beverly K. Brooks
                        2120 Accommodation Drive
                      Richmond, Virginia  23224-2037

Career Objective:   A secretarial position with opportunities to use typing
                    skills, transcription skills, display initiative, and
                    assume responsibility

EDUCATION

        Simmons Community College
        Richmond, Virginia
        Associate Degree in Applied Science, June, 1984

        Major Courses:

            Data Processing     Business Math I and II   Human Relations
            Word Processing     Secretarial Procedures   Machine Transcription
            Business Law        Business English         Oral Communications

        Secretarial Skills:  Shorthand dictation rate, 90 words a minute
                             Machine transcription rate, 40 words a minute
                             Typewriting straight copy rate, 65 words a minute

        Office Machines:  Lanier word processor, IBM Electronic 75 typewriter,
                          mimeograph, direct process duplicator, photocopier,
                          printing and display calculators

        Central High School
        Richmond, Virginia
        Business Diploma, June, 1982 (6th in class of 204)

WORK EXPERIENCE

        September, 1982--June, 1983   Work-study program   Office Assistant
        Simmons Community College                          Reading Center

        June, 1980--August, 1982      Part-time            General Office Clerk
        Hollister Corporation                              (typing, filing,
        Richmond, Virginia                                 stamping mail)

SCHOLASTIC HONORS

        1982  Scholarship Award, Simmons Community College
        1983  Outstanding Achievement Award, Philmont Corporation

REFERENCES

        Mr. Edward Reed, Manager of Reading Center, Simmons Community College
           1900 Vernon Road, Richmond, Virginia  23234-2150
           Telephone 782-5486
        Mrs. Irene Hogue, Personnel Director, Hollister Corporation
           2910 Clay Drive, Richmond, Virginia  23229-2043
           Telephone 782-3099
        Ms. Jean Christian, Business Teacher, Central High School
           4225 Brook Avenue, Richmond, Virginia  23224-2030
           Telephone 782-2728
```

Illus. 2-5
Personal data sheet

3. State the names and addresses of at least three people who can vouch for your ability and character. List people who are employed themselves because they are more familiar with what is expected of employees. It is good to include people who know you well that are in supervisory or managerial positions. Names of relatives should not be used. Always request permission to use names as references.

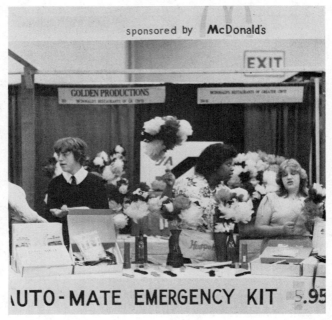

Illus. 2-6
Nonpaid work experience can be helpful in obtaining a job

The Application Blank

You send a letter of application and personal data sheet to get the opportunity to be interviewed personally for a position. Either before or after an interview, you may be asked to fill in an application blank. If an employer mails you an application blank prior to the interview, you should by all means type your answers in the blanks (unless it calls for your own handwriting). If you complete the application blank in the office at the time of the interview, use a good black or blue ink pen. Never use a colored or felt tip pen. Getting the job you want may depend on a well-prepared application. Consider the completion of an application blank as a sample of your work. It proves your ability to follow directions, to be neat, thorough, and accurate. An example of a typical application blank is shown in Illus. 2-7. The following additional suggestions will help you in completing an application blank:

EMPLOYMENT APPLICATION

ABACUS CORPORATION

Date of Application _____

AN EQUAL OPPORTUNITY EMPLOYER

PERSONAL INFORMATION

Name of
Applicant _____ Social Security No. _____
                First   Middle   Last

Present Address _____ Phone _____

City _____ State _____ Zip _____

Kind of _____ ☐ Full Time   ☐ 1st Shift

Work   _____ ☐ Part Time   ☐ 2nd Shift

Desired _____ ☐ Summer   ☐ 3rd Shift

MILITARY INFORMATION

Type of Work					Entered Mo. Yr.	Discharged Mo. Yr.
Special Training						
Branch:	☐ Air Force	☐ Army	☐ Coast Guard	☐ Navy	☐ Marines	

EDUCATIONAL INFORMATION

Type of School	Name and Address	How Many Years Attended	Graduated	Course or Major
Grammar or Grade			☐ Yes ☐ No	
High School			☐ Yes ☐ No	
College			☐ Yes ☐ No	
Postgraduate			☐ Yes ☐ No	
Business or Trade			☐ Yes ☐ No	
Other			☐ Yes ☐ No	

Illus. 2-7a
Application for employment

EMPLOYMENT HISTORY

(Please Complete Even If Supplemented by a Resume)

List Most Recent Position First	MONTHLY SALARY	EMPLOYED		TOTAL MONTHS
		FROM	TO	
1. Employer	$			
Address	REASON FOR LEAVING			
Name & Title of Supervisor				
Your Position and Duties				
2. Employer	$			
Address	REASON FOR LEAVING			
Name & Title of Supervisor				
Your Position and Duties				
3. Employer	$			
Address	REASON FOR LEAVING			
Name & Title of Supervisor				
Your Position and Duties				
4. Employer	$			
Address	REASON FOR LEAVING			
Name & Title of Supervisor				
Your Position and Duties				
5. Employer	$			
Address	REASON FOR LEAVING			
Name & Title of Supervisor				
Your Position and Duties				
6. Employer	$			
Address	REASON FOR LEAVING			
Name & Title of Supervisor				
Your Position and Duties				

List any other experience that you feel would be significant in our evaluation of your capabilities. Attach an additional sheet if necessary.

In signing this application you hereby authorize the company to conduct investigations including verification of prior employment history and education. Your signature indicates your awareness that false statements or failures to disclose information may be sufficient to disqualify you for employment; or if employed, may result in your dismissal.

_____   _____
Date   Signature of applicant

Illus. 2-7b
Reverse side of application for employment

1. If you are to fill in the form in your own handwriting, do so carefully, using your best penmanship. Print if you are so directed.
2. Answer every question. If there is a question that does not apply to you (such as military service) put *NA*, meaning *Not Applicable*, in the space provided. As an alternative you may draw a straight line through the blank, but most employers prefer a specific response. Leaving something completely blank may give the impression that you missed the question.
3. Be sure you spell accurately. Carry a pocket dictionary to ensure that you will not make a mistake or have to ask the receptionist how to spell a word.
4. Be prepared! Have all information with you that you will need: dates you attended all schools, dates of employment, and complete addresses of previous employers and references. You will also need your social security number.
5. List complete information about references. Be sure that you have obtained permission to use their names as references.
6. Some application blanks provide space for additional comments or special information. This is your chance to say something special about yourself. Use this opportunity to emphasize your abilities, your desire to work for that company, or your outstanding achievements.

The Interview

If you have done well thus far in the application process, you may get the opportunity you've been hoping for—the chance to meet the employer face-to-face. It is the interview that gives you the best opportunity to sell your abilities to the employer. Your preparation and self-confidence will be fully tested at this point.

Be sure you know the exact time and location of the interview. Do not rely on your memory; write the time, address, and person's name you are to see on paper and take it with you. Most of all, allow time for unexpected delays. You will not want to be late for your interview. Excuses for being late will not be received kindly.

Remember that the interviewer is probably as uncomfortable about the interview as you are. More than likely you will not know each other. Your bid for the position may very well be won or lost during the first few minutes of the interview. If you enter making a good impression, you have set the stage for the interview. If you make an initial unfavorable impression, it may be impossible to undo a mistake or indiscretion. For the most part, however, interviewers are tolerant people and are inclined to overlook minor breaches of conduct, attributing them to nervousness or inexperience on the part of the applicant. They prefer to withhold judgment until they have had an opportunity to talk with the applicant. But a good first impression will put you at ease and enable you to answer the questions of the interviewer in a relaxed and pleasant manner.

In many cases interviewing is a process of elimination to determine the person best suited for the job. Once the number of possible applicants is narrowed, interviewers set up second interviews with the potential candidates for the position, the purpose being to select the right person for the job. An opportunity for a fine position with an excellent future may depend on how you handle yourself in the time given to the interview.

Illus. 2-8
Get the interview off to a good start by a favorable first impression.

Helpful Hints. Be prepared. Appearance and enthusiasm are extremely important in the interview. With this in mind, here is one expert's advice.

1. Dress appropriately.
2. Give a firm handshake.
3. Maintain good eye contact.
4. Control your energy—try not to act nervous.
5. Display good humor and a ready smile.
6. Show a genuine interest in what the interviewer says and be alert to all questions.
7. Demonstrate pride in your past performance.
8. Try to understand your prospective employer's needs and show how you can fill them.
9. Express yourself clearly and with a well-modulated voice.
10. Do not smoke or chew gum.

Interviewers can more easily evaluate your personality than any other trait during the interview. From your application, your personal data sheet, your educational background, your achievements, and company tests that may have been administered, an interviewer can determine your specific skills. What must be determined, however, is your ability to project yourself through your use of good grammar, your knowledge of current events, your hobbies and interests, and your attitude toward people and work in general.

An interviewer needs to know what *you* want and why. Your goals and how you plan to accomplish them may be an influencing factor in whether you are offered the job. In this brief time, an interviewer evaluates your drive, poise, ability to communicate, basic social skills, and your general personality. So be sure to accentuate your positive qualities!

Commonly Asked Questions. Being prepared for the interviewer's questions will aid you in expressing yourself properly. Sample questions from an interviewer may include the following:

Questions for Openers
1. Did you have any trouble locating us?
2. Are you familiar with our company?
3. How did you learn of this position?
4. Why do you think you are qualified for this position?
5. Why are you interested in joining this company?

Questions Regarding Motivation
1. Are you presently employed?
2. Is your present employer aware of your interest in changing jobs?
3. Why do you want to change jobs?
4. What caused you to enter this field?
5. What is the ideal job for you?
6. If you could have any position, what would it be? Why?
7. What would you like to be doing three years from now? five years from now?

Questions Regarding Education
1. What formal education have you had?
2. Why did you choose your major area of study?
3. What was your academic average or class standing when you were in school?
4. What honors did you earn?
5. Were you involved in extracurricular activities in school?
6. Did your grades adequately reflect your full capability?
7. Which courses did you like the best? the least? Why?
8. What special training have you had that is required for this position?

Questions Regarding Experience
1. Have you ever been fired or asked to resign from a position?

2. Why did you leave your previous job(s)?
3. Have you had any problems with previous supervisors?
4. Which supervisor did you like the best? Why?
5. Which duties performed in the past have you liked the best? the least? Why?
6. What kind of people do you prefer to work with?
7. What are your greatest strengths?
8. What are your weaknesses?
9. Have you had any military service?
10. How do you fit the requirements for this position?
11. What has been your greatest accomplishment thus far?
12. Why should I hire you?

Eventually the interviewer will say, "Now what questions would you like to ask me?" In addition to getting specific information not already covered, this is the opportunity for the applicant to control the conversation. Your ability to communicate effectively and to initiate conversation will be evaluated at this point. Always be prepared for this part of the interview. Never say that you have no questions; but, by the same token, do not ask too many questions. Here are some questions that you may ask the interviewer.

1. Would you like for me to explain anything on my personal data sheet in more detail?
2. Would you please describe the specific duties of the job for me?
3. What characteristics are you seeking in the person to fill this position?
4. Is this a new position?
5. What do you consider as ideal experience for this job?
6. Was the person previously in this position promoted?
7. Is there anything unusually demanding about the job I should know about?
8. Could you tell me about the primary people I would be working with if I were accepted for this position?
9. Can you tell me the prospects for advancement?
10. Can you tell me the pay range for someone with my qualifications?

Preparing for an interview takes quite a bit of work. Don't try so hard that you overdo it. You can overdress, use too much makeup, talk entirely too much, and virtually ruin a good job opportunity. If you believe in your ability to be a good employee, prove it in the interview.

The Follow-Up

After you have completed the interview, it is your responsibility to thank the interviewer for the time spent with you. You should thank the interviewer in person when leaving the interview. Within the next day or two it is appropriate to type a short letter to the interviewer expressing your appreciation for the interview. Remind the interviewer of the position for which you applied and the date of your interview. Illus. 2-9 is an example of a thank you letter for an interview.

A letter of this nature serves two purposes. It is a courteous gesture, and it reminds the interviewer of you and your interest in the position. After following up with a thank you letter, it still may be necessary in a week or ten days to call the interviewer about the position. Do not just sit back and wait for a prospective employer to call you—go after the job!

JOB PERFORMANCE

The true reward for completing the application process successfully will be getting the position you want. Maintain the same enthusiasm you had when you applied for the position. Getting off to a good start at a new job is very important to your future success with that company. You have been selected because *you* are considered the right person for that job. Now is the time to prove what you said you can do in the interview. Some advice at this point may help you with that successful start. Listen to what co-workers and supervisors tell you. Observe and learn what is expected and what is accepted in the office. Ask questions when you do not understand something you have been instructed to do.

Performance Evaluations

Immediate supervisors generally evaluate the performance of employees. As a new employee, you may be evaluated at the end of your first three months on the job, again at the end of six months, and thereafter at the end of each year. One type of evaluation is called merit rating. *Merit rating* is a procedure by which an employee is measured on certain traits and qualities that the employer thinks are important for job performance. These periodic ratings are intended primarily to help employees improve job performance. If the rating shows that you need to improve certain aspects of your work or your attitude toward your work, the evaluator will discuss them with you. Accept any suggestions as an attempt to help you be more effective in your job rather than as a criticism of your work.

2120 Accommodation Drive
Richmond, VA 23224-2037
July 17, 1984

Mr. Joseph Ryland
Personnel Director
Abacus Corporation
475 Finley Avenue
Richmond, VA 23219-2001

Dear Mr. Ryland:

Thank you for allowing me to discuss my qualifications
and my interest in working for Abacus Corporation. The
interview which I had with you on Monday, July 16, was
very informative. You described thoroughly the requirements for the secretarial position.

I am eager to prove my abilities to be a good secretary.
My skills are above average, and I believe I am capable
of being an asset to your firm.

Again, thank you for your time. I look forward to hearing from you soon.

Sincerely,

Beverly K. Brooks

Beverly K. Brooks

Illus. 2-9
Thank you letter

Advancement on the Job

Soon you will be thinking of ways that you can improve yourself so that you will be eligible for promotion when the opportunity arises. Do not let ambitious thoughts interfere with the performance of current duties, or you will become unhappy and frustrated. Remember that you gain valuable work experience on whatever job you are assigned. Your first job, in all likelihood, will be at an entry level. Do not be too eager to move up. Take time to learn your job well, to work well with others, and to find out what you do not know and need to learn. Advancement and promotions are earned through hard work and experience.

In some companies the procedure for selecting the person to be promoted is well established. In other companies there is no fixed policy. Usually a promotion is made upon the recommendation of an immediate supervisor or department head. Your immediate supervisor knows best your work record, your ability to get along with others, your willingness to accept responsibility, your loyalty, and your eagerness to advance.

Be ready for a promotion should the opportunity present itself. Learn as much about other jobs in the company as you can. Acquaint yourself with people that work in other departments. Know how your present position fits in with the overall organizational structure. Stay informed of the changes in personnel, of the installation of new equipment, and of the development of new procedures in your company. In all, be an efficient employee.

PROFESSIONAL POINTERS

Can you accept an adverse performance evaluation about your job performance? Although constructive criticism is difficult to take sometimes, it can be helpful. Here are some pointers to help you in accepting a difficult evaluation.

1. Listen to what the evaluator is saying.

2. Earn the evaluator's respect by remaining silent. Do not defend yourself by offering excuses and arguing.

3. Look at the evaluator. Maintain eye contact.

4. Find no fault with the evaluator. Keep in mind that the evaluation reflects your performance—not the evaluator's.

5. Accept an adverse evaluation as a criticism of your performance, not of you as an individual.

6. Resolve to correct your mistakes. Use your mistakes as learning tools.

7. Respect your evaluator's position and stick with the subject. Do not try to sidestep the issue.

8. Accept an adverse evaluation as the company's way of emphasizing your strengths, pointing out your weaknesses, and helping you to improve.

9. Thank the evaluator for an honest and unbiased evaluation— even if it was painful.

10. Use your evaluations to improve your performance and advance your position.

These pointers can be wisely applied in any situation in your career where you find yourself in the position of having made a mistake that requires correction and/or criticism from your supervisor or employer.

FOR YOUR REVIEW

1. What should you know about yourself in order to determine your career goal?

2. List sources that can be used to obtain job information.

3. Give two reasons why you need knowledge about a company before you apply for a position.

4. List five *musts* for writing a good letter of application.

5. What categories of information should be included on a personal data sheet?

6. Give three tips for correctly completing an application blank.

7. What are five considerations in preparing for an interview?

8. List five questions you can ask the interviewer about the job.

9. What courteous act can you perform after an interview?

10. What can you do to enhance your chances for promotion once you are employed?

CASE PROBLEM

Jane Harris has completed her secretarial studies at Buxton Business College and has recently applied for a position as secretary at two local firms: Dobson Industries and the Sawyer Corporation. Jane was first interviewed by the Sawyer Corporation to fill a secretarial vacancy in the public relations department. The job sounded exciting, and the beginning salary was very good. The personnel director at the Sawyer Corporation was to let her know by phone if she was selected for the position.

While waiting to hear from the Sawyer Corporation, Jane was interviewed by Dobson Industries. At the conclusion of her interview, she was offered a position as stenographer in the collection department with the understanding that she would report for work in one week. She was so thrilled with the offer that she accepted and agreed to start work the following Monday.

Three days before Jane was to begin working at Dobson Industries, the personnel director at the Sawyer Corporation called to inform her that she had been chosen for the secretarial position in the public relations department. Since the salary at the Sawyer Corporation was considerably higher than that at Dobson Industries, she was tempted to change her mind. She was confident that she would get more experience as a secretary in the public relations department at the Sawyer Corporation than as a stenographer in the collection department at Dobson Industries.

1. What should Jane do under the circumstances?

2. What would you do in a similar situation? Why?

PRODUCTION PROJECTS

PP 2-1

(Objective 1)

Choosing a career that is best suited to your interests and abilities will be a major factor in your success and happiness. Use the evaluation chart in the Supplies Inventory to rank items in terms of their importance to you. Be prepared to discuss your ranking of items with members of the class.

PP 2-2

(Objective 2)

Choose one or more of the following sources of job information. Find out from one or more of the sources what secretarial positions are open for someone with your skills and qualifications. Write at least a paragraph explaining the requirements for the secretarial positions available to you.

1. School placement office

2. State operated employment agency

3. A private employment agency

PP 2-3

(Objective 2)

For this project use the classified section of your local newspaper. Circle the secretarial advertisements that are blind and put a *B* beside them. Circle all signed advertisements and put an *S* beside them. Disregard signed advertisements of private employment agencies. Select two of these advertisements—one blind and one signed—and complete the form in your Supplies Inventory.

PP 2-4

(Objective 3)

A friend, Malynn Jones, has worked for Bradford & Associates for six years. Her duties with the company include the following:

1. Answering the telephone for the accounting department

2. Handling general typing for the four accountants in the department

3. Taking shorthand dictation and transcribing it for the department manager

4. Filing for the department

5. Handling inquiries from customers about their accounts

6. Handling miscellaneous office duties such as photocopying; scheduling appointments for the manager; and recording vacation, sick leave, and personal leave days for members of the department

She has handed in her resignation to accept a position as an office supervisor with another firm. She tells you about this opening and advises you to apply for the position. The contact person is Charles Rice, Personnel Director, Bradford & Associates, 3520 North Broad Street, Richmond, VA 23240-2208.

Write a letter of application for the position. Type the letter in final form and sign your name. Assume that you will complete your school program in three weeks.

PP 2-5

(Objective 4)

Prepare a personal data sheet to go with the letter of application in PP 2-4. Type your personal data sheet on plain white paper.

PP 2-6

(Objective 5)

Assume that Bradford & Associates responded to your letter of application and personal data sheet with a letter requesting that you complete their application form prior to coming in for an interview. Complete the form for the position for which you applied. Use the application form in the Supplies Inventory.

PP 2-7

(Objective 6)

Even though you cannot anticipate every question an interviewer may ask, you can prepare yourself mentally for the interview. Writing your answers to the anticipated questions will help you answer the difficult questions in the interview. Use the form in the Supplies Inventory to answer questions frequently asked during a job interview.

PP 2-8

(Objective 7)

Your job performance affects your opportunity for promotion in either a positive or negative way. Evaluate yourself according to the criteria on the chart in the Supplies Inventory. After you have evaluated yourself, list some steps you plan to take to improve yourself in areas that you rated unsatisfactory.

Chapter 3

MANAGING YOUR WORK EFFICIENTLY

As a secretary, you must be able to manage your work efficiently. However, the demands made upon the secretary in today's world make this a complex and even awesome task. Consider this situation. You have been given a rush report to type. All day you have been diligently trying to get it typed; but the telephone has rung continuously, and numerous people have interrupted you with crisis-type tasks. It is now the end of the day, and you still have three pages of the report to type. For many secretaries, a situation of this kind is not unique but commonplace.

It is your responsibility to bring order to chaotic situations. To do so requires that you use good work management techniques. You need to be able to make good use of your time, to minimize stress, and to make sound decisions. This chapter will give you insight into how to manage your work more efficiently.

General Objectives

Your general objectives for Chapter 3 are to:

1. *Determine the importance of time management for the secretary*
2. *Prepare a time log and analyze the expenditure of time*
3. *Establish an action plan for increasing time efficiency*
4. *Identify the factors that contribute to negative stress*
5. *Determine how stress may be minimized*
6. *Explain the steps in the decision-making process*
7. *Commit yourself to managing time, minimizing stress, and making effective decisions*

TIME MANAGEMENT

Time management has always been important for the secretary. Yet in the past relatively little emphasis was placed on its usefulness outside the office. Today there are dozens of books and hundreds of articles written on the advantages of time management for everyone. Why? What has happened in the last few years to bring about this change? First, we live in an age that is more complex than ever before. We are faced with technological changes daily. Understanding and dealing with these changes takes time. As a prospective secretarial employee, you should become aware of these changes in the office. The machines that you use today are much different from the machines used several years ago. And, as technology continues to change, the machines that you will use in the future will change dramatically. Not only must you be aware of these changes, but you must be able to operate new machinery and understand new methods. Learning new procedures takes time from the other duties and responsibilities that you have in life.

Second, we live in a competitive age in which organizations demand much of their employees. Effective time management allows us to gain some control over our workday. Secretaries who have control over their workday are highly productive. Successful secretaries know that time is an important resource to be managed carefully. And effective time management involves getting the most out of our workday by arranging tasks according to priority.

Time—A Unique Resource

In order to better control time, we must understand something about time. We never seem to have enough time, yet we have all the time there is. Time cannot be bought, sold, rented, borrowed, saved, or manufactured; but it can be spent. It is spent by each of us, even if we accomplish nothing. Everyone receives an equal amount of time each day, although often it does not appear to be equal since some people can accomplish more in a day than others. Time itself cannot be changed, converted, or controlled. Managing time means managing yourself so that you utilize the time that you have to the optimum.

Time Misconceptions

There are several misconceptions about time. Recognizing these misconceptions will allow you to understand the concept of time and to manage yourself more efficiently in using time. Here are a few of these misconceptions.

Time problems can be solved by working harder. It is often believed that trying harder will prompt you to do a better job and quickly finish your work. This assumption is not necessarily true. Certainly there are times when you should try harder to complete a job satisfactorily, but trying harder is not always the answer to time management problems. To work smarter not harder usually is a wise motto. To work smarter is to find ways to reduce the number of tasks that you have to do. Analyze your work flow. Determine what you can do in a more efficient manner. Try to eliminate some of the steps you take in completing a task.

Supplied by International Paper Company

Illus. 3-1
Work smarter not harder.

It is impossible to plan your activities and set priorities. Many office support workers accept crises and confusion as part of the job. They are resigned to hectic days as the norm for their positions. In other words, their work load controls them rather than vice versa. However, this situation is not an absolute. It is possible to control your work by planning ahead and establishing priorities. Emergencies can and do arise that cause hectic days and then other work must be put aside and the emergency matters given priority. You must continually ask yourself, How can I use my time effectively today? What is the most important task that I have to do?

People know how they spend their time. Right? Wrong! Most people have very little idea of how they actually spend their time. Try to write down how you spent your time last week. You will probably be unable to remember many of the things that you did—let alone the time that it took you to do them. If you will keep a record of your activities for one week, you will probably be amazed at the way you actually spent your time and how much time you wasted.

Managing time means reducing the time spent in creative activities. Another misconception is that time management is boring and mechanical and that people who concentrate on time management have little time for creative activities. Actually the opposite is true. People who manage their time well have more time available for creative activities. They have established routines which enable them to finish necessary tasks and thus increase their discretionary time.

Time Wasters

In addition to having misconceptions about time, most people are guilty of wasting time. Understanding how time can be wasted will encourage more effective time management. Here are several common time wasters.

Socializing. If you presently have a job, do you go to work and get busy accomplishing the tasks of the day? Or do you report to work promptly and then spend the first thirty minutes of your workday talking to your co-workers about what happened the night before, drinking coffee with the secretary in another department, and making personal telephone calls? Certainly it is important that you communicate with your co-workers and that you have some time in which you are free to talk about something other than work, but too much time can be wasted during the workday in excessive socializing.

Disorganization. "I had that letter just a few minutes ago, and now I can't find it. It couldn't have disappeared into thin air." Have you ever made such a statement and then proceeded to rummage through the clutter on your desk in an attempt to find the paper that you had just a few minutes ago? A disorganized and cluttered desk can be a major time waster for a secretary. You should know what goes into your desk and what stays on top of your desk. Do not clutter your desk with papers that should be in file drawers. Organize efficiently incoming and outgoing materials; then organize your workday as you do your desk.

If you try to type a report, plan a meeting, do a month's filing—all at the most hectic part of the day—when the telephone is ringing constantly and callers are coming and going, the result will be time wasted, nothing accomplished, frayed nerves, and total frustration.

Ineffective Communication. As a secretary, you will communicate both orally and in writing with people in the office—your employer and co-workers and possibly with customers. It is important

Illus. 3-2
Disorganization can be a major time waster.

that the lines of communication between yourself and others are open and easily understood. Think of the time you will waste if you type a report incorrectly because you misunderstood instructions from your employer. Or think of the profits the company may lose if you make a customer unhappy and lose an account.

Procrastination. Have you ever been guilty of procrastination? *Procrastination* means trying to avoid an unpleasant task by putting it aside with the intention of doing it later. It can be a No. 1 time waster. Procrastination takes many forms, but people who habitually procrastinate actually invite interruptions. They will prolong telephone conversations, talk with co-workers, take a long coffee break, or seek all kinds of excuses to avoid doing what must be done.

Time Inventory

Now that you have examined a few misconceptions about time, how do you spend yours? Until you know how you spend your time, you cannot expect to become more efficient in managing it.

Time Log Preparation. One way to determine how you spend your time is to chart the amount of time you spend each day in various activities. Illus. 3-3 shows a time log.

TIME LOG

Monday, Oct. 25

	Total Time per Day	Total Time per Week
Typing *9:20-10:05, 11:00-11:30, 1:00-2:15, 4:00-5:00*	3 hrs., 30 min.	17.5 hrs.
Filing *10:15-10:25, 11:30-11:40, 12:00-12:10, 2:15-2:25*	40 min.	3.33 hrs.
Dictation *8:10-8:25, 3:05-3:20*	30 min.	2.5 hrs.
Transcribing *8:25-9:15, 3:20-4:00*	1 hr., 30 min.	7.5 hrs.
Incoming mail *10:25-10:40, 3:30-3:45*	30 min.	2.5 hrs.
Outgoing mail *11:40-12:00, 3:45-3:55*	30 min.	2.5 hrs.
Incoming calls	21 min.	1.75 hrs.
Outgoing calls *9:16-9:18, 10:40-10:44, 2:37-2:40*	9 min.	.75 hr.
Financial records		.5 hr.
Office host duties		.5 hr.
Duplicating		
Working with others		.5 hr.
Miscellaneous		.17 hr.

Illus. 3-3
Time log

Log Analysis. Your next step is to analyze your time log in an attempt to discover ways in which you can improve the management of your time. Ask yourself these questions:

1. What was the most productive period of the day? Why?
2. What was the least productive period of the day? Why?
3. Who or what accounted for the interruptions?
4. Can the interruptions be minimized or eliminated?
5. What activities needed more time?
6. On what activities could I spend less time and still get the desired results?
7. Do I have all my supplies and materials ready before beginning an activity?

Action Plan. Your next step is to do something about how you spend your time. Make an action plan for yourself. Determine the positive steps you will take to increase your time management efficiency. In deciding how you will manage your time more efficiently, you may want to use some of the time management techniques given here.

Effective Time Management Techniques

Here are several positive steps that you can take as a secretary to manage your time.

Establishing a Daily Schedule.
Consult the tickler, or follow-up file, for all matters that must be taken care of that day. A *tickler file* is a chronological record of things to be done. Notice the illustration of a tickler file in Illus. 3-4. A guide for the current month is placed in the front of the file followed by a separate guide for each day of the month. At the back of the file are guides for each month of the year. Any matter that needs future attention is written on an individual file card, and the card is placed behind the guide for the appropriate day or month.

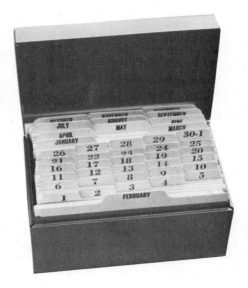

Illus. 3-4
Tickler file

Next, consult the schedule of appointments. Your employer may have special instructions to give you regarding some appointments. Certain people may be allowed to stay for only a specified time, or information from the files may be needed for some of the appointments. Even if your employer does not definitely ask for this information, you should know whether or not special information will be needed for certain appointments. Then you should place the necessary information on your employer's desk. A little forethought in this respect may save numerous interruptions during the day.

Setting Priorities. Many times it will be impossible for you to do everything that you are asked to do in one day. But you must be able to determine the most important items—which jobs should be done first. Know also which jobs can wait for a day or a week. If you are unable to establish priorities, ask your employer to assist you.

Maintaining a Weekly Schedule. In addition to a daily schedule, it is helpful to make a weekly schedule. For example, on Friday afternoon, you might check the tickler file to see what must be accomplished during the next week. A weekly schedule for October 15-19 may include the following.

1. Board of directors meeting, October 15—take notes at the meeting and type report of meeting.
2. Ms. Elliott will be leaving for Chicago on October 19—prepare itinerary, confirm travel arrangements, pack briefcase.
3. Type and distribute monthly sales report on October 17.
4. During slack periods this week (a) check supply cabinet and order necessary supplies, (b) clear files of inactive materials, and (c) read company periodicals.

Notice that priority items are included in the weekly schedule. In addition, jobs to be done during slack periods are also listed. It is an extremely good idea to plan for your slack periods. It is easy to put off or never get around to a job such as cleaning out the files since it is usually considered routine and monotonous. But it is a necessary and important job since cluttered, disorganized files contribute to inefficiency. If you plan for jobs such as this, you will get them done without too much pain. Reading company periodicals is also one of the activities planned for slack periods. You will be a better secretary if you are knowledgeable and up to date concerning what is going on in your own company. If your company does not have a periodical, you might read periodicals such as *The Secretary, The Office,* or *Modern Office Technology.*

Organizing Your Work Station. Organizing yourself and your work is not an easy task, but it must be done if you are to make the most efficient use of your time.

Your Desk. When you are working on a project, clear your desk of materials that relate to other projects. Put these materials in a file folder, label the folder with the name of the project, and place the folder in your drawer. It is not easy to work with stacks of paper around you. You need a flat, uncluttered surface on which to work. The only items that should be on your desk, other than those for the project on which you are working, are the telephone, a message pad and pencil, a desk calendar, a stapler, a tape dispenser, desk references, and in/out trays.

Your In *and* Out *Trays.* Label the trays on your desk so that it is clear which is for incoming material and which is for outgoing material. If space permits, you may wish to have a file tray on your desk. Keep an alphabetic file sorter in your desk so that all materials to be filed can be quickly put in alphabetical order for ease in placing in file cabinets.

Your Supplies. The center drawer of your desk should hold frequently used supplies, such as pencils, pens, erasers, and paper clips. The top side drawer is generally equipped with sloping partitions for paper. Divide your paper into letterhead, plain bond, onionskin, and carbon paper. Keep your carbon paper in a box or manila folder so that it will not curl or wrinkle. Notice how the desk drawer is organized in Illus. 3-5.

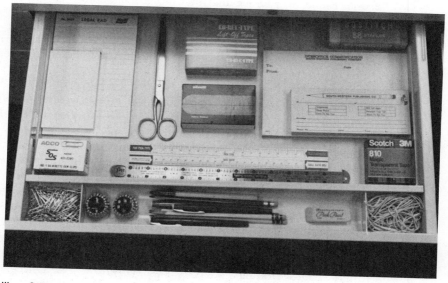

Illus. 3-5
Organize your supplies.

Your Work Area. The way you arrange your work area will have much to do with your efficiency in getting work done. Much is being done to make office work areas as efficient as factory areas, which depend on time and motion studies to eliminate unnecessary work. You will undoubtedly find that on your first job you can eliminate many unnecessary steps and wasted motion by properly arranging your equipment and supplies. For example, if you frequently must leave your desk to refer to material in a file cabinet in another part of the office, it might be more convenient to have a desk-high file cabinet alongside your desk or to incorporate a file drawer in your desk.

Your Filing System. When you are setting up a filing system, set up one that is most appropriate for your office—subject, numeric, alphabetic, or geographic. You will learn more about these filing systems in Chapter 20. Keep your files neat. If labels become torn or difficult to read, replace them. If file folders become dog-eared, replace the folder. When a folder becomes crowded, divide the folder into two. Set up the appropriate number of primary and secondary guides so that you may find materials quickly and easily. To ensure an efficient filing procedure, it is wise to set a particular time of the day to take care of your filing duties; however, this should be scheduled at a time when your mind is free to concentrate on your filing. Set up a sign out procedure so that you know where materials are when they are taken from the files. Determine with your employer how long materials should be kept in the active files and when materials should be stored.

The Mail. In most offices, procedures for handling incoming mail are well established. The following procedures will help you efficiently process incoming mail.

1. Sort according to personal or company mail, separating envelopes of different size, telegrams, and special delivery mail. Be sure to check the wrappers that are used for mailing some magazines. Occasionally mail slips inside the wrapper.
2. Open the envelopes except for personal correspondence. Either a letter-opening machine or a hand opener may be used.
3. Remove the contents from the envelopes. Check the envelopes carefully for enclosures. If there is no letter address, the envelope should be attached to the correspondence. Envelopes are frequently kept for several days to check enclosures that may have been missed or to verify the postmark date on the letter.
4. Time stamp and date all correspondence. As this is done, sort the correspondence by department or individual.
5. Distribute the mail to the proper department or individual.

Arrange outgoing mail properly. Be certain that all envelopes are addressed correctly and that the appropriate enclosures are inserted in the envelopes. If material is being sent by a special service, be sure that the mailing notation is on the envelope. Use the proper postage on all mail.

Your Reading. In your secretarial position, numerous items to be read will pass your desk. It is your responsibility to know what is happening in the office. In reading the correspondence and other materials, practice speed-reading techniques. Do not move your head from side to side as you read. Take in groups of words rather than a single word each time your focus shifts. Read for the main thought or idea. If you are reading a periodical or company literature, scan the table of contents first. Then practice selective reading techniques. Read carefully only the sections that will enhance your knowledge of your job and the company for which you work and any other information that is of importance to your employer.

Using Good Communication Techniques. Get complete and accurate data on a subject. If your employer asks you to do something, be sure that you understand exactly what you are to do and how you are to do it. Don't be afraid to ask questions. It is better to ask a question than to waste time doing something incorrectly.

Transmit ideas in simple, clear terms. Define terms if necessary. Don't try to impress people with your vocabulary. Frequently a communication breakdown can be attributed to the fact that the communicators are talking about two different things. Repeat what you think you have heard. For example, say, "This is what I understand you want me to do." Then repeat your understanding of the communication.

Listen carefully when someone is talking. When you are communicating with an individual face-to-face, look at him or her. Be sensitive to the person's body language as well as to his or her words. Keep an open mind to new ideas. Refrain from passing judgment on what you think the speaker is saying.

Reducing Interruptions. Interruptions can be frustrating time wasters. Controlling or minimizing interruptions is crucial to efficient time management. Here are some suggestions.

The Telephone. The telephone can be one of your greatest time savers; it becomes a time waster when you do not use it properly. As a secretary, you should screen calls for your employer. It is important that you give and record correct information during telephone calls. When taking incoming calls, find out who is calling and the nature of the call. When placing calls, identify yourself, your employer (if you are placing a call for him or her), and what you need. If the person called is not in, find out when the person will return. If you are taking a call for your employer who is not in, let the person know when your employer is expected. If you take a message, write the message accurately. Repeat the name, number, and message to the caller to confirm your understanding of it. When you have several calls to make, group them and make the calls when the persons are likely to be in the office. Early morning is usually a good time to reach people. Keep your personal calls to a minimum. Let your friends know that they should not call you at the office.

Visitors. Set up appointments for visitors. Discourage people from dropping by unexpectedly to see you or your employer. If a visitor drops by to see your employer and he or she is busy, ask, "May I help you?" or "May someone else help you?" If no one else can help, ask, "May I set up an appointment for you on Tuesday at 2 p.m.?"

Make visitors to your office welcome, but do not feel that you must make small talk with them. Provide them with reading materials, and then continue with your duties. Discourage your co-workers from dropping by to socialize with you. Breaks are usually provided in the morning and in the afternoon. If you want to socialize, meet your co-workers for a break or for lunch. Make it clear that during working hours you think that it is your responsibility to work.

Meetings. You may be responsible for conducting a meeting or helping your employer plan a meeting. Here are several suggestions that will keep the meeting from being a time waster.

1. Start the meeting on time.
2. Determine who should come to the meeting. Limit the number of participants.
3. Distribute an agenda in advance.
4. Follow closely the agenda during the meeting.
5. Control interruptions.
6. Accomplish the purpose of the meeting.
7. Conclude the meeting as scheduled.
8. Send out concise minutes within 24 hours after the meeting.
9. Follow up promptly on any items that need to be handled after the meeting.

SECRETARIAL STRESS

In addition to time management, your ability to manage and control stressful situations is extremely important to your effectiveness as a secretary. You need to understand the nature of stress and how to cope with it.

Stress Defined

Stress is the response of the body to a demand made upon it. Wants, needs, and desires are derived from stress of some kind. You cannot avoid stress. But you do not necessarily want to avoid it since stress does not always have a negative effect. If you didn't feel a need for friends, you wouldn't join a club or social group. If you didn't feel a need to achieve, you wouldn't go to school or take a challenging job. If you didn't feel a need to pass a test, you wouldn't study. All these situations are examples of stress that can make a positive impact on your life. However, stress can be harmful also. In fact, some writers distinguish between positive stress and negative stress, calling negative stress *distress*. Just as you face situations in life that cause positive stress, you may also face situations that cause distress. Illness is a distressful situation. When someone you love is sick or dies you experience distress. How we cope with and adjust to the stresses in our lives is extremely important. If we are unable to cope with our stresses, then we can become physically, mentally, and/or emotionally ill. This section will help you understand more about stress and how to deal with it.

Illus. 3-6
Sometimes even getting to work can cause stress.

Contributing Factors

Some of the factors that contribute to stress on the job are role ambiguity, job insecurity, working conditions and relationships, work overload, and personal problems.

Role Ambiguity. Role ambiguity exists when an individual has inadequate information about his or her work role—when there is a lack of clarity about work objectives and expectations. As a secretary, you may experience some role ambiguity. You may not understand exactly what is expected of you. When this situation occurs, it is up to you to find out what your job is. Many companies write job descriptions for various positions. If one exists for your position, read it. If your employer has not told you what he or she expects of you, ask for a job description.

Job Insecurity. Another factor that contributes to stress on the job is job insecurity. Perhaps your company has had recent serious losses and is in the process of laying off employees. You may wonder, Will I be the next to go? If you have these thoughts, you probably are not able to give your best efforts to your job. You are in a distressful situation which can cause reduced productivity.

Working Conditions and Relationships. A number of studies have shown that there is a relationship between working conditions and an employee's physical and mental health. Physical health is impaired in a dehumanizing environment—an environment in which the job is extremely routine and people are treated as objects rather than as individuals. Studies have also shown that poor working relationships with employers and colleagues can lead to distress on the job. Lack of trust among people who work together can lead to inadequate communication and to job dissatisfaction. An inconsiderate superior can be a source of job pressure. Lack of adequate support from co-workers can also cause a distressful situation.

Work Overload. Studies have also shown that too much work or work that is too difficult can cause negative stress. One study of a sample of 1,496 employed persons found that work overload was significantly related to such indicators of stress as drinking, absenteeism from work, low motivation to work, and lowered self-esteem.[1] Both qualitative (difficulty of work) and quantitative (amount of work) factors can produce psychological and physical strain and stress.

Personal Problems. Personal problems are another cause of negative stress. If someone in your family is sick or if you are disturbed by other family problems, you are likely to feel distressed. These negative stresses affect not only the quality and quantity of your work and your interactions with co-workers, but they also affect your home life.

Types of Stress

How do you know when you are experiencing negative stress? There are two types of negative stress: acute stress and chronic stress.

Acute stress occurs when a person has to respond instantaneously to a crisis situation. For example, if your car goes into a skid on an icy road, you must react quickly. As you experience acute stress, two

---

[1]B. L. Margolia, W. H. Kroes, and R. P. Quinn, "Job Stress: An Unlisted Occupational Hazard," *Journal of Occupational Medicine*, Vol. XVI, No. 10 (1974), pp. 654-661.

chemicals are produced in your body—adrenaline and noradrenaline. These chemicals have stimulated people to perform incredible acts in a crisis. They have impelled persons to lift extremely heavy objects off injured people (objects that they would not be able to lift in an ordinary situation) or to fight off ferocious animals. Immediately after the crisis, however, these heroic persons become weak, their hands shake, their knees quiver; they have been known to collapse.

Chronic stress occurs when a distressful situation is prolonged with no rest or recuperation for the body. Chronic stress triggers the production of different biochemicals in our bodies. While adrenaline and noradrenaline can be broken down by our bodies, the chemicals produced by chronic stress cannot be broken down and remain in our system where they are capable of damaging our bodies. Chemicals produced by chronic stress can cause high blood pressure, kidney damage, increased likelihood of cardiovascular disease, migraine headaches, ulcers, and numerous other problems.

Chronic stress can also cause emotional problems, such as depression, withdrawal, deep-seated anger, and loss of self-esteem. Have you ever had the blues? Most people have. When the blues last for weeks or months, however, they frequently are diagnosed as chronic stress. Chronic stress can also cause people to become extremely irritable— not only with others but with themselves. They may lose their self-esteem and suffer serious self-rejection.

Cost of Stress

What is the cost of negative stress? The price is high for both the individual and the organization. For the individual the price can be illness and temporary loss of work; for the organization the price can be absenteeism and loss of productivity.

To the Individual. Stress related illnesses recently cost workers $8.6 billion in lost wages in one year. Other health related costs to workers include the physical problems already discussed (high blood pressure, ulcers, migraine headaches, and emotional problems), not to mention boredom, frustration, and anxiety. Chronic stress victims tend to feel burned-out. Life can become too much for them so they drop out. They no longer participate as producing members of society.

To the Organization. The organization, too, sustains a monetary loss when individuals suffer from chronic stress. High absenteeism and low-quality work are the invisible costs to the employer. The

---

[2] Jere E. Yates, *Managing Stress* (New York: AMACOM, 1979), p. 1.

visible cost has been estimated by one source at $17 billion annually in decreased production resulting from stress related mental disorders. Estimates on productivity losses as a result of stress related physical illnesses are even higher—as much as $60 billion.[3]

Coping with Stress

Since stress is so costly to the individual and to the organization, can steps be taken to cope with it? Definitely. You can lessen the negative stress in your environment. Here are some suggestions.

Maintain a proper diet. What you eat or do not eat affects your overall health. Excessive intake of fat, sugar, salt, and caffeine contributes to poor health and to certain diseases such as hypertension and heart disease. The average cup of coffee contains 100 to 150 milligrams of caffeine. Nervousness, insomnia, headaches, sweaty palms, and perhaps ulcers have been related to as little as 250 milligrams of caffeine. Excessive amounts of caffeine may cause an individual to exhibit the same clinical symptoms as an individual suffering from anxiety.

The average American consumes more than 126 pounds of sugar a year. Excessive sugar consumption can lead to an increase in triglyceride levels in the blood which can cause cardiovascular disease. Too much salt can lead to an increase in blood pressure and to the development of hypertension. The wisest course of action for an individual is to lower the intake of fat, sugar, salt, and caffeine in the diet.

To maintain a balanced diet, you should follow this plan:

1. Eat appropriate portions from the four basic food groups
   a. Milk group—two portions
   b. Meat group—two portions
   c. Fruit and vegetable group—four portions
   d. Bread and cereal group—four portions
2. Use polyunsaturated oils in cooking rather than shortening or lard
3. Limit the number of egg yolks you eat each week
4. Increase the amount of poultry and fish in your diet
5. Do not add salt to your food
6. Decrease your caffeine intake

Set up an exercise program. Cardiovascular specialists have found that regular exercise can lower your blood pressure, decrease fats in the blood, reduce joint stiffness, control your appetite, and decrease fatigue. What type of exercise should you do? There are many exercises that are good for your body—swimming, bicycling, jogging, walk-

---

[3] Ibid.

ing, to name a few. Participate in an exercise that you enjoy. Determine a regular time of the day that you will exercise and then do it. When you begin exercising, go slowly. Train your body—don't strain it. If you have any medical problems, be sure to consult your doctor about the type of exercise that is best for you.

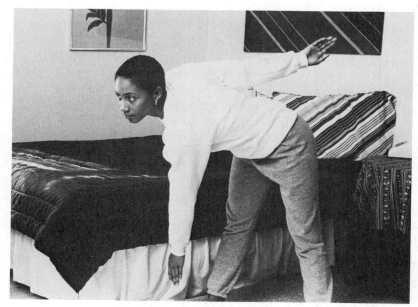

Illus. 3-7
You can lessen the negative stress in your environment.

Use visualization. Visualization means using your imagination to help you relax. It helps you block out unwanted thoughts. Settle into a comfortable position, relax any muscles that feel tense, and visualize a pleasant scene. Imagine a sky of white fluffy clouds, ocean waves licking a golden beach, the sun glistening on a snow covered mountain, or whatever to you is a relaxing, pleasant scene. Focus on this scene for several minutes to block out the tensions of the day.

Clarify values. Assess your values. Take a few moments to analyze what is important to you. Determining what you really value in life will help you establish your priorities and thus reduce stress. For example, assume that you are working and going to school, too. There never seem to be enough hours in the day to get everything done. Ask yourself if you really value your education, if it is important to you to go to school now, and if your education is worth the sacrifice. If your answers are yes, then put education in its proper perspective in your life. Evaluate the situation to determine which activities you can give up that will provide you with the additional time that you need.

Clarify your work environment. Know what is expected of you on the job. Read the job description if one exists. Ask your employer to clarify your role and what is expected of you.

Reduce organizational dependency. Do not depend totally on the organization. Educate and train yourself to be employable by a number of companies. Engage in continual education. This education may be formal education at a college or university, informal education such as reading professional books and periodicals, attending workshops and seminars, and/or participating in company staff development programs.

Understand role relationships. Be sensitive to the needs of your employer and your co-workers. Know what they expect of you. Know how you fit into the organizational structure. Be familiar with the organization chart; know who reports to whom. Accept people for who they are. Be tolerant. Strive to communicate openly and honestly with your employer and co-workers.

Conduct a self-analysis. Be aware of the negative and positive stresses in your life. Know when you are under stress. Take the time to analyze why that stress is occurring. Then take steps to manage and minimize that stress.

DECISION MAKING

Just as it is important for you as a secretary to manage time and minimize stress, it is also important that you learn to make responsible decisions. As the secretarial role increases in complexity, the secretary is being groomed to make decisions—decisions which can be of great importance. Thus, you must understand the basis of decision making and the steps in the decision-making process.

Your Approach to Decision Making

Do you ever have trouble making decisions? Most of us have at one time or another in our lives. It isn't always easy to make a decision. Why is it sometimes difficult? Most of the difficulty centers on fear: We are afraid of making a mistake or taking a risk. Our behavior and actions are the product of the decisions we have made or have allowed someone else to make for us. Thus, the way we approach decision making definitely affects our lives.

Your Values and Your Decisions. Your values are closely linked to the decisions that you make. Consider your values and how they affect your decisions. You have made a decision to further your education; the fact that you are in this course is evidence of that. This decision to further your education is probably influencing your life in certain ways right now. For example, you are spending time in school. That time could have been spent at work or in leisure activities. You have also chosen to invest money in pursuit of your education and to give up money that you could have made working. Thus, you have chosen to invest your time and money to advance your education. Why? What do you value? One of your values must be education. Another value may be the status that you think you can gain in society through higher education. Still another value may be the higher income you think you will realize from your career by continuing your education. Whatever your values, the decisions that you make reflect those values. Understanding this association will help you understand the decision-making process.

An Educated Approach. Certainly at sometime in the past you have made a quick decision without giving sufficient thought to the consequences. No doubt your decision was sound, but there are times when a cautious approach to decision making is necessary. You will need to identify the problem, gather the facts (determine the criteria), search for solutions (consider alternatives), test the alternatives, and determine the best possible solution. In other words, using an educated and systematic approach to decision making will assist you in making correct decisions.

Decision-Making Steps

A decision is the outcome or end product. The process by which a decision is reached involves problem solving which comprises five steps. When you make decisions from an educated and systematic approach, you should understand and follow these steps in arriving at a decision.

Define the problem. The first step is to define the problem. This step may sound simple, but it is usually the most difficult of the steps. Consider this situation.

Ms. Angela Pickens is the office manager for a medical equipment and supplies firm. Two secretaries, one clerk, and one receptionist report to her. Rona, one of the secretaries, has been an employee in the office for two years. She has always been a good employee, turning out quality work in a short period of time. For the last two weeks there has been a noticeable difference in Rona's work and attitude. She has been thirty minutes late for work three mornings. She has made numerous mistakes on several reports; and when these mistakes have been called to her attention, she has not seemed concerned about them.

What is the problem? A newcomer to the office may determine the problem to be Rona's incompetence. Yet Ms. Pickens knows that is not true because of Rona's past performance. Another person may decide that Rona does not care about her job. Yet, from past experience, that does not seem to be the case either. To identify the problem you need to ask several questions.

1. Why is Rona behaving in this manner?
2. What is not the problem? (Rona is not incompetent; she has the ability to do the work.)
3. What is happening? (Rona is turning out poor work; she is not coming to work on time; her attitude seems to be poor.)
4. What should be happening? (Rona should be a productive member of the team as she has been in the past.)

The identification of the problem is the most critical step in the decision-making process. It is also the step most often neglected. Many people think that they know what the problem is and start looking for solutions. With such an approach, they often find solutions to the wrong problem. Hasty decisions are made by not properly examining the problem. Sound decisions require a thoughtful analysis. When the problem is stated too narrowly, the search for solutions is restricted. The more broadly a problem is stated, the greater the chance for finding a solution that will meet all needs. It is helpful to state the problem as a question. This question format will assist you in solving the problem.

In the case just described, the problem might be stated in this manner: Why has Rona's job performance and attitude deteriorated? This statement is relatively broad. It does not confine Rona's problem to job performance. Job performance could be merely a symptom of the real problem. The real problem may lie in stressors in Rona's personal life which are influencing her work. By including attitude in the problem statement, you allow yourself the flexibility of considering this dimension.

Gather the facts. The next step in the decision-making process is to gather the facts or to determine the criteria you need to make a sound decision in the situation. In setting your criteria, here are three questions that will help you.

1. What do you want to achieve?
2. What do you want to preserve?
3. What do you want to avoid?

In Rona's situation, the answers to Ms. Pickens' questions might be:

1. She wants Rona to be a productive employee again.

2. She wants to preserve a good working relationship between them.
3. She wants to avoid a situation in which Rona's work and attitude continue to deteriorate.

Search for solutions. The next step in the decision-making process is to begin looking for solutions to the problem. Searching for solutions involves developing alternatives based on the goals and objectives that you have determined. For example, in the case given, since Ms. Pickens wants to maintain a good relationship between manager and employee and to prevent a situation in which Rona's work and attitude continue to deteriorate, she should avoid certain alternatives. She should not fire Rona. She should not berate Rona for her poor job performance. But she might (1) ask Rona if there are problems or concerns on the job or in her personal life that are affecting her job performance, (2) observe how Rona is responding to her co-workers in an attempt to determine if there is a problem among the co-workers, (3) talk with Rona's co-workers about any problems of which they may be aware.

Test the alternatives and implement the decision. The decision maker tests each alternative, using this system:

1. Eliminate ideas that are unrealistic or incompatible with your values or the situation.
2. Give more thought to the alternatives that seem most appropriate in the situation.
3. Select the alternative that appears the most realistic, creative, or appealing.

In the example given, Ms. Pickens must reject talking with other employees. This alternative could cause problems between Rona and her co-workers. Given the other two alternatives, Ms. Pickens may decide that the better approach is to discuss the problem openly with Rona.

Once the alternative is selected the next step in the process is to implement the decision. Assume that Ms. Pickens decides to talk privately with Rona about the situation. As they talk, Ms. Pickens learns that the following stressors have been affecting Rona's work: (1) Her husband has been ill, and Rona has been trying to take care of him and work, too and (2) she has had a serious confrontation with one of her co-workers. Both of these factors have affected Rona's concentration and her ability to produce quality work.

Evaluate the decision. Once a decision has been made, you need to evaluate whether you have made the right decision, how you can improve your decision-making skills for the future, and what you have learned from the process. Here are some questions you can ask yourself.

1. What was right about this decision? What was wrong?
2. How did the decision-making process work? How can it be improved in the future?
3. What was learned from the decision? What changes should be made for the future?

Ms. Pickens might ask herself if, through talking with Rona, she has learned the real reason for Rona's poor job performance. If she has, has Rona agreed to improve? In other words, did Ms. Pickens gather all the facts and achieve the goal she established? Did Rona's job performance and attitude improve? Is there still a good relationship between Ms. Pickens and Rona?

Creativity and Decision Making

As you have learned, decision making usually involves choosing one of several solutions to a problem. Creativity is also involved in finding solutions to problems. What is the relationship between creativity and decision making? How is creativity important in the decision-making process?

Relationship Between Creativity and Decision Making. In making decisions, many times we use past experiences and/or knowledge in arriving at a decision. However, you may confront situations for which you have no past experience or knowledge on which to base a decision. Creativity is required when there is no one best answer or when there is no known solution. Creative problem solving involves formulating new ideas or alternatives rather than relying on preconceived notions for making decisions. Creative decision making requires *divergent thinking*—thinking in which the mind is encouraged to travel in many different directions.

Characteristics of the Creative Decision Maker. You may be thinking, How can I be a creative decision maker? I am not creative. Most people perceive a creative person as an artist who paints a memorable portrait or a musician who composes a magnificent cantata. Certainly these people are creative, but creativity is not confined to persons with purely artistic abilities. *Creativity* is the ability to combine already existing elements in new ways. A creative spark exists in everyone. However, most people seldom if ever utilize their creative ability. Consider some characteristics of the creative individual.

- *Flexibility. Flexibility* is the capability of responding to change and adapting to different situations. A flexible person has the ability to see various options and is able to choose the best solution from this variety. This type of person can adapt easily to new situations.

- *Curiosity.* Creative people are not afraid to be curious. They are not afraid to ask naive or even ridiculous questions. They have childlike curiosity. They have not let their senses be dulled to what is going on around them.
- *Independent thinking.* Creative people often see problems or solutions where other people cannot. They are not afraid to view a problem from different angles. Creative people are often compulsive problem seekers, not so much because they enjoy problems but because they enjoy putting ideas and solutions together in different ways.

WORK MANAGEMENT ADVANTAGES

Throughout this chapter, you have looked at ways that you can become a better manager of your work. You have learned how to manage your time, how to control or minimize stress, and how to make effective decisions. Efficient management of these aspects of your work can make you a happier and more productive person both on the job and in your personal life. There can be a ripple effect, too—that is, how you manage your work can have an effect on other aspects of your job. For example, greater job productivity can mean

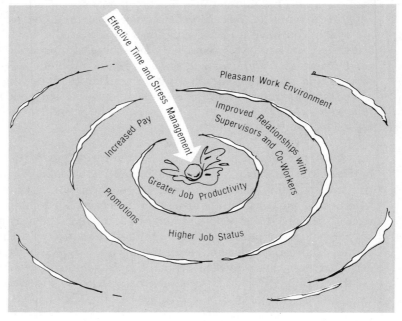

Illus. 3-8
The ripple effect of efficient time and stress management

increased pay, promotions, and higher status on the job; management of stress can contribute to more effective relationships with your supervisor and co-workers and thus result in a happier work environment for you. A happy and productive work environment means that less worry and negative stress are carried into your personal life. Managing these areas of your work will free you to use your resources more effectively. It is important that you, living in a complex, rapidly changing world, use your resources to the best of your ability.

PROFESSIONAL POINTERS

Try these time and stress management suggestions to help you work more effectively.

1. Clarify your values. Periodically record and analyze them.

2. Clarify your objectives. Put them in writing.

3. Set priorities.

4. Periodically analyze the way you spend your time by keeping a time log and determining ways you can improve your time management.

5. Eliminate at least one time waster from your life each week.

6. Make a list of things to do every day. Mark off items on your list as you accomplish them.

7. Take time to do things right the first time. Then you will not waste time doing things over.

8. Get plenty of exercise.

9. Maintain a proper diet.

10. Eliminate recurring crises from your life by analyzing why things go wrong and then confronting the situations before they become crises.

11. Do not procrastinate. Do the difficult task first.

12. Schedule some time for yourself each day.

13. Finish what you start.

14. Know what is expected of you on your job.

15. Record the sources of interruptions for a few days. Determine which interruptions can be eliminated and which are necessary but can be handled more efficiently.

FOR YOUR REVIEW

1. Why is time management more important today than ever before?

2. What characteristics make time a unique resource?

3. Identify three time wasters.

4. Explain how a time log is used.

5. Is there a difference between stress and distress? If so, explain.

6. List four factors that contribute to negative stress.

7. Explain five ways to reduce negative stress.

8. How do your values relate to your decisions?

9. Define the steps in the decision-making process.

10. What is the relationship between creativity and decision making?

CASE PROBLEM

Victor Silvia has been working as a secretary for Lone Star Lumber Company for two years. He has always enjoyed his job; he considers himself a happy, outgoing individual. Recently, however, several of Victor's co-workers and his employer have made remarks to him such as:

"What's wrong with you today, Victor? Did you get up on the wrong side of the bed?"

"What a grouch!"

"You don't smile anymore."

Victor has been having problems both at work and at home, but he thought he was hiding his problems from his employer and co-workers. Apparently he is not. Victor realizes that his attitude is poor; most days he would rather not go to work. However, Victor needs his job; so he must correct his attitude.

Victor's job responsibilities have increased recently. A new district manager has been hired who gives Victor numerous pieces of correspondence to handle. To compound the problem, Victor doesn't like the person. Every job that the district manager gives Victor to do is a crisis job which must be completed immediately. Victor has been doing the work immediately, but he is beginning to feel pressured. Many times he misses his lunch hour or his breaks in order to accommodate this person. Victor has been planning to be married in two months; however, he and his fiancee have been having problems. She wants a big wedding; he wants a small one. She wants to rent a house; he wants to rent an apartment. They can't seem to agree on anything. Victor is beginning to wonder if he should be getting married at all.

1. Is Victor experiencing stress? If so, identify the stress. Is it positive or negative stress?

2. What steps would you suggest Victor take to help alleviate his problems?

PRODUCTION PROJECTS

PP 3-1

(Objective 1)

Do you manage your time well? Take the self-assessment inventory in the Supplies Inventory to determine how you presently manage your time. Use the space below the self-assessment to identify problem areas and how you can improve your time management.

PP 3-2

(Objective 1)

Review two articles on effective time management for the secretary. Type a summary of the articles on plain paper, giving the reference sources you used.

PP 3-3

(Objective 2)

Use the time logs given in the Supplies Inventory to record your activities for three days. If you have a part-time job, log the time you spend in various activities at work. If you are not employed at present, log the way you use your personal time.

PP 3-4

(Objective 3)

Analyze the way you spent your time during the three days you made recordings in the time logs. Answer these questions as you analyze your time logs:

1. What patterns and habits are apparent from the time log?

2. What was the most productive period of the day?

3. What was the least productive period of the day?

4. Who or what accounted for the interruptions?

5. Can the interruptions be controlled or minimized?

6. What were the biggest time wasters?

7. How can the time wasters be eliminated or minimized?

8. On what activities can less time be spent?

9. What activities need more time?

Now prepare an action plan using the form in your Supplies Inventory to show how you can improve the way you spend your time.

PP 3-5

(Objective 4)

As honestly as you possibly can, answer the questions in your Supplies Inventory. Your answers will not be turned in to your instructor. This exercise is for you to determine where the negative stress factors are in your life.

PP 3-6

(Objectives 4 and 5)

Analyze the case below; then respond to the items following the case.

Maria has been working as a secretary for Edwards Freight Company for six months. The company is small, and there have been several personnel cutbacks since Maria started. There were three secretaries in the office, but two months ago one of the secretaries was laid off. Since that time Maria has been getting the work that the other secretary did. Maria's employer did not tell her that she would have an increased work load; but one day Mr. Bateman, whose secretary was laid off, came to Maria and said that he expected her to do his work, too. Maria merely smiled and said nothing. Maria is a fast typist and has good secretarial skills. She has always prided herself on being able to do lots of work. For the last two months, however, she hasn't been able to see the top of her desk. Also, she has been skipping her breaks in an attempt to get the work done. There never seems to be an end—she can't get caught up. Recently Maria hasn't been feeling well, nor has she been sleeping well. She wakes up two and three times a night thinking about the office.

1. Identify the factors that have contributed to negative stress for Maria.

2. How can Maria minimize her stress?

PP 3-7

(Objective 6)

Identify one decision that you have made in the last week. Think through the steps that you followed in making that decision. How could your decision making have been improved? What steps should you have taken that you did not take? Use the form provided in your Supplies Inventory to answer the questions.

PP 3-8

(Objective 6)

Analyze the following case and respond to the items at the end of the case.

Josephine has recently completed her postsecondary education in office procedures and is interviewing for a full-time job with a growing company. Two companies have offered her a job, and she must decide which job to take. One company is a medium-sized electronics firm. The company has been in business for five years, and during that time it has grown tremendously. The growth for the future also looks promising. Josephine has been offered a secretarial position in the manufacturing department. The other company is a small printing company. This company has been in business for twenty years; in fact, the owner of the company lives on the same street as Josephine. Josephine has known the owner for approximately five years, and she thinks that she would enjoy working at the printing company. She has been told that salary advancements at the printing company will be good, and she has been offered $75 more per month at the printing company than at the electronics firm. Josephine will be the only secretary in the printing company.

If you were Josephine, what decision would you make? Explain the steps you would follow in making your decision. At each step explain the process in relation to this situation. For example, what is the problem? Define the problem by stating it in a question format. Next, determine Josephine's criteria, and then consider the remaining steps in arriving at a decision.

PP 3-9

(Objective 7)

As you have learned in this chapter, being an effective secretary means efficiently managing your time, minimizing stress, and making sound decisions. What do you plan to do in the future to be effective in these areas? Write a short paragraph for each area, explaining what your commitments will be to achieve improved effectiveness in these areas. Use the form in your Supplies Inventory for your answer.

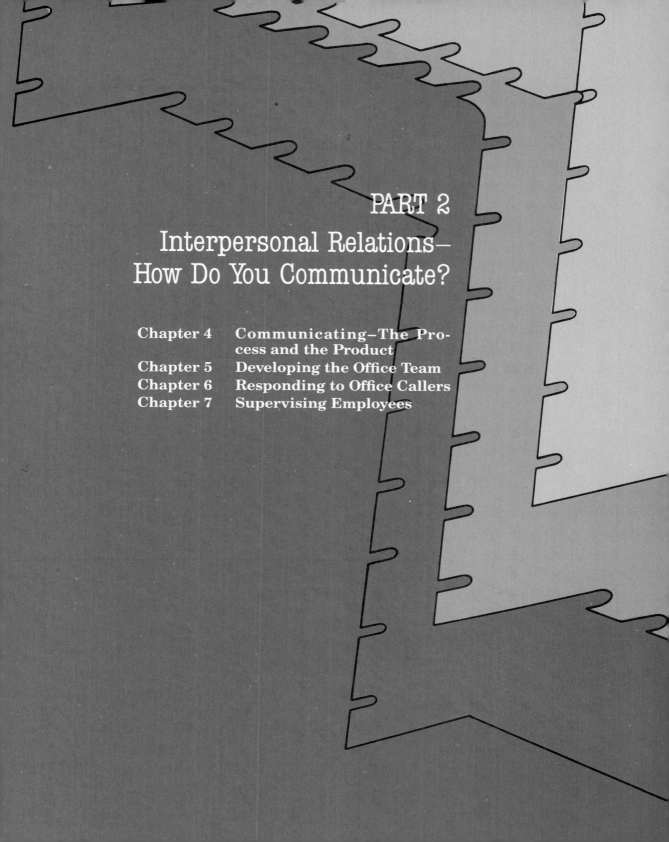

PART 2
Interpersonal Relations—
How Do You Communicate?

Chapter 4   Communicating—The Process and the Product
Chapter 5   Developing the Office Team
Chapter 6   Responding to Office Callers
Chapter 7   Supervising Employees

Chapter 4

COMMUNICATING—THE PROCESS AND THE PRODUCT

"You did not understand what I said." "We must have a communication problem." These are familiar statements. Research statistics show that most people spend 70 percent of their total waking hours in some form of communication—either writing, reading, speaking, or listening. As a secretary, you will spend much of your time in the communication process.

The dictionary definition of the word *communicate* is "to make known; to impart; to transmit information, thought, or feeling so that it is adequately received and understood." That definition seems simple. If you want someone to know something, you merely tell the person. But this is not as easy as it sounds. When people talk, write, read, or listen, communication barriers often develop. What one person meant to say is not understood by the person receiving the message. Communication problems are frequent among individuals and in business organizations. This chapter will help you understand the importance of communication, become aware of communication barriers, and discover ways to reduce these barriers.

General Objectives

Your general objectives for Chapter 4 are to:

1. *Explain the relationship between self-concept development and communication patterns*
2. *Identify self-concept strengtheners*
3. *Explain the communication process*
4. *Explain the types of nonverbal, or nonoral, communication*
5. *Identify and explain ways to eliminate communication barriers*

SELF-CONCEPT AND COMMUNICATION

The way you communicate reveals something about who you are. It tells others, at least to a degree, how you think of yourself. If someone says to you, "I don't want to do this because I'm sure I will fail," it reveals that the person has a low self-concept of his or her abilities. Maybe he or she does not feel qualified or is afraid of possible failure. Each statement that a person makes tells you something about that person. Self-concept is an important element in the communication process. Let's look at how self-concept is formed.

Self-Concept Development

Self-concept is the way you see yourself. You may see yourself as attractive or unattractive, smart or stupid, witty or humorless, athletic or nonathletic, and so forth. Every characteristic you think you have goes into the formation of your self-concept. You have decided these things about yourself based on your experiences and the feedback you have received from others.

Experience. Through experience you learn your strong points and your likes and dislikes. Each day you have different experiences which contribute to your self-concept. For example, if you excelled in chemistry at school, most likely you decided that you were good at chemistry, that you liked it, and that you would continue to take similar courses. On the other hand, if you did poorly in chemistry, you probably considered it your worst subject and avoided taking additional courses if possible. Do you remember the first time you participated in sports activities? If your experiences in sports were good, you probably decided that you had some athletic ability. You may have become quite active in sports and spent a large part of your leisure time engaged in participative sports. If you were not skilled in sports activities, you probably convinced yourself that you were not athletic and quit participating in physical sports.

Feedback from Others. Your self-concept is also a reaction of how others see and respond to you. Suppose that you are constantly told that you are attractive, good looking, or beautiful. If so, you probably look at yourself in the mirror and feel good about what you see. Suppose you are told that you are a good speaker. After hearing that several times, you probably decide that you do have ability in public speaking and this encourages you to improve your presentations before groups. Other people's comments can validate, reinforce, or alter the perceptions of who you are and what you can do. The more positive comments you receive, the more positive your self-concept. Conversely, negative comments destroy your self-esteem and you develop a negative self-concept.

Illus. 4-1
Your self-concept is formed from your experiences and the feedback you receive from others.

Communication Patterns

Your self-concept affects your choice of vocabulary, your tone of voice, your self-image, and your relationships with others.

Your Vocabulary and Tone of Voice. There is a definite connection between one's self-image and one's speech habits and voice inflection. Self-pitying remarks such as "I never could do that," "I just can't seem to get anything right," or "No wonder no one likes me, I do everything wrong," reveal that a person does not have a positive self-concept. Constant deprecation of the accomplishments of others may also be a sign of a low self-concept. People with low self-esteem frequently voice complaints such as "Sue got the promotion only because her uncle is president." (The fact that Sue attended night school for five years is not mentioned.) "Of course John can travel every summer; he makes more money than I do." (The fact that John lives frugally all year in order to afford those trips is overlooked by the complainer.)

In contrast, people with positive self-concepts make statements such as "I can't wait to try that; I know I will be successful," "I'm always eager to try something new; I may not win but it's fun to try," and "This job is going to be a challenge, but I love a challenge." Their voice is enthusiastic and their manner self-confident. No wonder they succeed!

Your Self-Image. Another indication of your self-concept is your impression on others. The higher your self-concept, the more likely you are to make a positive impression. Conversely, the lower your self-esteem, the more negative the image you are likely to present. For example, if you believe that you can be successful as a secretary, you approach each task with self-confidence. You soon impress others with your ability to accept responsibility. But if you believe you do not have the skills necessary to be successful in secretarial work, you reveal by your actions a lack of confidence in yourself.

Interpersonal Relationships. Have you ever awakened in the morning full of misgivings about the day ahead? Have you verbalized your fears by thinking, This is going to be a bad day; I know it; I may as well not even get up? On such days you probably want to withdraw from the world and have as little contact with others as possible. A person with a negative self-concept experiences such self-defeating emotions frequently. Such a person wants to withdraw into a shell. This person seems to feel that he or she is not worthy of the company of others.

The reverse is true of the person with a positive self-concept. This person seeks out others and enjoys interpersonal relationships. If you have a positive self-concept, you will interact easily with others and you will enjoy their company. You will benefit from the feedback that other people give you about yourself and your work, and this feedback will reinforce your self-concept and influence it in a positive way.

Self-Concept Strengtheners

You know that self-concept is important in the communication process. You understand how self-concept is developed and how it influences your speech habits, your tone of voice, your self-image, and the way you interact with others. Now consider how you might strengthen your self-concept.

Be open to new experiences. You have discovered that your self-concept has been shaped in part by the experiences you have had in your life. Also, you should continually be open to new experiences. For example, your experiences may have made you believe that you were not capable of creative thinking. Perhaps when you were young a teacher asked you to write an essay. You couldn't think of anything to write, so you labeled yourself uncreative. Since then you have had other experiences that have reinforced your sense of inadequacy. Recently, however, you solved an office problem in a unique way. Your employer complimented you on your creative approach to the problem. Absorb this experience into your consciousness. Be aware that your previous experiences do not necessarily have to control the rest of your life. Believe in the feedback you received from this new experience, and allow yourself to test your creativity further with additional creative experiences.

Illus. 4-2
New experiences help build your self-confidence.

Set your own directions. You have also learned that self-concept is a result of what others tell you about yourself. As you have matured, however, you have probably discovered that others are not always right. The way they perceive you and the feedback that they give you is colored by their own self-perceptions. It is your responsibility to realize that the perceptions of others may be inaccurate. Too many people accept others' perceptions without question.

If you want to strengthen your own self-concept, you must start by recognizing that perceptions can be wrong. If someone says to you, "You do not play volleyball very well," you may ask yourself, What do my past experiences and knowledge tell me about how I play volleyball? If you have always been successful at this sport, you should conclude that you may have had a bad day or for some unexplained reason this person does not think you play well. But you do not have to accept every statement that others make about you. You should evaluate their statements based on what you know about yourself and your experiences. You should decide whether or not the statements of others are accurate. To do this you must be able to think independently and rationally and sort out the valuable feedback from the erroneous feedback. In other words, set your own directions.

THE COMMUNICATION PROCESS

Now that you have considered how communication and self-concept are related, take a look at the process of communication. This process involves the exchange of ideas and feelings through the use of symbols, such as words or gestures. It contains several elements—the originator, the message, the receiver, and the response.

The Originator

The originator is the sender of the original message. The originator transmits information, ideas, and feelings through speaking, writing, or gesturing. Although the originator is often one person, the originator may be a company, a committee, or even a nation. For example, in the advertisements you see on television about a particular product, the company is the originator of the communication. Through this advertisement, the company transmits information about the product.

The Message

The message is the idea being presented by the originator. The process of turning an idea into symbols that can be communicated is called *encoding*. The symbols used are usually words; but they may be hand signals, gestures, or a combination of words and gestures.

After the originator mentally encodes the message into symbols, these symbols are transmitted. You will usually be involved in transmission which takes place in the form of face-to-face interchanges, telephone conversations, or written correspondence such as letters and memorandums. Other forms of transmission are radio and television.

The Receiver

The person for whom the message is intended is the receiver. The receiver takes the symbols that are transmitted and *decodes* these symbols into meaning. The message that is decoded by the receiver may not be the same message that was encoded by the originator.

Consider an example of how everyday communication can be misunderstood. Assume that John tells Bob to turn down the air conditioner. The room temperature is 72 degrees. John is cold and intends for Bob to turn the air conditioner to a point where the room will be warmer. Bob assumes that John wants the air conditioner turned to a lower temperature. Thus, Bob turns the air conditioner to 68 degrees. About 20 minutes later when the room has become even colder, John yells at Bob, "Why didn't you do what I asked you to do?" Bob cannot understand why John is upset; he had turned down the air conditioner. An unusual situation? Not at all. What one person considers a simple communication is often misunderstood by another person, thus resulting in misunderstandings, frustrations, and unhappiness for both persons.

The Response

A receiver decodes a message and responds to the message. The response (feedback) of the receiver lets the originator know whether the communication was understood. The response may be verbal or nonverbal (a nod of the head, a smile, a lifting of the eyebrows). If the

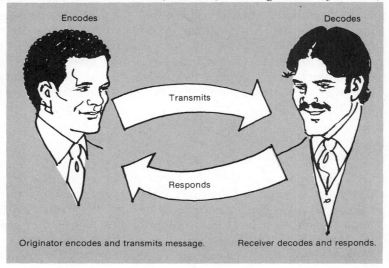

Encodes

Decodes

Transmits

Responds

Originator encodes and transmits message.   Receiver decodes and responds.

Illus. 4-3
The communication process

response of the receiver indicates to the originator that the communication was misunderstood, then the originator can send the message again, perhaps in a different manner. However, in some instances, it may take some time to determine the response of the receiver. In the previous example, John did not know that Bob had misinterpreted the communication until 20 minutes later. Although it is not always possible to get an immediate response, the communication improves markedly as more interaction takes place.

NONVERBAL COMMUNICATION

Although what we say and what we write are important parts of communication, another important area concerns nonverbal communication. We use a variety of nonverbal communication methods to convey meaning. Consider the following.

Body Language

Various body motions or gestures have meaning. Notice in Illus. 4-4 that the verbal communication of the originator and the receiver

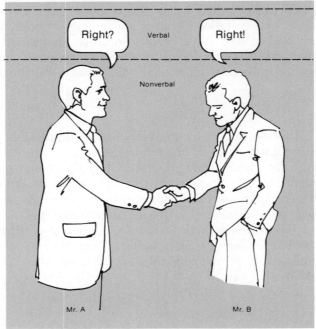

Illus. 4-4
Body language

is the same, yet there are clues from the nonverbal behavior which help to determine something about each person. For this illustration, answer these questions: Who is more aggressive? Who is more persuasive? Who is more approachable?

You probably have decided that Mr. A is more aggressive and more persuasive. Mr. A's nonverbal behavior—the jutting jaw and the positive facial expression—symbolizes assertiveness and authority. You probably have decided that Mr. B is more approachable. His meek and tractable expression indicates that he is compliant and docile.

Although body language is extremely important, one gesture cannot be taken as having meaning of itself. All gestures that a person makes must be considered along with what is being said. The study of body language is useful because it points out that a person actually communicates through gestures as well as words.

Voice Quality

A loud tone of voice is usually associated with anger, a soft tone of voice with calmness and poise. Two people talking softly with each other usually indicates that they are at ease. The loudness or softness of the voice and the pitch of the voice are nonverbal behaviors that reveal something about an individual. A person's voice will usually be pitched higher when he or she is tense, anxious, or nervous. And a person usually talks faster when angry or tense. In contrast, a low pitch and a slow pace usually indicate an intimate or relaxed tone. Other forms of nonverbal voice communication include the nervous giggle; a quivering, emotional voice; and a breaking, stressful voice.

Time

Another important nonverbal communicator is time. Think about the implications time has for the American people. In a school situation, a late term paper or project usually results in a penalty for the student. In a business situation, habitually late reports usually cause dire consequences. After fair warning, the employee may be fired. An applicant who fails to notify an interviewer that he or she will be late for a job interview may forfeit the chance of getting the job. An uninformed interviewer may conclude from the nonverbal behavior that the applicant is undependable, unconcerned about others, and uninterested in the job.

Space

Do you have a certain desk in a classroom which you consider yours? Do you feel pushed out of your place if someone else occupies that desk? Do you consider particular areas in your home your territory? The act of laying claim to and defending a territory is termed *territoriality*. People of different cultures use the space within their territories in various ways. *Proxemics* is the study of the personal and cultural use of space.

Americans tend to divide space equally. In a business office each individual usually has the same amount of space for his or her desk. A new employee also receives an equal amount of space. But an American working in France will encounter an entirely different situation. A new person becoming part of an office in France is usually given a small desk facing the wall. The French are used to this working arrangement and readily accept such working conditions. However, an American working in such a confined area would probably feel isolated and unwanted unless the American understood the French use of space.

Consider another example of the way different cultures use space. Latin Americans come close to an individual when talking on an impersonal basis. On the other hand, people in the United States usually do not get close to each other when talking unless there is an intimate relationship.

Illus. 4-5
Americans use space to protect their privacy in impersonal communication.

ARRIERS TO EFFECTIVE COMMUNICATION

In order for a company to function productively, there must be effective communication. The information transmitted among employees must be sufficiently received and interpreted. However, this is not always the case since employees come from various educational, social, and cultural backgrounds. As a result, communication barriers exist. Consider the following barriers.

Noise

Communication theorists refer to the noise that gets in the way of communication. This noise may be external or internal.

External Noise. External noise refers to the physical sounds that stand in the way of communication. For example, if someone is talking while several people around you are typing and you cannot hear, then external noise—the typewriters—is clogging the communication channel. Or if you have ever listened to someone speaking and started counting the times the person said "ah" rather than hearing what the person was saying, then external noise was involved. This annoying speech mannerism is a form of external noise, and it gets in the way of what the person is actually saying.

Internal Noise. Internal noise comes from different backgrounds, experiences, and perceptions which cause a person to interpret a communication in a certain way. In other words, internal noise is a learned response—learned through environment, culture, and the significant people in a person's life. Consider this example. Jane and Jim see a group of office workers laughing together. Jane thinks, What a great place to work; the employees enjoy their work and cooperate with each other to get the job done. Jim thinks, I bet that department is extremely inefficient; no one is working. They are just standing around telling jokes. Jane's perception is that work can be fun while Jim's interpretation is that if you are having fun you can't be working. Internal noise has affected how Jane and Jim have responded to the situation.

Language Usage

The language we use often prevents clear communication. Words of themselves have no meaning; they have meaning only because people have agreed upon a particular meaning. You may say, "But what about the dictionary? Doesn't it contain the correct meaning of words?" Yes, it contains the correct meaning as agreed on by *etymologists* (specialists in the study of words). This meaning can be called the objective meaning of a word, and we use the dictionary to determine this meaning. But meanings change with time. New words come into existence, and other words become obsolete because of their lack of usage.

For example, the computer era has generated different applications for certain words. The word *terminal* to a computer operator, programmer, or analyst means an input/output device that enables a user to have direct contact with a computer. However, if you look up the word *terminal* in the dictionary, you find definitions such as "pertaining to, situated at, or forming the end or boundary of something; growing or appearing at the end of a stem, branch, stalk, or similar part; any ornamental figure or object situated at the end of something; a position in an electric circuit or device at which an electric connection is normally established or broken." Certainly these definitions are correct, but you can readily see the problems that can occur with the various meanings of the word.

Another problem with the English language is that words may mean different things to different people. Meanings of words are often subjective because they are based on our experiences and backgrounds. Consider this conversation between an employer and an employee.

> The employer said: Type this report as soon as possible.
> The employee interpreted: Type this report as soon as you finish what you are working on.
> The employer meant: Drop everything and type the report.

A half hour later the employer comes back for the report, discovers that it hasn't been typed, becomes upset, and says to the employee, "Why didn't you do what I asked?" The employee, frustrated, says, "But I am going to type it as soon as I finish this project." Thus, a communication problem has occurred over words that have different meanings to the employer and the employee.

Evaluation

The tendency to evaluate other people often gets in the way of communication. The following conversation occurred between Ruth Lyons and Elsa Spofford. Elsa took the CPS (Certified Professional Secretary) examination for the first time two years ago. The first year Elsa passed two parts of the examination and failed four parts. The second year, she passed the remaining four parts and is now a CPS. Ruth is taking the examination for the first time next month.

Elsa: Ruth, I just heard that you are going to take the CPS exam next
      month. Good luck!

Ruth: Thanks, but I feel quite confident. I don't think I will have any
      trouble passing the exam. I have taken several review courses
      and have been studying all year.

Elsa: If I were you, I don't think I would be so confident. It really is a
      stiff exam.

What has Elsa done? She has immediately evaluated Ruth. Elsa's experience has led her to believe that the examination is difficult; she has trouble believing that anyone can be so confident. She probably did not even hear Ruth say that she has been studying for a year and has taken several review courses.

One of the major barriers to communication is the tendency to judge, to evaluate, and to approve or disapprove of the person making the statement. This evaluation is made from the listener's frame of reference and experience. If what is said agrees with the listener's experience, the listener tends to make a positive evaluation of the person making the statement. However, if what is said does not agree with the listener's experience, then a negative evaluation occurs.

Illus. 4-6
Evaluation is a communication hazard.

What can be done to prevent or reduce the tendency to evaluate other people? You need to listen with understanding. What does this mean? It means seeing ideas from the other person's point of view and trying to sense how the other person feels. If you listen with understanding, you may begin to comprehend the idea as the speaker comprehends it; you may find that your attitudes and ideas have been influenced. If you have the courage to listen with understanding, communication will be improved greatly. You may even find that you have learned and grown in the process.

Inference

Read these statements: You arrive home from work late one evening and see that all the lights are on in your home. A car is parked in front of your house with the words Chris Smith, M.D., in small letters on the door on the driver's side.

Now determine if the following statements are true or false.

1. The car parked in front of your house has lettering on the door on the passenger side.
   (False. The statement says the lettering was on the driver's side.)
2. Someone in your family is sick.
   (May be true or false. Someone may be visiting a member of your household and that person may have become ill. The doctor may be making a social call. The doctor may be seeing someone next door. There may not be a doctor driving the car at all; someone may have borrowed the car from the doctor.)
3. No car is parked in front of your house.
   (False. The statement says there is a car parked in front of your house.)
4. The car belongs to a man named Smith.
   (May be true or false. The doctor may be a woman. The car may not belong to someone named Smith. The car may have been recently sold or stolen.)

What do the statements illustrate? People sometimes jump to conclusions or infer things that are not true. People often make an inference, fail to recognize that an inference has been made, and proceed to act upon the inference as if it were a certainty.

The first step in correcting inference problems is to be aware that you may be making an inference. Know the difference between an inference and an observation. Ask yourself, Did I observe this event or did I infer that it happened? And, if you inferred that it happened, what are the probabilities that your inference is correct? Certainly there are times when you personally cannot observe an event, and it is necessary for you to infer its occurrence. But it is important to recognize inferences and to realize that inferences aren't always correct.

Allness

Communication theorists refer to a communication problem called *allness* which means that an individual presumes that what he or she says or knows is complete, absolute, and all inclusive. To demonstrate this concept, listed below are a few details about one individual. This person is a:

Female
Secretary
Sister
Member of Professional Secretaries International
Tennis player
Pianist

Do these details list all there is to know about this person? No. There is much more to know about the person. An individual cannot take one characteristic, idea, or detail and assume that he or she knows all or has said all there is to say about a person, subject, or concept. However, that is exactly what we do sometimes in communicating. Or two people may take different details from a given situation and assume that they know all there is to know. Then when these two people begin to talk about the situation, a tremendous communication problem results.

What can you do to lessen this communication problem? Be aware that you can never say or know everything about anything. Realize that you select and omit details when you communicate. In listening to others, you should use questioning and restatement techniques to be sure all essential information is obtained. If you are talking or writing, make it a habit of adding (at least silently when talking) an "etcetera" to remind yourself that you do not have all the information.

Body Motions or Gestures

Realize that nonverbal communication can contradict verbal communication. Be sensitive to the nonverbal behavior of others because a person's every move talks. Also, pay attention to your own nonverbal communication so that you are aware of the signals you are sending.

Numerous studies have been conducted on the impressions formed from certain body movements. For example, a person may lean back in a relaxed manner in a chair if in agreement with what a speaker is saying. Arms folded firmly are usually a gesture of refusal. On the other hand, if a person's arms are folded gently and loosely, this usually is a sign of relaxation and an attitude of friendliness. The person who stands erect with shoulders upright may communicate determination, pride, grace, or courage in the face of tragedy. On the other hand, a person with hunched shoulders may communicate a lack of ambition, discouragement, depression, or weariness.

Illus. 4-7
What are these people communicating?

Categorization

Categorization is the ability to compare, contrast, and classify objects, persons, or ideas. For example, as a small child you learned what a dog looked like and how a dog sounded. As you discovered different breeds of dogs, you were able to see the similarities and the differences in the generic category *dogs*. Just as categorization is useful to a child in learning about the world, it is also useful to an adult in acquiring new information. Categorization provides the means to classify new information with other similar facts.

As categorization can assist in the learning process, it can also block the communication process; for example, the tendency to categorize people by their sex. All women may be considered more emotional than men. All women may be considered superior in language skills and all men superior in math skills. Or all scientists may be considered extremely intelligent and all athletes stupid. Obviously such categorization is a communication barrier. Through categorization, it is difficult to understand who an individual really is and how that individual thinks and feels. It is possible to miss valuable interaction with others through categorization—interaction that can broaden one's perspectives and make one's life more meaningful.

REDUCING COMMUNICATION BARRIERS

If you want to communicate successfully, you must learn to reduce communication barriers. It is difficult to eliminate all communication barriers because you encounter different people in different situations every day. You are constantly faced with different language usages, with your individual internal noise which affects the way you respond, with the internal noise of others, with categorization, and with nonverbal gestures and motions. But you should be alert to these barriers and should take steps to reduce them. Here are some techniques that will help you communicate better.

Use Active Listening

Studies show that most people spend 70 percent of their time communicating. Of that 70 percent, 45 percent is spent listening. Since such a large percentage of time is spent listening, it may be assumed that listening is the most effective part of the communication process. However, most authorities agree that listening is the weakest factor in the communication process. Hearing someone say something does not constitute listening. A person can hear the sounds that come from another's mouth and yet not understand the words. Active listening requires that you listen for the words as well as the meaning of the speaker. Here are some techniques which will help you become an active listener.

Prepare to listen. Daydreaming is one of the leading causes of poor listening. Drive distracting thoughts from your mind. Direct your full attention to the speaker.

Knowing when to stop talking is essential to the listening process. In fact, the very nature of the listening process demands that you stop talking; it is impossible to listen when you are talking. Be a good listener; know when to stop talking!

Listen for facts. Mentally register the key words that the speaker is using. Between the time the speaker says the words (average 125 WPM) and the time it takes you to comprehend them (at a rate of 500 WPM) review the key ideas presented. Raise questions in your mind about the subject. Assimilate what the speaker is saying with your own experiences. Mentally repeat key ideas or related points. Listening is not a passive activity. Good listening requires concentration and active participation. A listener who is able to identify the speaker's main points and the pattern of the speaker's remarks certainly has an advantage over the listener who is simply listening to words.

Listen for feelings. Search beneath the surface. Listen to what the speaker is not saying as well as what he or she is saying. What does the speaker really mean when he or she says, "I will be glad to retype the report a third time"? Does the statement mean that the speaker feels good about redoing the report? that the speaker is unhappy about having to correct another person's errors? that the speaker is feeling a great deal of stress with retyping a report three times? A comment such as this can have many meanings which only an alert listener can grasp.

Minimize your mental blocks and filters. Everyone has certain biases and prejudices. Being aware that these blocks exist will make them easier to control. You may hear people say such things as "You can't talk with CPAs (Certified Public Accountants); they only know how to deal with figures," "Don't try to reason with a union representative," or "Give me the old equipment any day; it was much better." These statements reveal prejudices. Each speaker is judging an entire group of people or things on the basis of one individual or product. Your listening behaviors will improve if you become aware of your own blocks and filters as well as the speaker's blocks and filters.

Use mnemonic devices. A *mnemonic device* is a formula, word association, or rhyme used to assist the memory. For example, if an individual finds jogging *b*oring, *e*xhausting, and *t*ime-consuming, that person could create a mnemonic device such as BET to act as a memory trigger in voicing opposition to jogging programs.

Take notes. When listening to a presentation or a lecture, you may find it beneficial to take notes. Here are some suggestions for effective note taking:

1. Determine whether you need to take notes. Consider your goals, your concentration and retention abilities, and whether you will use the information immediately or at a later date.
2. Identify the pattern of the message and reflect that pattern in your notes.
3. Write only the main points of the message. Do not attempt to record each word.
4. Keep your notes clear. Avoid doodling or making other marks on your notes which may confuse you when you review them.
5. Read your notes immediately after the presentation and expand on any points you think necessary.
6. Categorize and file your notes so that they can be found easily when you need them.

Try Empathy

Literally place yourself in the other person's shoes. Try to identify with the feelings and ideas that a person is communicating. Attempt to see the world as others see it. To communicate effectively, you should realize that everyone sees the world differently. And when two persons' views differ, it does not mean that one is right and the other is wrong; it merely means that they are different. Accept these differences and you will avoid unnecessary disagreements that could lead to serious confrontations.

Be Person Oriented

As you have learned, words do not have meanings by themselves. They have meanings only because word specialists have agreed upon a particular meaning, and this meaning is not the same for all groups of people. Alert communicators ask, "Do you understand what I'm saying?" They check to see that the meaning of the words they are using is understood by the persons receiving the message.

Question and Paraphrase

Ask questions when you don't understand what you have heard, when you think that there may be more than one legitimate interpretation of what is being said, and when a statement seems out of line with your knowledge of the facts or the situation. Put the speaker's communication in your own words (*paraphrase*), and ask the speaker if your paraphrasing is correct. Paraphrasing will help you remember and understand the speaker's message.

Analyze the Signals You Are Sending

Everything you do—the way you talk, walk, gesture, or stand— communicates information about you. Sensitivity to nonverbal behavior should be of major importance to anyone who wants to work more effectively with people. Impressions left through nonverbal behavior, regardless of their validity, play a significant role in our relationships and communication with others.

Use Your Perception

Perception is to nonverbal communication what paraphrasing is to verbal communication. Be alert to how others react when you communicate. Test your perception skills. For example, if a person frowns while you are talking, you may say, "I'm not sure what your frown means. Are you confused or do you disagree with what I'm saying?" If a person uses a sharp tone of voice, you may say, "I get the impression that you're upset with me." Confirming perceptions gives the originator the opportunity to verify or correct what has been received.

Reduce External and Internal Noise

Eliminate external noise if possible. For example, turn off the stereo or radio; move to a quiet location. Turn on your power of concentration; attempt to block out noise through concentrated effort. Remember that your background and experiences (internal noise) affect the way you view a situation. As an originator of a communication, examine what you intend to say so that those persons who receive your communication are able to understand and interpret the language you are using.

Reserve Judgment

Try to understand the message as the speaker intends it. Avoid arguing (overtly or covertly) with the speaker. If you are opposed to an idea which a person is conveying, try not to argue or become emotional. Work hard at being objective. Control your reaction at least until you have heard all the speaker has to say. You may find that your views change or broaden by what the speaker says. Or you may find that what the speaker says is not relevant to you. Regardless of your acceptance or rejection of what a speaker says, your knowledge will increase when you listen—even if you only learn another person's view on a subject.

PROFESSIONAL POINTERS

Do you have high communication ability? Can you answer yes to most of these statements?

1. I realize that what I see is an incomplete picture of what may be observed.

2. I realize that my experience and background may affect what I see, hear, or say.

3. I realize that what a person says to me about a situation is merely one version of what might be said.

4. When I speak, I take into account the danger that some of my words may be misinterpreted.

5. I am alert to the nonverbal behavior of others and incorporate the nonverbal behavior with the verbal behavior.

6. I try to use the most up-to-date meaning of words.

7. I avoid using words that threaten the self-concept of the listener.

8. I am aware that my opinions may be different from those of another person.

9. I realize the difference between facts and inferences.

10. I am people oriented rather than word oriented.

FOR YOUR REVIEW

1. How is self-concept related to communication?

2. What contributes to the development of self-concept?

3. Explain two ways to strengthen your self-concept.

4. Identify and explain the elements of the communication process.

5. List and explain three types of nonverbal communication.

6. Explain the difference between internal and external noise.

7. How is language a communication barrier?

8. Define *allness,* and explain how it is a communication barrier.

9. Describe three effective listening techniques.

10. Identify and explain four ways (other than active listening) in which communication barriers can be reduced.

CASE PROBLEM

Marcia Allen's employer was recently promoted to vice-president, administration. Marcia was transferred with her employer. Jack Babb previously held the position of secretary to the vice-president, administration; but, when his employer retired, Jack was given a secretarial position at a lower level although his salary was not cut. Jack has been upset about the situation and, according to Marcia, "Jack publicly snubs me and is always disagreeable. He never speaks to me; and when he needs to see my employer, he walks directly into the office without consulting me first. On several occasions I have requested information from him about letters from his files, and he has told me that I have no need for it."

Marcia has tried to ignore the situation, hoping that it would get better. But it has been going on for six months now.

1. What should Marcia do?

2. Should she continue to ignore the situation, or should she take action?

PRODUCTION PROJECTS

PP 4-1
(Objective 1)

Study the following conversation, and then answer the questions that follow.

Christine: Would you like to play tennis with me?
Elaine: I'm not good at sports. I have never played tennis, and I know I would be terrible.
Christine: You should try it. It's a great game. Come on, let me help you. I'm a good player, and I'm a good teacher, too. What do you say?
Elaine: Okay, but don't say I didn't warn you.
(Later, on the tennis court)
Christine: That was a pretty good shot, Elaine.
Elaine: Thanks. This is fun!
Christine: Let me help you with your serve. I think that with a little help you can be a good player.
Elaine: No one has ever tried to show me how to play a sport before. Maybe I can learn to do something.
Christine: Of course, you can. All you need is a little help and a lot of practice.
Elaine: Do you really think I can be a good player?
Christine: Well, maybe not a Martina Navratilova, but better than average. Would you like to play again Wednesday?
Elaine: Yes. This has been fun.

1. How do you perceive Christine's self-concept?

2. Why do you think Christine feels this way?

3. How do you perceive Elaine's self-concept?

4. Why does Elaine feel this way?

5. Did Elaine's perceptions change during the game? If so, how and why?

PP 4-2
(Objective 1)

As you learned in this chapter, individuals do not always perceive people, situations, or ideas in the same way. To demonstrate this concept, participate in this exercise with your classmates.

1. Divide into groups of eight members.

2. Choose three members from each group who will leave the room. (Person A, Person B, and Person C)

3. Your instructor will show the rest of the members of the groups a picture. Examine the picture, but do not write down what is in it.

4. Call in the Person A from each group. Each group describes the picture to Person A. Person A cannot ask questions; he or she merely listens to the description the group gives.

5. Call in the Person B from each group. Then Person A describes the picture to Person B but without the group's help.

6. Then Person C from each group is called in, and Person B describes the picture to Person C. Person C goes to the chalkboard or flip chart and draws the picture from Person B's description. Compare the drawings with Person C's in each group. Then compare these pictures with the original picture.

Each group should then discuss the following questions:

1. How did the differences in the perceptions of various members interfere with the communication process?

2. What contributes to these various perceptions of individuals?

PP 4-3
(Objectives 1 and 2)

To function effectively as a secretary in a modern office, you will need to have an adequate self-concept in order to perform job related tasks, help others with their duties, and get along with all personnel. What characteristics must a secretary develop and strengthen if he or she is to function effectively in an office situation? List the personal qualifications and skills that a secretary who possesses a strong self-concept should have.

PP 4-4
(Objective 3)

In this chapter you learned about the elements that make up the communication process. Expand your knowledge of these elements by researching two articles or books that discuss the elements of the communication process. Write a summary of your findings, and include a bibliography of the reference sources that you used.

PP 4-5
(Objective 4)

In this chapter you learned about nonverbal behavior. Use the form provided in your Supplies Inventory to record your responses to the following:

1. List five types of nonverbal behavior by which you reveal who you are. After each nonverbal form of behavior, describe a specific situation in which you use this behavior.

2. Spend twenty minutes in the school cafeteria, library, or similar place observing nonverbal communication. Select two persons whom you do not know and observe their nonverbal behavior. Describe their nonverbal behavior and give your interpretation.

PP 4-6
(Objective 4)

Choose two or three people to work with you on these projects.

1. Discuss the following: How do you perceive space and time? Are you offended when someone gets too close to you to talk? Are you offended when someone makes an appointment with you and is late? Do you have your own "territory" at home? If you work in an office now, are there certain areas which you consider yours? Do your perceptions about space differ when you are talking with a teacher? a good friend? a person you have just met? Are your attitudes the same as those of the other members of your group? If not, how do they differ?

2. Have each member of the group choose one area of nonverbal communication to research. Find at least one article or book containing information on an area of nonverbal behavior. Present your findings in a group report before your class. Incorporate the group's feelings which were discussed in Question 1 above.

PP 4-7
(Objective 5)

Work with one member of your class in analyzing this case: La-Ton Electronics has a word processing center. There are four word processing operators in the center. Their desks are lined up one behind the other. The first desk has always been occupied by the person with the most seniority with the company. When this person is promoted, the other people in the center move up a desk. The new manager of the center, Dollie Kildrow, has decided that this game of musical chairs is ridiculous. When a new word processing operator, Rachael Rodriquez, was employed, Dollie gave the new operator the first desk.

There has always been a friendly, teamwork approach in the word processing center with good-natured bantering between the operators and the manager. Since Rachael has been employed, the friendly bantering has stopped. Rachael seems very capable and is trying hard to get along with everyone in the office. However, none of the other operators will have anything to do with her. Dollie is puzzled. She doesn't understand what has happened.

1. Is there a communication problem here?
2. If so, what is it?
3. How could the problem have been avoided?
4. What can be done to avoid this type of problem in the future?

PP 4-8
(Objective 5)

This conversation takes place in the office of Patricia Martin, office manager for Bauer Industries. Donald Smith, a secretary, has been reported as doing unsatisfactory work by Mr. Wilson, to whom he reports. Mr. Wilson has requested that he be transferred to another department.

Martin: Mr. Smith, you will remember we talked together last month. At that time I told you that Mr. Wilson was not entirely satisfied with your work. He has reported to me that he is still not satisfied.

Smith: He hasn't told me that. In fact, he told me that I was doing a good job.

Martin: Well, Mr. Wilson has written a report about your work. I am going to read it to you. Please tell me whether you agree with the report. ". . . does not keep the filing current."

Smith: I don't like to file, and I wasn't hired to file. I was hired as a secretary.

Martin: Filing is part of your job.

Smith: But I wasn't told that it was part of my job.

Martin: ". . . writes personal letters during business hours."

Smith: I have done that only once, and it took only 10 minutes.

Martin: ". . . is always behind in his work."

Smith: Mr. Wilson asked me to help him on a project. I told him I would be glad to, but I couldn't keep up with my regular work and work on the project, too. He said he would get someone to help do the regular work, since he wanted me to help him on the project.

Martin: ". . . leaves the office 15 minutes before lunch and leaves 20 minutes before quitting time."

Smith: I have done that only two or three times in the two years that I have worked here.

Martin: Do you have any differences with Mr. Wilson?

Smith: I'd rather not say.

Martin: Don't you get along?

Smith: Oh, sometimes we don't.

Martin: Please tell me about it.

Smith: I want to leave this position. Please transfer me to another department.

Martin: This is the third department you have worked in at Bauer. We can't continue to transfer you from department to department. Do you think your work load is too heavy?

Smith: I get behind sometimes.

Martin: Do you leave work early?

Smith: Only the two or three times that I mentioned before. And I have worked overtime many times. Also, I've noticed that other secretaries leave early.

Martin: Do you get along with the other secretaries?

Smith: Yes.

Martin: You can go back to your department now. I will let you know what we plan to do in two or three days.

Select one class member to work with you, and analyze this conversation. What communication problems do you see? What mistakes has Ms. Martin made? What mistakes has Mr. Smith made? Do communication barriers exist between Ms. Martin and Mr. Smith. If so, what are they? Are there communication problems between Mr. Wilson and Mr. Smith? If so, what are they? Prepare a joint report on the communication problems in this case; type the report; sign both names. Do the following in your report:

1. Suggest ways that the communication problems could have been avoided.

2. Determine what steps can be taken now to reduce the communication problems.

Chapter 5

DEVELOPING THE OFFICE TEAM

As a member of the office team, you may handle scientific, legal, technical, or financial documents as well as correspondence. However, none of your responsibilities will be more challenging than the complex task of understanding, working with, and relating to people inside and outside the organization. In the previous chapter you learned about ways to deal with communication barriers and how to reduce these barriers in order to communicate effectively. But there are still other factors to be understood if you are to perform effectively as part of the office team.

In this chapter you will learn about the formal and informal communication channels of an organization as well as other factors that contribute to your effectiveness as a member of the office team. Some of these factors are acceptance and understanding of others, loyalty and dependability to the people within the organization, tactfulness and fairness, the elimination of discrimination on the job, and a pleasant and safe working environment.

General Objectives

Your general objectives for Chapter 5 are to:

1. *Understand the composition and needs of the office team*
2. *Understand the differences between formal and informal communication in an organization*
3. *Explain the role that effective communication plays in the development of the team*
4. *Discover the nature of discrimination in the workplace*
5. *Understand the role of ergonomics and safety in the office*

THE OFFICE TEAM IS . . .

The office team is a group of individuals who work together with defined goals. There are three important elements in this definition: (1) a group of individuals, (2) who work together, (3) with defined goals. The three elements of the office team will be examined separately in the following paragraphs.

A Group of Individuals

The office team comprises a group of individuals who have various physical characteristics that range from differences in height, weight, and general appearance to differences in age, sex, and race. In addition to physical differences, the office team is composed of people who possess diverse mental and physical abilities, such as intelligence, aptitudes, physical strength, manual dexterity, knowledge, and skill. Perceptions may also vary. Each person sees the world from a perspective determined by that person's background and experiences. And, just as background and experiences influence perception, they also influence values. *Values* are principles and qualities that you consider important and are learned from the significant people in your life and from your experiences. For example, belief in hard work and individual freedom are values passed down from one generation to the next.

The United States was settled by people who believed that, through hard work and endurance, they could improve their standard of living. Certainly that aspiration has been realized. The pioneering spirit of individuals or small groups who set out to conquer frontiers is a rich ingredient of our heritage. Those individuals who, through hard work and perseverance, not only developed the natural resources of this country but also served in government and steered the nation to its greatness will always be a part of America's success story.

Today, however, some traditional values have changed. People want jobs with potential—jobs offering participation in company decisions and management opportunities. Many companies are now realizing the importance of teamwork between management and talented employees in accomplishing company goals. Certainly the entrepreneur still has an important function in American business, but cooperation and team effort are now held as important as individual effort in the success of a company.

Individuals also have different needs. Everyone has certain primary needs (the need for food, water, rest, safety and security, and acceptance by others), but even these primary needs differ in intensity among individuals. For example, you may have an intense social need (acceptance by others; friendship). To satisfy this need, you constantly join groups, seeking the companionship of others. Whereas another individual may enjoy the company of others but rarely join social groups. The person with a low social need may prefer to work alone and refrain from participating in organized activities—business or social.

What do these differences in individuals mean to you as a potential office worker? To get along with people, you must recognize, understand, and accept differences in people in order to be an effective member of the office team.

Working Together

Individuals on the office team form a working unit. The design of almost all offices forces individuals into a close physical working relationship. Although a company may be housed in a large building, each office team within the company is usually grouped together. Thus, the organization of a company brings individuals in proximity to each other.

In addition to working together in physical proximity, the office team shares similar job tasks. These tasks depend on the nature of the work done by the office team. For example, secretaries in a law office produce similar legal documents and correspondence. Secretaries in educational institutions work on the same types of forms and correspondence. Business offices are arranged by departments so that all persons work in areas designated by the name of the department: Accounting, Billing, Marketing, Filing, Word Processing, and so on. Therefore, by the nature of the physical location and the type of work done, groups of individuals work together. But working together has much broader implications than proximity and similar job tasks. To work together effectively, the group must have a common purpose. This common purpose is considered next.

Illus. 5-1
Individuals on the office team form a working unit.

With Defined Goals

What are the goals of the office team? Two groups of goals to consider are individual goals and organizational goals. You do not join a company without certain goals of your own. Your goals are probably both short- and long-term goals. For example, one of your short-term goals may be to learn your job as quickly as possible or to be highly productive in your job. One of your long-term goals may be to be promoted to a high-level secretarial job in the company.

In addition to individual goals, the organization has goals. A major long-term goal of all businesses is to make a profit. A short-term goal of a company may be to increase sales by $200,000 over the next six months. In order to do so, the company must engage in numerous activities such as producing its products quickly and at a low cost, acquiring its share of the market, and keeping labor costs low.

For an individual to work effectively as a member of the office team, the individual's goals and the organization's goals should be compatible. But this is not always the case. Consider this example.

Assume that one of your goals is to develop social relationships with your co-workers. To achieve this goal you make it a habit to go to lunch each day with a group of people with whom you have identified as satisfying your social needs. After several months on your job, the Advertising Department in which you work is developing a major advertising campaign to market a new product. The campaign is behind schedule and your department head has asked you to shorten your lunch hour by thirty minutes and work overtime for two hours every evening for a week.

At this point your goals and your employer's goals are conflicting. By working overtime you will not be able to engage in your usual social activities. You can reconcile your goals and the organization's goals only by postponing your social activities for a week and by adjusting your schedule to meet the demands of your job. Reconciling conflicting goals may require adjustments on both your part and that of the organization. For the long pull, however, this may be a small price to pay in becoming a productive and essential team member who will be given first consideration when opportunities arise for which you are qualified by reason of your efficiency, loyalty, and ability to adjust to inconveniences when they occur.

THE OFFICE TEAM IS MADE UP OF . . .

In addition to understanding the definition of the office team, you must also understand the composition of the team. You and your employer compose one part of the team; you and your co-workers compose another part of the team. In each of these relationships, you have certain rights and responsibilities.

The Secretary and The Employer

As an employee, what do you owe your employer? What does your employer owe you? Your relationship with your employer is of primary importance. Unless it is satisfactory, neither of you will perform at top capacity.

The Secretary's Obligations to the Employer. Every employer wants to be accepted and respected. Employers also want employees who are loyal, dependable, and understanding.

Acceptance. Who is your employer? He or she is a person just as you are with the same basic needs that you have. Your employer must satisfy physical and safety needs. He or she needs to feel important and to be accepted as an individual. Your employer also has personal needs. Try to accept your employer.

Do not categorize your employer because of sex, age, race, or other single characteristic. You cannot put people into categories and expect that they will react a certain way because they are male or female, young or old, or black, brown, or white. One example of this is the male/female role in society.

In the past executives have usually been males who were seen as tough, able to make decisions quickly, unemotional, and intellectually superior. Females were seen as highly emotional, unable to make hard decisions, dependent, noncareer oriented, and intellectually inferior.

Today that picture is changing. More and more women are entering the job market. Women are staying in positions longer and are actively pursuing careers. And women are proving that they can indeed handle positions in management. This illustrates conclusively that we cannot fit people into predetermined molds based on characteristics which we presume they have. Individuals grow and develop differently based on different environments, social customs, and time periods.

Respect. You owe your employer respect simply because he or she is another human being. Each individual should value and appreciate other individuals. Because of individual ability, your employer has risen to a responsible position in the company. You need to respect his or her decision-making ability although you may not always understand or agree with the decisions made. Your role as a secretary is to respect and support your employer's decisions.

Loyalty. Have you seen the word *loyalty* in lists of desirable traits so often that you reject it as old-fashioned and not worthy of your attention? Don't. Loyalty between secretary and employer is a must. What does it mean? It means that you do what is asked of you to the best of your ability.

Loyalty means that you handle office matters confidentially. A person who cannot keep business or personal secrets should not expect to advance to a responsible secretarial position. If your employer cannot give you confidential work with the assurance that information will not be divulged, you will never have his or her full confidence. When other employees question you about subjects that are none of their business, or if they question you about personal affairs of your employer, you should not discuss these topics but should try to change the subject. The personal affairs of your employer should never be the subject of gossip—in or out of the office.

You are responsible for helping your employer better perform office duties. As a secretary, you are not in a position to make major decisions which affect company policy. This is an executive's role. However, your support role does not mean that you are subservient. You are a valuable assistant to your employer. And, as you develop more experience in the secretarial field, your employer will rely on you for your advice and opinions.

Dependability. Dependability in the office means that you observe the company rules. These rules include office hours, coffee breaks, sick leaves, vacations, and the like. When you are employed,

Illus. 5-2
Dedication on the job includes observing company rules at break times.

company policies are made clear. You are expected to work during the hours set by the company and to observe the designated break times. You are also expected not to abuse the sick leave or vacation policies. The company expects you to abide by these and other rules.

Understanding. Obtain as much information about your employer as possible. Being alert to your employer's likes and dislikes will make you an efficient and indispensable worker.

- *Business Background.* You should know something about the business experience and education of your employer. Find out your employer's length of time with the company, starting position, present position, and previous employer. You may obtain information from company publications, other employees, or your employer.
- *Personal Interests.* Not only is it important to find out the hobbies or interests of your employer, but it will also be helpful if you learn something about these interests yourself. For example, if your employer is an avid tennis player, you might learn something about the game. Remember that one of the best ways to get along with other people is to take an active interest in the activities that interest them.
- *Personal Traits.* Your employer will not always take time to explain in detail the things to be done and when to do them. After you have been on the job a short time, you will be expected to anticipate some of your employer's wishes. How can you learn to anticipate these wishes? The likes and dislikes of a person can best be learned by observation.

    Is your employer a fast thinker and ready to make quick decisions? a deliberate thinker and slow to make decisions? a person eager to complete a job once it is started? or a person who has a habit of putting off things?

    Does your employer get upset easily? When your employer is in an irritable mood, you should make a special effort to keep cool and to exercise self-control. Your empathic understanding will help you to exercise this self-control.

    Is your employer a person who is neat and orderly both in personal appearance and work habits? Or is he or she inclined to be careless and disorderly?

    Regardless of strong or weak personal characteristics, the average business executive expects you to be able to interpret and carry out orders when given. If you do not understand a request or an order, remember to ask questions; do not proceed blindly.

The Employer's Obligations to the Secretary. The secretary/employer relationship is not one-sided. There are certain things that your employer owes you, too.

Respect. Your employer should be aware of your needs and show respect for you and your ability. You were hired because you had the qualifications to handle the job. Your employer must give you the chance to prove that you can.

Sincerity. Your employer should let you know how your performance is being evaluated. If you have done something well, you should be told. If you have not performed satisfactorily, your employer should honestly tell you about it. You, in turn, must be able to take constructive criticism. It is much better to know exactly where you stand than to presume that you are doing a good job and later discover that you were wrong. If your employer honestly and sincerely tells you about your progress or lack of progress, you will benefit in the long run.

Illus. 5-3
Your employer should give you a sincere evaluation.

Loyalty. Just as your employer deserves your loyalty, you deserve your employer's loyalty. Your employer should present you in the best possible light to all individuals. For example, loyalty means that your employer does not criticize you either professionally or personally to other people. And, if your employer overhears gossip about you, he or she attempts to stop it. Your employer understands that the secretary and executive respect and help each other. The two of you are a close working team. Without loyalty on both sides, this team cannot operate at maximum efficiency.

Understanding and Acceptance. You, as a normal human being, will have times when you do not perform to capacity. Most people have days in which they are not, for some reason, equipped physically, mentally, or emotionally to handle a job at top capacity. Your employer should understand and accept this. This statement does not imply that you can bring all your personal problems to work. Certainly you should not! On your bad days, however, your employer should accept and understand you just as you accept and understand your employer on bad days.

The Secretary and Co-Workers

What type of relationship should you have with other office employees? Have you ever been in an office where one secretary (even though that person had nothing to do) refused to help another secretary who was overloaded with work? Have you ever been in an office in which coffee breaks and lunch hours were spent gossiping about other office employees? Have you ever been in an office where small cliques existed? Ridiculous? Yes, but if you have worked at all, you have probably encountered these situations. These problems can never be avoided entirely, but they can be reduced considerably if you apply what you know about human relations.

Acceptance. You will come in contact with many different people in an office. Their backgrounds and interests may be quite different from yours. You may not understand many of these people at first. And, because you do not understand them, you may dislike or disapprove of them. As a successful secretary, you need to accept other employees without judging them. You should recognize and respect people who are different from you. If you sincerely listen to others, you will learn more about them and avoid conflicts that result from a lack of understanding.

Cooperation. You should have a cooperative attitude in working with other employees in the office. Since few jobs are performed in isolation, cooperation is necessary in order to attain company goals. You should willingly assist other employees in meeting job deadlines when the situation demands. For example, if one secretary has a rush job that cannot be finished without help, you should help your co-worker finish the job provided you have no top priority work to complete. Through cooperation secretaries establish informal working arrangements for such responsibilities as answering the telephones, bringing supplies from the stockroom, or covering the reception desk during lunch.

Tact. *Tact* is skill and grace in dealing with others; it means having a sensitive perception of others. You should consider the impact of what you say, and try to avoid statements that will offend people. The tactful secretary emphasizes others' positive traits rather than their negative traits. If you are tactful, you think before you speak. For example, if one of your fellow employees has just returned to the office after a serious illness, let the person know that you are happy that he or she is back; but avoid asking prying or possibly upsetting questions about the illness.

Fairness. The fair person does not take advantage of others. For example, you may get an idea from someone else. But if you are fair, you will not take credit for the idea. Instead, you will give credit to the individual who gave you the idea. You also assume your share of responsibility without attempting to get co-workers to do jobs that are yours.

FACTORS THAT CONTRIBUTE TO THE GROWTH OF THE OFFICE TEAM ARE . . .

Now that you have considered the definition and the composition of an office team, consider the factors that contribute to the growth of the office team.

Effective Organizational Communication

In Chapter 4 you learned about communication in your professional and personal life. Now you will learn about the characteristics of organizational communication. All organizations have formal and informal communication channels, and you should understand how these channels function. Also, you should be aware of communication techniques that will help you communicate effectively within an organization.

Formal Communication. Formal communications such as written and oral messages are the lifeblood that gives the company vitality. For example, if your employer asks you to take a letter, the request is a formal communication between your employer and you. The letter which you take, type, and send out is a formal communication between your employer and the person to whom it is written.

The formal communication channels in an organization may be upward, downward, or horizontal. Downward communications consist of messages that flow from management to the employees of the company. Upward communications are messages that travel from the employee to the supervisor, manager, or employer. In all organizations there are extensive downward communications in the form of memorandums, letters, job descriptions, objectives, performance appraisals, oral assignments, directions, orders, and the like. Communications from management are necessary and important. Unless the lines are open for upward communication also, severe problems may result. The employees of an organization need to know that their opinions matter. They need to know that their work is appreciated and that they have a voice in the organization.

Horizontal communication involves messages that flow from co-worker to co-worker. You work closely with your co-workers; you need to be sure that you belong to the group and that your ideas and opinions are heard and appreciated. Unless the horizontal communication lines are open, the teamwork and acceptance needs will not be satisfied.

Informal Communication. In addition to formal communication in an organization, there are also informal channels of communication often referred to as the grapevine. The origin of the term *grapevine* in reference to communication goes back to the time of the Civil War. Messages were transmitted by telegraph wires which were strung like a grapevine from tree to tree. These messages were often garbled, and today the grapevine has come to mean messages that may or may not be true and that originate from an unknown source.

Illus. 5-4
The grapevine can carry correct as well as incorrect information.

The grapevine is a natural and normal outgrowth of people working together. Probably the worst feature of the grapevine is the untrue communication or rumor that is often started. An organization and its employees can be hurt by untrue communications that spread. Rumors can never be squelched entirely; the best way to reduce the number of rumors is to be certain the lines of formal communication are open—upward, downward, and horizontally. Employees need to be kept informed about what is happening in the company.

Communication Techniques. An awareness and understanding of the organizational structure and climate, the grapevine, and status differences can help you communicate effectively in an organization. Several techniques specifically related to organizational communication are given in this section.

Understand the organizational structure. When you join a company, ask for an organization chart if one is not made available to you. This chart will show you the structure of the company, the relationship between each department or division, and the levels of administrative authority. It will also help you learn the names of the various executives in the company. With such a chart, you will be able to understand the formal communication flow (both upward and downward) in the organization. A portion of an organization chart is given in Illus. 5-5. Notice that the general accounting office reports to the assistant controller, the assistant controller reports to the controller, and the controller reports to the president.

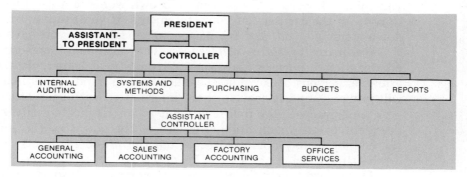

Illus. 5-5
Organization chart

Understand the organizational climate. The top and middle managers of an organization can have a considerable influence on the amount and type of communication in an organization. The managers of one organization, for example, may encourage individuals to express themselves and to participate in the decisions of the company. This leadership style is called participative, and the climate in such an organization is usually open and communicative. The managers of another organization may perceive their role as telling the employees what to do, discouraging participation and freedom of expression. This leadership style is known as autocratic. In such an organization, frequently the informal communication channels are often much stronger or more active than the formal communication channels. As a result, workers are more likely to receive inaccurate information about company procedures from informal channels. To be an effective communicator, you should understand the nature of the organizational climate and its effect on the communication channels. You will learn more about leadership styles in Chapter 7.

Verify the grapevine. You have already learned that the grapevine can carry correct as well as incorrect information and rumors. Your responsibility is to verify the information that you receive through the grapevine. Do not assume that all information is true. Ask questions such as Who told you? How do you know that? Where did you hear it? Be hesitant about what information you pass on from the grapevine. Pass on only valid information.

Write and speak clearly. As a secretary you will frequently engage in both spoken and written communications. Be certain that your communications are as clear as possible. Keep your words simple. Refrain from using difficult words to impress others. You usually do not impress people—you just confuse them. Express your thoughts, opinions, and ideas concisely. Be specific. Tell others exactly what you mean. If you think you do not understand the speaker, repeat what you think the person has said in your own words and ask the speaker to confirm the accuracy of your statements. If you think a listener has not understood you, ask the person to repeat what you have said.

Be aware of status differences. The position of persons in the organization influences the type and quality of communication. For example, persons of equal status—such as two middle level managers—will probably find it easy to share information with each other. However, an employee may find it difficult to communicate easily with the president of an organization. Because of the status of the president, the employee may not feel free to tell the president exactly what he or she thinks.

Downward communication from the president to the employees can also be difficult. As the communication is passed downward from one manager to another, a certain amount of dilution takes place. In other words, important information may be omitted and the communication does not reach the workers in the form that was intended by the president. Also, managers may be tempted to color or filter facts or events to make the manager writing the communication appear more competent or knowledgeable. For example, assume top management has said that the company profits increased by 10 percent during the last year with only one subsidiary (the plastics subsidiary) losing money. Then the manager of the plastics subsidiary reports to the employees that the company profits increased by 10 percent last year. The manager has filtered the facts by failing to report that the plastics subsidiary was the only subsidiary that lost money during the last year.

Employees and managers should be aware of the effect differences in status may have on communication. Pay particular attention to avoid diluting or filtering communication as it travels from one level to another, and be certain to communicate your thoughts and opinions accurately.

Be word conscious. You learned in Chapter 4 that words mean different things to different people. You need to consider how the communicator interprets and uses words. The intended meaning of a supervisor may be misinterpreted by an employee unless both persons are using the same point of reference. For example, if an employee is told by the supervisor that productivity must be increased to a higher level, the employee may think that *higher* means *unrealistic.* The supervisor, however, may merely mean that each employee must work to capacity. The employee may visualize the supervisor demanding more and more work, while the supervisor sees each employee using his or her full potential to attain maximum production.

Technological changes have also contributed to communication problems. As a secretary, you may use word processors, OCRs, and intelligent copiers. Unless these terms are familiar to you, you will have difficulty understanding instructions. You hear the words, but the terms used are a barrier to understanding. To help you overcome word barriers, listen carefully to the communicator. Try to understand what he or she means by the words that are being used. If you don't understand the meaning of a technical term, ask the communicator to define the term.

Lanier Business Products

Illus. 5-6
It is important to use good communication techniques on the job.

Elimination of Discrimination

Obviously there are many groups of people—whites, blacks, Mexican-Americans, men, women, older workers, religious groups, the handicapped—that face discrimination in the workplace. Only sexual harassment and racial discrimination will be considered in depth in this section.

Sexual Harassment. Surveys show that sexual harassment is a serious social problem. One national survey by a women's periodical reported that of the 9,000 women responding, 88 percent stated that they had experienced one or more forms of unwanted sexual advances on the job. Other available statistics indicate that seven out of ten women are sexually harassed in some way during their working lives. Since it is a serious problem, you should consider what it is, what your legal rights are, and how you can handle it.

What is it? Sexual harassment is a form of sexual discrimination. It has been defined by the Equal Employment Opportunity Commission (EEOC—an office of the federal government) as harassment on the basis of sexual conduct which is unwelcomed by the recipient and which may be either physical or verbal in nature. Three criteria for sexual harassment are set forth:

1. Submission to the sexual conduct is made either implicitly or explicitly as a condition of employment.
2. Employment decisions affecting the recipient are made on the basis of the recipient's acceptance or rejection of the sexual conduct.
3. The conduct has the intent or effect of substantially interfering with an individual's work performance or creates an intimidating, hostile, or offensive work environment.

Thus, sexual harassment in the office can take many forms. Forms of sexual harassment are verbal in nature (suggestive comments and demands, sexual jokes), pressure for sexual activity, unwanted body contact, or attempted or actual rape.

Professional Secretaries International has considered the issue of sexual harassment in the office today and believes that the problem is widespread enough to make this public statement.

1. Sexual harassment is an affront to secretaries and must be faced as a discriminatory employment practice.
2. Awareness needs to be expanded of the intimidation factor and the full scope of harmful practices of sexual harassment in the secretary's workplace.
3. Instances of sexual harassment should be documented, disclosed, and reported to appropriate persons as counteraction.
4. Compliance with EEOC guidelines regarding sexual harassment is urged by PSI.

5. Support from other concerned individuals and organizations should be enlisted to diminish the occurrence of sexual harassment.[1]

Racial Discrimination. In addition to sexual harassment in the workplace, racial discrimination also exists. *Prejudice,* defined as an adverse opinion or judgment formed without sufficient knowledge or examination of the facts, has resulted in discriminatory employment practices which have often denied certain people employment because of their race.

Why does racial prejudice occur? Racial tensions have occurred in the United States from the time the first white settlers drove out the native Americans and set up a system of labor based on black slavery. Then the settlers migrated to areas held by Spanish settlers, forced them from their territory, and thus continued discriminatory practices. Consequently, racial prejudice has a history in this country that dates back to its beginning. Prejudice is based partially on observation but mainly on ignorance, fear, and cultural patterns. As groups of people were viewed in certain roles and with certain characteristics, those attitudes were learned in one generation and passed on to the next. Changing learned attitudes is a slow process. However, strides in reducing racial prejudice are being made today, and it is imperative that even greater strides be made in the future.

What can be done about it? There are laws that prohibit racial discrimination, the most important being Title VII of the Civil Rights Act of 1964 which makes discrimination illegal if it is based on national origin, ethnic group, sex, creed, age, or race. Title VII was extended to cover federal, state, and local public employers and educational institutions by the Equal Employment Opportunity Act of 1972. This amendment to Title VII also gave the Equal Employment Opportunity Commission the authority to file suit in federal district courts against employers in the private sector on behalf of individuals whose charges were not successfully resolved. Under this act, businesses have also been asked to institute affirmative action plans under which employers must establish certain guidelines:

1. Identify all barriers in the personnel management system which limit the ability of applicants and employees to reach their full employment potential, without regard to race, sex, religion, national origin or other factors
2. Eliminate all such barriers in a timely, coordinated manner
3. Undertake whatever special programs are needed to accelerate the process

---

[1]"Sexual Harassment in the Secretary's Workplace," *The Secretary* (August/September, 1981), p. 10.

Action to Be Taken. Sexual harassment and racial discrimination are illegal, and many court cases have supported the illegality of these practices. Consider these steps which you may take if you are a victim of sexual harassment or racial discrimination.

1. Know your rights. Know what your organization's position is on racial discrimination and sexual harassment, what is legal under the EEOC guidelines, and what your employer's responsibility is. In addition to Title VII of the Civil Rights Act (1964), amended by the Equal Employment Opportunity Act in 1972, which prohibits discrimination based on sex as well as on race, color, religion, and national origin, there are two other laws that relate to sexual discrimination.
   - *The Equal Pay Act.* This act, a 1963 amendment to the Fair Labor Standards Act, prohibits pay discrimination because of sex. Men and women performing work in the same establishment under similar conditions must receive the same pay if their jobs require equal skill, effort, and responsibility.
   - *The Pregnancy Discrimination Act.* In 1978 this act amended Title VII to make clear that discrimination on the basis of pregnancy, childbirth, or related medical conditions is unlawful, including refusal to hire or promote pregnant women or to offer them the same fringe benefits or insurance program.

2. Keep a record of all sexual harassment and racial discrimination infractions, noting the dates, incidents, and witnesses (if any).

3. File a formal grievance with your company. Most companies have formal grievance procedures which employees can follow if they think an injustice has occurred. Check your company policy and follow the procedures. If no formal grievance procedures exist, file a formal complaint with your employer in the form of a memorandum describing the incidents, identifying the individuals involved in the sexual harassment or racial discrimination, and requesting that disciplinary action be taken.

4. If your employer is not responsive to your complaint, file charges of discrimination with the federal and state agencies that enforce civil rights laws. The Civil Rights Act of 1964 established the Equal Employment Opportunity Commission (EEOC) which serves as an agency to ensure that violations of the act are exposed, to hear complaints of employees who think that they are discriminated against, and to see that appropriate actions are taken. Check your local telephone directory for the address and telephone number of the EEOC office in your city. Your state may also have civil rights offices which can assist you; check your local directory for these offices.

5. Confront the harasser. Let the offender know in no uncertain terms that his or her behavior is unwanted and unacceptable. There is a chance that the harasser was not aware that his or her behavior was offensive.

6. Talk to friends, co-workers, and relatives. It is important to avoid isolation and self-blame. You are not alone; sexual harassment and racial

discrimination do occur in the work sector.

7. Consult an attorney to investigate legal alternatives to discriminatory behavior.

An effective office team is based on the fair and equal treatment of all team members regardless of race or sex. You have every legal, moral, and ethical right to expect and demand fair and equal treatment.

Pleasant Physical Environment

Everyone prefers to work in an attractive and safe physical environment, and studies have shown that physical surroundings can and do affect productivity. Thus, a pleasant work environment will contribute to the growth of the office team.

Ergonomics. *Ergonomics*, from the Greek words ergos (work) and nomos (natural laws), means the bringing together of the physiological factors that make an effective work environment and the psychological factors that explain how workers react to their environment. The physiological factors in the office include the utilization of space and color, the arrangement of furniture and equipment, and the regulation of lighting and noise. An attempt is made here to treat ergonomics succinctly; an in-depth approach would take several chapters. However, as an office worker, you should understand how ergonomics affects the office team.

Color. Color influences the way visitors regard a company as well as the health, productivity, and morale of its employees. For example, attractive, cheerful, and efficient looking offices tend to inspire confidence and trust. In contrast, drab or poorly painted offices can arouse doubt or mistrust. The use of light colors is essential in offices where detailed work on white paper is done. Tones of gray tend to put workers to sleep; warm colors such as yellow, red, and orange create cheerful surroundings; cool colors such as green and blue produce a calm and tranquil atmosphere.

Studies show that productivity increases from 15 to 30 percent with the effective use of color. One firm reported that absenteeism was reduced by 20 percent as a result of an improved color plan.

Lighting. In order to process information in an office, an adequate lighting system must be maintained. Improper lighting contributes to eyestrain, which can cause muscular tension, fatigue, and irritability. Natural light can be used in many ways in the office; however, it must be controlled. Direct sunlight can produce glare, discomfort, and eyestrain. Proper use of window screens and draperies that diffuse the light, deflect glare, yet provide a pleasant outside view are recommended. Research on the lighting needs of the office has established a unit for measuring illumination: the foot candle which is the amount of light produced by a standard candle at a distance of one foot. The higher the foot candle level of illumination, the better the health, morale, and efficiency of the workers.

Noise. Sound in the office can be good or bad. For example, background music and subdued conversation are necessary in the office and do not disrupt the workday; street sounds and clattering machines irritate and disturb employees. In the short run, office noise diminishes the worker's efficiency and decreases productivity. In the long run, noise can have serious effects on the employee's health. Noise interferes with communication, makes concentration difficult, and causes irritation and fatigue. High levels of noise impair hearing, cause sleep loss, and can induce emotional damage.

In contrast, the control of noise levels has positive results. One study showed that sound conditioning increased the efficiency of office employees by 8.8 percent, decreased typists' errors by 29 percent, and reduced turnover by 47 percent. To control noise, such measures as relocating the office, keeping doors and windows closed, segregating noisy departments, and using acoustical screen and sound-absorbing materials have proved effective.

Layout. The layout of the office is important since the flow of information in the office is similar to the flow of materials in a factory. There are aisles or routes along which information is transported. The amount of time necessary to transport information from one place to another should be minimal. Also, the number of work stations should be kept to a minimum without sacrificing accessibility to the information needed. The way the office is laid out affects the efficiency and productivity of the workers. In planning the office layout, here are some factors that need to be considered:

1. Sufficient space
2. Comfort and convenience of employees and customers
3. Work flow routes
4. Coordination of layout with color, lighting, and noise control
5. Flexibility to rearrange work stations if a change in work routes occurs
6. Interpersonal communication needs of the office staff (Desks should not be completely isolated.)

Temperature. It has been determined that the most comfortable and healthful temperature for sedentary work is about 70, assuming that proper humidity or moisture is maintained. Indoor comfort is the result of a proper balance in temperature, relative humidity, and air motion. High humidity makes one feel colder on a cold day and hotter on a hot day. Studies have shown that a person is more comfortable in a room with a temperature of 65 to 70 where the air is reasonably moist than in a room where the air is dry and the temperature is several degrees higher. In determining temperature settings, the number of lighting fixtures in the office, the number of occupants, the number of machines, the height of the ceiling, and the material used in constructing the building must be considered.

Furniture. Just as the other elements mentioned have an effect on productivity, the furniture in the office also affects the level of production. In choosing office furniture, consider these factors:

1. The furniture should be attractive in style and complement the decor of the office.
2. The furniture should be suitable for the work to be done and should be of good quality.
3. The furniture should be adaptable to multipurpose use whenever possible.
4. The furniture should fit the needs and preferences of the workers.
5. The furniture (chairs, desks, tables, and video terminals) should be designed so that they may be used for long periods of time without causing physical discomfort or fatigue to the employee.

Safety. Working in an office is not as dangerous as mining coal or forging steel, but neither is it always the safe, healthy environment that many people think. Statistics in one state for a year have revealed that there were almost 7,500 disabling injuries from sprains, strains, dislocations, and hernias among office workers. These statistics do not include the increasing numbers of allergies, respiratory diseases, and other problems resulting from health hazards at the office. These health hazards are costly both to management and to employees due to loss of time, loss of production, and loss of income.

In 1970 the Occupational Safety and Health Act was passed to ensure American workers a safe and healthy workplace. OSHA (the Occupational Safety and Health Administration), established by the act, was directed to encourage states to develop and operate their own job safety and health programs. OSHA requires that employers furnish a place of employment free from recognized hazards that are likely to cause death or serious injury. Employers are required to keep records of work related deaths, illnesses, and accidents; maintain records of employee exposure to materials that are potentially toxic; and notify employees of their exposure to such materials when the toxic effects exceed the set standards. Trained safety inspectors, employed by the government, make unannounced visits to companies to see that safety standards are being maintained. If problems are found, the company is required to correct the problems.

A number of potential hazards can be found in offices; for example,

1. Frayed or loose telephone cords and/or electric wires
2. Open file and desk drawers
3. Wires loosely secured to the floor
4. Spilled beverages and food on the floor
5. Paper cutters and spindle files
6. Loose floor coverings on stairs or floors
7. Equipment such as duplicating machines

In order to avoid these potential office hazards:

1. Floor coverings should be durable and in good repair.
2. Anti-slip protection (same as a rough surface mat) should be used at all building entrances.
3. Electrical equipment should be inspected regularly for damaged cords and improper placement.
4. Employees should be trained in the proper operation of equipment.
5. Only one file drawer should be opened at a time. (Some cabinets are manufactured so that it is impossible to open more than one drawer at a time.) File drawers should be closed immediately after use. File cabinets should be placed away from heavy traffic areas.
6. Office furniture should be checked for sharp edges that may scrape or snag clothing or skin.
7. Employees should be instructed in procedures to follow in case of accidents. First aid kits should be readily accessible to all employees.

PROFESSIONAL POINTERS

Following these suggestions will help you become an effective member of your office team.

1. Accept people rather than evaluate them.

2. Be loyal to your company and your employer.

3. Be dependable.

4. Refrain from participating in office gossip.

5 Verify information received through the grapevine.

6. Communicate clearly and concisely in both verbal and written messages.

7. Treat everyone with respect.

8. Work to reduce your prejudices.

9. Cooperate with others.

10. Concentrate on learning the facts rather than making emotional judgments.

11. Be sincere.

12. Do not take advantage of others; be fair.

13. Learn and use people's names.

14. Practice patience when someone is angry.

15. Become familiar with the organization chart.

16. Be aware of how status affects communication.

17. Consider what the communicator means by the words that are used.

18. Keep your sense of humor regardless of what is happening.

19. In your conversations frequently use words such as *please*, *thank you*, and *you're welcome*.

20. Avoid stereotyping (thinking of groups of people as all being the same—blacks, Germans, artists, Lutherans, and so on).

FOR YOUR REVIEW

1. Define and explain the three elements of an office team.

2. What are a secretary's obligations to an employer?

3. What are the employer's obligations to a secretarial employee?

4. List and explain three characteristics that will assist you in working with your co-workers.

5. Explain the difference between formal and informal communication.

6. List and explain three communication techniques that will assist you in organizational communication.

7. What is sexual harassment? What can be done about it?

8. Why does racial prejudice occur? What can be done about it?

9. Define *ergonomics*. Cite three factors that affect the office environment.

10. What is OSHA? What is its significance to a business office?

CASE PROBLEM

Carmen Lamas has been with Keyser Automotive for three months as a secretary in the sales division. Most of the sales representatives and the sales manager (as you would expect) are gregarious, friendly people. There are three men and two women sales representatives. Carmen's immediate superior is the sales manager, Raymond Meyers. He is approximately 30 years old, married, and has two small children. Carmen considers all the people in the division her friends. She enjoys talking and joking with them. Mr. Meyers has always been nice to Carmen, and she considers him fun and easy to work with. Recently, however, he has become overly friendly with Carmen. Carmen is 27 and unmarried. He has made several remarks such as, "My, you look beautiful today," and "If I weren't a married man, I would be calling you every evening." Carmen has thought that he was merely joking, and she has thanked him for his compliments and continued her work. Two days this week, however, Mr. Meyers has made what Carmen considers to be sexual advances toward her. On one occasion, he placed his arm around her shoulders when he made the remark. Carmen was embarrassed by his overtures, but she said nothing to him. This morning he asked her to go to dinner with him this evening. She told him very emphatically that she would not go to dinner with him. His parting comment as he walked from the room was, "Just wait until evaluation time."

1. How should Carmen handle the situation?

2. Should she quit?

PRODUCTION PROJECTS

PP 5-1

(Objective 1)

Interview three secretaries from different companies and ask them the questions given on the form in your Supplies Inventory. Report your findings to the class.

PP 5-2

(Objective 2)

Here are some communication situations that have occurred at Dennehy Corporation. Determine in each situation whether the communication is formal or informal. If it is formal, determine whether it is upward, downward, or horizontal communication.

Situation 1

Linda Morris (supervisor) says, "I need this report finished by tomorrow at noon. Do you think you can handle it?" Yoko Sumio (accountant) replies, "Yes, I can get it done. It will be on your desk at noon."

Situation 2

Jana King (secretary) states, "There are several letters on my tapes that need to be transcribed, but I am working on a rush project for Ann Evans now. Do you have time to transcribe the letters for me?" David Carpenter (stenographer) replies, "I will be free in 30 minutes, and I will be happy to transcribe the letters then."

Situation 3

Clarice Hamilton (clerk) writes a memorandum to Joanne Nelson (manager) requesting a leave of absence for two months.

PP 5-3

(Objective 3)

Jessica Nunnally has been working for Summit Advertising Agency for three weeks. During that time, several problems have occurred. Using the form in your Supplies Inventory, identify the communication problems. What are your suggestions for correcting the situations?

Situation 1

Carolyn Henson, Jessica's supervisor, told her to prepare the materials for the monthly board meeting. Jessica proceeded to check the files for examples of how the materials should be prepared. When she found no examples, she asked a co-worker how the materials should be prepared; but the co-worker didn't know either. Finally, in desperation, Jessica prepared the materials as she thought they should be done. When Carolyn received the materials, she returned them to Jessica with a note telling her that they were incorrectly prepared and asking her to be sure that she understood what to do the next time.

Situation 2

Jessica heard through the grapevine that one of the secretaries was being let go. She assumed it was true; and, trying to be sympathetic, she said to the secretary, "I hear you are leaving. We will miss you." The secretary replied, "What do you mean? I'm not leaving."

Situation 3

Carolyn told Jessica to use the word processing equipment when handling form letters. Jessica was not familiar with the term *word processing*, but she was reluctant to ask Carolyn to explain the term.

PP 5-4

(Objective 4)

Do you have prejudices based on sex, race, age, or other traits? Use the form in your Supplies Inventory to record your preconceptions about various groups. Be honest. Your form is confidential; you will not be asked to hand it in to your instructor. After you have identified your biases about various groups, analyze your intolerances. Then determine steps that you can take to reduce or eliminate your prejudices.

PP 5-5

(Objective 4)

Interview an executive and inquire what policies and procedures the company follows to prevent sexual harassment and racial discrimination. Record the responses, and report your findings to the class.

PP 5-6

(Objective 5)

Read four articles on ergonomics and safety in the office. Summarize your findings on plain paper and note your sources at the top of the paper.

Chapter **6**

RESPONDING TO OFFICE CALLERS

As a secretary, you will work with people much of the time. You will work not only with people in your office but with people outside the organization. You will respond daily to telephone callers and office visitors, many of whom are contacting the company for the first time. Your ability to receive these people in a pleasant and professional manner is necessary for your employer to maintain a favorable public image.

This chapter will help you become proficient in working with customers and other individuals who visit or telephone the company. You will learn effective techniques that will enhance both yourself and the company before the public.

General Objectives

Your general objectives for Chapter 6 are to:

1. *Discover the importance of good public relations*
2. *Learn how to be gracious and efficient with office visitors*
3. *Develop proper telephone techniques*

PUBLIC RELATIONS RESPONSIBILITIES

Public relations is defined as the technique of inducing the public to have understanding for and goodwill toward a person, firm, or institution. Favorable public relations are crucial to any organization. If prospective clients or customers have a favorable impression of a company, they will probably do business with it. In fact, organizations are so concerned about maintaining a favorable public image that most companies have established public relations departments or employ professional public relations firms to handle this aspect of their business. A considerable amount of money and energy is expended in creating a good public image of the company.

But, you may ask yourself, What is my role as a secretary in maintaining good public relations? Your public relations role is a crucial one. A company can spend thousands of dollars building goodwill, and this goodwill can be rendered ineffectual by one insensitive employee. If you are curt or rude to a customer, you can lose in a few seconds the goodwill that has taken years to build. It is also possible to lose business for the company by alienating a customer. As a secretary, you represent the company; you are responsible for making a good impression on visitors and telephone callers.

GREETING VISITORS

In many large organizations a receptionist initially greets all office visitors. The receptionist generally keeps a register in which the name of the visitor, company affiliation, nature of the visit, person the visitor wishes to see, and date of the visit are recorded. After obtaining this information from the visitor, the receptionist notifies the secretary that the caller has arrived. If this is a first time visit, your job as a secretary may include going to the receptionist area and escorting the visitor to your office.

In small companies, the secretary may also serve as the receptionist. In other words, the secretary has the responsibility of greeting all visitors to the company and seeing that they are directed to the proper persons. Regardless of whether you work in a large or small company, here are some techniques for receiving office visitors.

Knowing What Your Employer Expects of You

Determine your employer's preferences regarding visitors. Some people will have immediate access to your employer's office. The president of the company, a valuable client or customer, a representative of a competitive firm, a distinguished civic official—these people, because of their importance, are not kept waiting. They are given immediate attention. Here are some questions you can ask your employer in order to learn his or her preferences concerning visitors.

1. Do you have a list of certain persons whom you will see at once, regardless of how busy you are or what the circumstances are at the time?
2. Do you set aside a particular time of day for seeing people? Do you prefer certain periods for dictating and handling paperwork?
3. Do you have a list of relatives or friends who call on occasion without an appointment?
4. Do you have a list of persons you do not see under any circumstances: job applicants who should be referred to the employment office or personnel department? sales representatives who should be referred to the purchasing department?

5. How do you want me to announce callers? If you have not met the visitor as yet, do you want me to handle the introduction, or do you prefer to introduce yourself?

The answers to these questions will provide the information you need in assuring that all visitors are given courteous and efficient treatment and will enhance your importance to your employer and to the company.

Receiving the Visitor

Even though the visitor to a large organization has already been greeted by the receptionist, your role as secretary is to welcome the visitor to your office. Greet the person graciously with a simple "Good morning" or "Good afternoon." Welcoming the visitor by name is a courteous gesture.

When a visitor enters your office, give that person your immediate attention. It is discourteous to leave someone standing at your desk while you finish filing papers or typing a letter. Excuse yourself if you must answer the telephone when a visitor is at your desk. A visitor to the office should be treated as a guest and should receive your full attention. Receiving office visitors promptly and cordially promotes goodwill and enhances your professional image.

Illus. 6-1
Give an office visitor your immediate attention.

Determining the Purpose of the Visit

When a scheduled visitor (one with an appointment) comes to the office, you probably determined the purpose of the visit when you set up the appointment. When you receive an unscheduled visitor, however, you must also find out why that person is visiting. Your initial greeting may be, "Good morning (or Good afternoon), may I help you?" Such a greeting gives the person a chance to respond with his or her name and reason for the visit. If the visitor does not volunteer the information you need, you must ask for it. Avoid blunt questions: "What is your name?" "What do you want?" "Where do you work?" Use tact and patience in obtaining the information.

Keeping a register of office visitors on your desk is a polite, proven way to get the information you need. Merely ask the visitor to record the necessary information on the register. (See Illus. 6-2.)

REGISTER OF OFFICE VISITORS				
Date	Time	Name and Company	Person Seen	Purpose of Call
10-12	9:30	E. B. Williams, Darcia Corp.	S. D. Hill	Shipping Contract
10-12	11:00	R. J. Keller, Krueger Industries	M. J. Walker	New product
10-12	1:30	L. P. Alton, Peek Properties	S. D. Hill	Real estate

Illus. 6-2
With this register of visitors, the secretary can keep a daily record of information about office callers.

Notice that there is a place for the date, time, visitor's name and affiliation, person visited, and purpose of the call. Most people regard a register of office visitors as routine procedure and usually do not object to giving the information requested. The register provides a convenient record of all visitors. You may also diplomatically get information about a visitor by asking for the person's business card which usually contains his or her name, position, company name, address, and telephone number.

Sometimes the visitor's purpose in seeing your employer is outside the scope of your employer's duties. You will save the caller and your employer time by finding out the purpose of the visit and referring the visitor to the appropriate person. Be certain that you are considerate if it is necessary to refer the visitor to someone else. Call the office of the person to whom you are referring the visitor and explain the situation. If the person can see the visitor immediately, direct the visitor to the correct office. If an appointment must be made for another day, check with the visitor to set a mutually convenient time.

Remembering Names and Faces

You should learn the names of people outside the company with whom you will come in contact. The following pointers will help you learn names quickly:

1. Listen carefully to the person's name when it is pronounced.
2. If you do not understand a name, ask the person to repeat it.
3. Write the name phonetically if the pronunciation is difficult.
4. Use the person's name when you first learn it.
5. Address the person by name.
6. Ask the person for a business card; attach this card to an index card with notations about the caller; place the index card in a card file and refer to the file often to refresh your memory.
7. Use a mnemonic device to remember names.

If you receive an office visitor who has been in the office before but whose name you have forgotten, be tactful and say, "It's good to see you again." You will let the person know that you remember him or her; you can then check your appointment calendar or business card file for the person's name.

Making Introductions

You will probably be responsible for introducing visitors to your employer. Learning and practicing the proper techniques will enable you to handle this responsibility with poise and confidence.

The general rule for introducing people is that the most important person is named first, regardless of sex. In business, the person named first is usually the one in the higher position. For example, if the president of another company visits your employer, who is the traffic manager, you would say, "Mrs. Robbins, president of Cortez Equipment, Mr. Selden (your employer)." Or, since the visitor probably knows your employer's name, you might say as you introduce the two, "This is Mrs. Robbins, president of Cortez Equipment."

If an executive is introducing an office employee to a client, the client is named first. A young person is introduced to an older person. And the old rule that a man is always introduced to a woman is no longer invariable. A girl of eighteen is introduced to a man of fifty. A woman is introduced to a man of the same age who is more important (in offices held or achievements). The traditional rule for introducing a man and woman of approximately the same age and status still holds: the man is introduced to the woman. For example, "Melissa

Younger, this is Cecil Brewer." Notice that in this situation no titles were used. In view of our contemporary casual life-style, it is not always necessary to use *Mr., Mrs., Miss,* or *Ms.* However, you should use a title such as Doctor or Senator when introducing individuals.

Traditionally in this country the woman has remained seated when being introduced to someone unless that person is much older or very prominent. But today it is perfectly acceptable for a woman to rise for all introductions. It has been traditional for a man to wait until a woman extends her hand before he extends his; this practice is also changing. Whether you are a man or a woman, extend your hand. Make sure that your handshake is firm. Grasp the other person's hand and shake it sincerely. If you are wearing gloves, remove your right glove before shaking hands. The exceptions to this rule are when you cannot physically remove the glove because your hands are full of things or when you are outside and it is cold.

Making the Wait Pleasant

Often a visitor must wait, and it is your job to make the wait as pleasant as possible. If coffee is available, offer the visitor a cup of coffee. Explain approximately how long the wait will be. If possible, explain the reason for the delay—particularly if the visitor had an appointment. For example, you may say, "I'm extremely sorry, but Miss Rosenstein is tied up in an important meeting. It should be over in approximately 15 minutes." Such an approach lets the visitor know that you are concerned but that the wait is unavoidable.

See that the visitor has something to read so that the wait will not seem so long. You should have available business periodicals such as *Forbes* or *Business Week.*

After the office visitor is situated, you are free to go back to your work; you are not expected to chat. The visitor realizes that you have other duties. However, if the wait is longer than you anticipated, tell the visitor so that he or she can come back later or see someone else in the company if that can be arranged.

Handling Interruptions

You may need to interrupt your employer with a message when there are visitors present. Do so as unobtrusively as possible. You can knock on the door (or just open it, whichever your employer prefers) and hand him or her a note. Some callers overstay their welcome. You may help your employer by bringing a note or by telephoning. This approach provides your employer with a convenient means of letting the visitor know that there are other people waiting or other responsibilities that require attention.

Working with the Difficult Visitor

It is not always easy to be pleasant to visitors, especially those who are ill-tempered and discourteous. At such times, however, you must keep foremost in your mind your role as an ambassador of good-will.

Illus. 6-3
You must be tolerant and even-tempered when receiving a difficult visitor.

It is your job to find out the name of the caller and why that caller wants to see your employer. Be wary of an office visitor who tries to avoid your inquiries by evasive answers ("It's a personal matter." "I have reason to believe Mr. Moss will be interested in what I have to say.") You may respond, "I'm sorry, but Mr. Moss sees visitors only by appointment. He needs to know the purpose of a call before I'm permitted to schedule an appointment." If the visitor still refuses to reveal the purpose of the visit, you have several options. You may offer the visitor a sheet of paper and suggest that a note be written to the executive. Then take the note to your employer and ask if he or she wishes to see the visitor. If your employer is in a conference, you might suggest to the visitor that a letter be written to your employer requesting an appointment.

Do not disclose specific information about the company or your employer to unidentified visitors. If a person comes to your office and asks for specific information, your response should be, "I really don't know. Perhaps you would like to set up an appointment with Mrs. Browne so that she can help you."

Sometimes a visitor is upset or angry for reasons that have nothing to do with you or the company. Something probably happened on the way to your office that triggered this wrath, and the person is venting his or her frustrations on you. If you are curt and further provoke the visitor, the situation is aggravated. Let the visitor talk. You listen. Try to understand the visitor's viewpoint. Much of the caller's anger or frustration may vanish in talking. When an incident such as this occurs, it is important for you, as a secretary and a company representative, to be even-tempered and tolerant.

Scheduling Appointments

The secretary schedules appointments for the employer. These appointments may be scheduled in an appointment book or on a regular desk calendar. Illus. 6-4 shows a desk calendar with scheduled

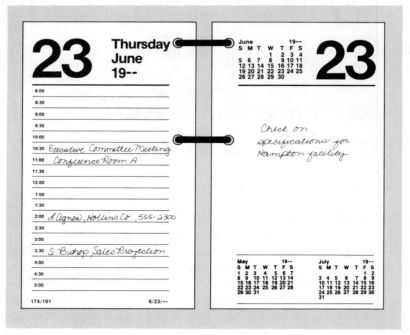

Illus. 6-4
Desk calendar with appointments

appointments. To help you in getting all pertinent and correct information, keep these questions in mind as you schedule appointments.

1. Who is the person? (Get the name of the person, the name of the company the person represents, and the telephone number.)
2. What does the person want? (Record the purpose of the appointment on the calendar or in the appointment book.)

3. When is the appointment and how much time is needed? (Block off the appropriate amount of time on the calendar.)
4. Where is the appointment to be held? (Is the appointment to be in your employer's office, in the client's office, or at another location? Record the place, also.)

Remember, there are four *W*'s to scheduling appointments—Who, What, When, and Where.

Your employer may also schedule appointments. If so, he or she occasionally may forget to tell you about these appointments. Each morning check your employer's desk calendar for additional appointments that do not appear on your desk calendar; add these appointments to your calendar. If some pertinent information about the appointment is missing, ask your employer for clarification. You will avoid embarrassing conflicts by keeping in close contact with your employer on business appointments.

Canceling Appointments

If your employer cannot keep an appointment, it is your responsibility to cancel it. Appointments may be canceled by a telephone call. Be sure to give a reason for canceling the appointment and offer to reschedule it. A detailed explanation for the cancellation is not necessary. You can say, "Mrs. Friedan has been called out of town unexpectedly, and she will be unable to keep her appointment. May I schedule another appointment for next week?"

If you must cancel an out-of-town meeting or a speaking engagement, it is usually best to call and then send a letter of confirmation, stating the reason for the cancellation. In the case of a canceled speaking engagement, your employer may suggest a replacement.

WORKING WITH THE TELEPHONE CALLER

A very important public relations tool is the telephone since a large number of communications are by telephone. No doubt you have been answering the telephone since you were very young. You may think you know all there is to know about using a telephone and want to skip this section. Don't! This section is quite important. You would be surprised how often people abuse the telephone.

What mistakes are usually made in using the telephone? People seem to forget that the person on the other end of the line is human, too. Somehow it is easier to be rude when you cannot see the person to whom you are talking. How many times have you been angered or hurt by rude treatment on the telephone? How many times have you been kept waiting for an indeterminate time by an inconsiderate secretary? How many times have you been told curtly by a secretary that the person you wanted to talk with was busy? The mistakes made by secretaries over the telephone are numerous and inexcusable. You, as a secretary, should put all callers at ease. Let them know you understand their needs and want to help them.

Think for a minute about the attitude you convey on the telephone. Are you a sincere person? Do you recognize that the person calling obviously thinks that you or someone in the company can be of assistance? Do you honestly attempt to help the person with the problem?

Practice Good Telephone Techniques

If you are to do an effective job on the telephone, there are several techniques which will help you. Study carefully the suggestions given in the following sections.

Develop a Pleasant Voice. Regardless of how busy you are, you should answer the telephone with a smile in your voice. How? One way to do so is to smile as you pick up the receiver to answer a call. If you have a smile on your face, it is reflected in your voice. Treat the voice at the other end as you would a person sitting across from your desk. Let the individual know that you are eager to help.

Illus. 6-5
Put a smile in your voice.

Even if you are busy, the caller has no way of knowing that you are "up to your ears" in work. If the person knew that, he or she could empathize with your problem. But, since the caller isn't aware of your agitation, you cannot answer the telephone by bellowing, "Why did you call? I don't have time to talk with you." Too often secretaries give callers this impression. When you are rude and curt in answering the telephone, you set the stage for a negative approach to the whole conversation. However, if you answer the telephone with a smile in your voice that says, "I am happy you called. How can I help you?" the conversation gets off to a positive start.

Speak Distinctly. Your voice is carried most clearly when you speak directly into the mouthpiece, keeping your lips about an inch away from the transmitter. Be certain that you do not have gum, food, or a pencil in your mouth when you answer the telephone. You cannot speak distinctly with something in your mouth. Speak in a normal tone of voice—do not shout and do not mumble.

Be Helpful and Discreet. When someone calls and your employer is not in the office, tell the caller approximately how long your employer will be gone or ask if someone else can help. Let the person know that you are trying to be of help. Consider this example. Mr. McArthur calls for Mrs. White. Mrs. White is out of the office, and the secretary knows that she will be gone for about two hours. The conversation goes like this:

Mr. McArthur:	This is Ralph McArthur. May I speak with Mrs. White?
Secretary:	Mrs. White is out of the office.
Mr. McArthur:	When will she be back?
Secretary:	I expect her back in about two hours.
Mr. McArthur:	Would you ask her to call me then?
Secretary:	Yes, may I have your number, please?

Analyze that conversation. You may wonder what is wrong with it. You may be thinking that you do not see any glaring errors. The secretary answered Mr. McArthur's questions. But that is exactly the point. Mr. McArthur had to pull the information from the secretary. Mr. McArthur probably thought the secretary was most uncooperative. Notice the improvement in this conversation:

Mr. McArthur:	This is Ralph McArthur. May I speak with Mrs. White?
Secretary:	I am sorry, but Mrs. White is out of the office at present. I expect her back in about two hours. May I have her call you then?
Mr. McArthur:	Yes, please. My number is 254-3456.
Secretary:	Thank you.

How is this an improvement over the previous conversation? The secretary has saved time for the two persons involved—herself and Mr. McArthur. No doubt, this approach left a positive impression on Mr. McArthur; he was aware that the secretary wanted to help him.

Another important point here is that you should be helpful but also be discreet. In other words, do not give unnecessary information to the caller. Consider the same situation.

Mr. McArthur: This is Ralph McArthur. May I speak with Mrs. White?

Secretary: I am sorry, but Mrs. White went over to see Carl Englewood of IPI about an advertising matter. She should be back in about two hours. May I have her call you then?

Mr. McArthur: Yes, please. My number is 254-3456.

Secretary: Thank you.

What went wrong? The secretary gave entirely too much information. Was it necessary to tell Mr. McArthur exactly where Mrs. White went? Certainly not! The secretary may have revealed confidential information. You want to help the caller, but you must also protect your employer.

Ask Questions Tactfully. It is your responsibility to learn the caller's name. Usually the caller will identify himself or herself; but if not, ask the name tactfully. Never say "Who is this?" Notice the difference between "Who is this?" and "May I tell Mr. Finley who is calling, please?" *May* and *please* completely change the approach. The caller understands that it is your responsibility to find out who is calling and usually does not resent your asking tactfully. Always try to put yourself in the other person's place, and ask questions the way you would want to be asked.

Take Messages Completely and Accurately. It is aggravating, to say the least, to have someone give you an incomplete message. Always get all the necessary information and get it accurately. You need to get the person's name, company, telephone number, time of the call, and the message. Offices usually supply message pads for recording telephone calls and office visits. If not, these can be purchased for a nominal price at a stationery or office supplies store. Illus. 6-6 shows one example. You merely fill in the blanks. If you cannot understand the person's name, ask that it be spelled. It is good to repeat the person's name and telephone number so that if you have misunderstood, you can be corrected.

Be Attentive. As you are talking with the caller, visualize him or her. Speak *with* the person, not *at* the telephone. Listen politely to

```
┌─────────────────────────────────────────────────────────────┐
│                        MEMO OF CALL                         │
│   To _Mrs. Valdez_____      5/4  19__               │
│   M _r. Robinson_____ called from _Office Supply Co.___  │
│   Telephone No.: ___291-8603_____│
│                                                             │
│   I TOLD THAT PERSON          THE REPLY WAS:                │
│   YOU WERE:                                                  │
│   Out _____ ☐   No message _____ ☐      │
│   Not in today _____ ☐✓  See message below ___ [ ]    │
│   Not in your office _____ ☑   Will call again _____ ☐      │
│   Talking on telephone____ ☐   Answering your call _ ☐✓     │
│   In conference_____ ☐   Please call back ____ ☑      │
│   Out of town _____ ☐   It is urgent _____ ☐      │
│                                                             │
│   ADDITIONAL REMARKS _He has a question_                    │
│   _about an order placed on 4/30._                          │
│   _____                  │
│                                                             │
│   _____                  │
│              Message taken by _Ken Stykes_____              │
│                    Time _2 p.m._____                  │
└─────────────────────────────────────────────────────────────┘
```

Illus. 6-6
Telephone message form

what the other person is saying. Don't interrupt. If the caller is unhappy about an experience with the company, let the person tell his or her story. It is easier to deal with a disgruntled caller after you have listened to what he or she has to say. Use good listening skills: listen for facts, search for veiled meanings, be patient, don't evaluate, try to understand the words the caller is using, and act on what the caller is saying.

Say *Thank You* and *You're Welcome.* People always appreciate courtesy, and it is especially nice to be courteous over the telephone. Use the words *thank you* and *you're welcome* frequently. Such words let the caller know that you are grateful and that you care.

Use the Caller's Name. It is flattering to the caller to be recognized and called by name. Use the person's name on the telephone. Frequent responses such as "Yes, Mr. Fitzgerald, I will be happy to get you the information" and "It was nice to talk with you, Mr. Fitzgerald" indicate to the caller that you are thoughtful and efficient.

Transfer Calls Properly. Frequently it is necessary to transfer a caller to another extension. Before you transfer a call, explain to the person why it is necessary and make sure the caller is willing to be transferred. You may say, "Miss Dyer is out of the office at the moment, but I believe Mr. Radman can help you. May I transfer you to Mr. Radman?" A thoughtful gesture is to give the caller the extension number in case there is an equipment malfunction and the transfer does not go through. The caller can then call that number without having to call you again.

Be certain that you know how to transfer calls properly. You may be able to transfer the call by merely depressing a receiver button (switch/hook) and dialing the extension, or you may need to go through an operator who will then transfer the call. In either case, stay with the caller until the transfer is completed.

Terminate Calls Courteously. Use elementary courtesy. Thank the person if a *thank you* is appropriate. Say *good-bye* pleasantly. Let the person who called hang up first. Treat the handset (receiver) gently; no one likes to have it slammed down in his or her ear.

Avoid Slang. It is neither businesslike nor in good taste to use slang.

Avoid	*Say*
OK	Yes
Yeah	Certainly
Uh-huh	Of course
Bye-bye	Goodbye

Keep a List of Frequently Called Numbers. A file of frequently called numbers is an excellent time-saver. You may keep these numbers in a 3-by-5-inch card file or listed in a special telephone file.

Receive Incoming Calls Correctly

As a secretary, you will be responsible for handling many calls. Here are some techniques to help you handle these efficiently.

Answer Promptly. When your telephone rings, answer promptly—on the first ring if possible. You may lose a potential customer if you are slow in answering the telephone.

Identify Yourself and/or the Company. The company for which you work will usually instruct you as to how to answer the telephone. In large companies the switchboard operator identifies the company and directs incoming calls. When your telephone rings, identify your office and possibly yourself. For example, "Mrs. Paul's office, Carla Geraci speaking" is a typical way to answer the telephone. If you are in a one-person office without a switchboard operator, you will identify the company. "Good morning, Jones Equipment Company" is an acceptable greeting.

Place Calls on Hold Only after Requesting Permission. A caller may sometimes request information which you do not have at your fingertips; it may be essential for you to check with someone else or go to the file cabinet to get information. When this happens, do not place the caller on hold without his or her permission. You may say, "I need to pull the information from my files. Would you like to hold for a moment while I get it, or shall I call you back?" If the caller agrees to hold, try to get back to the person as soon as possible. Nothing irritates a caller more than to be left on hold. When you return to the line, let the caller know you are back by saying "Thank you for waiting." If there has been an unavoidable delay, apologize immediately.

Leave a Message When You Leave Your Desk. If you have to leave your desk, tell the co-worker who will answer your telephone where you can be reached and the time you will be back. If your employer is also gone, tell the person in general terms where your employer is and when he or she will be back. There is no need to be specific. "Mr. Morgan is out to lunch and will be back about one" or "Mr. Morgan is in a meeting and will be back in the office around three" are informative but discreet messages to be left with a co-worker.

Follow Through on Promises. If you make a promise to call back with additional information, do it. A broken promise can cause a canceled order or a lost customer; a kept promise can enhance a reputation for reliability and trustworthiness. Help your employer remember promises that he or she may have made. If you know of information that your employer has promised a customer and has not followed through on, remind him or her tactfully of the need to follow through. Your employer will appreciate you for the reminder.

Handle Outgoing Calls Properly

As a secretary, you are often responsible for placing calls for your employer or for making business calls yourself. Just as incoming calls must be handled effectively, so must outgoing calls be handled efficiently. Here are some hints for facilitating outgoing calls.

Know the Number. Your file of frequently called numbers should be up to date and readily available at all times. If a needed number is not in your file or if you are not sure of the number you

have, check the telephone directory. If the number is not in the directory, check with directory assistance for the correct number and place
it in your file.

Allow Time to Answer. After you have called a number, give
the person you are calling at least eight to ten rings to answer. You
may be saved another call if you give the caller time to answer.

Plan Your Call. Take a few moments before you make your call
to plan it. Know the purpose of your call and what you intend to say.
Make notes in advance and follow them during your call. The person
you call will appreciate your organization, and you will save yourself
and the company time and money.

Place Long-Distance Calls Correctly. Although most calls
will be local calls, you may also be making long-distance calls. In
order to dial long distance correctly, you should be familiar with the
different types of long-distance services available. In most areas you
can call long distance by Direct Distance Dialing (DDD). You do not
have to go through an operator. The company you work for may have
a Wide Area Telecommunications Service (WATS) for making long-
distance calls. With such a service, the company is charged less per
call than the normal rate for a long-distance call.

If you are dialing long distance, you may wish to place the call
station to station or person to person.

Station-to-Station Calls. A station-to-station call is made when
the caller is willing to talk to anyone who answers. This type of call is
faster and cheaper than a person-to-person call. Charges start when
the called telephone is answered. In most areas station-to-station calls
may be made by dialing the prefix *1* plus the area code and telephone
number.

Person-to-Person Calls. A person-to-person call is made when
you must talk to a particular person. Charging begins when the called
person answers. In most areas person-to-person calls may be made by
dialing the prefix *0* plus the area code and the telephone number.
When you have completed dialing, the operator will come on the line
and ask for calling information. You then give the operator the name
of the person you are calling.

Remember Time Differences. It is important to remember
time zone differences in placing long-distance calls. There are four
standard time zones in the United States: Eastern, Central, Mountain,
and Pacific. There is a one-hour difference between neighboring zones.
For example, if it is 10 a.m. in New York City (Eastern Standard

Time), it is 9 a.m. in Dallas (Central Standard Time). If you are calling from New York to California, you would not want to call at 9 a.m. Eastern Standard Time since it would only be 6 a.m. in California (Pacific Standard Time) and the office would not be open. Also, you probably would not want to call New York from Colorado (Mountain Standard Time) at 10 a.m. since it would be noon in New York and the person may be out to lunch. Illus. 6-7 shows a map of telephone area codes and time zones.

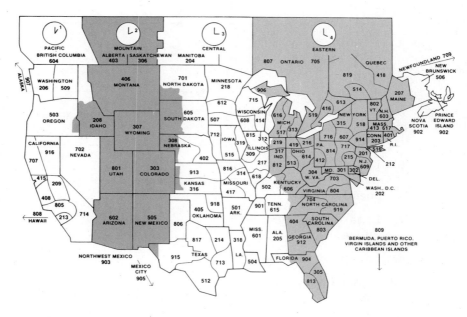

Illus. 6-7
Map of telephone area codes and time zones

There are also international time zones. For example, the person who places a call from New York to London must remember that when it is 11 a.m. standard time in New York, it is 4 p.m. in London. If you are placing many international calls, you need to become familiar with these time zones also.

PROFESSIONAL POINTERS

What is your public relations ability? Rate yourself on the following scale according to how you perform on the job you presently have. If you are not working at present, rate yourself on a job you have held in the past.

	Always	**Sometimes**	**Never**
1. I answer the telephone promptly.			
2. I am pleasant to telephone callers.			
3. I inform the caller before placing the person on hold.			
4. I return to a caller on hold often in order to keep the person informed.			
5. I terminate telephone conversations courteously.			
6. I say *thank you* and *you're welcome* frequently.			
7. I take messages accurately.			
8. I keep my promises.			
9. I make an effort to remember people's names.			
10. I use people's names when talking with them.			
11. I make visitors to the office feel welcome.			
12. I introduce people with confidence and poise.			
13. I offer reading material to visitors that have to wait.			
14. I listen to a disgruntled caller without evaluating the person.			
15. I keep an accurate record of appointments.			

FOR YOUR REVIEW

Technique for having goodwill ↔ toward a person, firm or institution.

1. Define *public relations*. What is the role of the secretary in public relations? *Responsible for making a good impression on visitors + tel. calls*

2. List three questions you might ask your employer concerning his or her preferences about office visitors?

3. How can you tactfully determine the purpose of a caller's visit? *Good morning may I help you?*

4. List four methods for remembering names.

5. Describe the proper way to introduce the following persons:
   a. A man and woman of the same age and status
   b. Two executives—one president of a large company, the other vice-president of another large company
   c. An office employee and a client of the company
   d. A young woman and an elderly gentleman

6. Should a woman offer her hand first in an introduction? Explain. *Yes, Extend your hand whether you are a man or woman.*

Who, what, where, when

7. What information should you obtain when scheduling appointments? *Who is the person. What does the person want, when, where*

8. What is meant by being discreet on the telephone? *don't give out any extra information.*

9. How should telephone calls be transferred? *Make sure caller is willing to be transferred.*

10. How should calls be terminated? *Person who calls hangs up first.*

11. Explain the importance of time differences in making telephone calls.

CASE PROBLEM

Lucia has been with Brower Electric for three months now as a secretary. Brower Electric is a small company; Lucia is the only secretary in the office. She has a front office and also functions as the receptionist for the company. This morning a shabbily dressed man came in and asked to see Lucia's employer. He identified himself as Jim and said that he needed to talk with Mr. Brower immediately. Mr. Brower was on the telephone when he came in. Lucia (in a pleasant voice) told Jim that Mr. Brower was on the telephone and asked that he be seated. Although Lucia was pleasant to the man, she thought that he couldn't be very important since he was dressed so shabbily and she wondered how she could get rid of him without bothering Mr. Brower. She didn't offer him coffee or reading material; she hoped that he would get tired of waiting and leave. After about 10 minutes of waiting, Jim said, "That phone conversation is certainly long; could you let him know that I am here." Mr. Brower had finished his first conversation but he was now on another call. Lucia informed Jim that she certainly could not interrupt Mr. Brower, but that when he was off the phone, she would let him know. Finally, after 15 more minutes (and two calls later), Lucia went in to tell Mr. Brower that a man named Jim was outside. She told Mr. Brower that she was sure he didn't want to see the man but that she didn't know how to get rid of him. Mr. Brower became very angry. He said, "What do you mean, I won't want to see him? That is Jim Books—one of our most important clients. Send him in immediately." Lucia meekly did as she was told, wondering how she could redeem herself.

1. What was Lucia's original mistake? *She felt he wasn't important cause of his books.*
2. How can she rectify her mistake now? *apologise.*
3. How should she have handled the situation? *Let Mr. Brower know Jim was waiting.*

PRODUCTION PROJECTS

PP 6-1

(Objective 1)

Read two articles in recent periodicals on the importance of public relations in business. Summarize these articles on plain paper and note your sources at the top of the paper.

PP 6-2

(Objective 2)

You have the following visitors in your office today. How would you handle each situation? (Your employer's name is Walter Pfeiffer.) Type your answers on a separate sheet of paper and turn in your paper to your instructor.

1. A sales representative comes in and asks for an appointment to see your employer; your employer has told you that he does not like to see sales representatives.

2. Your employer has been called out of town unexpectedly. Mr. Scheen (with whom your employer had scheduled an appoint-

ment but has failed to tell you about) shows up for an 11 a.m. appointment.

3. An associate of your employer comes by and asks you to set up a luncheon engagement with your employer. You know that your employer does not care for the person.

4. A woman comes in to see your employer. She refuses to give her name or the purpose of her visit. However, she says the matter is urgent. She seems upset.

5. Miss Nicole Botha comes in to see your employer. Miss Botha has an appointment at 11 a.m., and it is now 10:55 a.m. Your employer has had an extremely busy morning, and he is now in a conference that will last until 11:30 a.m.

6. A man walks into your office and asks to see your employer, but he does not give you his name or the company he represents.

7. Roger Shields, in a state of agitation, comes into your office. The company recently designed a microprocessor for his company which has not been working properly. Your employer was the principal designer of the equipment. As soon as Mr. Shields sees you, he starts bellowing at you about how incompetent and inept the company is.

8. Mr. R. T. Arlston is in your employer's office. He had an appointment at 2 p.m. It is now 3 p.m., and your employer has an appointment with Ms. Carol Haile. Ms. Haile has arrived.

9. Mr. George O'Casey arrives at 3 p.m. for his appointment with your employer. On checking your appointment book, you find that Mr. O'Casey's appointment really is for 3 p.m. the following day.

10. Dr. Allen Rouche arrives for his appointment with your employer. Your employer has not met Dr. Rouche.

PP 6-3

(Objective 3)

Team up with one of your classmates for this project. You are to evaluate each other's telephone voice. Call each other. Using the rating scale in your Supplies Inventory, rate each other's voice. You may find it convenient to read preselected material over the telephone rather than carry on a normal conversation. Select material with numbers in it. After you have rated each other, prepare an action plan on how you propose to improve your telephone voice. Submit the rating scale and action plan to your instructor.

PP 6-4
(Objective 3)

You receive the following telephone calls today. Determine how you would handle each call. (Your employer's name is Walter Pfeiffer.) Type your answers on a separate sheet of paper and turn in your paper to your instructor.

1. Miss Adams calls at 2 p.m. to talk with your employer. Your employer is playing tennis with a client and will not be back in the office today.
2. While your employer is out of the office, Alberta Edwards, of Edwards & Edwards, calls. You take the name of the caller and the telephone number. What is missing?
3. A man calls and asks to speak with Walter. Your employer is in the office and is available to take the telephone call.
4. Bill Stalets calls to talk with your employer. The conversation goes like this:

    Bill Stalets: This is Bill Stalets. May I speak with Walter?

    Secretary: Mr. Pfeiffer is out of town this week. May I take a message or help you?

    Bill Stalets: Perhaps you can help me. Can you give me the date of the AMS convention?

    Secretary: Yes, I believe I can. Let me check. (You place Mr. Stalets on hold. You return three minutes later with the information only to discover that Mr. Stalets has hung up.)

    Rewrite the conversation as it should have been handled.
5. Your employer's son has called the office three times in the last thirty minutes. Your employer is in a meeting with the president.
6. A person calls about an advertisement that appeared for a secretary. The department advertising for the secretary is the payroll department.
7. Your employer asks you to call California; it is now 3 p.m. in New York (where your office is located).
8. Your employer asks you to call Colorado; it is 9 a.m. in New York (where your office is located).
9. Mr. Robert MacDonald calls to talk with your employer who is out to lunch.
10. Mr. Michael Cohen, extremely upset, calls to inform you that your employer has not shown up for an important meeting; you forgot to tell your employer about the meeting.

Chapter 7

SUPERVISING EMPLOYEES

As you are promoted to higher level secretarial positions, your job may require that you supervise office support personnel. Supervision must be done effectively; consequently, it is important that you understand some of the responsibilities of management and how these responsibilities relate to the office employee. The supervision of personnel requires a knowledge of the principles of management and an understanding of how these principles may be applied to the management of people. Therefore, management principles are introduced in this chapter to help you understand management techniques. Practical suggestions are given as to how you can put these principles to work as you supervise people.

General Objectives

Your general objectives for Chapter 7 are to:

1. *Identify responsibilities of the supervising secretary*
2. *Understand how to use supervisory techniques in getting work done*
3. *Explain the qualities of an effective supervising secretary*

MANAGEMENT RESPONSIBILITIES

In order to fulfill your role as a supervisor, you need to have a thorough understanding of basic management responsibilities. *Management* can be defined as working with and through individuals and groups to accomplish organizational goals. Functions of management include planning, organizing, recruiting, training, controlling, and evaluating.

Planning and Organizing Office Operations

Two crucial managerial functions are planning and organizing. *Planning* involves setting goals and objectives for the organization and developing plans for accomplishing these goals and objectives. *Organizing* involves dividing into manageable units the activities performed by the organization and determining who is going to perform the activities.

The Planning Process. A major part of the planning process is the setting of goals and objectives. All organizations have goals and objectives. One of the major goals of any company is to make an adequate profit to enable it to stay in business and to grow and expand. In order to accomplish this major goal, however, certain objectives must be achieved. From this we can determine that an *objective* is a short-term end to be achieved, while a *goal* is directed toward long-term achievement. For example, assume that a company has a long-term goal of selling 24,000 calculators during the next five years. In order to attain this goal, the company objective must be to sell 4,800 calculators each year, or 400 every month.

Thus, although all organizations have goals and objectives, they may be very loosely defined or not defined at all in writing. The process of allocating time to determine the exact nature of the goals and objectives, putting them in writing for all managers, and using these goals and objectives in the management process is known as *management by objectives (MBO)*. This management theory was first suggested by Peter Drucker,[1] and it is used quite extensively in business today. The planning process in which goals and objectives are set is usually done for a one-year period, which is called *short-range planning*, and for a three-to-five-year period, which is called *long-range planning*.

The goals of a company are set by the top-level administrators; i.e., the board of directors, the president, and the executive vice-president. Once these goals have been determined, they are distributed to the managers and supervisors in the organization. Then the supervisors set objectives for their particular work unit, the managers for their particular division. The supervisors and managers are responsible for the contributions that their work units or divisions make to the departments above them and eventually to the entire organization.

Now that you have looked at why and how goals and objectives are set by organizations, look at what your role as a secretary supervising an office support unit might be in planning. You may be included in helping to set the objectives of the department in which you work. The responsibility for setting departmental objectives rests with the managers of the department, but some organizations include their employees in this planning process. If you have some management responsibilities, the possibility of your being included is greater.

---

[1]Peter F. Drucker, *The Practice of Management* (New York: Harper and Row, Publishers, Inc., 1954).

Once you have participated in the setting of objectives for your department, you will have a greater understanding of the objectives and goals of the company. However, even if you do not help set the objectives of your department, you will engage in planning the activities of your unit personnel. That planning includes setting objectives. Each person in the unit needs to understand what he or she is expected to produce.

Your role then as a supervisor of an office support unit is to help plan the work of the people who report to you. How do you go about this planning process? Studies have shown that most employees like to be involved in the decision-making tasks of their jobs. Thus, you need to involve the personnel that report to you. You should have a planning session at least once a year to look at what your unit should be accomplishing for the year. Some supervisors choose to have planning sessions more often, perhaps once every six months. During this planning session, you and the employees you supervise discuss what the unit should be accomplishing and how it should be accomplished. For example, assume that you determine that the amount of work produced by the word processing operators should be increased by 10 percent. The objective is then written in a statement such as this: Increase the productivity of Word Processing Unit by 10 percent. All objectives should be written in measurable terms. In the above objective, for example, you have stated that productivity should increase by 10 percent. Then, at the end of the month, year, or whatever period determined, you can measure whether productivity has increased by that level. Illus. 7-1 shows a set of objectives written for a word processing unit. As a supervisor, your duties include not only

```
                        WORD PROCESSING UNIT

                     Objectives for 1984-1985


        1.  Increase the accuracy of reports produced by
            20 percent

        2.  Increase the productivity of the entire unit
            by 25 percent

        3.  Expand the number of word processing machines
            by two in order to take care of increased
            production needs

        4.  Recruit, employ, and train two new word pro-
            cessing operators

        5.  Continue to build a team that respects each
            other and is able to work together harmoniously
            in the production of quality work
```

Illus. 7-1
Objectives for a word processing unit

planning but also controlling. In other words, you are not only responsible for planning and writing objectives for your unit but also for seeing that these objectives are accomplished. You will learn more about the controlling function of management in a later section.

Work Organization. Once the planning has been done, the work must be organized. Organization involves bringing together all resources—people and equipment—in the most effective way to accomplish the goals. It involves dividing the work into manageable jobs that can be performed by specific employees. As a supervising secretary, you will be responsible for dividing the work load. In order to do so, you need to be familiar with some of the concepts of organization.

Span of Control. First, it is important to know how many people you can effectively supervise. *Span of control* is a management term which refers to the number of employees who are directly supervised by one person. There is no formula that rigidly defines the span of control. Some management authorities have suggested that 12 to 15 employees is the maximum span at a low level of supervision. Other management authorities have stated that 5 to 6 subordinates is the maximum number at the top level of management. Even though there is no formula, certain factors must be considered; for example, (1) the skill of the supervisor and the employees being supervised, (2) the nature of the work, (3) the amount of time to be spent on supervisory activities, (4) the nature of the organization, and (5) the latitude extended to the employees in decision making.

Job Analysis. The second factor in work organization is a job analysis. To perform a job analysis a supervisor must determine the requirements of a job and the qualifications needed by personnel to get the job done. Once this information is determined it is usually compiled into a job description (Illus. 7-2). The job description includes skills, training, education necessary for the job, and a list of the job duties. Most companies have job descriptions for all employees. Such an approach not only is helpful in the hiring process since it forces the interviewer to focus on the skills needed for the job, but it is also helpful in letting new employees know what they are expected to do.

Work Periods. A third factor that you need to consider in organizing work is the time in which the work is to be performed. Traditional office hours have often been from 8 a.m. to 5 p.m. with an hour for lunch. This tradition is changing, however. The four-day week, flex-time, and job sharing are gaining acceptance where these arrangements improve employee satisfaction and productivity.

With a four-day week, employees usually work the regular number of hours determined by the company (35 to 40); however, the

JOB DESCRIPTION

Job Title: Secretary C

Company: Brewster Company

Department: Personnel

Reports to: Patricia LaFaver

Skills and Training

The position of Secretary C requires excellent secretarial and human relations skills. Training and experience in general office procedures are required. Exceptional courtesy and the ability to understand people are important. Because of the heavy work load, this position requires the ability to screen and establish priorities on projects.

Basic skills include accurate and fast typing (60 wpm with no more than five errors as demonstrated in a five-minute test), excellent grammar, accurate and fast transcription ability, calculator and copying machine operation, and filing competence.

Education and Experience

Four years of secretarial experience and some college are preferred.

Duties

1. Typing letters, reports, memorandums, and other correspondence

2. Transcribing machine dictation

3. Operating an electronic typewriter

4. Checking figures on a calculator

5. Filing correspondence

6. Working with executives in the company

Illus. 7-2
Job description

35 to 40 hours are compressed into four days. The 35-hour week consists of three days of nine hours each and the fourth day of eight hours.

Another departure from the eight-to-five workday is the flex-time approach (the staggering of working hours to enable each employee to work the full quota of time but at periods most convenient for the individual). Under this plan, all employees do not report to work at the same time nor leave work at the same time. For example, with a 35-hour workweek, one employee may come to work at 9:30 a.m. and work until 5:00 p.m. Another employee may come to work at 7:30 a.m. and work until 3:00 p.m. (with 30 minutes for lunch). Core hours (hours when everyone is at the office) in this company are probably from 9:30 a.m. until 2:30 p.m. Such a plan allows employees to adjust their work hours to accommodate their particular life-styles. Variations in arrival and departure times also help reduce traffic congestion at the traditional peak hours. Thus, less time may be required to commute, and the pressure and tension of meeting a fixed schedule are reduced.

Still another departure from the traditional workday is the job-sharing plan. Under this arrangement, two part-time employees perform a job that otherwise would be held by one full-time employee. Such a plan may be suitable for families having small children where one or both spouses want to work on a part-time basis. It can also be suitable for workers who want to phase into retirement by reducing the length of their workday.

Illus. 7-3
Work arrangements such as flex-time and job sharing allow employees to adjust their work hours to accommodate their life-styles.

Recruiting, Training, and Motivating

As soon as a secretary is given a position of supervisor, new responsibilities may be added, such as assisting in recruiting new employees and teaching them their jobs. If you are to get personnel to do their work well and at the same time help them to have work that is fulfilling and challenging, you must understand motivational techniques.

Recruit and Employ Workers. In recruiting office workers, a company makes use of several sources. One of these is the employment agency. In Chapter 2 you learned how you as a prospective job applicant can make use of employment agencies; the employer also may use these agencies in looking for an employee. The largest public employment agency is the United States Employment Service which is supervised by the Department of Labor. This service has branch offices in every state. No fees are charged either the employer or the applicant. In addition to this public agency, there are numerous private employment agencies. These agencies charge a fee which ranges from approximately one week's pay to a percentage of the employee's annual gross salary. This fee may be paid by the job applicant or by the employer.

Another method of recruiting employees is to advertise in the local newspapers. When placing advertisements, care should be taken to make sure that the wording of the advertisement does not conflict with fair employment practice laws. Discrimination statutes prohibit job descriptions in advertisements that show preferences in terms of race, religion, sex, or age. Thus, expressions such as *young person* or *retired person* cannot be used in advertisements.

Prospective employees may also be recruited through recommendations of qualified employees. Most colleges maintain placement offices. Employers frequently approach these offices in search of potential job candidates, or they may visit colleges and interview applicants on site.

Once applicants are recruited, there are three major tools for screening and selection:

1. Written application
2. Personal interview
3. Testing procedures

Review all applications and determine which individuals will be interviewed for the job. When you, the supervising secretary, analyze an application, ask yourself these questions: What type of person am I seeking? What qualifications does that person need to have? What education and experience does the person need? With your criteria in mind, screen the applications and select the most qualified individuals to interview.

Before you begin interviewing, consider exactly the type of person you are looking for and what that person's qualifications should be. It is a good idea to write out a list of questions that you will ask the individual. Then ask each individual whom you interview the same questions. With such a list of questions, you are able to objectively select the candidate by comparing the answers of various applicants. Commit yourself to allocating enough time for a thorough interview. You may need to spend an hour or more with each applicant. Don't consider this time wasted; it can be some of the most important time you spend. As you interview applicants be aware of the latest laws that apply to interviewing. For example, laws that prohibit discrimination based on age, race, religion, or sex make it unlawful for you to ask questions such as these:

1. What nationality are your parents?
2. Are you married? single? divorced? separated?
3. What is the date of your birth?
4. Is your spouse a United States citizen?
5. Where were you born?
6. To what clubs do you belong?
7. What are the ages of your children?
8. What church do you attend?

It is imperative that you keep up with the latest laws. Without the latest information, you may place the company in jeopardy of a discrimination suit.

The third screening tool is the test. Here, too, legal considerations are important. The use of tests in selecting office workers is not prohibited, but testing practices that have a discriminatory effect upon job applicants are prohibited. The important point for you to keep in mind is that the test must measure the person's qualifications for the job and not the person as an individual. For example, if you are employing an office worker and a requirement of the job is that the person be able to type at a certain rate of speed with a certain degree of accuracy, you can give the person a typing test to discover if he or she has the necessary skills. If a person is required to transcribe notes, you can give the person grammar and spelling tests to determine if the person has the necessary English and spelling skills to transcribe the notes. However, you cannot ask a person to take a math proficiency test unless the use of math is necessary in performing the job.

Train Personnel. Once the person has been employed, a training period is necessary. No matter how qualified a person is for the job (what skills and knowledge he or she may possess), procedures and policies of the company must be learned. As a supervisor, you must assist the employee in this job training.

Job training can be divided into three parts—entry level training, job up-date training, and promotional training. Entry level training makes the employee aware of the procedures within the company and how certain jobs are to be handled. For example, a new employee may be instructed in how to handle the incoming mail, the letter and memorandum style the company uses, and the way the telephone is to be answered.

With rapid changes in technology, it is also necessary to provide job up-date training for office workers. For example, the company may purchase new word processing equipment, and an employee may need training to operate the equipment. The manufacturers of the equipment usually provide training manuals and may provide seminars to help update the employee.

Still another type of training for which a supervisor may be responsible is preparation for promotion. Company programs for promoting qualified office workers improve employee morale. Supervisors should be constantly alert for employees who show promotion capabilities and should use every opportunity to encourage and develop these employees. Additional training may be available through company sponsored seminars, through tuition reimbursed courses at local colleges, or through job internship or rotation plans in which the employee spends a period of time learning various jobs.

Motivate Employees. Motivation comes from the Latin word meaning *to move*. Thus, *motivation* is the internal process that moves or energizes you to seek various goals. On page 156 are some techniques that can be used to move or energize others to perform work that will satisfy organizational objectives.

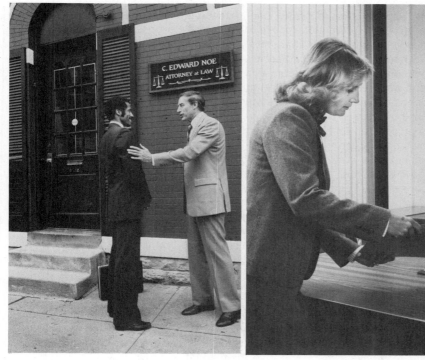

Illus. 7-4
Two techniques used to motivate employees include giving recognition for a job well done and delegating responsibility.

MOTIVATION TECHNIQUES

1. *Set Objectives.* Help the employees that you supervise to establish challenging, measurable objectives. Inexperienced supervisors frequently fail to motivate workers because they are afraid to demand enough. Once you have helped the employees establish these objectives, help them to commit themselves to achieve these objectives. This requires follow-through and planning on the part of the supervisor. You must not only know what the objectives are, but you must follow up to see that the employee has achieved these objectives.

2. *Give Recognition.* As a supervisor, you need to train yourself to become sensitive to the accomplishments of others. There are a number of ways that you can give recognition—verbal praise for a job well done, a thank you letter written to the employee, recognition in the company newsletter, and so forth. The effective supervisor will seek creative ways to give recognition.

3. *Enrich the Job.* Job enrichment is accomplished by giving employees a greater variety of duties to perform. Such enrichment can help make the job more challenging and prepare the employee for advancement. For example, one employee may have the title of receptionist with job duties of answering the telephone and greeting callers. Job enrichment will add more responsibilities to the receptionist's role. The person may also be asked to type correspondence. This additional responsibility can increase the employee's sense of satisfaction and also contribute to promotional possibilities since he or she will have learned new skills through the additional duties that were assigned.

4. *Develop a Team.* We need to be an accepted member of a group. As a supervisor, you can capitalize on this need by building a team of people who work together well. Productivity can be increased when each person in the group contributes to the overall effectiveness of the team. Become involved with the workers you supervise. Give them your undivided attention when they need it or ask for it.

5. *Pay for the Job.* Most companies have performance review evaluations at least once a year—some companies have these review sessions twice a year. At this point an employee is rated and a salary increase is generally recommended if the evaluation is satisfactory. As a supervisor, know what your employees do and then pay for the job. Reward the employees who consistently give you outstanding performance with good salary increases.

6. *Delegate Work.* Delegation is the process of entrusting the performance of some specific work to another person. Prudent delegation is one of the keys to effective supervision. Every supervisor knows this; but most supervisors also realize that it is not always easy to delegate properly. The reasons for not delegating are many and varied. Some supervisors may not understand their role well and thus cannot delegate what they do not understand. Other supervisors do not trust the people who work for them. They believe that the work will not be done properly unless it is done by them. Still other supervisors do not have the confidence they need to delegate. They fear competition or loss of credit and recognition if they delegate work to their subordinates. Delegation is vital not only to the supervisor because he or she cannot do everything, but because it is essential to delegate to key subordinates in order to motivate them and give them room to grow.

Controlling Production

The success of a business depends on its efficient operation. The paperwork of an office must be done correctly and must be completed in a time frame that satisfies the needs of company executives. Most work in an office is composed of systems which contain procedures and methods. In this context, the word *system* means related elements that interact to achieve a planned objective. For the supervising secretary, the elements of a system usually include personnel, the work to be performed, and the machines and equipment necessary to complete the office work.

Included in the system are *procedures* which are planned sequences of operations for handling the recurring transactions. For example, a written report is given to the supervising secretary who then delivers the report to the individual who will work on the report. There is also a method for accomplishing a particular phase of work. A *method* is the manual, mechanical, or electronic means by which each operation is performed. For example, the method used to produce the report may be to check the accuracy of all figures on the calculator, type the report at a typewriter, proofread the report, and make the necessary number of copies.

Each office system should function effectively to coordinate people, equipment, time, and money in order to increase productivity and reduce costs. In controlling work production, here are some questions that can be asked to determine if the system is working effectively.

1. Does the system furnish correct information?
2. Do the right people get the information they need?
3. Is the information received in an appropriate time frame?
4. Is duplication of work eliminated?
5. Is time wasted?
6. Are materials wasted?
7. Are repetitive, routine tasks mechanized when possible?
8. Do all personnel understand the system?
9. Are personnel adequately trained?

Evaluating

Performance evaluation occurs whether or not there is a formal evaluation program. It is a consequence of the way jobs are designed and organizations are structured. Superiors are constantly observing the way the people reporting to them are performing. Most companies do have formal evaluation periods in which personnel are evaluated every six months or every year. Sometimes new employees are evaluated every six months for the first year and then once a year thereaf-

EVALUATION TECHNIQUES

1. *Evaluate performance on a day-to-day basis.* Employees should always know how they are doing. If a report or letter is not typed as it should be, let the person know immediately. Praise a job well done. In other words, give the employee immediate feedback as to how he or she is doing. Do not save all criticism or praise for a yearly evaluation session.

2. *Know yourself.* Know who you are, what your needs are, and what your values are. If you come to the office tired or upset, don't vent your irritability on other employees. Realize that you are having a bad day. Psychologists call this phenomenon of transferring our problems to others *projection*. Although we can't eliminate completely this very human tendency, we can guard against it. The supervisor should understand his or her own wants, needs, values, reaction to authority, moods, and habits. Then he or she will be better able to look at other people honestly.

3. *Allow adequate time for the evaluation.* The performance evaluation is important for both you and the employee. Set aside enough time on your calendar to do it well. You need to spend an hour or two with each employee. Also, be sure that the place is appropriate. If you are using your office, it is best to have your telephone calls transferred to someone else so that you will not be interrupted as you talk with the employee. Usually it is best to close the door so that visitors will not drop in and interrupt you.

4. *Give credit where credit is due.* Be certain that you praise the employee for work well done. Too many managers consider an evaluation period a time for criticism only. It is not. It is a time to look at the total work of the employee. In what areas is he or she performing in an exemplary manner? an average manner? below expectations? Praise the employee for work well done as well as offer constructive criticism for work needing improvement.

5. *Be fair.* Anayze the employee's work based on an established criterion of performance, not on how well you like or dislike the employee. Stay away from personality traits. Stress job performance. In discussing errors, suggest ways that the work could have been performed satisfactorily. Give the employee an opportunity to suggest possible alternatives. Let the session be a growth experience for the employee. Stay away from statements such as, "Your poor performance is a problem." Instead say, "You are doing well in these areas (then identify the areas), and improvement is needed in these areas (identify these areas)."

6. *Listen to what the person is saying.* Too often we listen to others with only half an ear. The employee often comes in to an evaluation session with a certain amount of anxiety and perhaps even hostility. Let the person talk. By talking, the person can usually release much of the anxiety and thus be more receptive to constructive criticism.

7. *Avoid personal areas.* Sometimes a supervisor, even with the best intentions, will become too deeply involved in the employee's personal life. Don't try to counsel an employee about problems which should be handled only by a qualified professional.

8. *Establish attainable objectives.* Help the employee set realistic objectives for improvement. It is a good idea to ask the employee to put these objectives in writing as you discuss them. In fact, if there are several areas where the employee needs to improve, a plan of action for improvement may be developed, with dates set for the accomplishment of each objective. Then, as the employee works on a plan of action, your role as supervisor is to check the accomplishment of each objective and make suggestions or let the employee know that improvement is satisfactory.

ter. Whatever the time period for performance evaluations, it is a crucial management function and must be done well in order to achieve employee growth as well as increased productivity for the company. Illus. 7-5 shows a typical performance evaluation form. On page 158 are some suggestions for conducting performance evaluations.

Another part of evaluation in which you should be involved is the evaluation of the objectives that were set for your area. You will need to determine if these objectives were met. For example, using the

---

PERFORMANCE REVIEW FORM

Name _Joe C. Wilson_   Department _Word Processing_

Quality of Work	15 16 17	18 19 20	21 22 23	24 25 (26)	27 28 29
	Unsatisfactory	Below Average	Average	Above Average	Superior
Comments	_Seldom makes errors_				

Volume of Work	15 16 17	18 19 20	21 22 23	24 25 26	(27) 28 29
	Unsatisfactory	Below Average	Average	Above Average	Superior
Comments	_Works quickly and efficiently_				

Knowledge of Work	5 6 7	8 9 10	11 12 13	14 15 16	(17) 18 19
	Unsatisfactory	Below Average	Average	Above Average	Superior
Comments	_Has thorough understanding of departmental procedures_				

Initiative	5 6 7	8 9 10	11 12 13	14 15 (16)	17 18 19
	Unsatisfactory	Below Average	Average	Above Average	Superior
Comments					

Work Attitude	5 6 7	8 9 10	11 12 13	14 15 (16)	17 18 19
	Unsatisfactory	Below Average	Average	Above Average	Superior
Comments	_Learns new applications quickly_				

Attitude Toward Others	5 6 7	8 9 10	11 12 13	14 15 (16)	17 18 19
	Unsatisfactory	Below Average	Average	Above Average	Superior
Comments	_Always willing to assist colleagues_				

Promotional Potential	5 6 7	8 9 10	11 12 13	14 15 (16)	17 18 19
	Unsatisfactory	Below Average	Average	Above Average	Superior
Comments					

Add points in each area to determine overall rating; check appropriate rating below.

Superior (133-153 points) _✓ (134)_   Below Average (70-90 points) _____
Above Average (112-132 points) _____   Unsatisfactory (55-69 points) _____
Average (91-111 points) _____
Signature of evaluator _Mary Morgan_   Position _Supervisor_   Date _7/2/--_

Illus. 7-5
Performance review form (Notice that the scales in the form are weighted so that more emphasis is placed on the quality of work and the volume of work.)

objectives for the word processing unit established in Illus. 7-1 on page 149, was the accuracy of the reports increased 20 percent, was the productivity of the unit increased by 25 percent? If your objectives were not accomplished, you should ask yourself these questions: Why were they not accomplished? Did outside factors prevent me from accomplishing them? Did personnel inefficiency prevent me from accomplishing them? Are the objectives still worthy of accomplishment? If so, what will ensure their accomplishment during the next planning cycle? If the objectives were accomplished, determine what objectives to establish during the next planning cycle. A major part of the planning process is evaluating the results of the process and determining future directions for planning.

QUALITIES OF AN EFFECTIVE SUPERVISING SECRETARY

Getting work done through people requires continual analysis on your part of your own strengths and weaknesses and continual commitment to your personal growth. This commitment to growth can pay dividends to you as a supervisor of happy and productive people who work with you.

Know Your Leadership Style

Knowing something about leadership styles can help you to better understand how you work and how others around you work. Several management theories deal with leadership styles, the most popular of which are presented here—Theory X, Theory Y, and Theory Z.

Theory X and Theory Y. In 1960 Douglas McGregor classified the way in which organizations are traditionally managed as Theory X. He also presented Theory Y, which he suggested was more consistent with current research concerning motivation and the realization of both individual and organizational goals.[2] McGregor's writings have had a tremendous impact on management theory, and a brief explanation of his theories will help you understand how people perform in organizations.

According to McGregor, the assumptions upon which Theory X is based are the following:

1. The average human being has an inherent dislike of work and will avoid it if possible.

---

[2]Douglas McGregor, *The Human Side of Enterprise* (New York: McGraw-Hill Book Company, Inc., 1960), pp. 33-57.

2. Because of this inherent dislike of work, most people must be controlled to get them to put forth adequate effort toward the achievement of organizational goals.
3. The average person prefers to be directed and wishes to avoid responsibility.

In contrast, Theory Y is based on the following assumptions about people:

1. The expenditure of physical and mental effort in work is as natural as play or rest.
2. People will exercise self-direction and self-control toward achieving goals to which they are committed.
3. The average person learns, under proper conditions, not to reject but rather to seek responsibility.

The central principle of an organization which adheres to Theory X philosophy is one of directing and controlling employees; whereas the central principle of an organization which adheres to Theory Y philosphy is one of believing that employees enjoy work. The task of Theory Y management is to help these individuals achieve their own goals by directing their efforts toward the success of the business.

Theory Z. In 1981 William Ouchi formulated Theory Z which is based on a management theory used in Japan that has reportedly contributed to high productivity levels.[3] The assumption underlying Theory Z is that involved workers are the key to increased productivity. Some of the characteristics of a Theory Z organization are: (1) the decision-making process is typically participative; (2) concern for the welfare of subordinates and of co-workers is a natural part of a working relationship; (3) open communication, trust, and commitment are valued; (4) egalitarianism is a prominent feature; and (5) a close interchange between work and social life is fostered.

American business has not been able to keep pace with Japan in its productivity efforts; and, for this reason, Theory Z is receiving considerable attention among managers as to how it may be applied in the United States. The principal assumptions of Theory Z are that the worker does want to become involved and can be trusted as a valuable participant in the decision-making process of the organization.

Questions to Ask Yourself about Leadership Styles. These theories help you observe how people behave and how they can best be supervised. Some questions you should ask yourself are:

---

[3]William G. Ouchi, *Theory Z: How American Business Can Meet the Japanese Challenge* (Reading, Mass.: Addison-Wesley Publishing Company, Inc., 1981).

What do I believe about people? What are my basic assumptions about how people behave in organizations? The answers to these questions will help you discover your leadership style. And, as you have learned already, the more you know about yourself, the better able you are to relate to other individuals and thus the better able you are to attain company goals through directing other people.

Once you have discovered your most prevelant leadership style, the next question you might ask is: What style works best with the people whom I supervise? You have also learned that all people do not want and do not value the same things. Some people may work primarily for social or economic reasons, while others may work primarily for recognition and the opportunity for promotion. In fact, McGregor's Theory Y has been criticized because of the assumption that all people like to work and will exercise self-direction and self-control if they are committed to the objectives of the organization. People are different; they have different needs and values. And, as a supervisor, you cannot assume that all people will become involved in their work. You must consider each person individually and adjust your supervisory style to the needs of that person. Thus, you may find it necessary to use Theory Y or Theory Z principles with some people and the Theory X principle with others.

Is there a best style of leadership? No. The style used in any particular situation depends on a number of factors; however, your knowledge of these styles can help you apply the most appropriate style under any circumstance.

Practice Effective Communication

Your growth in supervision also depends upon your ability to communicate effectively. In Chapter 4 you learned about communication problems and techniques for minimizing these problems. The important thing to remember is that communication problems continue to surface. No matter what your communication skills, you will never become a perfect communicator. It is simply not possible because people and situations change constantly. You must be aware that people view things differently, come from different backgrounds, use language differently, and react to others differently. It is impossible to be a good supervisor if you are not an effective communicator. Practice effective communication techniques daily in order to fine tune your skills.

Be Flexible

Organizational goals change, personnel change, and equipment changes. As a supervisor you must be flexible. *Rigidity* is a trait that you should not possess. You must be able to respond to changes as they occur each day, and you must respond to these changes with effective decisions that benefit the organization and the personnel within the organization.

Continue to Learn

Continue to read and broaden your knowledge of supervisory techniques. Any number of management journals are available; for example, *Office Administration and Automation, Management Review*, and *Management World*. The company may provide periodic training seminars which you can attend, or you may be interested in taking courses on employee supervision at a local college.

PROFESSIONAL POINTERS

Follow these suggestions to help you become a better supervisor.

1. Maintain a positive attitude.
2. Establish measurable objectives and goals.
3. Set appropriate priorities.
4. Keep current on developments in your area of responsibility.
5. Know your preferred supervisory style.
6. Know each of your subordinates.
7. Listen to people and encourage expression of their views.
8. Develop team working commitments.
9. Stress job performance, not personal traits.
10. Employ the most qualified people you can find.
11. Communicate efficiently and logically.
12. Take some risks.
13. Delegate work.
14. Control your time.
15. Look for creative solutions to problems.
16. Participate in professional organizations.

FOR YOUR REVIEW

1. Define the term *management*.

2. List and describe the basic management functions.

3. What is likely to be a supervising secretary's role in the planning process?

4. What is meant by flex-time?

5. Define the term *motivation*. Describe two motivation techniques.

6. What are some suggestions for conducting performance evaluations?

7. List and explain two leadership styles.

8. Is there one best leadership style? Explain.

CASE PROBLEM

Because of a management problem, morale has been very low in the office of a large equipment manufacturer for several months. Stephanie Kootz was promoted to office manager from a secretarial position six months ago. Recently Stephanie asked for a transfer back to a secretarial position, stating that she had found a complete lack of cooperation and loyalty from the office staff. She also said that this taste of management convinced her that she would contribute more to the company—and be happier—as a secretary. Her immediate supervisor, Josephine Massie, accepted the resignation reluctantly. She was confident that Stephanie had potential and had not given the new position a sufficient trial.

Before choosing a replacement for Stephanie, Josephine Massie decided to talk with the office staff about the problem. They told her that they had been pleased when Stephanie had first been appointed office manager. They liked her and respected her work as a secretary; however, they had soon become frustrated by her supervisory style. They said that Stephanie certainly understood the job and the goals of the company, but stated that she didn't know anything about supervising people. Whenever a problem arose, she would quickly dictate action without getting all the facts. Opinions that differed from her own would be quashed by references to her status as manager. Soon the office staff was doing precisely what Stephanie dictated, regardless of their ideas or preferences. Everyone stopped making suggestions about work improvement and did as they were told. Stephanie drove the office staff hard; even though morale was low, productivity was relatively high. However, in the last two weeks productivity had dropped off to some extent.

1. What is Stephanie's preferred style of leadership?

2. What seems to be the secretaries' preferred style?

3. Do you think there is a leadership style that would get the most work accomplished in this situation?

4. Should Stephanie have submitted her resignation? What could have been done to help Stephanie?

PRODUCTION PROJECTS

PP 7-1

(Objective 1)

Interview a secretary who supervises other employees. Ask the secretary the following questions:

1. How many people do you supervise?

2. What types of supervisory responsibilities do you have? (For example, do you recruit and employ personnel? Do you evaluate personnel? Are you responsible for setting objectives for your department?)

3. How do you motivate your employees?

4. Is there a certain type of leadership style that works best for you? If so, what is it?

Give an oral report of your findings to the class.

PP 7-2

(Objective 1)

Read two articles on office management. Summarize your research on plain paper and note the sources used. Answer the following question at the completion of your research: What are the responsibilities of the office manager?

PP 7-3

(Objective 2)

Answer the questions at the end of each of the following cases. Use a separate sheet of paper and type your answers.

Case A

Betty Freudiger, the supervising secretary, was conducting the yearly performance evaluation with one of the office support workers, Thomas Garcia. Here is how the evaluation went:

Betty: Thomas, I've just been reviewing your job description. There are some problems here. It seems that you have been having trouble getting out the monthly reports on time. In fact, in the past ten months, not one single report has been out on time. I'm getting complaints from other departments about your work.

Thomas: Well, I've been meaning to talk to you about these reports.

Betty: What were you going to say?

Thomas: For one thing, I have too much to do. I work constantly. None of the other employees has as much to do as I have. And ...

Betty: (Interrupting Thomas) What do you mean you have too much to do. You don't have as much to do as the other employees. In fact, Sherrie has twice as much work as you and she is twice as efficient.

Thomas: If you would just listen to me for a minute, maybe I could explain what I am talking about.

Betty: I'm tired of listening to you, Thomas. Either you produce or you get fired. That's all I have to say to you.

Rewrite this performance evaluation using the effective techniques you have learned in this chapter.

Case B

Zena Privett is an office manager. Here is her story:

"Six months ago I hired and trained my replacement as secretary. My job presently is to manage the office and coordinate the work between the president and vice-president, plus supervise five office workers, including the one that I hired to replace me. This secretary, Ann Baker, has been causing me some problems. I see copies of all the correspondence she prepares after it leaves the office and she makes numerous typographical and grammatical errors in almost everything she types. I have given her work back to her to redo two and three times before it is right. Her filing is never up to date, and she spends numerous hours on the telephone about personal matters. I have discussed her job performance with her on three occasions, but lately I have just been giving most of the work to the other secretaries. After our last conversation, she went to see the president and complained that I had not helped her enough on the job; she also stated that I was picking on her. She said that I never bothered the other secretaries. The president called me in and asked me what was going on. I tried to explain the situation, but I am not sure that he understood."

1. Should Zena discharge the secretary, or should she try to work with her?

2. How do you think she could help the secretary?

3. Can Zena use more effective management techniques? If so, what would you suggest?

Case C

Eunice Rogers has recently assumed a supervisory role. She now has a staff of three employees to supervise. One employee has recently resigned and Eunice's job responsibilities include recruiting and interviewing the replacement. Eunice placed an advertisement in the local newspaper which read:

> Secretary needed. Good skills essential.
> Woman needed who is willing to work overtime;
> would prefer mature woman in her 40s.

This is the way Eunice conducted the first interview.

Eunice:	Tell me about yourself.
Susan Day (Applicant):	Where should I begin?
Eunice:	Well, just any place; I want to learn more about you.
Susan:	(She then begins a ten-minute talk starting with her high school years.)
Eunice:	(Eunice notices that Susan has on a wedding ring.) What does your husband do?
Susan:	He is an engineer.
Eunice:	Do you have any children?
Susan:	Yes, two.
Eunice:	Who will keep them while you are working?
Susan:	My mother.
Eunice:	Why do you want to work for this company?
Susan:	It seems to be a company where job advancement is good.
Eunice:	What skills do you have?
Susan:	I can type 80 words a minute, use word processing equipment and a transcription machine.
Eunice:	Thank you. I will contact you as soon as I have made a decision.

1. How should the job advertisement be written?

2. Are there other sources of recruitment that could have been pursued?

3. What mistakes did Eunice make in the interview?

PP 7-4

(Objective 3)

Read the following case and suggest solutions. Your solutions should be based on the assumptions stated below the case, not on how you personally would handle the situation.

Case A

You are responsible for supervising three secretaries. In the past all have produced at a satisfactory level, but during the last six months something seems to have gone wrong with everyone. One secretary has had numerous personal problems which have affected her work. Because of these problems, she has been absent frequently. The second secretary has been quarreling with the third secretary over work assignments, and the production of both secretaries has decreased drastically. Managers are complaining to you that their work is not being done well.

Assume that you believe the following things to be true of people:

1. People like to work.

2. People will exercise self-direction and self-control if given the opportunity.

3. The average person seeks responsibility.

Based on these assumptions, how would you handle the problems? Type your answers on a separate sheet of paper. What leadership style is assumed?

Case B

The situation is the same as in Case A above. Assume that you believe the following to be true of people:

1. People are lazy and dislike to work.

2. People must be controlled and disciplined to get them to perform their jobs.

3. The average person has little ambition.

Based on these assumptions, how would you handle the problems? Type your answers on a separate sheet of paper. Indicate what leadership style is assumed.

PP 7-5

(Objective 3)

Use the rating scale in your Supplies Inventory to rate your supervisory potential.

PART 3
Correspondence Responsibilities— What Skills Do You Need?

Chapter 8   Using Typewriting Equipment and Supplies
Chapter 9   Preparing Office Correspondence
Chapter 10   Utilizing Dictation and Transcription Skills
Chapter 11   Processing Mail and Using Shipping Services

Chapter 8

USING TYPEWRITING EQUIPMENT
AND SUPPLIES

An interesting fact, though it may not surprise you, is that more people are trained to operate a typewriter than any other machine today. Typing skill requires more than knowing how to type if quality work is to be produced. If you are to be competent in secretarial work, you must be an expert in the use of typewriting equipment and supplies.

This chapter is designed to review the typing procedures that will enable you to be a competent typist. A variety of typewriting equipment will be covered as well as the use of typewriting supplies.

General Objectives

Your general objectives for Chapter 8 are to:

1. *Identify the typewriting equipment used in most offices today*
2. *Name the sources from which documents are created*
3. *Demonstrate the use of proper typing techniques in preparing mailable documents*
4. *Explain the typing supplies that a secretary commonly uses*
5. *Type lined business forms*

THE EVOLUTION OF TYPEWRITERS

The invention of the typewriter has greatly transformed the preparation of business correspondence. Communications that were originally handwritten have been expedited and made more uniform by typewriting.

Manual Typewriters

Not until 1868 when Christopher Sholes patented a typewriter did this machine become popular as an acceptable alternative to handwriting. This early typewriter had upper and lowercase letters on typebars that were activated by a person forcefully depressing the keys. The carriage was manually returned by a typist reaching with the left hand and swinging a lever to the right. Even though a machine of this nature was slow compared to today's equipment, the manual typewriter improved the quality and quantity of work prepared by secretaries for many years.

Illus. 8-1
Early model manual typewriter

Electric Typewriters

A major improvement in typewriting equipment came during the 1930s when the International Business Machines Corporation (IBM) marketed the first electric typewriter. Two revolutionary improvements in the electric typewriter were ease in key stroking and the elimination of the manual carriage return; the carriage was returned to the left by lightly touching a key with the right little finger. It became unnecessary for a typist to remove his or her hands from the keyboard while using the typewriter.

Element. A major change in electric typewriters came in the early 1960s when IBM replaced electrically powered typebars with a round, ball shaped mechanism called an *element*. This element was constructed to contain all the letters, symbols, and numbers previously contained on separate typebars. The carriage of the typewriter was designed to remain stationary while the element moved back and

Illus. 8-2
Stationary carriage electric typewriter

forth across the *platen* (the roller against which the paper rests in a typewriter) striking the paper through an inked or carbon ribbon.

Although some typing elements may be interchanged from one brand of typewriter to another (for example, IBM Selectric II with a Remington Rand), other elements cannot be interchanged even on models of the same manufacturer (for example, IBM Selectrics I and II with the Selectric III model).

Interchangeable Type. An element, or *typing font* as it is called by some manufacturers, can be removed and replaced by one with a different letter style. Because of this "selection" feature, typists can choose from a variety of type styles for use in specialized typing. Elements have even been created for mathematical symbols and technical equations as well as for foreign languages.

Typists like the convenience of changing type styles. It is important, however, to exercise good judgment when choosing a type style for a document. A standard type style (such as prestige elite) should be used for all general correspondence, while other styles should be reserved for special projects or effects.

Pitch. The size of typewriter print is referred to as the *pitch.* For the first hundred years or so, typewriters were made to type in one size. The lettering was known as pica type, and it contained ten char-

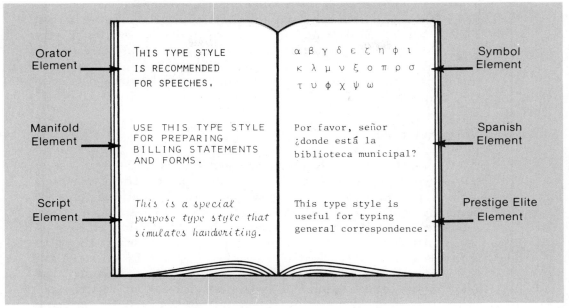

Illus. 8-3
Interchangeable elements have greatly increased the variety of type styles available to the secretary.

acters in one inch of type. Resourceful manufacturers later reduced the pitch to twelve characters to an inch and called this type *elite*.

In the 1970s typewriters were introduced with the capability of dual pitch. Typewriters that have dual pitch can be used for either pica or elite type by simply positioning the pitch selector lever and inserting either a pica or elite element. Many of the typewriters on the market today have dual pitch. Some typewriters are equipped with a proportional pitch, which allows a different amount of space for each character in order to *justify* the lines (make the right margin even).

Self-Correcting. Electric typewriters that have a mechanism for error correction are called *self-correcting*. Special correcting tape positioned between the typewriter ribbon and the platen is activated by a specially marked correcting key. The typist uses the correcting key to backspace to an incorrectly typed character and then restrikes the incorrect character to delete it. The correcting tape either covers up the error with a chalklike substance or literally lifts the error off the paper when that character is restruck. The typist can then type the correct character.

Some portable typewriters require that you remove the ink ribbon and insert the correcting ribbon in order to make the correction.

These machines are not as popular for high-volume office work as those that contain the correcting tape adjacent to the inked or carbon ribbon. Making corrections with a self-correcting typewriter is very easy. Usually these corrections are undetectable. If a correction is noticeable, however, it is your responsibility to use additional correcting techniques. Some of these techniques will be covered later in this chapter.

Electronic Typewriters

The 1980s will surely be remembered for the widespread use of automated equipment in the office. Just as electric typewriters replaced manual typewriters, typewriters with automatic features are becoming commonplace in offices today. You will learn more about sophisticated equipment such as word processors in Chapter 17.

Electronic, or intelligent, typewriters perform basically the same functions as electric typewriters. However, when you lift open the top of an electronic typewriter, you'll find the inside nearly empty. The many levers, springs, gears, and screws found inside an electric typewriter have been replaced by circuit boards that tell the machine what to do when your fingers hit the keys. Flip the *ON* switch and

Exxon Corporation

Illus. 8-4
Electronic typewriter

you will not hear a humming motor but only a click each time you strike a key. An occasional beep will occur to warn that you're near the right-hand margin or have pressed an incorrect function key. Some special functions performed by electronic typewriters are:

1. Automatic correction of a full line of type
2. Automatic setting of frequently used margins and tabs that can be recalled for repeated use
3. Automatic centering and underscoring
4. Automatic alignment of decimals in columns of numbers
5. Storage of frequently used phrases
6. Storage of a limited amount of characters for automatic playback
7. Automatic carriage return

Electronic typewriters commonly use a *print wheel* rather than a ball shaped element. The element looks like a flattened daisy with characters (letters, numbers, and symbols) at the end of each "petal" on a multispoked, rimless wheel. The print wheel rotates vertically until it arrives at the selected character; then a hammer hits the character against the paper to print through a ribbon. Xerox Corporation produced the first daisy wheel printer in 1974. There are 96 characters on the wheel, each character on a different spoke. Print wheels also come in a variety of type styles and pitches.

SOURCES FROM WHICH DOCUMENTS ORIGINATE

Most secretaries do a considerable amount of typing. Documents frequently typed include letters, memorandums, reports, forms, and tables. In whatever manner a document originates, the secretary must type it in usable form. The final copy must be error free, appropriately arranged on the page, complete, and grammatically correct. The ultimate responsibility lies with the secretary to see that every typed document is accurate.

Handwritten Copy

Many documents that must be typed by the secretary are handwritten. Some originators have unintelligible handwriting; others clearly print each character. It is not always easy to prepare typed copy from handwriting. The writer often depends on the secretary to supply correct punctuation and spelling. You may need to decide which format is proper for certain documents. Your judgment and often your patience may be tried when you type from a handwritten original.

Dictation

Machine dictation is frequently used in offices today. Machine transcription is a learnable skill that enables a secretary to transcribe dictation into typed, mailable copy. Chapter 10 will cover transcription techniques that will help you in typing documents from machine dictation.

Composition

As a secretary, your employer may say to you, "Answer this letter," or "Type a memo in reply to this request." Routine correspondence is composed and typed by many secretaries. Composing a document at the typewriter saves time. Secretaries that are responsible for originating documents find the typewriter a useful tool. Information and suggestions for composing original correspondence are included in Chapter 9.

Rough Drafts

Rough drafts should not be typed for all documents. In fact, you should strive to type a final copy on your first attempt. In some instances, however, a rough draft should be prepared. If you have been asked to compose a memorandum, letter, or report, your employer may want to review a rough draft of your work before the final copy is prepared. Some employers like to see a rough draft of certain dictated correspondence in order to review the content, shorten or lengthen the letter, consult with a colleague, or change the format before deciding on the final revision.

When typing a rough draft, consider these helpful suggestions:

1. Double-space to allow room for revisions.
2. Unless you are using a self-correcting or an electronic typewriter, simply X out errors instead of erasing.
3. Allow for wider margins so that notations or additions can be made.
4. Type a rough draft at your fastest speed. The time you save will be used for preparing the final draft of the document.

Final Copies

A final copy should be typed with extreme care. Any corrections that must be made should be undetectable. Always keep your typewriter clean—especially the typing element. The final copy must be accurate and have an attractive appearance before it is submitted to your employer for signature. The typing techniques discussed later in this chapter will aid you in preparing final copies.

Proofreading

Proofreading is of great importance in preparing mailable documents. A mailable document is one that—in its final form—is error free and ready for mailing or distribution.

You should recognize errors as they are made, and make corrections as you type. You may make errors that you are not aware of, and these errors are often difficult to detect when you proofread. Also, proofread each page before you remove it from the typewriter to make error correction easier.

As you proofread, look for errors in word endings. These errors are often missed because the typist does not proofread for meaning. Look for the *s* or *ed* on the end of words. Has a word been omitted, or is the same word typed twice? It is important for you to proofread and not just scan a page after you have typed it. Additional tips for proofreading are included in Chapter 10.

TYPEWRITING TECHNIQUES AND SUPPLIES

An outcome of office automation technology has been the development of sophisticated typewriting equipment that allows typists to produce correspondence or documents more accurately and quickly. Today's equipment can help a secretary achieve a high level of performance. However, it is still the secretary's responsibility to learn effective ways to prepare mailable documents. To do this, you should have an understanding of typewriting techniques and supplies.

Machine Parts

Always become well acquainted with your typewriter. Learn the features that are unique to the typewriter you will be using. Review thoroughly the manufacturer's booklet that accompanies your typewriter. You may even find it necessary to have a representative of the manufacturer give you a demonstration on how to operate a particular model. Knowing how to use all the parts of a typewriter will help you be a more efficient typist.

Formatting

Formatting means determining the appropriate style and placement of a document. Originators sometimes instruct typists on the format they should use when typing documents. Many offices provide style manuals, which contain the preferred styles for company or department usage. Quite often, however, you will make formatting decisions for yourself. Formatting may include such techniques as determining top, bottom, and side margins and vertical and horizontal placement.

Determining Margins. Use good judgment when deciding what side margins to set and how much top and bottom margins to leave. Unless you are typing a document that is to be bound, the left and right margins should be equal. The right margin should be kept as even as possible. Remember that margins frame the typed material on a page.

Centering Vertically and Horizontally. You will need to understand how to center material both horizontally and vertically on a page. Try to practice these methods of centering vertically and horizontally.

To determine the first line of type when centering vertically, follow these steps:

1. Determine the number of lines available on the paper (66 lines on a standard sheet of 8 1/2-by-11-inch paper).
2. Count the number of lines to be centered vertically (lines to be typed and blank lines in between typed lines).
3. Subtract the number of lines to be centered vertically from the number of lines available. The difference gives you the number of unused lines.
4. Divide the number of unused lines by two. (If a fraction results, disregard it). This figure will give you the number of lines for the top and bottom margins.
5. Space down from the top edge of the paper *one* more line than the number of lines to be left in the top margin.

Most electronic typewriters permit automatic horizontal centering. By positioning the element carrier at the center point or middle of the paper and giving the typewriter a "center" instruction, the word or words will be automatically centered. Notice that you must start the procedure from the proper centering point. If you are centering manually, you will find that the backspacing method described here is generally faster than the mathematical method.

Backspacing Method:
1. Position the carriage at the center of the paper.
2. Depress the backspace key one time for every two characters and/or spaces. Disregard a leftover character.
3. Begin typing.

Mathematical Method:
1. Determine the center point of the paper (not the typewriter).

2. Count the total number of characters and spaces in the line to be centered, and divide by two. If a fraction results, disregard it.
3. Using the margin scale, subtract this amount from the center point to get the exact number on which you should begin typing.

Correction Tools

There are a variety of correction tools to aid you in making corrections. The following paragraphs provide an explanation of those correction materials.

Eraser. You can make good corrections with a typing eraser. Choose an eraser that is not too abrasive. Erase in one direction. Be careful not to make a hole in your paper by erasing too vigorously. A hole in your paper makes retyping the document necessary. Most people prefer the stick or pencil-type eraser rather than a circular one.

An eraser is an effective tool when erasing a few characters or a short word. It is very difficult to erase several words without the correction being noticeable.

Eraser Shield. A plastic or metal shield with different size holes will allow you to erase an error without erasing the adjacent characters. The use of an eraser shield will also prevent fingerprints and smudges around the area of the correction.

Correction Paper. Correction paper is coated with a chalklike substance. Place the correction paper over the error with the coated side down and type the incorrect character that is to be covered up. Remove the correction paper, backspace, and type the correct character. Correction paper, in sheet or roll form, is an acceptable choice if you have only one or two letters to correct. It is not effective, however, for correcting long words or phrases. Another disadvantage in using correction paper is its lack of permanency. If the original document is retrieved for reading after a long period of time, the chalk may have flaked off, thus revealing the error.

Correction Fluid. A white liquid, which is sold in small bottles with an applicator brush, can be used to cover up errors. When correction fluid is carefully applied over a small area, such as a few characters, it is an acceptable method of correction. Rarely, though, should this fluid be used on original documents. If you are typing a document that is to be photocopied, and the copies are distributed instead of the original, correction fluid is a good choice for error correction. If you use colored stationery, you can order correction fluid that is blended to match the color of the paper.

Correction Tape. Also known as cover-up tape, correction tape is white, self-adhesive paper that is available in a variety of line widths. The tape comes in a small box with an opening and cutting edge. To use the tape, simply pull the tape from the box to the desired length, tear it off, and tape it over the area to be corrected. Corrections are then typed on top of the tape. This method is effective for correcting errors where appearance is not too important since the tape is visible.

Lift-off Tape. Lift-off tape, activated by a self-correcting typewriter correction key, allows the typist to lift the error off the page. Lift-off tape has a sticky substance which literally lifts the ink off the paper and makes an almost undetectable correction. A special typewriter ribbon, usually referred to as a correctable film or correctable ribbon, must be used with lift-off tape.

Error correction using lift-off tape applies to originals only. If you are typing carbon copies, you will need to correct them with other materials after deleting the characters from the original.

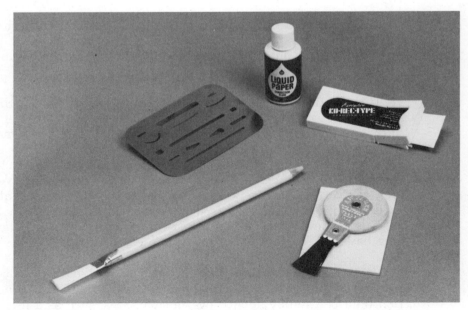

Illus. 8-5
Some of the tools used to correct typewritten errors include (clockwise from top) correction fluid, correction paper, circular and stick erasers, and an eraser shield.

Exact Positioning for Corrections

Try to correct errors as soon as you make them. You may not detect some of your errors until you proofread the document. When you must return to a line or reinsert your paper to correct an error, you may find it more difficult to make an unnoticeable correction. Exact positioning to make corrections is a typing technique that you must perfect.

Many typewriters have a ribbon position called *stencil*. As you depress the keys, no characters are printed. You may find the stencil position helpful if your paper slips, or if you lose your original typing line when you make a correction. Your first step will be to erase or remove the incorrect character or characters. To realign for exact typing position, change the ribbon position selector to the stencil position. Strike the key you want to type. You should be able to see a light impression of the character. If the character is correctly positioned, you are ready to return to the normal ribbon position in order to type the character. If the character is not correctly positioned, make necessary adjustments. This technique may take you additional time, but the quality of your correction will be better.

Typewriter Ribbons

Ribbons vary with different brands of typewriters. Learn right away what type of ribbon fits your typewriter, and how it is installed. Ribbons are made of different materials. You should be familiar with the different types of typewriter ribbons available in order to select the ribbon that fits your needs.

Fabric Ribbons. Generally nylon or cotton is used to make fabric ribbons. The cloth is coated with ink; and, because of its durability, it can be reversed for repeated use. The ink quality of the ribbon deteriorates after repeated usage. Fabric ribbons are less expensive than ribbons made of other materials.

Film Ribbons. Film ribbons are made of an ink coated plastic or paper that resembles carbon paper. The print quality of carbon or film ribbons is very good. They can be purchased in different colors, and they can be used only once. After the ribbon has wound itself from one spool to the other, it is discarded. Most film ribbons are contained in a cartridge that is easily inserted in the typewriter.

Correctable Film Ribbons. A correctable film ribbon does not dry immediately after imprinting on paper, allowing the ink to be easily erased or lifted off the paper. Use correctable film ribbons on self-correcting typewriters to ensure undetectable corrections. Because most film and correctable film ribbons are contained in similar cartridges, they can be easily confused. Both kinds of ribbons will fit the same typewriters. To avoid confusion when replacing ribbons, look carefully for the identification of the ribbon usually printed on the top of the cartridge. Some manufacturers do not print the type of ribbon on the cartridge but use a color-coding system for different kinds of typewriter ribbons.

Multistrike Film Ribbons. Most film ribbons are designed to move forward as each character is struck. A multistrike film ribbon moves more slowly and allows more than one character to be printed before winding; it therefore lasts longer. Some multistrike ribbons will yield as many as 580,000 typed characters compared with 150,000 to 300,000 typed characters from other film ribbons.

Multistrike film ribbons are preferred over regular film ribbons if confidentiality is required. Since a regular film ribbon winds forward as each character is typed, words can actually be read from the ribbon. A multistrike ribbon cannot be read because several characters are typed on top of each other or very close together.

Multistrike ribbons are made with a quick-drying, permanent ink. Lift-off tape cannot be used with multistrike ribbons for correcting errors. Cover-up, or correction, tape can be used on typewriters with a correcting feature when a multistrike ribbon is used.

Stationery

As a secretary, you will handle a variety of office correspondence, reports, and forms. The type of paper that is used for office correspondence and other documents affects the overall appearance and effectiveness of those documents. Quality, weight, and finish of paper vary.

Plain Bond Paper. Plain bond paper is used for all documents that do not require a printed form or letterhead. Plain bond paper is also used for the second and subsequent pages of a business letter.

The paper is made from cotton and/or wood. The amount of cotton in a certain grade of paper is referred to as its *rag* content. Paper with a high rag content is of good quality and is more expensive than low rag content paper. High quality bond paper usually has a "watermark." The *watermark* identifies the name of the manufacturer, the brand name, and the rag content of the paper. Paper with a watermark has a right and wrong side as well as a top and bottom. The watermark should be readable when the paper is held up to the light.

The lesser grades of paper that may be used for duplicating or for copying purposes will not have a watermark.

Finish refers to the surface texture of the paper. Bond paper comes with a smooth, cockle, or erasable finish. Paper with a smooth finish has a smooth texture; a cockle finish has a slightly pebbled or rippled texture and appearance; erasable paper has been coated with a substance to prevent immediate ink penetration and drying so that a soft eraser can be used to make a correction. After the ink from a typewriter ribbon has dried on erasable paper (about a half hour), the ink will not smear and will not be much easier to erase than the ink on nonerasable paper.

Paper is packed in reams which consist of 500 sheets. The weight of the paper is referred to as its *substance*. Standard weights for paper used for office stationery are 16, 20, and 24 pounds. Pounds represent the weight of a ream (500 sheets) measuring 17 by 22 inches. This large size ream is known as a *printer's ream*. When this ream is cut into four equal parts, the result is four reams of 8 1/2-by-11-inch paper. A printer's ream of paper weighing 20 pounds, for example, will produce four reams of standard size paper weighing 5 pounds each. Paper that is 16 substance is lightweight, while 24 substance paper is heavyweight paper.

Letterhead Paper. Most companies use stationery that has the name of the firm, the mailing address, and phone number printed at the top. Paper with this heading is called a *letterhead*. Letterhead stationery should be used for the first page of correspondence that is mailed outside the office.

Letterhead designs differ considerably. Some are very colorful and include engravings or the logo of the firm; others are simple. The current trend leans toward simple business letterheads. A letterhead design can range from one inch to three inches in depth across the top of the stationery. Most designs, however, average two inches. Letterhead stationery usually answers the following questions:

1. WHO? The name of the firm or organization.

2. WHERE? The location of the firm or organization with the complete mailing address and sometimes the phone number.

3. WHAT? The nature of the business or organization.

Interoffice Memorandum Forms. Many businesses use printed interoffice memorandum forms which have TO, FROM, SUBJECT, and DATE lines. Sometimes the interoffice memorandum will match the letterhead paper with these headings added. If you do not have printed interoffice memorandum forms, you may use plain paper and type the appropriate headings.

Most printed interoffice memorandum forms are 8 1/2 by 11 inches, which is standard size. Some companies also use half-sheet forms (8 1/2 by 5 1/2 inches). Although the half-sheet forms help to conserve paper, they can be lost in the files because of their small size. More will be said about interoffice memorandums in Chapter 9.

Carbon Paper. Very thin paper with an ink coated side is called regular carbon paper. Carbon paper also comes in different qualities, weights, colors, and sizes. Carbon copies are made as the original document is being typed. Secretaries in many offices use carbon paper to prepare a limited number of copies of an original document instead of using the copying machine to make copies.

A tissue-thin sheet of ink coated plastic is known as *carbon film.* This film resists smudging and is extremely durable. Carbon film produces high quality copies but is more expensive to use than regular carbon paper.

Paper that is treated with a special chemical designed to duplicate the original (make a copy of the original) is called *NCR* or *no carbon required* paper. You must know which side of the paper has been treated so that you type on the untreated side. NCR paper is considerably more expensive than plain and carbon paper and is especially effective for preassembled business forms.

Illus. 8-6
A secretary may use a carbon paper to prepare a limited number of copies of an original document.

Second Sheets. The paper used for carbon copies is called second sheets. Second sheets usually are yellow or white. Second sheets may be *onionskin*, which is a high quality, cockle finish paper used for copies that must be preserved. Second sheets may or may not have the word *COPY* printed on the face. Second sheet paper is lightweight so that copies will take up little filing space and may be mailed at low cost. It comes in 8- to 13-pound weight, with 9-pound weight being the most frequently used. In addition to white and yellow, second sheets are available in other colors—blue, pink, and green, for example—for an office that uses a color-coding system in routing copies.

Second sheets are manufactured in smooth, glazed, or cockle finish. When you need to make a large number of copies with high quality results, you should select a smooth finish. Glazed second sheets should be used when you must make a maximum number of copies. Cockle finish onionskin second sheets make attractive carbon copies that resist smearing. Fewer copies can be made on onionskin than on smooth or glazed finishes, since the cockle finish cushions the typing blow.

Envelopes. Envelopes come in a wide variety of sizes but only a few are well suited for office use. The envelope used most frequently in an office is the No. 10 size (4 1/8 by 9 1/2 inches). It usually will have the company name and return address in the upper left-hand corner and will sometimes include the company logo. Envelopes for mailing business letters usually match the letterhead stationery in weight, color, rag content, and finish. Envelopes are also made of kraft brown paper for sending bulky materials or padded kraft paper suitable for mailing books. Information about addressing envelopes and folding correspondence for insertion into an envelope will be given in Chapter 9.

Special Business Forms

In most businesses a variety of printed forms are used to authorize, direct, and control procedures and operations. The majority of business forms are typed. Secretaries must use their best typing techniques to produce neat and accurate business forms.

Business forms are often designed without the typewriter in mind. The spacing between lines or columns, for example, may not be adequate for typing all the information required. You will need to be skillful in typing just above lines and utilizing the space available so that your typing can be contained within the space on the form.

On invoices, purchase orders, and other business forms that have columns for numbers, be sure to align numbers from the right. If money amounts contain decimals, always align the decimals. Columns that contain words, such as descriptions, should be aligned on the left.

Business forms may be preassembled in a unit or set. It may be necessary for you to insert carbon paper for the multiple copies, or the paper may be chemically treated and require no carbon paper. Some business forms require that multiple copies be made, but the units are not preassembled. You must be very careful when assembling business forms for typing to ensure that the copies are aligned with the original form.

Business forms can be purchased in a continuous roll. They are perforated for easy separation after they are typed. A continuous roll is useful when processing forms in a large volume.

Knowing all the parts of your typewriter and how to use them properly will aid you in typing business forms. Although typewriters differ, you will find the following information on how to use certain parts of the typewriter helpful in typing business forms.

- *Variable Line Spacer.* Pressing in the left platen knob of the typewriter allows you to vary the space between lines. Once you change the spacing with the variable line spacer, it is very difficult to go back exactly to your original line position. The line spacer is useful when typing forms, especially when the lines are not spaced an even distance apart.
- *Line Finder.* When you need to change the line spacing temporarily but will need to return to your original line, use the line finder. By using this device, you will be assured of returning exactly to the previous line position.
- *Impression Control.* Most typewriters have a mechanism that allows the typist to control the force with which the typing element or keys strike the paper. A medium setting should be appropriate for most typing. When typing business forms with multiple copies, be sure to set the impression control for a heavier setting. The last copy should be clear enough to read without any misinterpretation.

PROFESSIONAL POINTERS

Learn more efficient and less expensive means of producing and handling the paperwork generated in your office and share your ideas with your supervisor and co-workers to improve office productivity. The following pointers can help you become a more productive secretary.

1. Practice your typing skill. You may type a lot, very little, or in spurts on a day-to-day basis. Use slack periods to practice your typing. Identify the areas which may need to be improved. Practice typing drills to increase your speed and improve accuracy. Proofread everything you type.

2. Set up a master copy of business forms that you frequently type. Keep this file of master forms handy for quick reference so that format, placement, or spacing will not have to be figured each time.

3. When you type columns of figures, add the columns twice to determine if you made an error.

4. If a document is to be photocopied or sent to a printer, you can cut and paste the original when making revisions. If a portion of a page is usable, cut and paste the usable portion to a clean sheet. Insert the pasted-up sheet in your typewriter, and type the part that needs revising.

5. Legal size paper, which measures 8 1/2 by 14 inches, is no longer allowed in federal courts. Effective January, 1983, all legal documents presented in the federal court system must be typed on standard size paper (8 1/2 by 11 inches). Legal size paper requires the use of larger filing cabinets and file folders.

FOR YOUR REVIEW

1. Name some features of electric typewriters.

2. List five functions of an electronic typewriter.

3. What is a print wheel?

4. Give three methods for the origination of documents to be typed as final copy.

5. When should a rough draft of a document be typed and submitted?

6. List three helpful suggestions for typing a rough draft.

7. Name two important factors to be considered in preparing a final copy.

8. What is determining the appropriate style and placement of a document called?

9. Which two methods can be used to determine how to horizontally center on a typewriter without an automatic centering feature? Which method is generally faster?

10. List four correction tools.

11. Name and describe three kinds of typewriter ribbons.

12. What kind of ribbon does lift-off correction tape for self-correcting typewriters require?

13. What is meant by paper substance?

14. What three questions do letterhead designs usually answer?

15. What is the difference between regular carbon paper, carbon film, and NCR paper?

16. Name two techniques that you can use to type neat, legible business forms.

CASE PROBLEM

Charlotte Lewis has been a secretary for 15 years. Her neighbor, Mary Sanders, is setting up a business in her home and is counting on Charlotte's help in establishing an office.

Mary wants to sell women's skirts on which she handpaints designs. She would like to market the skirts at local craft and women's apparel shops as well as in the major tourist centers throughout the state. Mary's business will require a lot of correspondence as she strives to advertise her product and obtain orders from existing shops.

The cost of office equipment and supplies must be kept to a minimum, but she must get everything that she will need. Mary already has all the equipment and materials necessary to make the skirts, since she has been making them on a limited basis for sometime.

1. Keeping cost in mind, what office equipment should Charlotte suggest that Mary purchase?

2. If you were Charlotte, what office supplies would you tell Mary that she will need to begin her business? Make a list.

3. Design a letterhead that would be appropriate for Mary's business.

PRODUCTION PROJECTS

PP 8-1

(Objective 1)

From the sources available to you—the library, vendors or manufacturers, magazines—collect as many pictures of different typewriters as you can find. Assemble them in a folder and give a short description of each picture. Include the make and model of each typewriter as well as something about the features of each typewriter. If you can obtain the price of each model, include it in your description.

PP 8-2

(Objectives 2 and 3)

In your Supplies Inventory you will find a letter in rough draft form. Using the letterhead also found in your Supplies Inventory, type the letter in final form.

PP 8-3

(Objectives 2 and 3)

Prepare in final form the rough draft memorandum in your Supplies Inventory. The memorandum is from Alan Compton to all department managers. Since there are 18 department managers, the company photocopy center will make the copies from your typed original. You decide on the format for the memorandum and use the appropriate correction materials. Also, correct any errors that you find in the handwritten copy. Use the memorandum form in your Supplies Inventory to prepare the original.

PP 8-4

(Objective 4)

The company for which you work wants to redesign its stationery. You have been asked to prepare a written report on various letterheads used in your local area. Collect the letterheads of at least four different companies. Compare styles and formats used as well as quality, finish, and weight of the stationery. In your report point out the major differences in the four letterheads.

PP 8-5

(Objective 5)

You will find a certificate of achievement in your Supplies Inventory. An employee of Eastern Electric, Patricia Peden, has completed training, and you are to type her certificate. The names of the training sessions, which should be typed in the middle section, are Punctuation Pitfalls, Time Management, and Using Reference Aids for Better Secretarial Performance. Use a type style that would be attractive for a certificate. Be sure to center properly, and type on the lines correctly.

PP 8-6

(Objective 5)

Office equipment needing repair that is not covered by a maintenance agreement must be reported to Albert Roark in the purchasing department. Use the following information to type the Office Equipment Repair Form in your Supplies Inventory. Prepare one carbon copy of the form. The following items need repair:

1. IBM Selectric II typewriter, Model 238, Serial No. 45-89001, Blue—tab key stuck

2. IBM Selectric II typewriter, Model 410, Serial No. 2-45587, Blue—motor makes loud, scraping noise

Both typewriters were purchased in May, 1982, from IBM Corporation, Purchase Order No. AZ 230, Requisition No. 47810. They are located in the accounting department, 2nd floor, Budget Code 178. Eva Shipley is the office supervisor; so list her name on the form.

Find two companies that repair office equipment from the Yellow Pages in your local telephone directory. List their names and addresses in the Suggested Repair Facility section of the form.

Chapter 9
PREPARING OFFICE CORRESPONDENCE

More than likely, one of your major responsibilities as a secretary will be to prepare office correspondence. You must be familiar with business letter styles and parts, envelope address formats, and interoffice memorandum forms. Your employer will expect you to know the correct procedures for preparing office correspondence. In this chapter you will learn about the preparation of the two kinds of correspondence most often handled by office personnel—business letters and interoffice memorandums.

General Objectives

Your general objectives for Chapter 9 are to:

1. *Demonstrate the ability to compose office correspondence*
2. *Apply effective writing principles when composing office correspondence*
3. *Fold letters correctly for standard business envelopes*
4. *Identify letter parts and styles*
5. *Set up and type office correspondence and envelopes*
6. *Analyze office correspondence to determine its effectiveness*

THE COMPOSITION OF OFFICE CORRESPONDENCE

The success of a business can be greatly influenced by the correspondence mailed from its offices. Even interoffice memorandums circulated within a company affect the efficiency of operations. The reader's reaction to a memo or a letter will quickly determine whether the message was interpreted as intended.

Common Office Correspondence

The different kinds of office correspondence that you can expect to write and/or type as a secretary are letters and memos that do the following:

1. Request information
2. Transmit documents
3. Acknowledge or cancel meetings and appointments
4. Place orders
5. Express appreciation
6. Answer inquiries
7. Acknowledge the receipt of information or materials

If you believe that office correspondence is routine and unexciting, the messages you compose will probably be unimaginative and ineffective. You may use previously prepared correspondence to guide your thinking but do not fall into the trap of preparing stereotyped or unoriginal correspondence. Never copy a letter exactly from a book or from one in the files. Strive to prepare office correspondence that is original and straightforward.

The Organization of Office Correspondence

Correspondence that is well planned and organized will be effective. Just as a builder needs a blueprint to build a house, you should develop an outline before you begin to write a letter or memorandum. You may find that making notes on a scratch pad or in the margins of a letter to which you are responding will help you in organizing your thoughts. As you become more experienced in writing, you may make only a mental outline of what you want to write. In any case, plan what you want to say.

Before writing a letter, you should ask yourself: What effect will this message have on the reader? Will the reader react favorably or unfavorably to the message? Human nature supports the belief that people react favorably to good news, unfavorably to disappointing news, and negatively (at least initially) to an unusual request. Based on the expected reader reaction to the message, there are three psychological patterns into which letters may be grouped: direct, indirect, and persuasive.[1]

Direct. If the reader's reaction to your message will be favorable or neutral, you should use the direct approach. Many of the routine letters that you will write as a secretary fall into this category. Examples of direct letters are (1) letters of inquiry, (2) letters answering inquiries, and (3) letters making appointments. These letters are concise and to the point. The direct letter should:

---

[1]Mary Robertson and W. E. Perkins, *Effective Correspondence for Colleges* (5th ed.; Cincinnati: South-Western Publishing Co., 1983), pp. 67-82.

1. Begin with the reason for the letter. If you are making a request or inquiry, state that request or inquiry.

    Do you publish a secretarial handbook?

2. Continue with whatever explanation is necessary so that the reader will understand your message.

    If so, I would like to know the title, author, and price of the book and where an order should be mailed.

3. Close the letter with a courteous thank you for action that has been taken or a request that action be taken by a specific time.

    Thank you for responding promptly to my order.

Indirect. When your message to the reader will cause an unfavorable reaction, your best approach is an indirect one. There are times when you have to write a letter refusing a request or an appointment or in some way saying no to a person. Even so, you want the person to accept the decision and to understand that you are concerned. You want to leave the person with a positive impression of the company and of you. The indirect letter should:

1. Begin with an opening statement that is pleasant but neutral.

    Thank you very much for your order for our new electronic calculator.

2. Then review the circumstances and give the negative information.

    As a manufacturer, we have found that customers prefer doing business with local retailers. For this reason, our excellent product is marketed in your area through Electra Supply, 700 Main Street, Dallas, TX 75201-7251, telephone number 746-2524. A telephone order or an order by mail will be efficiently processed.

3. Close the letter on a pleasant and positive note.

    It is our hope that you will soon own and enjoy one of our fine calculators.

Persuasive. Use the persuasive approach when you want to change an indifferent or negative reader reaction. By using this approach, you hopefully change the reader's initial negative or indifferent attitude to a positive position. The persuasive letter should:

1. Open with a *you* approach; get the reader's attention.

    Would you like to know all the latest secretarial techniques? how to screen your telephone calls with poise and tact? how to refresh your memory on grammar and punctuation rules?

2. Continue by creating an interest and desire.

    If you answered yes to the above questions, let us tell you how you can accomplish this. We publish a monthly handbook which is packed with simple but effective suggestions and techniques. By studying this handbook, you will improve your communication skills, your grammar, and your telephone techniques. This publication is a *must* for a good secretary.

3. Close by asking directly for the action desired.

     All this valuable information costs you only $2.50 a month. What a small amount to pay for information that will help you perform more efficiently on the job! To get this handbook, just fill in the information on the enclosed coupon, and we will send you a free examination copy of *The Secretary's Handbook.*

The *C*'s of Office Correspondence

     There are several characteristics that are necessary to produce an effective letter. They may be summarized as follows:

1. Is the letter *complete*?
2. Is the letter *clear*?
3. Is the letter *concise*?
4. Is the letter *correct*?
5. Is the letter *courteous*?

     Completeness. Correspondence must be complete. The best way to check the completeness of a memo or letter is to put yourself in the reader's position. A written message should not leave the reader guessing or needing to write or call for additional information. When necessary information is left out or pertinent facts omitted, additional correspondence will need to be generated to make the message complete. Because of the high cost of producing correspondence today, you must consider completeness an essential characteristic.

     Clarity. After reading a message, the reader should be able to determine without doubt the purpose of the correspondence. Messages that are clearly written will reflect clear thinking. Writing clearly requires good organization and simple expression. The rule of one thought for each sentence, one purpose for each paragraph enhances clear writing. You should use words that *express* rather than *impress.* Writing so that the reader understands your message is important. It is even more important, however, to write so that the reader does not *misunderstand* your message.

     Conciseness. Being concise means being direct and to the point. You can be concise without being abrupt, however. Unnecessary words, phrases, sentences, and paragraphs waste the reader's time as well as cause confusion. Use words that are easily understood. There is no point in using a long word when a short word will convey the meaning.

     Correspondence with unnecessary information is also more costly to produce because of its length. When many details must be included, list or enumerate them. The reader will find a list of facts easier to read, understand, and remember. While brevity is important in a good business letter, it is equally important to remember that in an effort to achieve conciseness the writer must be certain that no details are omitted and no questions are left unanswered.

Completeness and conciseness are both necessary in business writing and do not in any way conflict with each other. Conciseness guarantees that unnecessary words and expressions have been eliminated, while completeness guarantees that the reader will understand the message as it was intended.

Correctness. It is important to produce error free correspondence. Because the success of a business may rely on the effectiveness of its correspondence, the correct use of grammar, punctuation, and spelling is essential. Correctness also implies that the information given in written correspondence is accurate. Proper planning and diligent proofreading will help ensure that correct information is transmitted.

Courtesy. Do you know persons who are friendly, sincere, and caring when you meet them face-to-face but who write letters that are formal, mechanical, and even rude or discourteous? Keep in mind that writing is like talking. When dealing with people face-to-face, courtesy and consideration are necessary in order to develop and maintain goodwill. The same or perhaps greater concern must be evident in written correspondence since only the written word conveys the message—the added use of a smile, a nod, or a friendly gesture cannot be seen.

You should develop a conversational style in letters. Do not try to imitate someone else. Be natural and let your personality show. Here are some suggestions that will help you write more effectively.

1. Use conversational rather than formal words.

Formal words	*Conversational words*
forward	mail, send
peruse	read, study
procure	get
terminate	end
ascertain	find out
consummate	finish

2. Eliminate worn-out phrases.

Wordy, unnatural phrases	*Direct, natural phrases*
Acknowledge receipt of your letter	I received your letter
Attached please find	The bill is attached
Enclosed you will find	Enclosed is
In compliance with your request	As you requested

I should like to say	(You don't need to ask permission; say what you want to say.)
Same was shipped	The booklet was shipped
Due to the fact	Because

3. Keep sentences short. Long sentences are difficult to read. Notice the difference in these two examples.

Wordy: We wish to acknowledge receipt of your letter of November 25 in which you ordered several items listed in our new spring catalog and asked that we send the shipment by parcel post.

Better: Thank you for your order of November 25. We are sending your shipment today by parcel post.

4. Vary your sentence structure.

Do not write: Please send me an application for credit. I shop at Harpers frequently. A charge account would be convenient for me.

But: Please send me an application form for a Harpers' credit card. Since I shop at Harpers frequently, a charge account would be much easier than carrying cash.

5. Think and write positively.

Negative	*Positive*
You failed to tell us about	Would you please tell us Please indicate
You neglected to send your check	Your check should have been received by

6. Be specific.

Nonspecific	*Specific*
We shipped the order yesterday	We shipped your order on May 2
Let me know at your earliest convenience	Let me know by June 30

7. Use the *you* attitude.

We attitude: We are having a sale on our appliances on Monday, January 10.

You attitude: You can get top savings on all your appliances by buying during our sale on Monday, January 10.

BASIC BUSINESS LETTER TYPING

Not only must a letter be well written, but it should also be arranged attractively on the stationery. The attractive appearance of a business letter increases its effectiveness. It is the secretary's responsibility to know how to type business letters so that they make a good impression on the reader.

Appearance

What is one of the first things you notice about a letter? Its appearance? First impressions are important not only when you are meeting someone in person but when you are writing a letter. If a letter has messy corrections, typographical errors, unbalanced margins, or is an incorrect letter style, the reader's first impression is negative. The letter may be worded well, but it is hard to overcome the negative impression that the reader has received.

The placement of a letter on a page affects its overall appearance. Because placement is the most noticeable feature of a letter, it is a major factor in influencing the reader's first impression. Make sure that your letters are well balanced. The top, bottom, right, and left margins should resemble a frame around a picture. Try to keep the right margin as even as possible. When you look at a well-balanced letter, all margins should appear to be an equal distance from the edge of the page. Try to limit word divisions at the end of lines. Never have more than two end-of-line word divisions in a row.

Even a letter that is properly typed and well placed on a page can still be marred by smudges and fingerprints. A marred letter may be construed as an example of a disorderly business. Secretaries may find that having a package of finger wipes handy will prevent this problem.

One of your goals as an effective secretary is to ensure the attractive appearance of your letters. You should pay careful attention to the letter style, the placement of the letter on the page, correction procedures, envelope addresses, and how to fold and insert the letter in the envelope. Illus. 9-1 should help you in learning how to fold a letter for two standard size business envelopes. You will become proficient in properly folding and inserting letters only if you practice. After you have correctly folded a letter, *insert it in the envelope by placing the last folded edge in first.*

Letter Parts

Business letters are different from personal correspondence in that an acceptable format must be followed. In order to type mailable and effective letters, you should become familiar with the parts of a business letter. Common parts of a business letter include the dateline, letter address, attention line, salutation, subject line, body, second page heading, closing, reference initials, and notations.

Dateline. All letters should include the current date. You should spell out the name of the month rather than abbreviate it. Never use an ordinal number (for example, 1st, 2nd, 3rd, 4th, etc.) in the dateline of a business letter. Refer to these examples.

Use: November 2, 1983
Avoid: 11/2/83
Avoid: November 2nd, 1983

Standard Business Envelope (No. 10)

1. Use this size of envelope for standard business letters.

2. Check the letter address with the address on the envelope to be sure they correspond.

3. Be sure that the letter is properly signed.

4. Place the letter face up on the desk.

5. Fold slightly less than one third of the letter up toward the top edge of the sheet. With the edges even at the sides, crease the fold.

6. Fold the top downward so that the top edge of the letterhead is within one-half inch of the bottom fold. With the edges even at the sides, crease the fold.

7. Insert in the envelope with the last crease toward the bottom of the envelope.

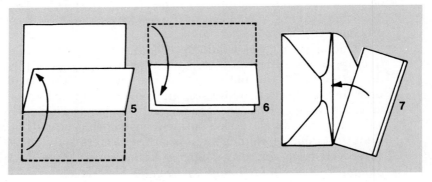

Illus. 9-1a
Folding a letter for a No. 10 envelope

The two methods that can be used to determine the placement of the dateline are fixed and floating. A *fixed dateline* is always typed on the second line below the letterhead. The number of lines between the date and letter address vary depending on the length of the letter. When using a *floating dateline*, the length of the letter determines how far down from the top edge of the paper to type the date. For a short letter, you may type the date on line 18; for a long letter you may float the date up to line 12.

Letter Address. The mailing address of the firm or person to whom the letter is being sent is typed below the date. When using a floating dateline, the letter address is typed four lines below the date. Refrain from using abbreviations, and be sure to spell all names correctly. When a person's title is used, type it on the first line with the

Small Business Envelope (No. 6 3/4)

1. This size envelope rarely is used in a business office, but it is an acceptable size.

2. Check the letter address with the address on the envelope to be sure they correspond.

3. Be sure that the letter is properly signed.

4. Place the letter face up on the desk.

5. Fold the letter from the bottom to within half an inch of the top edge. With the edges even at the sides, crease the fold.

6. Fold from right to left a third of the sheet width.

7. Fold from left to right to one-half inch of last crease.

8. Insert in envelope with last creased edge inserted first.

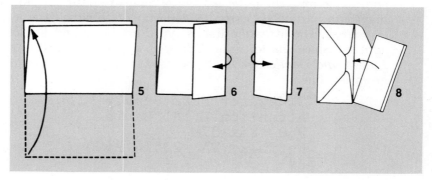

Illus. 9-1b
Folding a letter for a No. 6 3/4 envelope

name. If the title makes the first line too long, put the title on the second line (but do not use a comma after the name). The complete mailing address including the city, state, and ZIP Code must be used. You may type the two-letter state abbreviation, or you can spell out the state name. Refer to Illus. 9-2 for appropriate letter address styles.

```
Richard K. Alexander
Chief Environmental Technician
United Utilities Corporation
9 North Grande Boulevard
Kansas City, MO  64110-9881
```

Illus. 9-2a
Letter address

Some companies have a post office box number as well as a street address. The post office box number is generally used for correspondence. The street address is used for shipments of products or supplies made to a specific location.

```
Sylvia Brooks, Staff Assistant
Information Systems, Inc.
P.O. Box 6890
Newark, New Jersey   07112-0432
```

Illus. 9-2b
Letter address with post office box number

Attention Line. An attention line can be used to direct a letter to a particular person or department within an organization. The name of the company or organization is listed as the first line of the address because the letter addresses company business. However, there may be a particular person or department to which the letter should be routed. The attention line is typed as the second line of the letter address. Since the letter is addressed to the company, the salutation *Ladies and Gentlemen* would be used. Illus. 9-3 gives examples of an attention line.

```
Tidewater Farm Supply, Inc.
Attention L. H. Davis
P.O. Box 37M
Norfolk, VA   23514-2490
```

```
Miller, Landow & Associates
Attention Supplies Department
2511 Summit Avenue
Canton, OH   44708-4225
```

Illus. 9-3
Letter addresses with attention lines

Salutation. Most business letters have a salutation that greets the reader. The salutation should be typed a double space below the letter address. Make sure the salutation agrees with the first line of the letter address. When addressing a company or group, use a plural salutation such as *Ladies and Gentlemen*. When writing to an individual, use the person's name in the salutation. For example, write *Dear Mr. Smith* or *Dear Ms. Jones*. If you have addressed a letter to a title such as *Personnel Director*, you must use a singular salutation. In this case write *Dear Sir or Madam*. Whatever title a woman uses—Miss, Mrs., or Ms.—be sure to respond in a like manner. In a business letter where the writer knows the addressee personally, the salutation is less formal and written using just a first name, such as *Dear Martin*.

Some writers of business letters do not use a title in their signature. If you are uncertain whether the writer is a male or female, you can use the individual's first and last names in the salutation. For example, you would write *Dear Kendal Tucker*.

Subject Line. A short phrase that describes the subject or content of a letter can be typed a double space below the salutation. The subject line can be typed even with the left margin, or it can be centered horizontally. (See Illus. 9-4.)

```
October 15, 19--


Kendal Tucker, Secretary/Treasurer
Real Estate Brokers Association
123 Addison Avenue, NW
Washington, DC  20006-1950

Dear Kendal Tucker

MEMBERSHIP TRAVEL DISCOUNTS

We are pleased to announce that effective . . .
```

Illus. 9-4
Portion of a letter with a subject line

Body. The body of the letter, which is typed a double space below the salutation or subject line, contains the message and is the reason for the letter. The body consists of well-constructed paragraphs that develop the message. A paragraph develops a single idea or part of an idea. From the mechanical point of view, a paragraph helps create an impression of clearness. The paragraph is vital in developing a letter plan.

In letter writing, keep your paragraphs as short as possible. This is particularly true of your opening and closing paragraphs. An opening paragraph containing vital information but consisting of two to five lines will make an effective impact on the reader. Avoid long, involved paragraphs; but do not break the material into too many short paragraphs. Also, leave one blank line between paragraphs in a letter.

Second Page Heading. Letters that are longer than one page require a heading on all pages after the first one. Plain bond paper is usually used for subsequent pages, and the heading is typed one inch (6 blank lines) from the top edge of the page. After you type the second page heading, triple-space, and continue typing the body of the letter. Illus. 9-5 shows the two styles of headings.

```
Dr. Jonas Smith                    2              July 1, 19--
```

```
Dr. Jonas Smith
Page 2
July 1, 19--
```

Illus. 9-5
A second page heading can be typed in horizontal style (top) or block style (bottom).

Complimentary Close. The closing lines consist of a gracious ending and the signature line. Endings are less formal today and are usually a matter of preference. The most popular letter endings are *Sincerely, Sincerely yours, Yours truly,* and *Cordially.* Notice that only the first word in the closing is capitalized. The complimentary close is typed a double space below the body of the letter.

The writer's name (and title, if used) is typed four lines below the complimentary close. The three blank lines in between the complimentary close and the writer's typed name allow room for the signature.

You may be asked to type a letter that has been written by two persons. If both names are to appear in the complimentary close, refer to Illus. 9-6 for two possible formats.

```
     Yours truly

     Mary K. Lyon, M.D.

     Mary K. Lyon, M.D.
     Pediatrics

     Calvin LaLansky

     Calvin LaLansky, Ph.D.
     Chief Administrator


     Sincerely

     Leona P. Davis            Joe Zinberg

     Leona P. Davis    and    Joe Zinberg
     Vice-President           Director
```

Illus. 9-6
Possible formats when two names appear in the complimentary close

Reference Initials. Reference initials are typed at the left margin a double space below the typed name and title in the closing. Reference initials are used for identification, and there are several ways to use them. When the typed name, title, and signature of the dictator appear at the end of the letter, it is unnecessary to include the initials of the dictator; and most secretaries type only their initials in lowercase. If you work for an executive who wants his or her initials to appear on the letter, type them in solid caps, then a colon, and your initials in lowercase. If you compose the letter for your employer's signature, you might type your initials in solid caps to indicate that you were the author of the letter. This identification might prove helpful later if your employer sees the file copy and asks, "Did I say this?" If such a reference identification is used, you can tell very easily whether you or your employer composed the letter.

In some business situations, outgoing letters may bear the name and signature of a person in authority such as the director. This individual may not have actually composed the letter, however. It would be appropriate in this case to include the writer's initials as well as the signer's and typist's initials for reference purposes. Refer to Illus. 9-7 for examples of reference initials.

Sincerely

Ervin L. Russell

Ervin L. Russell, Consultant

jdh (Typist's initials)
OR
ELR:jdh (Writer's and typist's initials)
OR
JDH (The typist is also the writer of the letter.)
OR
ELR:WRS:jdh (Signer's, writer's, and typist's initials — Signer's
initials may be omitted.)

Illus. 9-7
Reference initials

Notations. Some letters require special notations for the reader's benefit or for reference purposes at a later time. Following are some commonly used notations.

Enclosure/Attachment. If additional material is sent with a letter, type *Enclosure* at the left margin a double space below the reference initials. If a document is stapled or clipped to the letter, you may prefer to use *Attachment.* Be careful, however, not to clip or staple bulky documents that might damage the mail and/or postal equipment. An enclosure or attachment notation will signal the person opening the letter to look for additional material. This notation will also serve as a reminder to you to include the enclosure when you fold the letter and insert it in the envelope for the outgoing mail. (See Illus. 9-8.)

Enclosure	Enc. (Certified check)
Enclosures (2)	Att. (Annual report)
Attachment	

Illus. 9-8
Enclosure and attachment notations

Copy. Often when a copy of a letter is sent to another person, a notation is typed on the letter. A copy notation is located a double space below an enclosure notation if there is one. The letters *cc* meaning carbon copy are used to indicate that another person will receive a carbon copy of the correspondence. With the extensive use of copiers today, many secretaries prefer to use *pc* (meaning photocopy) or *copy* when actual carbon paper is not used. In any case, always designate to whom the copy is being sent.

At times you may send a copy of a letter to someone without the knowledge of the person to whom the letter is addressed. A *bcc* (blind carbon copy) notation is made in this instance. Do this by placing a card in front of the original so that the notation will appear on the copies but not on the original correspondence.

Whether or not carbon copies are signed is up to the writer. Most copies are not signed. A check mark (✓) is usually placed beside the name of the receiver of each copy before distribution. Illus. 9-9 gives examples of copy notations.

cc Mr. Harrington	cc: Felix Cruz
pc Maxine Reynolds	copy to Art Department
bcc: Legal Department	

Illus. 9-9
Copy notations

Letter Styles

Some offices require one established letter style. Some, however, may leave style decisions to the secretary. You should know the standard letter styles and how to arrange each correctly.

Block. The block letter style is the most used letter style in business offices today. It is the easiest letter style to type. All the letter parts are typed flush with the left margin, and paragraphs are not indented. (See Illus. 9-10.)

Modified Block. In a modified block letter, the dateline and closing lines are typed at the horizontal center of the paper. Paragraphs can be typed flush with the left margin or indented five or more spaces. (See Illus. 9-10.)

AMS Simplified. In the AMS (Administrative Management Society) Simplified letter style, two major letter parts are omitted: the salutation and the complimentary close. A subject line is typed in all capital letters a triple space below the letter address. The body of the letter is started a triple space below the subject line. Only the writer's name and title, which are typed in all capital letters, are used in the closing. Three blank lines are left between the last line of the body and typed name for the writer's signature. The AMS Simplified style solves the problem of a correct or appropriate salutation: no salutation is used. The subject line is useful for informing the reader of the letter's content and provides help for filing purposes. (See Illus. 9-10.)

Mixed and Open Punctuation. There are two basic punctuation styles used in business letters today. In mixed punctuation a colon is typed after the salutation, and a comma is typed after the complimentary close. When open punctuation is used, there is no punctuation after the salutation or complimentary close. Today open punctuation is a commonly used form of punctuation.

Envelopes

Most companies use envelopes with the return address printed in the upper left-hand corner of the envelope; therefore, you need to type only the mailing address and any special mailing instructions. It is a good practice to type the sender's name or department one line above the printed return address on the envelope. If the letter is returned for any reason, the envelope can be directed to the sender unopened.

Bennett Electronics Corporation

899 Claremont Boulevard
Phoenix, AZ 85019-8276 (602) 555-7400

January 5, 19--

Kodelski Van Lines
Attention Mr. William Fallen
402 DuBuys Road
Biloxi, MS 39571-3331

Ladies and Gentlemen:

The modified block style letter may be written
with indented paragraphs as well as blocked paragraphs.
Notice that this letter has paragraphs which are indented
five spaces. The date and the closing lines start at the
center.

An attention line is included in this letter. It
is typed below the company name in the letter address.

The carbon copy notation is typed a double space
below the reference initials.

Sincerely,

Cecil M. Wells

Cecil M. Wells
Vice-President

nr

cc Miss Ethel Fairley

Letter A
Modified block style, mixed
punctuation, indented paragraphs

Webber Industries

500 Ferguson Drive
Atlanta, GA 30310-3301 (404) 555-0433

May 5, 19--

Ms. Q. Annette Lofton
Victory Advertising Agency
1131 Eighth Avenue
Melrose Park, IL 60162-6210

Dear Ms. Lofton:

THE MODIFIED BLOCK STYLE LETTER

This letter is typed in modified block style with blocked
paragraphs and mixed punctuation. Notice that a colon
follows the salutation and a comma follows the complimentary close.

The date and the closing lines begin at the horizontal
center. The subject line is typed a double space below
the salutation. It may be typed flush with the left
margin, at paragraph point, or at the horizontal center.

Sincerely,

Jeff C. Key

Jeff C. Key
Office Manager

wf

Letter B
Modified block style, mixed
punctuation, blocked paragraphs

EDWARDS CORPORATION

2456 Abrams Avenue Arlington, TX 76011-7741 (817) 555-3146

September 2, 19-- .

Mrs. Rose Davis
37 Duke Street
Boston, MA 02126-0117

Dear Mrs. Davis

All lines in the block style letter begin at the left
margin. In open punctuation, as this sample letter
shows, there is no punctuation after the salutation
and complimentary close.

The block style letter is efficient since no time is
spent in setting tabulator stops for indentions or in
striking the tabulator key when typing the letter.

You will find this letter style used quite often in
business correspondence.

Sincerely

Amanda C. DeVault

Amanda C. DeVault

gt

Letter C
Block style, open punctuation

DAWSON PRINTING COMPANY

1155 Matthews Road
Dallas, TX 75217-7270 (214) 555-8136

November 12, 19--

Miss Josephine Neely
Rollins Business Association
356 First Avenue
Irving, TX 75061-7215

AMS SIMPLIFIED LETTER STYLE

This letter is typed in the style recommended by the
Administrative Management Society. There are several
interesting features about it.

Block format allows for speedy typing. All capital
letters in the subject line and in the writer's name
and title also simplify the typing process. The subject line is typed a triple space below the letter
address and a triple space above the body. The
writer's name and title are typed four lines below
the body.

Since this arrangement saves time, the AMS Simplified
letter style is an efficient letter form.

Lydia Scarlato

LYDIA SCARLATO, OFFICE MANAGER

pf

Letter D
Simplified style

Illus. 9-10
Business letter styles

Standard Sizes. The standard size envelope, which is 9 1/2 by 4 1/8 inches, is referred to as a No. 10 envelope. A small envelope that is also considered standard size is the No. 6 3/4 envelope, which measures 6 1/2 by 3 5/8 inches. The No. 6 3/4 envelope is often used as a business reply envelope for customers or clients.

Address Formats. Typing envelopes for mailing requires following standard procedures. Because a great deal of the mail today is processed by machines, you should learn to type envelope addresses according to U.S. Postal Service requirements.

Addresses should be single-spaced on envelopes. The Postal Service prefers that addresses be typed in all capital letters with no punctuation. The only mark of punctuation should be the hyphen separating the five-digit ZIP Code from the four-digit add-on. Do not alter spacing because of the omission of punctuation except on the last line of the address; there should be two spaces between the last character of the state name or abbreviation and the first digit of the ZIP Code.

To type the mailing address, space down 12 lines from the top edge of a small (No. 6 3/4) envelope and 14 lines for a standard (No. 10) envelope. Set a tabulator stop ten spaces to the left of the horizontal center of a No. 6 3/4 envelope and five spaces to the left of the horizontal center of a No. 10 envelope; type all lines of the address at this tabulator stop position. Leave at least one inch of space at the right edge and 5/8 inch of space at the bottom of the envelope.

The Postal Service uses optical character recognition in many large post offices to sort and direct mail to its destination. Optical character readers electronically scan typewritten addresses. They are

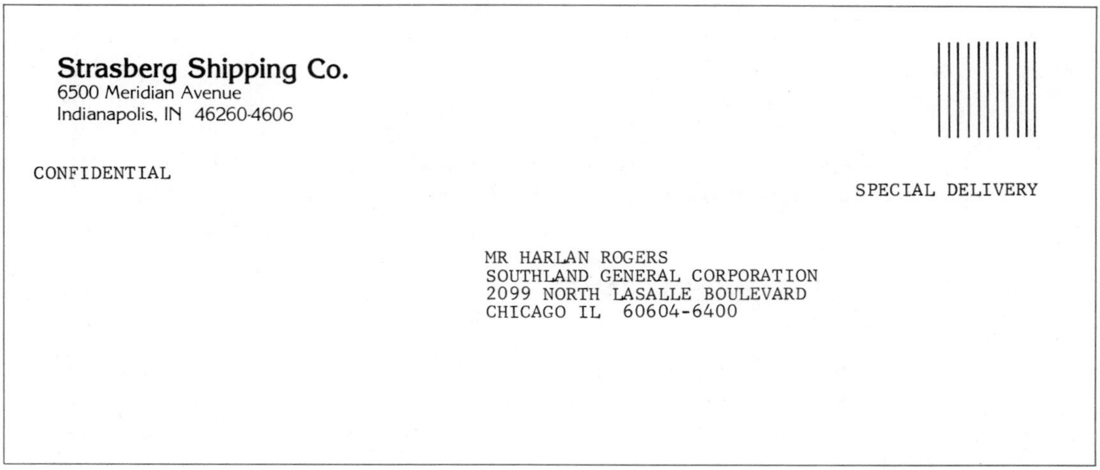

Strasberg Shipping Co.
6500 Meridian Avenue
Indianapolis, IN 46260-4606

CONFIDENTIAL

SPECIAL DELIVERY

MR HARLAN ROGERS
SOUTHLAND GENERAL CORPORATION
2099 NORTH LASALLE BOULEVARD
CHICAGO IL 60604-6400

Illus. 9-11
Properly addressed envelope

programmed to scan a specific *(read)* area on all envelopes by reading envelopes from left to right and bottom to top. The address must be within the read area, single-spaced, and in block style. Type an attention line immediately below the company name in the address. Special mailing instructions should be typed two or three lines below the stamp. Place a personal or confidential notation a triple space below the return address and three spaces from the left edge of the envelope.

The Preparation of Business Letters—Costs and Responsibilities

Business letters are costly to prepare. Every year since 1930 the Dartnell Institute of Business Research has conducted a survey to determine the average cost of preparing a business letter. The cost of a letter has risen from 29 cents in 1930 to $7.60 in 1983. Letters dictated to a secretary are more costly than letters dictated on recording machines. Because the secretary does not need to be present when a letter is dictated on a machine, the cost of the letter is reduced to $5.70 (in 1983).

The cost of preparing a business letter can be reduced in several ways. The use of standard formats for letters and memos saves typing time. Even the use of a standard line length has proven helpful in keeping down the cost of preparing office correspondence. The fewer decisions a typist must make about letter styles and margin and tab settings, the greater the amount of work that can be produced. When secretaries are capable of preparing certain office correspondence on their own, the cost is reduced further because no dictation time is required.

As a secretary, you should establish the level of responsibility your employer wants you to assume in preparing correspondence. Some employers may not delegate the writing of correspondence to their secretaries but ask instead that they only edit and type the copy. Others require their secretaries to compose letters and memos based on information supplied. When you prove your ability to prepare effective, well-constructed correspondence, you will be entrusted to handle more difficult or involved correspondence responsibilities.

INTEROFFICE MEMORANDUMS

Correspondence to individuals within an organization is usually typed as an interoffice memorandum. Most businesses use printed memorandum forms with the headings TO, FROM, DATE, and SUBJECT.

Align properly the information you type with the printed heading on the memorandum form. Space twice after the colon in the TO, FROM, DATE, and SUBJECT lines. On these printed forms, the left margin is usually flush with the name of the addressee.

Memos are usually typed in block style. Triple-space between the heading and the message. Single-space the paragraphs, but double-space between them. Reference initials are typed a double space below the message at the left margin.

Frequently interoffice memorandums are addressed to several people. It is best to alphabetize the names or list them according to rank or position. Omit personal titles such as *Mr., Miss, Mrs., Ms.,* and the like, when typing the heading.

Specially designed envelopes are used by most businesses to transmit interoffice correspondence. These envelopes are reusable and are generally large enough so that standard size stationery can be inserted without folding. An example of an interoffice memorandum and envelope are shown in Illus. 9-12.

The Pruett Company

TO: Barry Bomboy, Wallace Carroll, Patty Shaw INTEROFFICE MEMO

FROM: Bernard Kaplan

DATE: December 3, 1984

SUBJECT: ARMA Conference

At yesterday's staff meeting, it was recommended that three individuals from our department attend the Association of Records Managers and Administrators conference in Atlanta on February 11-14, 1985. Since the three of you will be actively involved in the implementation of our new records management system, I would like you to attend.

Please attend a meeting in my office on Wednesday, December 5, to discuss the details of the trip.

ahr

Illus. 9-12a
Interoffice memorandum

INTEROFFICE CORRESPONDENCE

TO	DEPT.	TO	DEPT.	TO	DEPT.

Illus. 9-12b
Interoffice envelope

PROFESSIONAL POINTERS

Effectively written communication is free of sexually biased terminology which can be offensive to a reader. In some instances, sexist terminology can have a devastating effect on the development of good business relationships. Whatever your writing responsibilities, be sure to eliminate these words or expressions from the written correspondence in your office.

Terms such as these involve implied or overt stereotyping and should be avoided:

1. chairman

2. mailman

3. stewardess

4. a secretary, she

5. a janitor, he

6. the nurse, she

7. the boss, he

There are ways to structure the English language to avoid male/female stereotyping. Here are some guidelines:

1. Use plural nouns to avoid having to use a singular pronoun.

    Example: secretaries, they

2. Use general titles rather than specific ones. Refer to the *Dictionary of Occupational Titles* for updated titles.

    Example: mail carrier or postal worker NOT mailman

3. Use the passive voice in order to avoid having to use a personal pronoun.

    Avoid: Have each floor nurse check her staff records on a monthly basis.
    Use: Staff records should be checked by each floor nurse on a monthly basis.

FOR YOUR REVIEW

1. What is a secretary's major responsibility for the preparation of correspondence?

2. List at least three kinds of office correspondence that secretaries may be required to prepare.

3. What is the first step in composing a well-organized letter?

4. Explain the three letter patterns that influence the reader's reaction to a message. When is each used?

5. Name the five *C*'s of good written correspondence.

6. Name three factors that affect the appearance of business letters.

7. List six business letter parts.

8. Name three business letter styles.

9. What format requested by the U. S. Postal Service should be used when typing envelopes for mailing?

10. Where should a confidential notation be typed on an envelope?

11. When an interoffice memorandum is addressed to several people, what are two ways the names can be listed?

CASE PROBLEM

Darlene Hughes began her career six years ago as a clerk-typist at Penningdale Corporation. For the past four years she has been a stenographer at Penningdale. Darlene has an excellent work record and exceptional composition, typing, and organization skills.

Two months ago quite a few administrative changes occurred in the company. Some managerial positions were eliminated, others were consolidated, and new ones created. Mike Urbane was promoted from field engineer to associate director of research and design. Darlene was given the position of administrative assistant to Mr. Urbane. She was quite pleased with the increase in salary and looked forward to the added responsibilities and the challenge of a new job.

Mr. Urbane's new responsibilities include introducing new product designs, completing routine forms for patents, handling inquiries for research data, and responding to requests for information on new products. In addition to tackling such a demanding job, Mr. Urbane has also been appointed chairperson of the committee to improve productivity in the manufacturing of new and established products.

Mr. Urbane has been so busy with his new job duties that he has failed to realize how Darlene can be an efficient assistant and thus lessen his work load. Darlene has done an average amount of typing; otherwise, her work load has been relatively light. Mr. Urbane composes in handwriting all his correspondence. Many of the letters he writes are replies that could be routinely handled by Darlene.

1. Should Darlene admit that she doesn't keep busy and that her work load is too light?

2. How could Darlene approach Mr. Urbane to discuss a better utilization of her skills?

3. What specific responsibilities could Darlene assume for Mr. Urbane?

4. How would you react to a situation such as this? Would you want to increase your work load?

PRODUCTION PROJECTS

PP 9-1

(Objectives 1 and 2)

Compose a letter to your teacher. Include an assessment of your own writing ability and a statement about how you can work toward improvement. Make your letter a minimum of three paragraphs but no longer than one page. Type your letter in an acceptable letter style on plain paper.

PP 9-2

(Objectives 1, 2, 3, and 5)

Assume that you are the administrative assistant to Mr. Mike Urbane, associate director, research and design, Penningdale Corporation. He asks you to write a letter to a colleague confirming the annual meeting of research and design directors which will be held on the first Tuesday of next month. Send the letter to:

Ronald Sanderson, Vice-President
National Distributors, Inc.
5612 Grayland Avenue
Cincinnati, OH 45227-4408

The meeting will begin at 10 a.m. in the Commonwealth Conference Room at the Holiday Hotel West on Main Boulevard. Remind Mr. Sanderson to present the report of the long-range planning committee.

Compose the letter at the typewriter. After making the necessary revisions, prepare the letter in final form and address an envelope. Make the proper notation to show that you composed the letter for Mr. Urbane. Use the letterhead in your Supplies Inventory; supply your own No. 10 envelope.

PP 9-3

(Objectives 1, 2, 5, and 6)

Analyze the memorandum in your Supplies Inventory. List words or phrases that you consider inappropriate on the special form also provided in your Supplies Inventory. Revise the memorandum keeping in mind the principles of effective writing. Type the memo on the form in your Supplies Inventory.

PP 9-4

(Objective 4)

Using the form in your Supplies Inventory, label the appropriate placement of the letter parts given below. Identify at the bottom of the form the letter and punctuation styles used in this skeleton letter.

Writer's name
Body

Dateline
Copy notation
Writer's title
Enclosure notation
Letter address
Reference initials
Salutation
Complimentary close

PP 9-5

(Objectives 3, 5, and 6)

In your Supplies Inventory is a handwritten letter that must be prepared for mailing as soon as possible. Select the style that will allow you to type the letter in a short time. Address a No. 10 envelope. Edit the letter for redundant or overused expressions, and rewrite the letter if necessary.

Chapter **10**

UTILIZING DICTATION AND
TRANSCRIPTION SKILLS

In the preceding chapters you have learned about a secretary's responsibilities and duties. The ability to prepare mailable documents has been emphasized. You know that secretaries type from handwritten copy, rough draft copy, or copy they have composed themselves. Secretaries may also prepare documents from shorthand notes, or they may transcribe material that has been recorded on dictation equipment.

The ability to take shorthand is certainly an asset. However, not all employers dictate correspondence directly to their secretaries. This chapter will discuss machine dictation and machine transcription as well as shorthand dictation. Also, suggestions are given that will help prepare you for the dictation/transcription process.

General Objectives

Your general objectives for Chapter 10 are to:

1. *Describe situations where shorthand may be required*
2. *Demonstrate the use of good techniques in taking dictation*
3. *Name the types of dictation equipment available*
4. *Discuss the advantages and disadvantages of machine dictation and shorthand dictation*
5. *Employ proper techniques in transcribing dictation*
6. *Demonstrate the ability to dictate effectively*

PREPARING FOR DICTATION

If you can take shorthand, you may be called on to take dictation at almost any time and for a variety of purposes. Because shorthand is an acquired skill, you will need to work at keeping it sharp. Practicing this skill will ensure its usefulness when you need it.

There will be many occasions on your job where you will find the ability to take shorthand an asset. Always be prepared to use shorthand whether it is for business correspondence, a telephone message, the minutes of a meeting, or personal notes and reminders.

Employer Dictation

Many employers dictate correspondence and other documents to their secretaries. People vary in their ability to dictate material. Some organize their thoughts well and even furnish punctuation as they dictate; others often change their minds causing their dictation to be disjointed and irregular.

It is much faster to dictate material than to write in longhand. Secretaries often transcribe their shorthand notes faster than they can decipher their employer's handwriting. An employer can dictate a letter in about one fourth the time it would take to handwrite it. But some employers prefer longhand because they can see their thoughts on paper and make revisions immediately. Longhand, however, is often difficult to read and time-consuming to "transcribe."

In the interest of efficiency, office correspondents are encouraged to dictate rather than handwrite their mail. The ability to dictate effectively must be developed. Poor dictation usually results in a typed transcript that needs revision. As an administrative or executive secretary, you may dictate correspondence yourself. The dictation tips given below should aid you in dictating effectively.

1. Organize your thoughts before you start dictating.
2. Begin by indicating what you are dictating—a letter, memo, report, or a particular form—and the number of copies required.
3. Spell proper names and give appropriate titles and complete addresses if the person who transcribes your correspondence does not have access to this information.
4. Dictate unusual punctuation and paragraphs when possible.
5. Explain changes or corrections in your dictation.
6. Speak clearly.
7. Avoid eating, chewing gum, or smoking while you dictate.
8. Prevent interruptions if possible during dictation.

Telephone Messages

Shorthand is helpful when taking long or involved telephone messages. It is important for secretaries to take accurate and complete messages. Telephone message pads have only a limited amount of space for important information; so it is wise to keep a stenographic notebook by the telephone to take long messages. Transfer the necessary facts to the telephone message sheet with a note that you have additional information regarding the message.

Conferences

Secretaries may use shorthand to take notes at conferences or at meetings. Machines are often used as a backup for recording meetings, but the presence of a secretary is advantageous. Meetings are often noisy with many people talking at once. A secretary who is present at the meeting can determine what information is essential and should be recorded. A secretary can take notes on speakers, their speeches, or motions made and carried. A taped recording is of little help in distinguishing who is speaking. Taped recordings will assist the secretary in making sure nothing has been omitted from the notes and in determining the order in which the proceedings occurred.

Notes and Reminders

As a means of keeping organized, efficient secretaries make notes and reminders for their employers. Shorthand may be a helpful tool in jotting down notations about meetings or schedules that must be met. Just a short note on your desk calendar will help you remind your employer of important appointments or deadlines.

TAKING DICTATION

Being prepared to take dictation means that you must have the necessary supplies at hand and that you yourself are ready. You should be ready to take dictation at any time. You may be asked to take dictation standing by a desk, sitting at a desk or table, or with the telephone receiver in one hand and your pen in the other.

Supplies Needed for Dictation

In order to be prepared for dictation, keep your supplies readily available. When you are asked to take dictation, you should not have to hunt for the items you need.

Notebook. A stenographic notebook (or steno pad) is your most valuable tool. Efficient use of a steno pad can make a difference in a secretary's ability to record dictated material. The following suggestions will help you in using a stenographic notebook effectively.

Illus. 10-1   Western Electric

When your employer calls in dictation, you must have the necessary supplies at hand and be prepared to take the dictation.

1. Write the date you begin using your notebook on the cover. When the notebook is filled, write the final date on the cover, and keep your notebook on file for a year or longer if your employer requires.
2. Be sure the notebook has adequate pages for dictation. Keep an extra notebook readily accessible.
3. When taking dictation from several people, use a different notebook for each person. Clearly mark on the outside cover the dictator's name.
4. Record the current date on each page of the day's dictation.
5. Leave several blank lines before and after each dictated document. Additions or changes can be made in this space.
6. Number or identify each entry of dictation. If you use numbers in sequence or letters in alphabetical order, you will find it easier to refer to your notes or to see if you have omitted any dictated material.
7. Designate the end of each dictated item with an identifying mark, such as two parallel straight lines or a wavy line.

Pens/Pencils. Ball-point pens are best for taking shorthand notes since ink will not fade or be accidentally erased. A brightly colored ink pen or pencil—such as red or green—is good to use for making special notations or marking items *Rush.* Keep extra pens or well-sharpened pencils handy for emergency uses.

Paper Clips and Rubber Bands. Rubber bands can be put around the used portion of the stenographic notebook so that the unused portion can be turned to quickly. Keep several paper clips attached to the notebook cover to indicate specially marked pages or instructions.

Calendar. Tape or paste a calendar on the back of the notebook cover so that dates can be referred to correctly during dictation.

Office Dictation

If you are expected to take shorthand dictation, you must possess a skill that will enable you to take down everything that is said. How fast do you need to take shorthand? Studies have been made that indicate a speed of 80 to 100 words a minute is sufficient to record most business oriented dictation.

Dictation in a business office may be quite different from that to which you are accustomed in the classroom. In the classroom, instructors may dictate at a specific, even rate of speed and enunciate each word clearly. The executive in the office may dictate at an uneven rate of speed, sometimes at a rate of 40 to 50 words a minute, then increasing it to 120 to 200 words a minute. Sustained dictation speeds of more than 120 words a minute are unusual, however, because most people must pause to organize their thoughts. Your goal while you are in school should be to acquire as much shorthand skill as possible so that you will be able to meet any situation in the office.

Shifting to Longhand in Dictation

Because proper nouns are not always spelled as they sound, write names and addresses in longhand. Dictators do not always supply complete names and mailing addresses when dictating letters. You may need to get this information from incoming correspondence, the files, or from a mailing list. If this information is not available from these sources, ask the dictator. Be sure to spell names correctly and use the person's preferred title if known.

Asking Questions during Dictation

In some instances a simple question by the secretary will solve a host of problems later. If a secretary has the least doubt about the dictation, identify the doubt with a question mark in the margin and ask the dictator. Some dictators prefer to be interrupted when a question arises; others prefer to answer all questions at the end of the dictation. If you think you have made an error in recording the dictation, read that part back to the dictator to ensure the accuracy of your notes. Ask the dictator how to spell unfamiliar technical terms; clarify special instructions about which you are unsure.

You should perfect your skill so that too many questions will not be necessary. Don't be afraid to ask questions, however, when accuracy is at stake.

Tips for Taking Dictation

Here is a list of helpful suggestions that you can use as a guide for taking dictation.

1. Take your position for dictation quietly and at the part of the desk your employer prefers that you use. Make yourself comfortable.
2. Eliminate nervous habits that might distract the dictator, such as tapping a pencil, chewing gum, arranging your hair, fingering jewelry, or looking around the office.
3. Flopping the notebook to turn pages under is annoying to the dictator and may cause you to fall behind in recording your notes. Leave the notebook cover and used pages open. If the used page is merely turned up instead of under, it is easier to turn back to previously recorded dictation if necessary during the dictation period.
4. Mark shorthand notes with a check mark to indicate any obvious errors in dictation. Call these errors to the attention of the dictator after the letter is completed. Do not interrupt the dictator's train of thought during dictation. If a grammatical error is made in dictation, it is not necessary to bring it to the attention of the dictator. Simply make the necessary change when you transcribe the notes.
5. Be ready to proceed immediately after an interruption by giving the dictator the last few lines of dictation. Use an interruption to review your notes and to insert punctuation marks.
6. Concentrate on the dictation.
7. Write shorthand as accurately as possible. It is much easier to read "cold" shorthand notes when they have been clearly written.
8. If the dictator makes frequent changes, leave a blank line between each line of shorthand or leave the right column blank.
9. If the dictator receives a personal telephone call, leave the office quietly. Stay nearby so that you can return as soon as the conversation is completed. If a visitor comes in, leave quietly and start transcribing if you have any completed notes.
10. Devise shortcuts for frequently used titles and phrases. Practice difficult shorthand words which you have trouble writing. Keep a shorthand dictionary nearby so that you can look up the correct symbols for unfamiliar words.

TRANSCRIBING FROM SHORTHAND

The ability to take fast, accurate dictation is a highly important function of an efficient secretary; however, producing accurate mailable transcripts is equally important. A good secretary should transcribe from shorthand or machine dictated copy at a rate of about two thirds the speed of typing from straight copy.

Ordinarily the dictation should be transcribed as quickly as possible after it has been dictated. It is only natural that a customer should expect a prompt reply to a letter or an order.

Set Priorities

If you have marked your shorthand notes properly, you will know if any items are rush. Top priority letters and telegrams should be transcribed first. Try to meet the office time schedule for outgoing mail so that an urgent letter will arrive at its destination on time.

Some employers consider every item of dictation a rush item. Obviously you can transcribe only one piece of correspondence at a time; so use good judgment as to which item to transcribe first. Never delay transcribing your notes because the correspondence does not appear to require immediate attention. Employers appreciate your promptness in handling their work.

Edit Your Notes

Read your shorthand notes carefully before you begin to transcribe. Make sure that sentences are complete and that correct grammar and punctuation are used. If the dictator has specified paragraph breaks, make certain that the paragraphing is logical. If you must decide where to break paragraphs, remember the rule "one thought for each sentence, one purpose for each paragraph."

Always check the accuracy of specific references. Be sure that dates, times, and amounts are correct. If you find a discrepancy, make the correction and inform the dictator, or ask the dictator if a mistake was made. Your responsibility is to catch errors, and you will be considered a valuable secretary when your employer knows you can be relied upon to check the accuracy of dictation before transcribing your notes.

Prepare Your Supplies

Keep adequate supplies in your desk. You will use a variety of office supplies when you transcribe, such as letterhead and plain stationery, envelopes, carbon paper and second sheets, a typing eraser, paper clips, and replacement typewriter ribbons and correction tape.

Decide whether you need to make carbon copies of the document or whether additional copies can be made on a photocopier. Some offices permit the use of photocopiers for making multiple copies of correspondence. At all times follow the procedures established for the office in which you work.

Determine which stationery is appropriate for the correspondence you are transcribing. Remember that letterhead stationery is used only for the first page of a multipage letter. Subsequent pages are typed on plain bond paper that matches the quality of the letterhead. If you make carbon copies, you may use plain paper—either white or colored—or a thin paper called onionskin. Carbon copies are usually made on an inferior quality lightweight paper. If you are transcribing a memorandum, you may type it on a preprinted company memorandum form or on plain paper. Some memorandum forms do not require the TO, FROM, SUBJECT, and DATE headings; so you should type the memorandum in the style used in the office in which you work.

When you transcribe letters, be sure to prepare an envelope if one is required. Use a No. 10 envelope for letters that have enclosures. If the enclosures should not or cannot be folded, you may need to use a larger envelope. Use a paper clip to attach the enclosures to the letter, or put the letter and the enclosures under the flap of the envelope when submitting them to the dictator for signature.

Transcribe Your Dictation

Once you begin to transcribe, try to finish the entire document without interruption. If it is the end of the workday or time for your break or lunch, finish transcribing even if it means working late or missing part of your break or lunch. If you must defer transcribing shorthand notes to the next day, make sure you have read them over thoroughly. Write in longhand anything you may not remember so that you will not be faced with unreadable shorthand notes.

Transcribe phrases rather than one word at a time. Read for correct meaning as you type. Be on the alert for errors in your notes *before* you type them. Unless you have been asked to type a rough draft, you should strive for final mailable copy as you transcribe. Refer to page 223 for helpful transcribing suggestions.

The dictionary can be your most useful reference aid. Never guess how a word is spelled or how a word should be divided at the end of a line. A secretarial reference book is also a valuable tool for transcription.

Proofread Your Transcription

Don't make the mistake of thinking that the job is finished once you have transcribed your shorthand notes. Transforming shorthand

SUGGESTIONS FOR TRANSCRIBING SHORTHAND NOTES

1. Place your notebook in a convenient, easy-to-read position. Turn pages without lost motion.
2. Read through the correspondence before you begin to type. Insert punctuation, mark paragraphs, and correct grammatical errors and any reference errors. For example, if a date has been dictated Wednesday, June 31, when it should have been Wednesday, June 30, make the correction. Before you correct something, however, make sure an error has been made. If you are uncertain about the use of grammar or punctuation, check a reference source such as a secretary's handbook.
3. Transcribe in phrases and at a smooth pace. Make sure the dictated material is clear before you transcribe.
4. When you are uncertain about the proper spelling or an end-of-line word division, use the dictionary or a word division manual.
5. If the dictation contains long, involved sentences, break them into short sentences. Avoid making major changes or rewriting the dictation unless you have the dictator's permission.
6. Be sure you have not omitted any sentences or paragraphs. Also, check carefully for additions to the dictation to see that you have transcribed them in the appropriate place in the correspondence.
7. After a letter has been transcribed, proofread the copy before it is removed from the typewriter. It is easier to correct typographical errors while the letter is still in the typewriter.
8. Mark an X or a diagonal line through your notes when you have finished transcribing each letter.
9. As you proofread the letter for mistakes, make a list of the enclosures to be sent with the letter. Then you can easily assemble the proper enclosures after removing the letter from the typewriter.
10. Some employers prefer to have the enclosures listed under the enclosure notation at the bottom of the letter. Others, however, may wish the enclosures to be described on the file copy only. If more than one enclosure is included, it is wise to place a check mark by the notation on the file copy as you gather each item. If you have typed only *Enclosure* or *Enclosures* on the letter, you may place a check mark on the file copy opposite the sentence or paragraph in which each enclosure is mentioned. Either of these methods will ensure that you do not omit an enclosure.
11. If you are sending material in a separate package, be sure that the label is addressed properly and that the package is properly prepared for mailing. Suggestions for preparing packages for mailing are given in Chapter 11.

notes into properly arranged, attractive, and readable copy is challenging. However, the real test of your skill comes when you proofread the letter, memo, or report to be sure that it is absolutely free of errors. Good proofreading skill will ensure that your correspondence is mailable. Use the suggestions given on page 224 as a guide for efficient proofreading. The suggestions are excerpts from "Aids to Successful Proofreading," Ruth H. Turner, *The Secretary*, February, 1978.

SUGGESTIONS FOR PROOFREADING

1. Pay attention to dates. Do not assume that they are correct. Check the spelling of months, even the correctness of the year, especially if other than the current year is used. Be especially careful of the year during the months of January and February—until they can be retrained, our fingers automatically seem to type the previous year.
2. Do not overlook the date, subject, enclosure notation, or even the names of recipients of copies. Errors may occur in these letter parts, too.
3. When you read the body of the letter, examine the sentences to be sure words like *that* or *and* have not been overused.
4. Concentrate as you read for typing errors. Read slowly—this is no time for speed-reading.
5. In order to concentrate specifically on typographical errors, read backwards. Of course, this method will not reveal omissions or repeated copy and, therefore, must be followed by a second reading for content.
6. Make the dictionary your best friend. Is it privilege, privelege, or priviledge? gauge or guage? descresion or discretion? chief or cheif? Never hesitate to look up the correct spelling of a word.
7. Watch closely for omissions of *ed* or *s* at the end of words.
8. Study related words until you understand the differences in their meaning and usage: affect/effect, imply/infer, immigrate/emigrate, advice/advise, counsel/council/consul.
9. Mentally repeat syllables of long words containing many vowels: evacuation, responsibility, continuously, individual. It is easy to omit a vowel.
10. Be careful of words with double vowels. *Succeed, proceed,* and *exceed* are the only words that end in *ceed. Supersede* is the only word in the English language that ends in *sede*; all other words (*precede, recede,* etc.) end in *cede*. Also, be careful of words with double consonants, such as *occasion* and *occurrence* and *accommodation*. Look up the word in the dictionary if you are unsure of its spelling.
11. Be alert to silent letters in words, such as rhythm, rendezvous, malign.
12. If punctuation causes you difficulties, check these marks after you have completed all other proofreading. Be careful not to omit a closing parenthesis or quotation mark.
13. Be consistent in the use of commas. If you have to read a sentence more than once to get its meaning, inserting or deleting a comma may correct the problem. For want of a comma, the meaning may be lost.
14. Be consistent in the use of capital letters. Follow the practice established by your office or the rules in a reference manual or secretarial handbook.

Submit Your Work

Rush items are submitted to the dictator as soon as they are ready. Otherwise you may wait to submit your transcription until several items have been completed. Follow the procedure that the dictator prefers.

Place a letter (not yet folded) with its enclosures under the flap of the envelope. Copies of the letter should come next. If you have several letters or memos requiring signature, you may want to put them in a folder labeled *Signature Required,* and place them on the dictator's desk. Placing transcribed correspondence in a folder will keep it neat and free from smudges. Also, confidential material is less likely to be seen by others if it is placed in a folder.

The dictator may ask you to sign the correspondence in certain instances, and you should know which signature method is preferred. Generally there are two ways a secretary may sign a letter for the dictator: (1) sign the dictator's name and add your initials or (2) sign your name as secretary to the dictator.

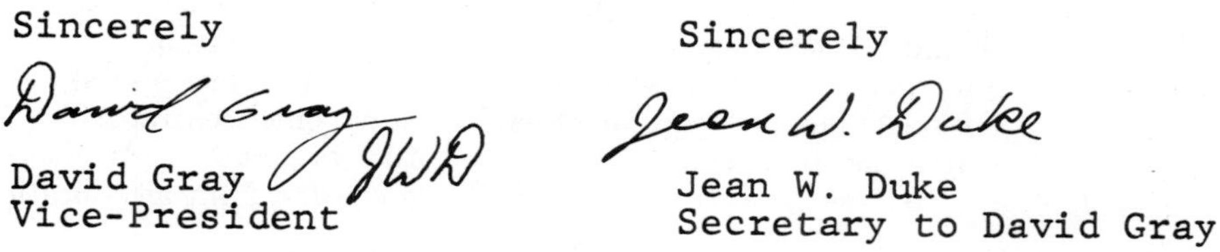

Sincerely

David Gray
Vice-President

Sincerely

Jean W. Duke
Secretary to David Gray

Illus. 10-2
Examples of a secretary's signature for an executive

HANDLING MACHINE DICTATION

Many companies use dictation systems for the majority of their dictation requirements. The use of dictation equipment has proven more efficient than utilizing both the employer's and the secretary's time. Executives who have heavy dictation find that machine dictation has advantages, one of which is to release the secretary to accept greater responsibilities.

In Chapter 9 you learned that the cost of producing a business letter is quite high. The Dartnell Institute of Business Research, which conducts an annual survey to determine business letter costs, has also found that letters dictated into recording machines cost less than personally dictated letters. In a recent survey, Dartnell found that 55 percent of employers use machine dictation. The overall cost of a letter dictated on a recording machine is $5.70, which is $1.90 less than a personally dictated letter. The main reason for the reduction in cost is the absence of the secretary, who can be handling other tasks while the employer is dictating.

Machine Dictation versus Shorthand Dictation

The three ways to originate correspondence are handwriting, dictating to a secretary, or dictating to a recording machine. We already learned that writing a letter in longhand takes four times longer than dictating it; so let's examine the advantages and disadvantages of shorthand dictation and machine dictation.

Advantages

Shorthand	Machine Dictation

Shorthand

1. Secretaries can ask questions during dictation if clarification is needed.
2. Secretaries taking shorthand at meetings or conferences can determine what information should be recorded.
3. Shorthand is useful when taking telephone messages or other verbal instructions.

Machine Dictation

1. The secretary does not have to be present for dictation.
2. A qualified person can easily transcribe machine dictation.
3. Faster typing speeds can be achieved when transcribing machine dictation.
4. With portable dictating units and some centralized systems, the originator can dictate at any time from any location.

Disadvantages

Shorthand

1. The time required of the secretary and the dictator for shorthand dictation is costly.
2. Not all secretaries are qualified to take shorthand.
3. Manual shorthand systems differ; therefore, secretaries may not be able to transcribe each other's notes.

Machine Dictation

1. There is the initial cost for dictation equipment as well as maintenance costs.
2. Some dictators never learn to dictate properly; therefore, efficiency is reduced.

Kinds of Dictation Equipment

There are basically three kinds of office dictation equipment: portable units, desktop units, and centralized dictation systems. Companies may utilize one of these dictation media or a combination of them. Maximum benefit can be derived from equipment that utilizes recording media that is compatible or interchangeable.

Recording Media. Dictation equipment will use either discrete media or endless loop media. *Discrete media,* such as a cassette or cartridge with magnetic tape or a magnetic disk, can be easily inserted and removed from a dictating machine. *Endless loop media* is inside the equipment and cannot be handled. Endless loop magnetic tape is often wound on spools and is spliced so that it is continuous. Because the tape is located inside the equipment, it does not require operator assistance and thus can accommodate many hours of dictation.

Illus. 10-3

Photograph courtesy of
Dictaphone Corporation

Technological changes have greatly improved dictation equipment. An early model dictation unit is shown here.

Portable Units. Portable units use discrete media. They are battery operated and are small enough to carry in a pocket or briefcase. Portable units have been improved so that they have many of the same features as large units.

The recording media used for most portable units are standard cassettes, minicassettes, or microcassettes. Equipment that uses the small size cassettes is popular because it is compact and lightweight. Standard cassettes measure 2 1/2 by 4 inches. Minicassettes are 2 by 1 1/4 inches, while microcassettes are slightly smaller at 1 3/4 by 1 1/4 inches. Even though microcassettes are approximately one third the size of standard cassettes, they can provide as much dictation time.

Portable units have built-in microphones, and the recorded voice quality can be quite good. They are relatively inexpensive compared with large model units. Portable units are versatile because they can be used in or out of the office. Portable units, however, can be misplaced easily because of their small size; and batteries must be replaced or recharged periodically.

Most portable units are used for dictation only. The cassette is removed from the portable unit after dictation and inserted in a transcription unit on the secretary's desk. The transcription unit is

Illus. 10-4

Lanier Business Products

A portable dictation unit is versatile and can be used whenever it is convenient for the dictator.

equipped with a headset, which the secretary uses to hear the dictation, and a foot pedal, which is used to control the starting and stopping of the tape. The foot pedal can also be used to advance or reverse the tape. In addition, the transcription unit is equipped with controls that regulate volume, voice tone, and the speed at which the tape is played.

Desktop Units. A desktop dictation unit is naturally one that fits on the top of a desk. It can be battery operated, but it is usually operated by electricity. Desktop units use discrete media and can be equipped for use as transcribing machines. Units that can be used for dictation or transcription are called *combination units.*

Combination desktop units are equipped for dictation by plugging in a microphone. Dictation is recorded on the cassette by talking into the microphone. The same unit is then used to transcribe the dictation. The microphone is unplugged, and the headset and foot pedal are attached to the unit. The secretary can then transcribe the dictation.

Illus. 10-5
Using a desktop dictation unit can save time and money since it
leaves the secretary free to perform other duties.

Centralized Dictation Systems. Unlike portable or desktop units, a centralized dictation system can be used by several dictators at one time depending on the size and features of the system. Dictators have access to the system from a microphone wired for dictation to a central unit or from the company telephone lines. In the latter case, the telephone itself is used to dictate to the centrally located dictation equipment.

Centralized dictation systems may use either discrete or endless loop recording media. The central recording equipment is stationary and is connected by either telephones or individual handsets (microphones) distributed to users. In a centralized system, transcription can begin while the dictator is still dictating, or it can be stored on the recording media to be transcribed later.

In most centralized dictation systems, the dictation is automatically forwarded to a central receiving station. Several secretaries may work in one center transcribing dictation. In this work arrangement, a few secretaries can transcribe the correspondence of many dictators.

Centralized dictation systems provide a way of managing dictation and transcription known as *word management*. Word management is accomplished through equipment that automatically logs in (records) dictation. Centralized dictation systems also have an optional feature called the *supervisor's control monitor*. This piece of equipment helps the supervisor manage the flow of work and provides a record of the dictation being transcribed. One concern is that centralized dictation systems may not facilitate confidentiality. This concern is not necessarily the case, however, because the supervisor can control the assignment of special projects to certain individuals.

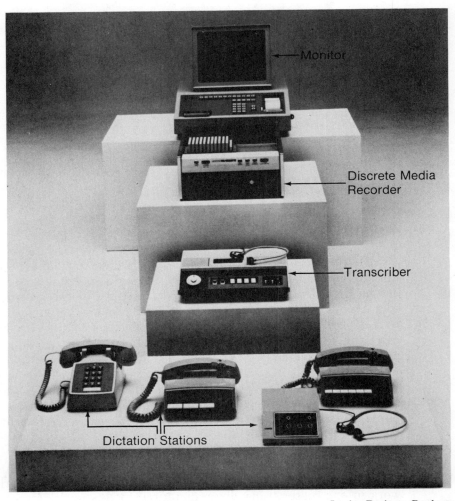

Lanier Business Products

Illus. 10-6
Centralized dictation system

Transcribing from Machine Dictation

Many of the same skills needed for transcribing from a machine are required for transcribing from shorthand notes. And the end result should be the same—that is, a correctly typed mailable document.

You should be familiar with the standard features found on most transcribing units. Of course, equipment differs; so be certain to read the manual from the manufacturer before using a transcribing machine.

Indexing or Queuing Feature. Dictating and transcribing machines contain a mechanism that indicates the beginning and end of dictated material. By depressing a special button or lever on the microphone, the dictator marks the number and length of dictated items on the tape, which enables the secretary to determine the amount of dictated material.

Older models of dictation and transcription equipment use paper index slips to indicate the length of dictation. The dictator marks the beginning and end of correspondence by depressing a button or lever on the microphone. Holes are then punched into the index slip. The number of holes indicates the number of documents, and the distance between the holes indicates the length of each document. (See Illus. 10-7.)

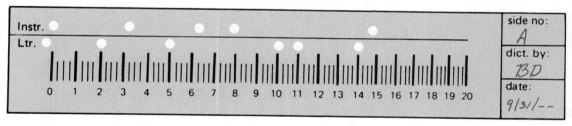

Illus. 10-7
Index slip

Recent models of dictation and transcription equipment use a digital counter in place of the index slip. The digital counter displays the amount of dictation in minutes or seconds. Some units have a window that actually displays the arrangement of the dictation on the cassette in addition to the total length of dictation. (See Illus. 10-8.)

Special Instructions. Dictators often instruct the secretary about changes to be made in dictated correspondence. The dictator may also request that a certain document be transcribed immediately. It is the secretary's responsibility to listen to any special instructions that have been given before transcribing recorded dictation.

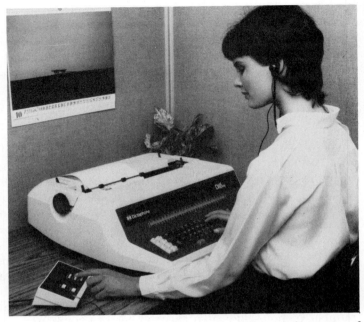

Photograph courtesy of
Dictaphone Corporation

Illus. 10-8
Recent models of dictation and transcription equipment use a digital
counter in place of the index slip.

The dictator can indicate special instructions in the dictation by
depressing a lever or button on the microphone at each special
instruction. For units that utilize index slips, a hole is punched on the
upper portion of the slip. The secretary looks for this special marking
in order to advance immediately to the point of the special instruction
in the dictation.

Late model machines that do not use index slips indicate special
instructions with a distinct tone. The depression of a button or lever
on the microphone will create an audible beep or tone to alert the secretary to the special instruction. Because special instructions may
occur anywhere in the dictation, the secretary must search, or scan,
the dictation before transcribing. Some machines have an automatic
scanning feature that quickly advances through the recorded dictation
and stops at the point where special instructions are given.

Organization of Work for Transcription. After you have
listened for special instructions and determined the order in which
dictated items should be transcribed, you are ready to transcribe the
dictation. Listen to just enough of the dictation to learn what the

first document is—a letter, memorandum, or report. You must then determine the appropriate style and arrangement for the document. (Review letter styles and placement in Chapter 9.) Your responsibility is to transform the dictation into a complete, appropriately arranged, grammatically correct, and perfectly typed document.

OPERATING STENOGRAPHIC MACHINES

Machines used by stenographers or secretaries to record dictation at very fast rates are called stenographic machines. The stenographer or secretary using a stenographic machine presses keys singly or in combination. One or more words may be recorded with a single stroke. The shorthand or abbreviations for the dictation are then recorded on a printed tape. The tape is read across and down, and often more than one word appears on a single line. Until recently these tapes have been transcribed at the typewriter just as shorthand notes are transcribed. It is now possible, through the use of a special steno-graphic machine, for a computer to transcribe the notes. This special stenographic machine has switches, or contacts, wired under each key that are connected directly to a magnetic tape recorder located in the base of the machine. As the notes are recorded on the paper tape, each stroke is automatically recorded on a cassette magnetic tape. This tape is then fed into a computer which prints out the notes.

Stenograph

Illus. 10-9
Stenographic machine

Fields Requiring Machine Shorthand

Although any secretary may use a stenographic machine to record dictation, secretaries in certain specialized fields regularly use stenographic machines. Some situations in the medical field require secretaries who can take machine shorthand. It is the legal field, however, that requires the extensive use of stenographic machines, since most court proceedings are recorded by an individual who uses machine shorthand.

Certification of Proficiency in Machine Shorthand

The National Shorthand Reporters Association offers a certificate of proficiency to individuals who demonstrate certain skill levels on a rigid examination. The examination includes a general knowledge section on English language skills and medical and legal terminology. Individuals must also record dictation using a stenographic machine at a minimum level of 225 words a minute. The development of good recording skill and a high rate of speed in using a stenographic machine takes time and a great deal of effort.

PROFESSIONAL POINTERS

How long has it been since you have critically evaluated the letters you prepare? Transcribing office correspondence, whether from shorthand notes or machine dictation, requires that you prepare satisfactory business letters. Keep the following points in mind as you type and then proofread correspondence.

1. Correct punctuation is very important. A comma in the wrong position can change the meaning of a statement completely. *Incorrect:* We are going to eat Mary before we discuss the matter. *Correct:* We are going to eat, Mary, before we discuss the matter.

2. Avoid outmoded expressions. These expressions tend to be wordy and unnecessary. *Outmoded:* As per your request . . . *Natural:* As you requested . . .

3. A positive tone is more effective than a negative one. *Negative:* We cannot ship the order before December 12. *Positive:* We will try to ship the order on or before December 12.

4. Very few people are perfect spellers. Make frequent use of your dictionary to check the words of which you are not completely sure.

5. Use more active than passive verbs. One way to shorten and strengthen your letters is by the more frequent use of active verbs. *Passive:* The conference was attended by Mrs. Andersen. *Active:* Mrs. Andersen attended the conference.

6. Few letters require more than one page. If they are often longer, perhaps too much detail or needless information is presented.

7. A paragraph should be fairly short (10 lines or less) and contain one specific thought. When you begin a new idea, start a new paragraph.

8. Too many words in your sentences may make your letter hard to read and understand. As a general rule, simple words have a more powerful impact than long ones that your reader may have to look up in a dictionary.

9. Make your letters more personal by using pronouns that add a personal touch. *Avoid:* applicants, claimants, etc. *Use:* you, he, she

10. Do not use a group of words when one word communicates the same meaning; for example, substitute *because* for *in view of the fact that.* Also, avoid using words that have the same meaning; for example, *each and every* or *exactly identical.*

11. Antagonistic words should not be used in business letters. *Examples:* complaint, failure, mistake, etc.

12. Be careful about using one word too many times in a letter. Correct this problem by using synonyms, changing your sentence construction, and using a pronoun (it) in place of a noun.

FOR YOUR REVIEW

1. List three situations where shorthand is an efficient means of recording information.

2. Give three suggestions for effectively using a stenographic notebook for dictation.

3. How is office dictation different from classroom dictation?

4. When should you use longhand in taking dictation?

5. List five suggestions that you consider helpful in taking dictation.

6. What does transcribing involve? Why is proofreading important for successful transcription?

7. List five suggestions that you consider helpful for transcribing.

8. Compare the advantages and disadvantages of shorthand dictation with machine dictation.

9. What are the two types of recording media used by dictation equipment?

10. List the three kinds of dictation equipment and the type of recording media used by each.

11. Name one field in which stenographic machines are used extensively. For what purpose is the stenographic machine used in this field?

12. What skills are tested for attainment of the National Shorthand Reporters Association's certificate of proficiency?

CASE PROBLEM

New Kent Corporation is a firm of average size. Two years ago, however, it was a small company with only 17 employees. Sales have almost doubled in the past two years, and New Kent Corporation now has over 50 employees.

Unfortunately the number of secretaries has not grown at the same rate as the number of salespeople; thus, there is a long turn-around time for receiving completed mailable correspondence. Four secretaries assist 23 salespeople, and only one secretary is qualified to take shorthand. Most of the salespeople write every letter and memorandum in longhand. Several salespeople ask the secretaries to compose correspondence, after providing them with the necessary facts. The four secretaries also answer the phones. They take a great number of telephone messages for the salespeople who are rarely in the office.

Since the organization is growing so rapidly, the sales manager has decided to hold a sales meeting every Monday morning. This policy will go into effect in two weeks. The minutes of the meetings will be recorded and submitted to the vice-president of the corporation.

1. If the secretarial staff cannot be increased for the next six months, what are your recommendations for accommodating such a heavy work load? Analyze the situation carefully, and give specific suggestions to improve the situation.

2. Do you see any opportunities where shorthand could improve efficiency?

PRODUCTION PROJECTS

PP 10-1

(Objectives 1, 3, and 4)

Conduct a small survey of your business community to find answers to the following questions:

1. Is shorthand a skill required by employers in your area?

2. In what situations are secretaries required to use shorthand?

3. Do most businesses in your area have dictation equipment?

4. What are the qualifications for transcribing from machine dictation? What are the advantages of machine dictation over shorthand dictation?

Type a report on your findings. Be sure to include the sources of your information.

PP 10-2

(Objectives 2 and 5)

Your teacher will dictate a memorandum for you to take in shorthand or give you an assignment to transcribe from machine dictation. Use the memorandum form in your Supplies Inventory for your final typed copy. Proofread carefully your transcription to be sure that it is error free.

PP 10-3

(Objective 6)

You are to dictate two letters to another student in your class. You may dictate the letters to be taken in shorthand, or you may dictate using a recording machine. Refer to the tips given on page 216 of the text before dictating the letters.

Suggestions for the letters you are to dictate are as follows:

1. A letter describing the three kinds of dictation equipment

2. A sales letter encouraging your friend to purchase a particular portable dictation unit

3. A letter of congratulations to your friend for achieving a good grade point average, receiving a special award, or obtaining a full- or part-time job

4. A letter to your friend explaining helpful suggestions for transcribing dictation

PP 10-4

(Objectives 2 and 5)

Record in shorthand and transcribe the letters in PP 10-3 as dictated to you by another student, or transcribe them from another student's dictation to a recording machine. Use plain paper. Proofread your transcribed copies to make certain that your letters will be completely error free.

Chapter 11

PROCESSING MAIL AND
USING SHIPPING SERVICES

In any company, communications by mail are a vital function. The way mail is prepared and processed can have a significant effect on operating costs. Company profits may suffer if mail operations are inefficiently handled. Efficient handling of office mail and the proper use of mailing and shipping services are expected of secretaries. This chapter will help you learn how to process mail and use shipping services effectively.

General Objectives

Your general objectives for Chapter 11 are to:

1. *Follow the steps involved in handling incoming mail*
2. *Process outgoing mail*
3. *Indentify various mail classifications*
4. *Describe the special services offered by the Postal Service*
5. *Discuss the different means of shipping parcels and freight*

HANDLING INCOMING MAIL

Secretarial responsibilities for handling incoming office mail will largely depend on the size of the company. As a secretary in a small firm, you personally may be expected to receive and process all the mail. Most large companies, on the other hand, have a central mail department that receives and distributes the mail.

You need to establish a schedule for handling incoming mail. Know when to expect the mail, whether it is delivered directly to you by the letter carrier or by the company's mail room attendant. Set aside time each day to handle promptly the incoming mail. Follow the steps described here when you process the mail.

Sort the Mail

When you receive the mail, you should immediately look through it for correspondence that requires immediate attention; for example, replies to letters regarding important pending matters. Registered, certified, insured, or special delivery mail should receive special handling. Mailgrams, telegrams, and express mail also deserve special handling. You should sort and process this mail first.

After you have taken care of the special mail, you are ready to sort the remaining mail. Separate the mail into stacks according to its purpose. You may find additional categories necessary, but generally mail can be sorted into these groups: (1) first-class mail—correspondence, orders or payments, bills or statements; (2) second-class mail—periodicals and newspapers; (3) third-class mail—advertisements, catalogs, and circulars; (4) fourth-class mail—packages; (5) interoffice mail. Mail that is marked *PERSONAL* or *CONFIDENTIAL* should be set aside for opening by the addressee.

After the mail has been sorted, it is ready to be opened. Open the envelopes carefully, using a standard letter opener or an electric letter opening machine. Remove the contents and inspect them to be sure that the sender's complete address appears on the letter. If it does not, the envelope bearing the return address should be stapled or paper clipped to the letter. If deadlines are a factor in the mail your office receives, retain the envelope as proof of the date of mailing. Any enclosed material should also be attached with a paper clip to the back of the correspondence. Turn the correspondence face down, and proceed until you have finished opening and inspecting all the mail in a particular category.

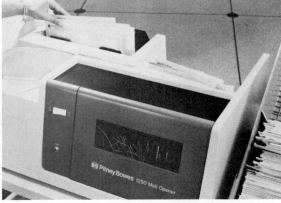

Pitney Bowes, Inc.

Illus. 11-1
Mail can be opened by hand using a standard letter opener or automatically using an electric letter opening machine.

Date and Time Stamp the Mail

Date and time stamping is an important step in handling incoming mail in most companies. After the mail has been opened and inspected, the stack of documents in each mail category is turned faceup. Each item in a stack is stamped in the upper left-hand corner to show the date and time received. A hand stamp usually prints the word *Received* and the date. You must set a hand stamp each day to show the current date. Machines can be used for date and time stamping. Most date and time stamping machines have a clock which automatically gives the exact time the letter was stamped as well as the date.

Stamping the incoming mail with the current date and time provides the recipient with important information. Occasionally deadlines are given for the receipt of payments, the processing of orders, or other services offered by a company; thus, date and time stamping verifies when a document was received. Some correspondence may not be dated; therefore, date and time stamping at the time of receipt will provide this information. Date and time stamping may also ensure a prompt reply to correspondence.

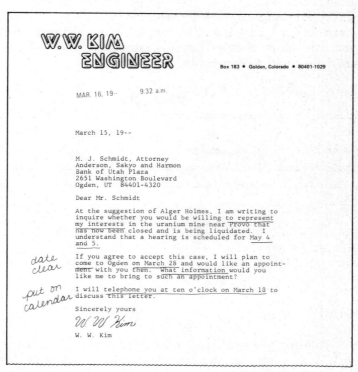

Illus. 11-2
Annotated letter with date and time stamp

Read and Annotate the Mail

You may be asked to read and annotate incoming correspondence as a part of your daily mail-handling responsibilities. *Annotating* means to underline with a colored pen or pencil the important elements of a letter. It also involves making notations in the margins to alert the reader to previous action taken or to facts that will assist the reader in making decisions or taking action. When you read correspondence, keep in mind any facts that would be helpful to the reader. You may want to attach related documents or even an entire file folder to a letter.

Keep a Log of Incoming Mail

You may be asked to keep a log (or record) of all incoming mail. Usually only first-class mail is recorded on the log sheet. A mail log serves several purposes. It shows the mail received on a given day and to whom it was directed. If a letter is lost or misplaced, the mail log verifies that the letter was received and identifies its contents and sender.

A printed form may be used for recording the mail you handle. If you think a mail log will be helpful, but no printed form is available, you can design a sheet for this purpose. Illus. 11-3 shows how necessary information is recorded in a mail log.

	FROM				ADDRESSED TO	
MAIL LOG						
DATE RECEIVED	NAME	ADDRESS	DESCRIPTION	DATED	NAME	DEPT.
2/26	Williams Assoc.	Chicago, Il	Certified letter -- Jones Contract	2/25	Ted Baxter / Legal Dept	
2/26	Jack Smith	Louisville, Ky	Package Cod $1.50 -- Replacement parts	2/23	Joan Brennan / Prod. Dept.	
2/26	Faye Steinburger	Chicago, Il	Special Delivery -- Rush order	2/25	Bill Crosby / Order Dept.	

Illus. 11-3
Mail log

Route the Mail

Routing the mail may mean you simply place it on the recipient's desk. If you are handling mail for several persons or departments, you may put the mail in separate boxes or trays marked for pickup by those individuals. It is very frustrating to receive someone else's mail; so be careful not to make errors in distributing mail.

If a document should be read by more than one person, you should attach a routing slip. A routing slip may contain the names of several individuals; in this case, place a check mark alongside the names of those persons who should receive the document. Some routing slips require that you write in the names of the individuals who are to receive the material. A routing slip should identify the location or person to whom the document is to be returned after it has completed its circulation. Because routing a document through several persons can take a lot of time, you may find it more efficient to make and distribute photocopies of the document. A routing slip should still be attached indicating to whom the photocopies are being circulated.

```
FROM
─────────────────────────────────────────
Albert Martin, Director
Public Relations Department

DATE   3/25/ - -
─────────────────────────────────────────


            ROUTING SLIP              Date
                                   Forwarded

_____  Everyone                  _____
_____  Babb, B.
___✓__  Gryder, H.                    3/25
_____  Igo, J.                   _____
_____  Mundt, K.
___✓__  Primrose, N.                  3/25
___✓__  Roehr, P.                     3/28
_____  Slaughter, G.
___✓__  Tucker, C.                    3/28
_____  Wingfield, M.
___✓__  Congdon, R.                   3/28


        Will you please:

_____  Read and keep
_____  Read and pass on
_____  Read and return
___✓__  Read, pass on, and return
```

Illus. 11-4
Routing Slip

HANDLING OUTGOING MAIL

A secretary's responsibilities for handling outgoing mail may vary. Even in companies that have a mail department, it is the secretary's responsibility to prepare the mail for the mail department. In small companies that don't have a mail department, the secretary may also assume the duties of preparing and processing outgoing mail. Several steps that will ensure that you handle outgoing mail properly are described here.

Check Enclosures

An enclosure notation at the bottom of a letter serves as a flag to the recipient. When you prepare documents for mailing, be sure to indicate any enclosures. If the enclosure is the same size as the letter, you can fold it with the letter. A small enclosure can be stapled to the back of a letter. Automatic canceling machines are equipped to process only envelopes containing flat contents. Do not enclose bulky items, such as pens, pencils, keys, etc., unless you write *HAND CANCEL* on the outside of the envelope.

Prepare Envelopes

Your responsibility as a secretary is to choose the correct size envelope for the correspondence that is being mailed. Envelopes that are too large for the items they contain not only cost the company extra postage, but they frequently get bent or torn as they pass through automatic canceling or sorting machines. Be sure that the envelope is the right size for its contents. Most outgoing correspondence will be mailed in No. 10 or No. 6 3/4 envelopes.

The Postal Service has requirements regarding the shape and size of envelopes. Place outgoing mail only in rectangular envelopes that measure between 5 by 3 1/2 inches and 11 1/2 by 6 1/8 inches. Additional postage will be charged for larger envelopes. Mail that is smaller than 5 by 3 1/2 inches will be returned to the sender.

Envelope Addressing. An incorrectly addressed envelope can cause the delay of an important letter or document and a consequent loss of money to the company. Always compare the letter and envelope address of outgoing correspondence. Check the address against the letterhead of previous correspondence to be sure the address is accurate. Don't guess at an address. If you keep a mailing list of frequently used addresses, be sure it is up to date; and, most of all, be sure you use it.

Requirements for Automation. As a secretary, you are responsible for seeing that outgoing mail is properly prepared for automated sorting equipment. The Postal Service uses automated equipment designed to handle the steadily growing volume of mail. Much of the sorting of letter size mail in large post offices has been accomplished by a person operating a semiautomatic letter-sorting machine (LSM). The machine moves envelopes at the rate of 60 a minute in front of the operator. The operator strikes a combination of keys according to the ZIP Code in the mailing address, and the envelope is quickly processed for delivery to its destination. Envelopes that are not legible or that do not contain a ZIP Code are removed for hand sorting.

Two new automated pieces of equipment being installed in large post offices throughout the country are the optical character recognition (OCR) and bar code sorter (BCS) machines. These machines, which are computerized, can process approximately 25,000 envelopes an hour. Only envelopes with typewritten addresses in block style and a ZIP Code can be processed by this fully automatic equipment. Avoid type styles such as italic, artistic, or script where any of the characters or numbers may overlap. Refer to Chapter 9, page 207, for the proper envelope address format.

The OCR machine reads, or scans, the address with its electronic eye and prints a series of short vertical lines at the bottom of the envelope. The lines or bar codes resemble the unit price code (UPC) on the items you purchase at the grocery store. The machine has actually converted your typewritten address into a code readable by the bar code sorter. This sorter processes all envelopes bearing a code at phenomenal speeds.

U.S. Postal Service

Illus. 11-5
An OCR machine can sort letters quickly and accurately.

State Abbreviations and ZIP Codes. The last line of the mailing address should include the city, state, and ZIP Code in that sequence. The Postal Service prefers that the standard two-letter state abbreviations be used in envelope addresses. The two-letter abbreviations for the United States are given in Illus. 11-6.

STATE ABBREVIATIONS

Name	Standard Abbreviation	Two-Letter Abbreviation	Capital
Alabama	Ala.	AL	Montgomery
Alaska	Alaska	AK	Juneau
Arizona	Ariz.	AZ	Phoenix
Arkansas	Ark.	AR	Little Rock
California	Calif.	CA	Sacramento
Colorado	Colo.	CO	Denver
Connecticut	Conn.	CT	Hartford
Delaware	Del.	DE	Dover
District of Columbia	D.C.	DC	Washington (National capital)
Florida	Fla.	FL	Tallahassee
Georgia	Ga.	GA	Atlanta
Hawaii	Hawaii	HI	Honolulu
Idaho	Idaho	ID	Boise
Illinois	Ill.	IL	Springfield
Indiana	Ind.	IN	Indianapolis
Iowa	Iowa	IA	Des Moines
Kansas	Kans.	KS	Topeka
Kentucky	Ky.	KY	Frankfort
Louisiana	La.	LA	Baton Rouge
Maine	Maine	ME	Augusta
Maryland	Md.	MD	Annapolis
Massachusetts	Mass.	MA	Boston
Michigan	Mich.	MI	Lansing
Minnesota	Minn.	MN	St. Paul
Mississippi	Miss.	MS	Jackson
Missouri	Mo.	MO	Jefferson City
Montana	Mont.	MT	Helena
Nebraska	Nebr.	NE	Lincoln
Nevada	Nev.	NV	Carson City
New Hampshire	N.H.	NH	Concord
New Jersey	N.J.	NJ	Trenton
New Mexico	N.Mex.	NM	Santa Fe
New York	N.Y.	NY	Albany
North Carolina	N.C.	NC	Raleigh
North Dakota	N.Dak.	ND	Bismarck
Ohio	Ohio	OH	Columbus
Oklahoma	Okla.	OK	Oklahoma City
Oregon	Oreg.	OR	Salem
Pennsylvania	Pa.	PA	Harrisburg
Rhode Island	R.I.	RI	Providence
South Carolina	S.C.	SC	Columbia
South Dakota	S.Dak.	SD	Pierre
Tennessee	Tenn.	TN	Nashville
Texas	Tex.	TX	Austin
Utah	Utah	UT	Salt Lake City
Vermont	Vt.	VT	Montpelier
Virginia	Va.	VA	Richmond
Washington	Wash.	WA	Olympia
West Virginia	W.Va.	WV	Charleston
Wisconsin	Wis.	WI	Madison
Wyoming	Wyo.	WY	Cheyenne

Illus. 11-6
State abbreviations and capital cities

The Postal Service has established a ZIP + 4 plan. The change increases the number of ZIP Codes from 40,000 to 20 million. Major mailers were notified of the new codes in the summer of 1981. National implementation of ZIP + 4 occurred in October of 1983. Just as the five-digit ZIP Code has allowed the Postal Service to increase productivity by using automated equipment, the new nine-digit Zip Code further identifies the destination of correspondence and permits even greater use of the new technology designed to improve efficiency. Use of the nine-digit ZIP Code by businesses is voluntary; large mailers will be encouraged to use this system.

The Postal Service will continue to publish the *National Five Digit ZIP Code and Post Office Directory* on an annual basis. This directory lists all five-digit ZIP Codes in the United States and can be purchased at your local post office. In order to determine an expanded ZIP Code, however, you must call a toll free number provided by the Postal Service.

Presort the Mail

Outgoing mail will be processed faster if it is presorted and bundled before it is taken to the post office. In a large company, this is usually done by the mail room personnel. To encourage presorting, the Postal Service offers a postage reduction of a few cents when 500 or more pieces of mail are presorted before they are deposited. Mail that is presorted by ZIP Code will also be processed faster. As a secretary, if you are responsible for mailing outgoing correspondence, separate first-class mail from other mail, and group it according to local or out-of-town mail. For further information on presorting mail, check a postal manual or call the local post office.

Establish a Schedule

Determine how often and at what times the local post office dispatches the mail. Outgoing mail can be delivered more quickly if it is deposited at the established collection times. If the company has a central mail department, there will be periodic pickups of outgoing mail from individual offices. In some offices there are outgoing mail trays (or a centrally located one) from which the pickups are made. Learn the schedule for these pickups, and strive to have your outgoing mail ready on time.

Determine Postage

If you are responsible for taking outgoing mail to the post office or nearest collection box, you must be certain that the proper postage has been affixed to the envelope. Postage for outgoing mail can be paid with adhesive stamps, a postage meter which makes an imprint on the envelope, or a special permit generally preprinted on the envelope. (See Illus. 11-7.)

Illus. 11-7
Postage for outgoing mail can be paid by using a postage meter, a special permit, or an adhesive stamp.

Many small companies and most mail departments have a postage meter. Envelopes are fed into the machine and are stacked, sealed, meter-stamped, and counted in one continuous operation. The metered mail imprint serves as postage payment, a postmark, and cancellation mark. A postage meter provides an accurate determination of postage since it either prints directly on envelopes or on adhesive strips which can then be affixed to packages.

A postage scale can calculate mailing cost based on weight, class of mail, destination, and any special service desired. Electronic mailing and shipping scales can compute weights and rates with unbelievable accuracy and speed. You can also *interface* (connect) many electronic scales with postage meters. After you choose a shipping method and weigh the package, you can generate the appropriate meter tape from the postage meter by pressing the print button on the scale keyboard.

The meter picks up a signal from the scale to imprint and dispense postage on gummed tape. The gummed tape is attached to the package. Electronic mailing and shipping systems can even be linked to a document printer to provide shipping documentation, such as invoices or bills of lading, at the same time metered postage is prepared.

Pitney Bowes, Inc.

Illus. 11-8
Electronic scale

USING POSTAL SERVICE MAIL CLASSIFICATIONS

If you work as a secretary in a small office, you may be required to know the current postal classifications and rates. Obtain pamphlets from the local post office about mail services and rates. Keep your information up to date, and call the post office if you have questions about mailing services or rates. The following is basic information on the different classes of domestic mail service.

Express Mail

The fastest mail service provided by the Postal Service is Express Mail Next Day Service. You can mail letters or packages at a designated express mail post office by 5 p.m. on any business day and be assured of delivery to the required destination by 3 p.m. of the next day. Express mail has a considerably higher postage rate than first-class mail; therefore, you should use it only for mail that must be delivered overnight. Letters and parcels sent by express mail are insured against loss or damage at no additional cost.

Illus. 11-9
Express Mail Next Day Service guarantees that a letter or package will be delivered the next day.

First-Class Mail

Mail that is sent first-class includes letters, greeting cards, personal notes, postal cards, bills, statements of account, and business reply mail. If you use an envelope larger than a standard No. 10 envelope, be sure to clearly mark *FIRST CLASS* on the envelope in the area below the stamp. You can obtain mailing labels free of charge from your post office to use when sending first-class mail that is larger than letter size. Mail sent as first class must not exceed 12 ounces in weight.

Priority Mail

First-class mail that weighs more than 12 ounces must be sent as priority mail. Priority mail cannot exceed 70 pounds in weight, and the maximum size for any item is 108 inches in combined length and *girth* (distance around the thickest part). Send items by priority mail if you need to have them delivered as quickly as first-class mail. You pay a higher postal rate for priority mail, so do not send packages by this class unless it is necessary.

Second-Class Mail

This mail classification is used to send newspapers, magazines, and other periodicals that are published at least four times a year.

Second-class publications may not be designed primarily for advertising purposes. No handwritten messages can be sent by second-class mail. Publishers and other mailers must obtain special authorization to mail materials at the second-class rate by submitting an application to the Postal Service.

Third-Class Mail

Mail that weighs less than 16 ounces and is not classified as first- or second-class mail is considered third-class mail. This category consists of catalogs, circulars, advertisements, photographs, keys, and lightweight merchandise parcels. There are two rate structures for third-class mail: a single piece rate and a bulk rate.

Fourth-Class Mail

Fourth-class mail, also referred to as parcel post, includes all mailable matter not in first-, second-, or third-class mail weighing 16 ounces or more. Packages weighing 16 ounces or more that are not marked *PRIORITY MAIL* are considered fourth-class mail. The amount of postage for fourth-class matter depends on its destination as well as its size and weight. The destination charge is determined according to the eight delivery zones in the United States. The zone chart for parcel post rates is available at your local post office.

SELECTING THE APPROPRIATE SPECIAL MAIL SERVICE

Not only will it be necessary for you to know the different classifications of mail, but you should be familiar with special postal services as well. Knowing what special services are available and how to use them will enable you to process more effectively outgoing mail.

Accountable Mail

For an additional fee the Postal Service offers to its customers certain services that enable mail to be handled in a special way. *Accountable mail* is mail that must be accounted for by each person in the Postal Service who handles it. A fee is charged to cover the cost of this extra handling. The following special services are available for all first-class mail as well as some other classes of mail.

Registered Mail. Registering mail is the safest way to send valuable items through the mail. Only first-class or priority mail can be registered. You may want to send by registered mail valuable and important documents or items such as stocks, bonds, or other records that cannot easily be replaced. Mail to be registered must be sealed (masking tape or transparent tape cannot be used), and it must carry the names and addresses of the sender and the addressee. Also, the value of the item must be declared when the item is registered.

The maximum indemnity for registered mail is $25,000. For items of greater value, the sender may wish to purchase additional private insurance. You will receive a receipt when you send an item by registered mail. For an additional fee you can receive a return receipt when the item has been delivered and accepted by the addressee.

Certified Mail. For materials that have no monetary value but for which you need a record of delivery, use certified mail. Certified mail can be used only for first-class and priority mail, and there is no insurance coverage provided. You will receive a receipt when you send an item by certified mail. The post office that delivers the certified mail obtains the addressee's signature and keeps a record of the date the material was delivered. The sender can also pay an additional fee for a return receipt that verifies the certified mail delivery. Illus. 11-10 shows a receipt for certified mail and a return receipt that can be requested for either certified or registered mail.

Special Delivery. Mail marked *SPECIAL DELIVERY* will be handled promptly by the post office. Mail sent special delivery will be delivered beyond the hours of regular mail delivery. At large post offices, special delivery mail is delivered even on Sundays and holidays. The special delivery service may not be available in some rural postal areas.

COD Mail. You may send letters or parcels by COD (collect on delivery) mail. The cost of the item plus the postage will be collected on delivery by the letter carrier. Merchandise cannot be sent by COD mail unless it has been ordered by the recipient or unless an agreement has been made between the sender and addressee. The maximum amount collectible on one package cannot exceed $400, and you may request that the package be delivered to a specific person. Mail that is sent COD is insured against loss. Only first-, third-, and fourth-class mail can be sent COD.

Insured Mail. You can obtain payment for mail that has been lost or damaged if you have it insured through the Postal Service. Third- and fourth-class mail can be insured for a maximum of $400. The post office will issue you a receipt for the item to be insured. If an insured item is lost or damaged, you will receive payment in the

```
P 379 830 294
RECEIPT FOR CERTIFIED MAIL

NO INSURANCE COVERAGE PROVIDED—
NOT FOR INTERNATIONAL MAIL

(See Reverse)
```

Sent to	
Street and No.	
P.O., State and ZIP Code	
Postage	$
Certified Fee	
Special Delivery Fee	
Restricted Delivery Fee	
Return Receipt Showing to whom and Date Delivered	
Return Receipt Showing to whom, Date, and Address of Delivery	
TOTAL Postage and Fees	$
Postmark or Date	

PS Form 3800, Feb. 1982

CERTIFIED
P 379 830 294
MAIL

UNITED STATES POSTAL SERVICE
OFFICIAL BUSINESS

SENDER INSTRUCTIONS
Print your name, address and ZIP Code in the space below
• Complete items 1, 2, 3, and 4 on the reverse
• Attach to front of article if space permits,
  otherwise affix to back of article
• Endorse article 'Return Receipt Requested'
  adjacent to number

U.S. MAIL®

PENALTY FOR PRIVATE
USE, $300

RETURN TO

_____
(Name of Sender)

_____
(Street or P.O. Box)

_____
(City, State, and ZIP Code)

Illus. 11-10
Receipt for certified mail and return receipt for certified or registered mail

amount of your insurance. You can also request that a return receipt be mailed to you when the insured item has been delivered.

Certificate of Mailing. A certificate of mailing is a receipt showing that a piece of mail has been received by the post office. The sender fills in the information required on the certificate, attaches the appropriate postage, and hands the certificate to the postal clerk with the piece of mail. The clerk cancels the postage and hands the certificate back to the sender as evidence that the piece of mail was received at the post office. A small fee is charged by the post office for handling the certificate.

Recall of Mail. Mail that has been deposited at a post office or in a collection box can be recalled by the sender. You must notify the post office from which the item was mailed as quickly as possible. You will be asked to complete a form entitled *Sender's Application for Recall of Mail,* and you must provide proper identification to prove that you are the sender. Expenses incurred for the recall of the item will be charged to you. Illus. 11-11 shows the form required for recalling deposited mail.

```
U.S. POSTAL SERVICE
SENDER'S APPLICATION FOR RECALL OF MAIL

Postmaster: Please intercept and return to me the mail described below:

□ LETTER         □ EXPRESS MAIL      □ APPROX. SIZE _____      □ REGISTERED NO. _____
                                                                 □ CERTIFIED NO. _____
□ PACKAGE        □ SPECIAL DELIVERY  □ COLOR _____             □ INSURED NO. _____
□ OTHER                              □ POSTAGE $ _____         □ C.O.D. NO. _____
  (Describe) _____                                             □ EXPRESS MAIL NO. _____

HOUR MAILED  A.M.   DATE MAILED    WHERE DEPOSITED    TIME APPLICATION  A.M.    DATE FILED
             P.M.                                     FILED             P.M.
REASON FOR RECALL OF MAIL


                        FACSIMILE LETTER, ADDRESS, OR ADDRESS LABEL

ADDRESS              _____        □          □               □
                     _____        ADHESIVE   POSTAGE         OTHER
□ HANDWRITTEN             (Return address)           STAMP      METER STAMP

□ TYPEWRITTEN        Name _____

   OR                Street and Number _____

□ OTHER (Describe)   Post Office _____

_____      State and ZIP Code _____

      I deposit herewith $ _____ to pay for all expenses incurred for telegrams, postage, etc., if
necessary, and will deliver to you cover of the mail so returned.

SIGNATURE OF APPLICANT (If signed as agent, include title and   APPLICANT'S ADDRESS      TELEPHONE NO.
firm)

       APPLICATION RECEIVED BY (Name of employee)        HOUR RECEIVED  A.M.   DATE RECEIVED
POST-                                                                   P.M.
MASTER
PORTION TELEPHONED TO              COPIES TO              RETURNED BY (Name of employee)
ONLY

                        INSTRUCTIONS TO DELIVERY OFFICE

     Please return the above-described mail to this office, if
found, or state on reverse of this form the action taken.

     Reply should be addressed to:                       ➡


    (Postmaster)                   (City, State and ZIP Code)

To:                                                      RECEIPT OF SENDER
                                                         DATE

                                                         NAME

                                                         ADDRESS


PS Form 1509
Jan. 1978                                                ✩ U.S. GOVERNMENT PRINTING OFFICE: 1981—751-385/106
```

Illus. 11-11
Form for recalling mail

The Postal Service and Electronic Mail

The Postal Service provides ways to transmit mail in addition to the conventional means described previously. The following services are offered by the Postal Service to help speed the delivery of mail.

Mailgrams. The Mailgram is the result of a service offered jointly by the Postal Service and Western Union. Mailgram messages are transmitted by the wire facilities of Western Union to any address

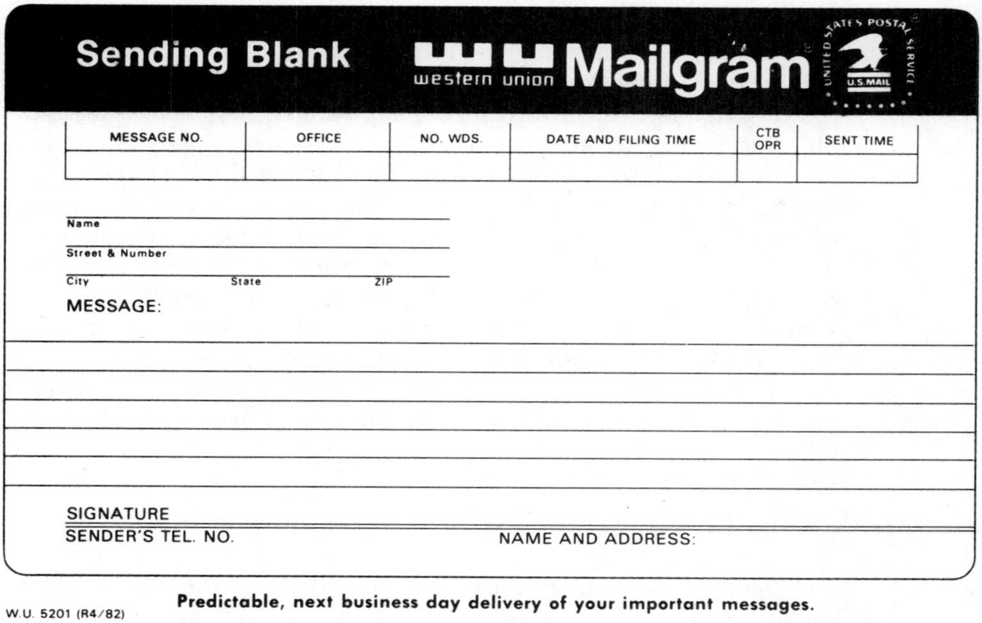

Sending Blank western union **Mailgram** UNITED STATES POSTAL SERVICE U.S. MAIL

MESSAGE NO.	OFFICE	NO. WDS.	DATE AND FILING TIME	CTB OPR	SENT TIME

Name

Street & Number

City State ZIP

MESSAGE:

SIGNATURE

SENDER'S TEL. NO. NAME AND ADDRESS:

W.U. 5201 (R4/82)

Predictable, next business day delivery of your important messages.

Illus. 11-12
Mailgram

in the United States for delivery the next business day. After the local Western Union office receives the message, it is sent electronically to the destination post office for delivery to the addressee. Western Union installs in certain post offices equipment that receives messages on a continuous roll of paper. A post office employee tears off the message, inserts it in a window envelope, and distributes it for delivery with the next morning's mail.

Electronic Computer Originated Mail. The newest service offered by the Postal Service is a system whereby messages are transmitted by computer. *Electronic Computer Originated Mail,* referred to as E-COM, allows a business to generate mail without using regular mail-handling procedures. E-COM messages can be sent 24 hours a day, seven days a week. Messages may not be more than two pages. E-COM service accepts messages in three different formats. *Variable messages* are those in which a unique text accompanies each address. *Common messages* are those in which a common text is accompanied by a list of addresses. *Personalized messages* have a common text accompanied by a list of addresses along with a unique message that is to be inserted in each printed message.

Certain post offices are designated as *Serving Post Offices* (or SPOs) to receive messages from the computers of client companies.

Under the E-COM system, a special transmission link sends computerized messages from the client company to one of several specially equipped Postal Service regional centers. The electronically transmitted message is transformed at the regional centers into a letter, a billing statement, an advertisement, or a notice. These documents are then inserted into special envelopes and marked with the proper postage for delivery by letter carriers. The Postal Service promises delivery within two business days anywhere in the 48 contiguous states.

A business must be certified in order to transmit messages to a Serving Post Office for E-COM preparation. Certification involves submitting sample messages prepared in the proper format. Postal E-COM personnel will determine whether the messages are appropriate for E-COM transmission and whether the necessary equipment connections are available between the client companies and Serving Post Offices.

Special Mailing Privileges

Special mailing privileges are provided by the Postal Service to certain mailers. You should be familiar with these special mailing privileges. More specific information about these services can be obtained from your local post office.

Overseas Military Mail. Our country has armed forces personnel stationed overseas. Mail sent to them is addressed to an Army Post Office (APO) or a Fleet Post Office (FPO) number. The city used in the address is the place from which the mail enters and exits our country. All mail is handled according to the standards for delivery from the post office. Be sure to type the city and country in all capital letters for mail you are sending out of the United States.

United States military personnel stationed in a foreign country that has been declared by the Department of Defense to be a combat zone can send mail to the United States free of charge. The words *FREE POSTAGE* must be written in the upper right-hand corner where the stamp would normally be placed. If the area has not been declared a combat zone, all mail must bear the proper postage.

Official Mail. United States government offices and officials send two types of official mail without affixing postage. The following is an explanation of the two types of mail.

Our laws permit members of Congress to send mail to their constituents without prepaying the postage. The correspondence that Congressional members send must relate to official government business. Instead of placing a stamp on the envelope, the sender's written signature or a stamped signature is placed in the upper right corner.

Mail sent by Congressional representatives and other authorized officials in this manner is called *franked mail.*

Postage for franked mail is paid quarterly in a lump sum to the Postal Service. Post offices serving the district offices of members of Congress and other Congressional officials entitled to use the franking privilege record the number of pieces of originating franked mail, the dollar value of fees for originating the special service, and the postage due.

Mail that is sent from offices of the federal government pertaining to official business is called *penalty mail.* Penalty mail is used by the executive and judicial branches of the government as well as other departments and agencies of the United States. Official government correspondence is sent in envelopes marked "Official Business—Penalty for Private Use" below the return address of the department or bureau sending the piece of mail.

Mail for the Handicapped. Materials that are for the use of the blind, or others who cannot read regularly printed matter, can be mailed free of charge. Individuals must be certified as unable to see normal reading material. Certain other restrictions may apply, so you may need to check with the local post office for further details.

International Mail

International postal service falls into two categories—postal union mail and parcel post. The following is an explanation of each classification of international mail.

Postal Union Mail. *LC Mail* (letters and cards) and *AO Mail* (other articles, such as printed matter, small packets, and the like) are the two categories of postal union mail. The postage for letters and cards mailed to Canada and Mexico is the same as for the United States. To other countries the rates are higher. Rates on letters to foreign countries are charged at a fixed rate for a half ounce (except to Canada and Mexico where rates are the same as in the United States—one ounce basis for a fixed rate).

Parcel Post. The Postal Service ships packages to foreign countries by two different methods: air parcel post and surface parcel post. Air parcel post ensures delivery in 10 days or less. Surface parcel post items are sent by boat and may take up to two months for delivery. Packages to be sent overseas by parcel post should be packed carefully and must be accompanied by a customs declaration document that describes the package's contents. Since rates, weight limitations, and other regulations vary from country to country, the secretary should obtain information from the post office about requirements for a particular shipment.

Philatelic and Other Postal Services

The Postal Service provides products and assistance to those people interested in collecting stamps. Philatelic products such as guides to stamp collecting, starter stamp collecting kits, all United States stamp issues, and annual mint sets of all the commemorative stamps issued in a given calendar year are offered for purchase.

Mail bags (often referred to as Jiffy Bags) can be purchased at your post office to use when sending items that would otherwise have to be boxed and wrapped. The post office also provides free adhesive stickers to place on outgoing mail or parcels that will call attention to special handling instructions.

Money orders in any amount up to $500 can be purchased from your post office. Money orders can be cashed at any bank or post office and are payable up to 20 years from the original day of issue. Money orders that are sent through the mail will be replaced by the Postal Service if they are lost or mutilated.

The Postal Service wants to assist its customers so that their mail will be handled efficiently and expeditiously. Therefore, free brochures and pamphlets are offered to help companies and individuals prepare their mail properly.

Postal representatives will visit companies at no cost to provide assistance on how to establish procedures for handling large volumes of mail. Training can also be offered to mail room employees free of charge. Postal representatives can point out how businesses can save money on postage.

When a company sends out a very large mailing to a few destinations, the post office may send a vehicle to the company to pick up the mailing. The Postal Service will also provide supplies such as mail trays, labels, and rubber bands to mailers who presort outgoing mail.

USING SHIPPING SERVICES

There are many common carriers that transport parcels or packages. The term *common carrier* refers to express agencies, railroads, trucking companies, airlines, and steamship companies. Every carrier does not serve all locations. Each carrier has its own standards of delivery and restrictions on the size of the parcels it will deliver. Services and costs vary greatly; so be sure to state clearly your needs when contacting a shipping service. Specify what is to be sent, the time requirements that must be met, and then allow the shipper to suggest solutions.

Express Shipments

Private carriers, such as United Parcel Service (UPS), Federal Express, and others deliver packets and packages from the shipper's door to the recipient's door. Look in the Yellow Pages of your local telephone directory under express and transfer services, messenger services, or delivery services for companies that specialize in the prompt delivery of materials. Each service has certain rules relating to the size, weight, shape and types of materials that they will handle. By calling the various shipping services, you can locate the services most suitable for your company's shipping needs.

United Parcel Service delivers packages throughout the United States. This carrier is not owned or operated by any agency of the United States government. UPS handles packages much like those that can be sent by fourth-class (parcel post) mail. Parcels are limited to 70 pounds per package and a combined girth and length of 108 inches. If a UPS driver is unable to make a delivery the first time, the driver will try twice more before a notice is given to pick up the package at a local UPS office. Their fastest delivery is known as *UPS 2nd Day Air*, and it ensures delivery within two days.

Federal Express offers free pickup service of letters and packages up to 70 pounds. The overnight letter can be placed in a special envelope for guaranteed delivery by 10:30 a.m. the next day. This letter may not exceed 10 pages of correspondence. Federal Express shipments must be made to specific locations. No shipments can be made to post office numbers. Federal Express operates its own fleet of vans and airplanes for the quick delivery of important documents and packages.

Arrangements can also be made with local offices of airlines, Amtrak, and bus lines for the transportation of packages. You must take the package to the shipping station and present the package well in advance of the scheduled departure time. Greyhound, for example, offers guaranteed 24-hour delivery service from one of its stations to any other station within a 500-mile radius.

Freight Shipments

Freight is generally considered to be a shipment sent by any method other than mail or express. If the company for which you work is involved in shipping products in large quantities, it will probably have a shipping department that handles freight. Still, you may be responsible for doing some paperwork involving the shipment of freight.

Methods of Shipping. Freight can be transported by rail, water, air, or truck. Freight is used for sending heavy, bulky goods in large quantities. Services and rates vary according to the type, quantity, weight, size, and destination of the merchandise being shipped. Goods are often shipped by freight because it is the most economical means. Water freight is usually cheaper than any other means of transportation, although the most expensive form of freight transportation, air freight, has grown in popularity. Air transportation provides fastest delivery. The high cost of air freight is partly offset by lower warehouse costs. If merchandise can be delivered quickly, not as much merchandise inventory must be kept on hand.

The Port Authority
of New York and New Jersey

Illus. 11-13
Shipping by freight is an economical way to transport heavy, bulky goods in large quantities. Water freight is usually the cheapest means of freight transportation.

Bills of Lading. A *bill of lading* (a written account of goods shipped) is the document that establishes a contract for goods to be shipped by a freight carrier. Either a straight bill of lading or an order bill of lading must be prepared for every shipment of freight.

A *straight bill of lading* is used for goods that are being shipped on open account; that is, the goods will not be paid for until after the merchandise has been received. An *order bill of lading* is prepared when a bank at the city where the goods are being shipped collects the amount due. The bill of lading with an attached *draft* (a written order for a certain amount of money) is sent by the seller to the bank in the town of the buyer. Once the freight has been paid for by the buyer, the bank gives the bill of lading to the buyer. The buyer gives the bill of lading to the freight carrier to obtain possession of the shipment. The freight carrier then delivers the merchandise to the buyer.

International Shipments

Many large companies ship freight to foreign countries. Foreign shipments can be transported by surface (ship) or air. Specific documents such as customs declaration, ocean bill of lading, or certificate of origin must be prepared in order to ship products abroad. You can obtain detailed information regarding international shipments from export companies or airlines that handle international cargo.

PROFESSIONAL POINTERS

These suggestions will help you with some of the special problems you may encounter in processing mail.

1. When mailing coins, tape the coins to a small card.

2. If you must mail a small amount of currency, fold the bills inside a sheet of paper. It is unwise, however, to mail money.

3. If you accidentally open confidential mail, write *OPENED BY MISTAKE* on the envelope before giving it to the addressee.

4. First-class mail may be forwarded by writing the new address on the envelope.

5. Second-, third-, and fourth-class mail may be forwarded, but additional postage is required.

6. Mail may be retrieved from the post office after it has been mailed by filling out the necessary form.

7. If mail has been lost, you can ask the post office to trace it.

8. If your company changes its address, fill out a change-of-address card available at the post office.

9. To help with your mailing procedures, you may purchase the *Domestic Mail Manual* from the Superintendent of Documents, U.S. Government Printing Office, Washington, D.C. 20401.

10. Packages should be wrapped and taped or tied securely enough to withstand frequent handling. If the contents are easily breakable, the package should be marked *FRAGILE*.

11. If stamped envelopes or cards purchased from the post office become damaged, you can exchange them for usable ones at your local post office.

12. Letters undeliverable as addressed and bearing no return address are sent to one of twelve dead letter offices throughout the United States. Authorized personnel in the dead letter office may open this mail, and if an address of the sender can be determined, the mail will be returned to the sender with postage due.

FOR YOUR REVIEW

1. List the five steps in handling incoming office mail.

2. What does annotating incoming mail mean?

3. Explain the purpose of a routing slip.

4. List the five steps to follow in preparing outgoing mail.

5. How can postage be paid for outgoing mail?

6. Explain the six classifications of domestic mail service offered by the Postal Service.

7. What services are offered by the Postal Service that enable mail to be handled in a special way?

8. State the purpose of a return receipt.

9. Name two electronic mail services provided through the Postal Service.

10. Name and explain three special mailing privileges.

11. Identify four ways that parcels can be shipped.

12. Name a special document that must accompany international shipments.

CASE PROBLEM

Rodger Boestic has been working as a secretary for two months for Mr. G. E. Griffin of Elrod Engineering Corporation. The business is small and Rodger is the only secretary in the office. The atmosphere at Elrod is warm and friendly. Rodger likes his job and enjoys working for Mr. Griffin. Rodger has one concern, however.

Since the business is small, there is no mail room. Rodger is responsible for processing the incoming and outgoing mail. He keeps a supply of stamps in his desk. One morning when he came to work, he found John Knowles, one of the engineers, getting some stamps from his desk drawer. When Rodger walked in, John said, "I forgot to buy stamps, and I need to mail these letters today. I'm borrowing four stamps from you; I'll repay you." Since then other employees have asked for stamps on several occasions, always with the remark, "I'll pay you back." But they never do.

Rodger has loaned employees a total of $20 worth of stamps during the last month. He doesn't think that Mr. Griffin knows the employees are using company stamps. But he doesn't want to cause trouble for anyone.

1. What should Rodger do in this situation? Should he refuse to give stamps to the employees? Should he ignore the whole situation?

2. Should he tell Mr. Griffin what is going on?

PRODUCTION PROJECTS

PP 11-1

(Objective 1)

Melanie Wong, the receptionist, is sick today, and you will be covering the front desk and handling her routine duties. One of these duties is to receive the morning mail for Mr. Frank Jamison, the company president, which is delivered at 9:30 a.m. (Assume that today is May 29.) Here is a list of the mail received.

1. The current edition of *Newsweek* magazine

2. A Mailgram dated May 28 to Mr. Jamison from the company's lawyer, Katherine Hill, regarding the Tupernic merger

3. A billing statement from an advertising company that recently did some work for the company

4. A certified letter dated May 27 to Mr. Jamison from Howard Doe of Chemsearch Corporation

5. The annual report for First City Bank for which Mr. Jamison is a stockholder

6. A sales catalog from an office furnishings store

7. A small package addressed to Mr. Jamison from his daughter Ann that has been insured and marked *PERSONAL*

8. A special delivery letter to Mr. Jamison from William Schmidt of Bangston Industries with a requisition for parts dated May 28 (No requisition was enclosed, however.)

List the important mail on the mail log in your Supplies Inventory. Also, annotate the two letters found in your Supplies Inventory. On a plain sheet of paper type your plan for sorting the mail to be placed on Mr. Jamison's desk.

PP 11-2

(Objective 2)

Type a letter to Mr. Howard Doe of Chemsearch Corporation from Mr. Frank Jamison thanking him for the contract to develop computerized monitoring systems for their assembly lines. Tell Mr. Doe that there is an error in the production cost figure in his letter. The proposal stated that production of the first monitoring system would cost $3,100, but Mr. Doe's letter stated $3,200 as the production cost. Also, tell Mr. Doe that the system will be completed within the 120-day deadline.

Use the letterhead stationery in your Supplies Inventory, and type an envelope in the proper format. Send the letter by special delivery mail so that no delay in delivery occurs.

PP 11-3

(Objective 3)

You are given the following items to be sent in the outgoing mail. Explain what type mail service you will use in sending these items.

1. A copy of *The Office* to be sent to Ms. Hilda McInnis in Oklahoma City

2. A letter to be sent to Mr. Ralph Walton, Pine Bluff, Arkansas

3. A book to be sent to Carter Electronics (The book weighs 18 ounces.)

4. A letter to Miss A. M. Andruss of Ames Company (You will need proof that Miss Andruss receives the letter.)

5. A circuit board worth $180 to be sent to Supreme Corporation

6. A contract to build a prototype of a process control unit for the assembly line of Eldridge Company

7. An important letter to Mr. H. N. Noel of Columbus, Ohio, that must reach him as quickly as possible

8. A check for $200 to be sent to Mr. Earl Cabel, president of the local chapter of AMS

PP 11-4

(Objective 4)

Yesterday (May 11) you mailed a contract for Mr. Robertson, your employer. The office mail had been collected; so you put the contract (with 40 cents postage) in the collection box on the corner of Franklin and Main Streets on your way home at 5 p.m.

The contract was addressed to Randolph Construction Co., 2314 Stafford Court, Richmond, Virginia 23224-2088. The contract was to authorize construction of a new wing of your office building. The contract was mailed in a 12 1/2-by-9 1/2-inch manila envelope with an address label. The mailing had no dollar value.

When you arrived at work this morning, you found the copy of the completed contract lying on your desk *unsigned*. In order to avoid an embarrassing situation between Mr. Robertson and Randolph Construction Co., you decide to recall the mailed contract.

The mail room attendant has given you the proper form that should be completed to recall mail. Complete the form in your Supplies Inventory with the information that you have. When you called the post office, you were told that it would cost approximately $2 to cover the expenses of recalling the contract. You will need to take the form, the money, and proper identification of yourself to the post office as soon as possible.

PP 11-5

(Objective 5)

Assume that you have a package that must be sent to someone in the town or city approximately 150 miles from where you are located. The package weighs 50 pounds and must be delivered before 5 p.m. tomorrow.

Identify the methods of shipment available to you in your locality. Determine which method would be the most economical and still deliver your package in the required time. State what the cost will be to send your package. Record your findings on a sheet of plain paper.

PART 4
Administrative Support Responsibilities—When and How Do You Provide Assistance?

Chapter 12   **Using Reference Sources and Preparing Reports**

Chapter 13   **Assisting in Meeting and Conference Preparation**

Chapter 14   **Providing Financial Assistance**

Chapter 15   **Making Travel Arrangements**

Chapter 12

USING REFERENCE SOURCES AND PREPARING REPORTS

Secretaries today are expected to be proficient in the mechanical preparation of business reports and, equally important, in assisting the executive in researching and compiling the information for reports. Secretarial duties may include (1) researching information at the company or public library, (2) preparing note cards, (3) assisting with the rough draft preparation of the report, (4) making the necessary revisions, and (5) typing the final report.

General Objectives

Your general objectives for Chapter 12 are to:

1. *Become familiar with various reference sources*
2. *Use the library in finding information*
3. *Type a business report that contains footnotes*
4. *Prepare and type an outline, a bibliography, tabulated material, and graphs*

IDENTIFYING REFERENCE SOURCES

"My secretary is a walking encyclopedia," boast many executives. Obviously no one can remember everything. So what those executives really mean is that their secretaries know where to find information. As a secretary, you need to be aware of the numerous reference sources available and how to use them. Reference sources are constantly being revised and updated. Thus, as you locate information needed in your day-to-day duties or assist your employer in researching a topic, you should search for the latest information available.

Dictionaries

Dictionaries are indispensable to a secretary. You should have on your desk, or easily available, a dictionary, a shorthand dictionary, a secretarial handbook, and a telephone directory with Yellow Pages.

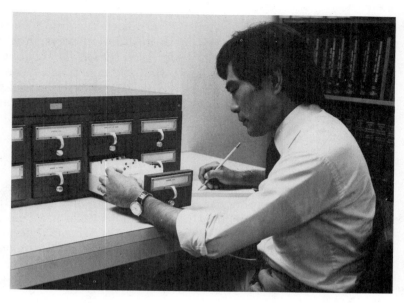

Illus. 12-1
Secretarial responsibilities may include researching and compiling information for reports.

You will find a good dictionary a valuable source of information not only for definitions, spellings, and pronunciations but also for information about syllabications, synonyms, and antonyms. Frequently a dictionary will also include an atlas or gazetteer, a list of colleges and universities, and occasionally a list of foreign words and phrases. Four recommended dictionaries are *Webster's New Collegiate Dictionary, The American College Dictionary, The American Heritage Dictionary of the English Language,* and *Funk & Wagnalls Standard College Dictionary.* Most desk size dictionaries provide the information ordinarily needed by the secretary. Some small dictionaries, however, do not give all the definitions of terms, the variations of pronunciation, or synonyms. An unabridged dictionary, which may be referred to as the final authority when questions arise, should therefore be available in every office. One unabridged dictionary is *Webster's Third New International Dictionary of the English Language.*

In addition to the dictionaries mentioned above, many specialized dictionaries are available. Some of these are *A Dictionary for Accountants; Dictionary of Personnel Management and Labor Relations; Dictionary of Computers; Dictionary of Insurance; Dictionary of Education; Black's Law Dictionary; Dictionary of Business, Finance, and Investment; Modern Dictionary of Electronics; New Dictionary of Physics;* and *Black's Medical Dictionary.*

Two additional valuable reference books are *Roget's International Thesaurus* and *Webster's New Dictionary of Synonyms.* The former is a collection of words and phrases arranged according to categories. If you need help in expressing ideas in different ways, *Roget's International Thesaurus* is a valuable aid. *Webster's New Dictionary of Synonyms* is useful when you wish to find the appropriate word to express a thought. Executives frequently find such reference books helpful in broadening their vocabularies and in providing a wide choice of words and expressions.

Almanacs and Yearbooks

Almanacs and yearbooks provide a record of notable events and statistical information, such as population and production figures. Some of the most frequently used publications are the *Information Please Almanac, Atlas, and Yearbook; The World Almanac and Book of Facts;* and the *Reader's Digest Almanac and Yearbook.*

Atlases

An atlas contains a collection of maps and statistical information regarding populations and geographic areas. The *Ambassador World Atlas* contains full-color maps with an index of world cities. The *New York Times Atlas of the World* contains, in addition to maps of every country, sections on the solar system, world energy sources, and world climates. *Rand McNally Commercial Atlas and Marketing Guide* contains geographic and economic maps of the United States and Canada. It also contains reference maps of the world. The *Oxford Economic Atlas of the World* contains topographic and economic maps and statistical information.

Government Publications

Numerous informational and statistical publications are available from the United States government. *The Monthly Catalog of U.S. Government Publications* provides a comprehensive listing of all publications issued by the various governmental departments and agencies. A semimonthly list of *Selected United States Government Publications* can be obtained free from the Superintendent of Documents.

Some of the publications available and a brief synopsis of what is contained in each are given here.

- The *Congressional Record* gives the proceedings and debates of Congress.
- The *Congressional Directory* gives the names and biographical sketches of all members of Congress.

- The *Congressional Staff Directory* publishes the names of staff personnel of the members of Congress.
- The *United States Government Manual* provides information on the purposes and programs of most government agencies and lists top personnel of those agencies.
- The *Statistical Abstract of the United States* gives statistics concerning population, climate, employment, military affairs, social security, banking, transportation, agriculture, and related fields.
- The *Guide to Foreign Trade Statistics* gives detailed records of the foreign commerce of the United States.
- The *Survey of Current Business* reports on the industrial and business activities of the United States.
- The *Monthly Labor Review* publishes labor statistics, standards, and employment trends.

Directories

You will frequently need to refer to directories of various types in your work as a secretary. Some of these directories are listed here.

City Directories. City directories, published by commercial enterprises, are available in many cities. This directory contains a listing of all residents and businesses within the city. To collect the information for the directory, the commercial enterprise goes door to door to all residences and businesses.

Ordinarily the residents and businesses are listed in three ways in the directory: (1) an alphabetic listing by name of the residents and businesses, (2) an alphabetic listing by street name of all residents and businesses, (3) a listing by the first three digits of the telephone number. If your company does not have a city directory, the local library should have a copy.

Business Directories. A general reference, *Guide to American Directories*, contains a descriptive listing of industrial, mercantile, and professional directories published in the United States. Over 300 major fields of public and private enterprise are covered.

Trade and Professional Directories. Most trade and professional associations also publish directories of members. Two references for locating associations are (1) *National Trade and Professional Associations of the U.S. and Canada and Labor Unions* and (2) *Encyclopedia of Associations*.

Biographic References

Frequently it is necessary to have more information about prominent persons than that found in ordinary business directories. *Who's*

Who in America is an alphabetic listing of notable persons living in the United States. In addition to this volume, there are a number of special volumes available, such as *Who's Who in Finance and Industry, Who's Who in American Politics, Who's Who in Electronics, Who's Who in Labor, Who's Who of American Women,* and many others. Special volumes are available according to geographic locations, such as *Who's Who in the South and Southwest.*

Reference Guides

Probably the most popular guide or index for reference reading is the *Readers' Guide to Periodical Literature.* The *Readers' Guide* is published semimonthly March, April, June, and September to December, and monthly January, February, May, July, and August. A selected list of magazines is indexed in each issue; and the articles, authors, and subject headings are cataloged alphabetically. Other periodical guides you may find helpful are the *Business Periodicals Index* and the *Index of Economic Articles.*

The New York Times Index is an index of material published in *The New York Times* newspaper, including *The New York Times Magazine.* A number of other leading newspapers publish similar indexes.

The *Cumulative Book Index* and *Books in Print* are listings of books in print in English. These indexes list each book by author, by title, and by one or more subjects. They also give the name of the publisher, the year of publication, and the price of the book. If you know the name of a book and wish to find out the name of the author or the publisher, you can obtain this information from these indexes. Similarly, if you know the name of the author, you can find out the titles of books written by that author.

There are also many special guides for reference reading. Some of these include the *Education Index,* the *Accountants' Index,* and the *Engineering Index Thesaurus.*

Financial Data

Various types of reference books are available that provide financial data and credit information. The following is a summary of some of the most popular financial reference books.

Moody's Investors Service publishes a series of books that provide financial information about all large firms and organizations in the United States, Canada, and foreign countries. Some of the publications include *Moody's Stock Survey, Moody's Bond Survey, Moody's Handbook of Common Stocks,* and *Moody's Handbook of OTC Stocks.*

Another company which publishes financial information is Standard & Poor's Corporation. Some of their publications are *Corporation Records, Daily Dividend Record,* and *Register of Corporations, Directors, and Executives.* Most public libraries and large financial institutions subscribe to some of the services offered by Moody's and Standard & Poor's.

Subscription Information Services

Managers of a company are interested in the latest information on labor, taxes, law, trade, real estate, and so forth. In order to obtain this information, companies often subscribe to services that provide specialized information on a frequent basis. These publishers usually use a loose-leaf format to keep the service up to date. Obsolete information can be destroyed and new pages easily inserted. It may be the secretary's responsibility to see that the new material is filed in the appropriate place in the loose-leaf binders. Some of the services available are listed here.

- The Bureau of National Affairs, Inc., reports government actions on management, labor, law, taxes, finance, antitrust and trade regulations, international trade, and patent law.
- The Conference Board, Inc., reports research in business economics, finance, personnel, marketing, international operations, and public affairs administration.
- Commerce Clearing House, Inc., covers such topics as federal tax, labor, trade regulation, securities, bankruptcy, trusts, and insurance.
- The *Real Estate Guide* covers all aspects of real estate operation.

Secretarial Handbooks

An extremely good general reference source for the secretary is a current secretarial handbook. Handbooks contain such information as letter styles, grammar rules, punctuation rules, postal regulations, report styles, telephone techniques, office etiquette tips, and the like. It would be to your advantage to keep a secretarial handbook on your desk for quick reference. The following is a list of a few of the available handbooks.

General Handbooks

- Esther R. Becker and Evelyn Anders, *The Successful Secretary's Handbook,* Harper & Row Publishers, Inc.
- James L. Clark and Lyn R. Clark, *How: A Handbook for Office Workers,* Kent Publishing Co.
- Clifford R. House and Kathie Sigler, *Reference Manual for Office Personnel,* South-Western Publishing Co.

- Lois Hutchinson, *Standard Handbook for Secretaries*, McGraw-Hill Book Company.
- J. Harold Janis and Margaret H. Thompson, *New Standard Reference for Secretaries and Administrative Assistants*, Macmillan Publishing Co., Inc.

Specialized Handbooks

- Myreta Eshom, *Medical Secretary's Manual*, Appleton-Century-Crofts.
- Besse Miller, *The Legal Secretary's Complete Handbook*, Prentice-Hall, Inc.
- John Smith, *The School Secretary's Handbook*, Prentice-Hall, Inc.

USING THE LIBRARY

Although many companies have their own libraries of technical materials related to their particular business, the secretary will find it necessary at times to visit the local public library or other special libraries for additional information.

If the special reference books or guides mentioned previously are not available in your office, you can usually find them at the public library. Such books often cannot be borrowed from the library but must be used there. In many instances, it is possible to get the required information by telephoning the reference department of the library.

The local chamber of commerce as well as certain professional organizations usually maintain libraries that are available to members. Most colleges and universities also have one or more libraries that may be consulted.

Finding Information

If you are not familiar with the library where you are doing research, ask the librarian to help you. He or she will gladly tell you where the reference section is located (which houses the sources referred to earlier in this chapter), explain how to use any media that you may need—microfilm readers, for example—and help you find any equipment that you may need, such as typewriters or copying machines. Once you are familiar with the arrangement and location of the materials in the library, you can work more efficiently.

Traditionally the library's index of books is located in a card file called a card catalog. Today, however, many libraries are installing other types of catalogs such as a microfiche catalog. Illus. 12-2 shows a microfiche catalog, and Illus. 12-3 shows a card catalog. The catalogs contain the title of the book, the author, a statement about the contents, and the call number by which the book is filed. The indexed information is filed in three ways: (1) by book title, (2) by author of the book, and (3) by subject classification.

Illus. 12-2
Microfiche catalog

Illus. 12-3
Card catalog

Taking Notes

Once you have located the information in the appropriate reference source, you are ready to record the data on cards or individual sheets of paper. Cards are frequently used since they are easy to shuffle and automatically control the amount of notes taken. Using large cards (4 by 6 inches or 5 by 8 inches) rather than 3-by-5-inch cards allows you to get more information on the card.

Compiling Reference Cards. Each reference card should include the reference source (author(s), title of publication, publishing information, and page reference), the topic, and the information taken from the reference source. You may also include the library call number on the reference card. Then, if you discover later that you need more information from a source, you won't have to go back to the card catalog or microfiche catalog to locate the call number. The format of a reference card may take various forms; one method of compiling reference cards is illustrated in Illus. 12-4. The information recorded may be written either as a direct quotation or as a summary statement. It is important that you specify direct quotations by enclosing the information in quotation marks. Any omissions from the original material should be indicated by ellipses (. . .).

(1)

House, Clifford R. and Kathie Sigler. Reference
Manual for Office Personnel, 6th ed. Cincinnati:
South-Western Publishing Co., 1981.

p. 180

Library call number: 651.4H175R

Business Reports

"Business reports are written to convey information in a clear, concise manner. They may be
formal or informal--but should always retain their
clarity and conciseness . . . ."

Illus. 12-4
A partial 4-by-6-inch reference card

Abstracting Articles. Many times it is necessary to abstract an article. An *abstract* is a brief summary that retains the sense of the original article. The principal aim in abstracting is to reduce the substance without distorting or changing the emphasis. When abstracting, read the entire article, looking for the core thought, the important facts, and the conclusion. Once you have determined what the author is saying, summarize it on a card or on a sheet of paper. Do not inject your own opinions or conclusions; carefully represent what the author has intended.

Illus. 12-5
When abstracting, read the entire article, looking for the important facts.

Copying Material. Most libraries provide typewriters and copying machines for a small fee. If time is extremely important to you, you may prefer to copy the material and then make any necessary notes after you return to the office. When library publications can be borrowed, you may take them to the office to type or reproduce the materials. Even if the material cannot be checked out, you may find that the library will lend you a noncirculating copy for a limited time. Libraries are eager to accommodate people and to have them take the greatest possible advantage of their facilities.

PREPARING REPORTS

As a secretary, you will play an important role in the preparation of reports. Once you have helped your employer obtain the information for a report, your next assignments are usually to type a rough draft of the report and then to prepare the final copy. In addition, it is your responsibility to edit the report for clear language, double-check the spellings and meanings of words, and double-check the accuracy of figures.

The Outline

An *outline* is a list of the important points to be covered in the report. Preparing an outline saves writing time since it provides a precise framework of the report. Although the general arrangement of the outline will vary with the type of report, the principal parts usually consist of an introduction, a body, and a conclusion. These words may not be used as such in the outline, but this design forms the basis for writing the report.

Notice the outline in Illus. 12-6. In order to type the outline properly, follow these instructions:

- *Title.* Use an appropriate title, and type it in capital letters. Center the title horizontally two inches from the top of the page. Leave a triple space after the title.
- *Main Headings.* Start main headings at the left margin and type them in capital letters. Roman numerals are used to identify the main headings.
- *First Level Subheadings.* The capital letter that identifies the first level subheading is typed under the first letter of the main heading. These headings are typed a double space below the main heading, with the first letter of important words capitalized.
- *Second Level Subheadings.* Arabic numbers are used for second level subheadings. These headings are typed a single space below the first level subheading with only the first letter of the first word capitalized.

```
                    PREPARING A BUSINESS REPORT

        I.  INTRODUCTION

            A.  Purpose of a Business Report
            B.  Role of the Secretary in Preparing a Business Report

       II.  THE OUTLINE

            A.  Using an Outline
            B.  Organizing the Information
                1.  Titles, headings, and subheadings
                2.  Parallel structure
                    a.  Definition of parallel structure
                    b.  Example of parallel structure
```

Illus. 12-6
Topical outline for a report

- *Third Level Subheadings.* Lowercase letters are used for third level subheadings. These headings are typed a single space below the second level subheading with only the first letter of the first word capitalized.

As you can see from the outline in Illus. 12-6, no main heading or subheading in an outline stands alone. For every *I*, there must be at least a *II*; for every *A*, there must be a *B*; and for every *1*, there must be a *2*. An outline can be written in topical form or complete sentence form. An outline in topical form gives only the topics or headings of the report. The sentence form uses complete sentences. If one part of the outline is in topical form, the other parts of the outline should be in topical form. The outline in Illus. 12-6 is easy to follow because each part is parallel. That is, since the first part of the outline is in topical form, the other parts follow in the same form.

The Rough Draft

When writing a report, it may be necessary to type one or more rough drafts of the report. The purpose of the rough draft is to get the writer's thoughts on paper so that they can be edited and improved. Follow these procedures when typing rough drafts:

1. Use inexpensive paper. There is no reason to use a high-quality paper, since it is going to be used as a working copy. Many executives prefer yellow paper for rough drafts, since this color is relaxing to the eyes.

2. Double-space the material and use wide margins (1 1/2 inches on both sides and at the top and bottom) to allow ample room for editing.
3. Date the rough draft in the upper or lower corner in case more than one draft is written.
4. Number each page of the rough draft for ease in handling.
5. Do not spend time in correcting errors; it is acceptable to X out errors and deletions in rough draft copy.
6. If insertions need to be made after the rough draft is typed, use separate sheets of paper to type the insertions and give them the same page number with letters added to indicate the position on the page. For example, the first insertion on page 5 should be numbered 5A and the second insertion 5B.
7. Quoted matter of four or more lines should be single-spaced and indented in the same form as it will appear in the final draft since changes are unlikely here.
8. Footnotes should be typed at the bottom of the page or on a separate sheet. They should be single-spaced and typed in correct form.
9. Make a photocopy of the rough draft in case the original is lost or misplaced.
10. Keep all rough drafts until the final draft is approved, since the writer may decide to include material from a previous draft.

Parts of the Report

A report may be formal, containing all or some of the following parts: a title page; letter of transmittal; a table of contents; an introduction; the body of the report; a list of tables, charts, and illustrations; a bibliography; an appendix; and footnotes. Or a report may be informal, containing only a title page and the body of the report. There is no one set format for typing a report; rather, there are several acceptable formats. Some companies have a preferred format for reports, which is usually detailed in the company manual. The information given here will familiarize you with the basic parts of a formal report.

Title Page. The title page contains the title of the report; the writer's name, title, and department or division; and the date the report is submitted. Each item is centered horizontally on the page. The title is typed approximately 2 1/2 inches from the top of the page in capital letters. The writer's name, title, and department or division are typed approximately 2 1/2 inches below the title, and the date is typed approximately 2 1/2 inches below the writer's identification. If the report is to be leftbound, one-half inch should be added to the left margin before horizontally centering each line. When adding one-half inch, the center point becomes 54 for elite type and 45 for pica type.

With a topbound report, an extra four to six lines should be left at the top before typing the title. Illus. 12-7 is an example of a well-balanced title page.

```
                        A BUSINESS REPORT




                               By
                      Joan Edwards, Manager
                      Accounting Department




                         April 16, 19--
```

Illus. 12-7
Title page of a report

Letter of Transmittal. Most business reports are presented to the reader with a letter of transmittal. The letter of transmittal introduces the report to the reader. The length and content of the letter will depend on the length and major subdivisions of the report.

The purpose of this letter is to help the reader understand the nature of the report and to arouse interest in studying it. The letter of transmittal may have one or a combination of the following components:

October 5, 19--

Mr. Edwin Marquez
Sun Air Conditioning, Inc.
10835 Gaston
Chicago, IL 60639-5124

Dear Mr. Marquez

The study of an information center which would have the capability of handling the correspondence and report needs of your organization has been completed.

Included in the study are a thorough survey of present correspondence and report requirements and a projection of your needs for the next three years. Also, attitudinal surveys were conducted with your executives and office support personnel. The survey results are included in the appendix of the report.

As a result of our study, we recommend that you establish an information center. Specifics as to the composition of the proposed center are included in the report. We also recommend that an evaluation of the center's effectiveness take place after six months of operation. This evaluation should include an analysis of the productivity of the center and its actual usage, along with personnel attitudes concerning the center. Our company will be happy to assist you in the evaluation of the center. We can design evaluation instruments unique to your situation at a minimum cost to you.

Thank you for giving us the opportunity to work with you on this study. Your staff was extremely cooperative. We look forward to working with you in the future.

Sincerely

Harold Eisman

Harold Eisman
Director of Research

Illus. 12-8
Letter of transmittal

1. Authorization for the report
2. Reason for the report
3. Explanation of the methods used to prepare the report
4. A general statement of the scope of the report

5. Acknowledgment of persons who contributed materials
6. Summary of the findings, conclusions, and recommendations
7. Suggestions how the report may be implemented or used
8. Other information that may assist the reader

A letter of transmittal should be typed the same as any business letter. If a letter of transmittal is to be placed in a leftbound report, one-half inch should be added to the left margin of the letter. With a topbound report, the dateline should be placed four to six lines lower on the page.

Table of Contents. A table of contents lists each major section in a report and the page number of the first page of that section. The table of contents is not required; however, when a report is long, it helps the reader find particular parts of the report. The margins used for the table of contents are the same as the margins for the remainder of the report. The title *TABLE OF CONTENTS* is typed in capital letters with a double space following the title and each major section and a single space within the section. *Leaders* (a series of periods with spaces between them) are used to help the reader follow the typed line. Illus. 12-9 shows a sample table of contents.

```
                          TABLE OF CONTENTS

                                                           Page

      I.  THE SECRETARIAL WORLD . . . . . . , ,, . . . . , . . . .    1

          A.  Defining the Secretarial Position . . . . . . .        4
          B.  Applying for a Position . . . . . . . . . . .          7
          C.  Managing Your Work  . . . . . . . . . . . . .         10

     II.  INTERPERSONAL RELATIONS . . . . . . . . . . . . .         12

          A.  Communicating . . . . . . . . . . . . . . . .         14
          B.  Developing the Office Team  . . . . . . . . .         17
```

Illus. 12-9
Table of contents

Body. The body of the report is where the facts and figures of a report are given. The body of the report should be typed in an attractive, easy-to-read style. The report may be single- or double-spaced. Double-spacing is easier to read, but single-spacing saves paper. Detailed directions for preparing the body of a report are given in the following sections.

Margins and Page Numbers. Illus. 12-10 gives the margin settings for the body of a report. The margin specifications are given for an unbound report (a staple is simply inserted in the top left-hand corner), a leftbound report (the report is bound at the left either with staples, a spiral, or other binding), and a topbound report (the report is bound at the top of the page).

It is not necessary to number the first page of a report; however, if it is numbered, the number is centered one-half inch from the bottom of the page. On leftbound and unbound reports, the second and subsequent pages are numbered one-half inch from the top of the page on line 4 at the right margin. A triple space follows the page number. On topbound reports, the page numbers are centered one-half inch from the bottom of the page.

BUSINESS REPORT MARGINS					
Type of Report	**Top**	**Bottom**	**Left**	**Right**	**Page Number**
Unbound					
First Page or Major Page Divisions	Pica: 1 1/2″ (Elite: 2″)	1″	1″	1″	None Necessary
All Other Pages	1″	1″	1″	1″	Top
Leftbound					
First Page or Major Page Divisions	Pica: 1 1/2″ (Elite: 2″)	1″	1 1/2″	1″	None Necessary
All Other Pages	1″	1″	1 1/2″	1″	Top
Topbound					
First Page or Major Page Divisions	Pica: 2″ (Elite: 2 1/2″)	1″	1″	1″	None Necessary
All Other Pages	1 1/2″	1″	1″	1″	Bottom

Illus. 12-10
Margin settings for the body of a report

Headings. The title is typed in capital letters and is centered over the line of writing. Subtitles are typed a double space below in capital and lowercase letters, followed by a triple space. If no subtitle is used, the title is followed by a triple space.

Side headings are typed at the left margin and are underlined. No terminal punctuation is used. The main words begin with a capital letter. A triple space precedes a side heading and a double space follows it.

Paragraph headings are indented five spaces, followed by a period, and underlined. Usually only the first letter of first words or proper nouns and adjectives are capitalized. Paragraph headings are preceded by a double space.

Illus. 12-11 shows various headings used in an unbound report. Read the report carefully because it contains many tips on report typing.

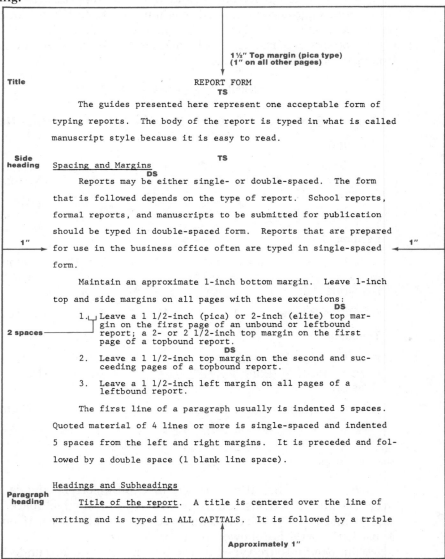

Illus. 12-11
First page of an unbound report with headings

Quotations. Material from other sources may be quoted directly or indirectly in a report. It is necessary to obtain permission to quote copyrighted material when reports are to be printed or duplicated for public circulation. If an indirect quotation is used, a footnote reference is all that is necessary. If the material is a direct quotation, it should be handled in the following manner:

1. Quotations of fewer than four lines are typed in the body of the report and enclosed in quotation marks.
2. Quotations of four or more lines are usually typed without quotation marks, single-spaced, and indented five spaces from both margins.
3. When the quotation consists of several paragraphs, quotation marks precede each new paragraph and follow the final word in the last paragraph only.
4. A quotation within a quotation is enclosed in single quotation marks.
5. Omissions are shown by *ellipses*—three spaced periods (. . .) within a sentence, four spaced periods at the end of a sentence.
6. Italicized words in the quotation are underlined.

Footnotes. Footnotes are references that cite the source of any quoted or paraphrased material for the reader. Traditional footnotes begin a single space below the last line of the typed copy at the left margin with a solid typed line 1 1/2 inches long. A double space follows the solid line, and the first line of the footnote begins five spaces from the left margin. Footnotes are single-spaced with a double space between them. Footnotes are numbered consecutively throughout the report with a superior numerical reference (raised a half line above the line of type). Illus. 12-12 shows an example of a traditional footnote.

> When tables are used to illustrate information, they should be listed on a separate sheet. This list of tables is similar to the table of contents and, in fact, the spacing of the list of tables follows exactly that used for the table of contents.[1]
>
> ―――――――
>
> [1]Clifford R. House and Kathie Sigler, Reference Manual for Office Personnel (6th ed.; Cincinnati: South-Western Publishing Co., 1981), p. 183.

Illus. 12-12
Traditional footnote

Another way of noting references is the scientific system of citation. With this system, all references are listed in alphabetical order at the end of the report with Arabic numbers assigned to each reference. Within the report, when quoted or paraphrased material is used, the reference is indicated in parentheses in the body. Illus. 12-13 shows the use of the scientific system of citation within the body of a report and the manner in which references are handled at the end of the report.

The appendix is a consolidation of examples, charts, graphs, memoranda, etc., to further support the recommendations made in the report. Each appendix item may be different in format, depending on the type of information included. As much as possible, however, the format should follow that recommended by the bibliography (3. p. 188).

REFERENCES

1. Burtness, Paul S., and Alfred T. Clark, Jr. Effective English for Business Communication, 7th ed. Cincinnati: South-Western Publishing Co., 1980.

2. House, Clifford R., and Kathie Sigler. Reference Manual for Office Personnel, 6th ed. Cincinnati: South-Western Publishing Co., 1981.

3. Johnson, Mina M., and Norman F. Kallaus. Records Management, 3d ed. Cincinnati: South-Western Publishing Co., 1982.

Illus. 12-13
Scientific system of citation

Bibliography. The bibliography identifies all sources used, quoted, or paraphrased within the report. The title *BIBLIOGRAPHY* is typed 1 1/2 inches to 2 inches from the top of the page, depending on the size of type used and whether or not the report is topbound. A triple space follows the title; each reference is single-spaced, and there is a double space between items. The first line of the reference begins at the left margin and subsequent lines are indented five spaces. When there are more than three authors, the phrase *et al* follows the name of the first author. Illus. 12-14 shows a bibliography.

Graphic Aids

Graphic aids such as statistical tables, line graphs, bar graphs, and circular graphs are frequently used in business reports to illustrate data.

BIBLIOGRAPHY

Janis, J. Harold. <u>Writing and Communication in Business</u>, 3d ed. New York: MacMillan Publishing Co., Inc., 1978.

McConnell, James V. <u>Understanding Human Behavior</u>, 3d ed. New York: Holt, Rinehart & Winston, Inc., 1980.

Popham, Estelle L., et al. <u>Secretarial Procedures and Administration</u>, 8th ed. Cincinnati: South-Western Publishing Co., 1983.

Illus. 12-14
Bibliography

Tables. Preparing statistical information in the form of tables requires knowing how to tabulate data. By this time you probably have had considerable experience in tabulating data. Tabulation is mastered only by practice. In addition to the ability to prepare tabulated material neatly, you must also know how to organize tabulated material. As a secretary to a sales manager, you may be asked to prepare tabulated figures showing sales, cost of sales, gross margin on sales, and net profit. As secretary to a purchasing agent, you may be asked to assist in preparing tabulated reports showing various costs relating to purchasing functions. As secretary to a personnel manager, you may be asked to tabulate information regarding salaries, turnover of employees, and other personnel information. You may be expected to know the fundamentals of preparing tabulated data without being given detailed explanations of how to do the job. Often it will be left to your judgment to prepare the data so that the figures will show the desired information.

For most of the tabulated material to be typed, you will find that you can use a standard typewriter. A wide-carriage typewriter may be necessary if the columned presentation of the material is unusually wide. Special attachments and devices for simplifying the typing of tabulated work are easy to obtain. For instance, a special decimal tabulating device, which is available on some typewriters, is helpful in lining up the material properly. The index key on an electric typewriter is also a helpful device. Special care should be taken to avoid errors in tabulated material. Tabulated work should be done at a time when you are free from interruptions and are not pressed for time. Concentration on getting the information in the proper column and on spacing properly can be accomplished more easily if you work without interruptions. Every effort should be made to type the work accurately the first time because tabulated work requires considerable time and is a costly procedure especially if the work must be retyped.

Titles in Tables. An appropriate title explaining the purpose and content of a table of figures should accompany the table. If a table is prepared on a separate sheet, the title may be typed either above or below the table. If the table is incorporated in the body of a report, the title is usually placed above the table. The title and the column headings in tables should be selected carefully. Column headings must sometimes be abbreviated so that the headings will fit into the columns. Although it is best to have the column headings written horizontally, it is sometimes necessary, when there are many narrow columns, to insert the column headings vertically.

Footnotes in Tables. Footnotes are sometimes necessary to explain column headings or figures used in tables. If only one or two footnotes are used, single or double asterisks are satisfactory identification. An asterisk should be placed after the heading or figure that requires explanation. The footnote giving the explanation should be preceded by an asterisk. In Illus. 12-15 an asterisk is used after the name of Mr. Caldwell to refer to the footnote, which states that Mr. Caldwell's sales were low because he worked only part-time during 1978 and 1979. If several footnotes are needed to explain information in a table, superior numbers or letters may be used. The objection to using numbers for footnotes is that if a footnote pertains to numeric data, there is a possibility that the number referring to the footnote will be confused as being part of the numeric data.

SALES BY PERSONNEL (COMPARATIVE ANALYSIS)					
Year	Ms. Joseph (No. 1)	Mr. Caldwell* (No. 2)	Miss Glass (No. 3)	Mr. Wilson (No. 4)	Total
1978	$ 22,000	$ 16,000	$ 25,000	$ 28,000	$ 91,000
1979	26,000	18,000	29,000	33,000	106,000
1980	34,000	27,000	38,000	36,000	135,000
1981	32,000	29,000	36,000	35,000	132,000
1982	28,000	30,000	38,000	40,000	136,000
1983	31,000	28,000	42,000	38,000	139,000
Total	$173,000	$148,000	$208,000	$210,000	$739,000

*Mr. Caldwell was employed on a part-time basis during 1978 and 1979.

Illus. 12-15
Table with footnote

Sometimes breakdowns of main totals are requested in listing information in a table. Illus. 12-16 shows such breakdowns. This table includes an analysis of sales by territories and states over a period of three years. In this particular instance, a territory consists of several states. The totals for the entire territory worked by a salesperson are determined by adding the totals for the individual states worked by that person.

SALES BY TERRITORIES AND STATES (CENTRAL REGION)			
Salesperson and State	Sales 1983	Sales 1982	Sales 1981
Brown			
Indiana	$ 60,550	$ 63,995	$ 59,000
Michigan	54,327	56,100	53,800
Ohio	78,641	80,763	79,045
Total	$193,518	$200,858	$191,845
Callaway			
Illinois	$ 57,462	$ 59,888	$ 56,741
Missouri	45,875	48,052	47,726
Wisconsin	48,345	51,678	50,321
Total	$151,682	$159,618	$154,788
Simpson			
Iowa	$ 52,918	$ 51,000	$ 50,025
Kansas	55,273	57,645	56,000
Nebraska	42,900	44,192	43,837
Total	$151,091	$152,837	$149,862

Illus. 12-16
Table showing breakdown of sales by territory and state

Graphs. Although statistical information and other figures prepared in tables can be interpreted rather easily if the tables are properly prepared, some information is more easily understood if it is prepared in graphs or illustrative charts. You should know how to

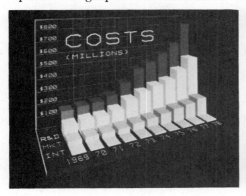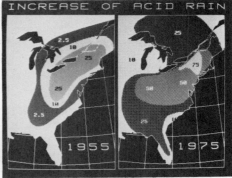

Photos courtesy of
Hewlett-Packard Company

Illus. 12-17
Today computers can produce easy-to-read graphs and charts.

interpret various kinds of graphs and know enough about the use of graphs to decide which kind can best illustrate certain information.

The most common types of graphs are line graphs, bar graphs, and circular graphs.

Line Graphs. A line graph is the most commonly used graph and is often found in business and financial magazines. *Line graphs* are generally used to indicate changes or trends over a period of time. When the trend of the line in the graph is upward, quantities or numbers are increasing; when the trend of the line in the graph is downward, quantities or numbers are decreasing. A series of line graphs can be used together to show the relationship of one factor to another. The line graph in Illus. 12-18 illustrates the figures from the table in Illus. 12-15.

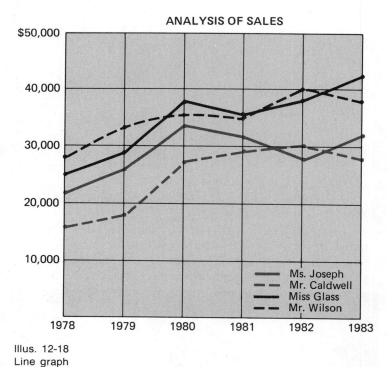

Illus. 12-18
Line graph

The best type of paper for making line graphs is graph paper. It can be purchased at most stationery stores where you will also be able to purchase other graphing supplies. If graph paper is not available, however, plain paper can be used and lines can be inserted to take the place of the main divisions found on printed graph paper.

One of the first steps in preparing a line graph is to decide what information will be shown on the horizontal scale at the bottom of the graph and what information will be shown on the vertical scale at the left side. Usually periods of time are recorded on the horizontal scale while variations in quantities or numbers are recorded on the vertical scale.

In Illus. 12-18, instead of using every other vertical line to indicate each year shown in the graph, 1978 has been moved to the extreme left-hand side of the graph, and each successive vertical line is used for the remaining years. Similarly, the horizontal scale could have been set up differently. The scale that is used, however, is satisfactory because each horizontal line represents $10,000 in sales. More horizontal lines could have been added so that each horizontal line would represent $5,000 in sales. It is important to select logical scale divisions so that the graph can be interpreted easily.

After determining the vertical and horizontal scales to be used in the graph, the next step is to *plot* the figures. For example, in plotting Ms. Joseph's sales, a small dot should be placed on the intersecting lines of 1978 and $22,000. Another dot should be placed at the intersecting lines of 1979 and $26,000. The same procedure should be followed in plotting the other figures for Ms. Joseph and for the other sales personnel. After all the figures for each salesperson are plotted, the dots are connected with a line to show the sales trend for that salesperson. Although an ordinary pen and a ruler with a metal edge can be used in drawing lines in ink, it is better to use a special ruling pen if many graphs are prepared. A ruling pen is adjustable for lines of different widths. India ink should be used in drawing lines on graphs because of its durability.

A different line should be used to represent each salesperson. Color may be used as well as a variety of dots, dashes, or solid lines. In Illus. 12-15, each salesperson is given a number. These numbers should appear on a graph prepared in one color so that anyone comparing the graph with the table of sales figures will know which line represents the sales trend of each salesperson. The key in the lower right-hand corner of the graph in Illus. 12-18 identifies the sales trend of each person by color. A key showing the name and number should accompany a graph when only one color is used.

Although the table in Illus. 12-15 gives an analysis of the sales for each person and makes it possible to compare the sales for any year or for a period of six years, the graph in Illus. 12-18 gives a better picture of the general trend of sales. In looking at the graph, you can see that over the period of six years the general trend of sales is upward in spite of the fact that sales decreased for two people and increased for the other two.

Bar Graphs. Bar graphs are generally used to show contrasts. For example, the bar graph in Illus. 12-19 compares the sales shown in the table in Illus. 12-15 for each year. The period of time is again

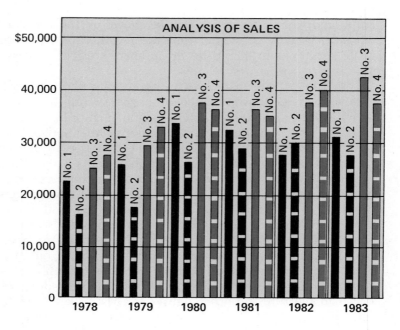

Illus. 12-19
Bar graph

charted on the horizontal line while the quantities are charted on the vertical line. This results in the bars appearing in a vertical position. The years might have been charted on the left-hand vertical scale and the sales for each on the lower horizontal scale. If this had been done, the bars would have been horizontal.

The bar graph in Illus. 12-19 shows the same information as the line graph in Illus. 12-18. It will be observed, however, that the trend of the sales for each salesperson can be observed less easily in the bar graph than in the line graph. At a glance the bar graph shows which salesperson had the highest volume in each year, but this same information can also be obtained by referring to the line graph. The use of the bar graph here points out that more than one type of graph may be used to illustrate the same information, but one type is usually preferable for the particular information. In this instance the line graph is more easily interpreted and is much easier to prepare than the bar graph.

The bar graph in Illus. 12-19 is sometimes called a *columnar bar graph*. There are also other types of bar graphs. For example, Illus. 12-20 shows a *component bar graph* that illustrates the relationship of parts to the whole. The entire column represents sales of Brunning Electronics Corporation. The sections of the graph are broken down into various parts representing manufacturing cost, selling expense,

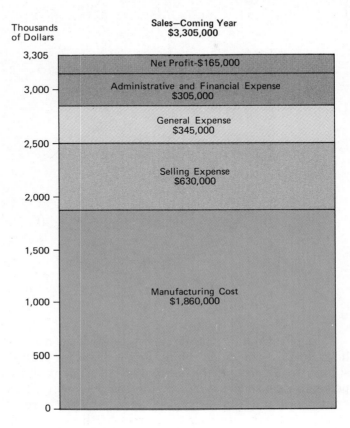

BRUNNING ELECTRONICS CORPORATION

Thousands of Dollars

Sales—Coming Year
$3,305,000

Net Profit-$165,000

Administrative and Financial Expense
$305,000

General Expense
$345,000

Selling Expense
$630,000

Manufacturing Cost
$1,860,000

Illus. 12-20
Component bar graph

general expense, administrative and financial expense, and net profit. In a component bar graph, extreme care should be exercised in marking off each component segment so that the column is divided into the proper proportions.

Circular Graphs. *Circular graphs*, sometimes called *pie charts*, are especially valuable in illustrating percentages or the relationship between parts and the whole. In a circular graph, the complete circle represents the whole, and the divisions within the circle represent the parts. A typical circular graph is shown in Illus. 12-21. Usually in preparing a circular graph, it is desirable to show in the various sections the percentage of each section to the whole. Illus. 12-21 shows the percentages of costs and profit in relation to sales. This circular graph is based on the same figures used in the component bar graph in Illus. 12-20.

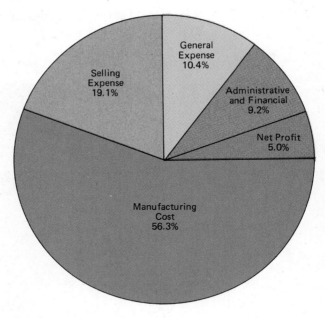

Illus. 12-21
Circular graph

In constructing the circular graph, it is necessary to determine how much of the circle should be set aside for each division. The first step is to determine the percentage of each part to the whole. This percentage is then used to divide the 360-degree circle into parts. By multiplying the total degrees in a circle by the percentage of each part of the circle, the number of degrees of the circle that should be allocated to each part can be determined. The table in Illus. 12-22 shows the calculations for finding the number of degrees in each section of the circular graph in Illus. 12-21.

CIRCULAR GRAPH CALCULATIONS

Classification	Amount	Percent of Sales	Number of Degrees
Manufacturing Cost.............	$1,860,000	56.3	360 × 56.3% = 203°
Selling Expense	630,000	19.1	360 × 19.1% = 69°
General Expense	345,000	10.4	360 × 10.4% = 37°
Administrative and Financial Expense	305,000	9.2	360 × 9.2% = 33°
Net Profit	165,000	5.0	360 × 5.0% = 18°
Sales........................	$3,305,000	100.0	360°

Illus. 12-22
Circular graph calculations

A device called a *protractor* is convenient in figuring the number of degrees for each part of the circular graph. Although several kinds of protractors are available, the one used in Illus. 12-23 is one of the most popular and easy-to-use protractors. This protractor covers 180 degrees or half of a circle. In preparing a circular graph with a protractor, the steps outlined below should be followed.

1. Draw the circle.
2. Insert in the circle a *radius* (a line segment extending from the center of the circle to the outer edge) to be used as a base for dividing the circle.
3. With the base of the protractor on the radius line and the middle of the protractor at the center point of the circle, measure the degrees to be allocated to the first part of the graph. Insert a dot at the edge of the protractor to indicate where the line should be drawn. With the dot as your guide, draw a line from the *circumference* (outer edge) to the center point of the circle.
4. Place the base of the protractor on the line just drawn, with the middle of the protractor at the center point of the circle, and measure the degrees for the next portion of the circle. The same procedure should be followed until the entire circle has been divided.

Illus. 12-23 shows how a protractor is placed to divide the circle used in preparing the circular graph in Illus. 12-21.

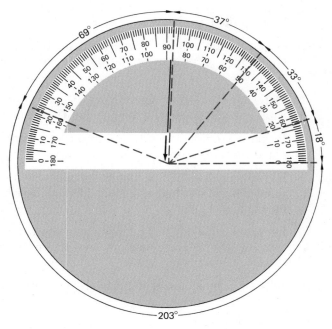

Illus. 12-23
Dividing a circle with a protractor

If a protractor is not available, the circumference of the circle should be divided into four equal parts, each part representing 25 percent. These parts may in turn be divided into halves, which represent 12 1/2 percent sections. This division plan should be followed until the size of the section desired is obtained.

PROFESSIONAL POINTERS

If you have the ability to assist your employer in researching, writing, editing, and typing reports, your worth as a secretary is enhanced. Here are some suggestions to help you become more effective in this area.

1. Become knowledgeable of the resources available to you. Ask the librarian for assistance when you begin to research a report; be certain that you are using the best and most current resources.

2. Abstract information carefully. Do not insert your personal opinions as you abstract material.

3. Carefully record reference sources on all notes that you take.

4. Enclose a direct quotation in quotation marks; it is extremely important to give credit for material which you use that has been quoted from another source.

5. Organize the report; prepare an outline first. Follow correct techniques in preparing the outline; for example, use parallel structure.

6. Determine whether the report is to be bound or unbound. Then set appropriate margins for the report.

7. Prepare a guide sheet to help you keep margins accurate and place footnotes properly on the page.

8. Review proper format before typing the report; if the company has established a certain format, be certain that you are familiar with it.

9. Decide which tables or graphs are needed to clarify the content of the report; use an attractive format in preparing tables or graphs.

10. Edit the report for grammatical correctness and proper use of words.

11. Double-check the accuracy of any figures in the report.

12. Proofread the report carefully; if the report is technical, it is a good idea to get a second person to proofread it with you.

FOR YOUR REVIEW

1. In order to obtain the following information, which reference source will you use if you
   a. Need help in expressing an idea
   b. Wish to improve your choice of a word
   c. Wish to employ maps of the United States with population figures of selected areas
   d. Need the name of a member of Congress from your area
   e. Need information on a prominent person
   f. Need financial information on stocks and bonds
   g. Need information on letter styles

2. Explain what information should be on a reference card.

3. What does abstracting mean? How is it used?

4. Explain how an outline is typed.

5. What margins should be used on leftbound, unbound, and topbound reports?

6. Where is the page number typed on reports?

7. How should quoted material of fewer than four lines be treated?

8. How should a bibliography be typed?

9. What do line graphs indicate?

10. When are bar graphs generally used?

CASE PROBLEM

Sylvia Myers worked for Mr. Albert Ector, president of Stanolind Oil Company, for seven years. Mr. Ector retired six months ago and was replaced by Mr. Jose Perez. Sylvia has had difficulty adjusting to her new employer. According to Sylvia:

"Mr. Ector and I worked very well together. As Mr. Ector's secretary, I assumed a great deal of responsibility. I answered much of his correspondence, prepared reports, assisted in doing research on new projects, kept personal financial records, and so on. Naturally I know the company procedures well, and I can almost run the president's office by myself after being in this position for seven years. In fact, Mr. Ector used to tell me that I knew as much about the company and his job as he did. I admired and respected Mr. Ector as president, and he admired and respected my ability as secretary.

As much as I hated to see Mr. Ector retire, I knew it was best for him; and I was looking forward to working for Mr. Perez. Mr. Perez came to Stanolind Oil from Sunshine Oil Company (he had been a vice-president there). I have tried to be helpful and show him the ropes. I have told him how Mr. Ector handled the job. Unfortunately he doesn't seem to appreciate my efforts and wants to change just about everything. When I tell him how Mr. Ector handled a job, he always thanks me but then informs me that he intends to do it his way (which is always different). I am beginning to think Mr. Perez does not like me and does not think I know how to do anything. What should I do? Should I ask for a transfer to another department? Or should I look for a job in another company?"

1. What do you regard as Sylvia's shortcomings?

2. In what way is Mr. Perez at fault?

3. How can the situation be remedied?

PRODUCTION PROJECTS

PP 12-1
(Objectives 1 and 2)

Prepare a table of the fifty largest cities in the United States as of 1980. List them alphabetically by city. List the city and state; give the 1980 and 1970 population figures; list each city's ranking in the top fifty. Provide an appropriate title, and type the table in proper form.

PP 12-2
(Objectives 1 and 2)

Your employer has discovered that the secretaries in your office frequently misuse words. You have been asked to help clarify the correct usage. Look up the definition for each of the following words; then type each word, followed by a brief definition.

1. bail	10. personnel	18. less
2. bale	11. principle	19. effect (noun)
3. core	12. principal	20. effect (verb)
4. corps	13. compare	21. affect (verb)
5. accept	14. contrast	22. correspondents
6. except	15. continual	23. correspondence
7. formerly	16. continuous	24. practical
8. formally	17. fewer	25. practicable
9. personal		

PP 12-3

(Objectives 1 and 2)

Using an almanac or similar reference source, look up the following information and type your answers on a sheet of plain paper.

1. Who are the two United States senators from your state?

2. List the United States representatives from your state.

3. Give the names of the presidents of the United States who served from 1940 to the present. After each name indicate whether he was a Republican or a Democrat and the years he served as president.

4. Who was secretary of the Treasury when Jimmy Carter was president of the United States?

5. Which teams played in the baseball World Series in 1980? How many games were played?

6. How much did the public debt of the United States increase from 1930 to 1980?

7. What were the occupations of employed women as of 1980? Give the percentage of women employed in each occupation.

8. Name the county seats of the following:
   a. Houston County, Georgia
   b. Logan County, Colorado
   c. Alameda County, California
   d. Marion County, Illinois
   e. Erie County, New York
   f. Lehigh County, Pennsylvania

9. What is the birthstone for the month of May?

10. What is the lowest point in altitude in the United States?

PP 12-4

(Objective 3)

Your Supplies Inventory contains a rough draft of a short report that your employer prepared for the local chapter of the Administrative Management Society. Use plain paper to type an original and a carbon copy of the report. Make the corrections indicated.

PP 12-5

(Objective 4)

Using a reference source, prepare and type an outline on the subject *How to Type a Business Report.*

PP 12-6

(Objective 4)

Here is a list of reference books on how to succeed on the job. Use a plain sheet of paper and arrange the references as a bibliography.

The Executive's Guide to Finding a Superior Job, William A. Cohen, AMACOM, 1978, New York

Making It on Your First Job: When You're Young, Inexperienced & Ambitious, Peggy J. Schmidt, New York, Avon Books, 1981

Women on Top, Jane Adams, New York, Berkley Publishing Corporation, 1981

Getting What You Want, J. H. Brennan, New York, Stein & Day, 1977

Survival in the Office: How to Move Ahead or Hang On, Andrew J. DuBrin, Van Nostrand Reinhold Company, New York, 1977

Fast Track: The Super Achievers & How They Make It to Early Success, Mary Alice Kellogg, McGraw-Hill Book Company, New York, 1978

PP 12-7

(Objective 4)

Prepare a table showing estimated sales and actual sales for a period of one year based on the following information.

Estimated Sales:

January, $221,000; February, $213,000; March, $244,000; April, $245,000; May, $262,000; June, $262,000; July, $249,000; August, $234,000; September, $211,000; October, $211,000; November, $218,000; December, $227,000.

Actual Sales:

January, $228,000; February, $210,000; March, $246,000; April, $258,000; May, $271,000; June, $268,000; July, $247,000; August,

$236,000; September, $221,000; October, $218,000; November, $220,000; December, $223,000.

1. Use plain paper and make two copies of the table. Hand in the original copy to your instructor and retain the carbon copy for use in PP 12-8.

2. Select an appropriate heading for the table.

3. The table should contain three columns: *Month, Estimated Sales,* and *Actual Sales.* Total the estimated and actual sales on the last line of the table.

PP 12-8

(Objective 4)

Based on the table prepared in PP 12-7, use the graph paper in your Supplies Inventory to prepare a line graph of estimated and actual sales. Use different types of lines to show the trend of sales and the estimated sales.

PP 12-9

(Objective 4)

Use the form in your Supplies Inventory to prepare a circular graph. Show the breakdown of sales from the following figures:

Cost of Goods Sold....................................... $1,971,000
Selling Expenses 470,000
General and Administrative Expenses 195,000
Net Profit from Operations 210,000
Net Sales $2,846,000

1. Net sales represent 100 percent or the entire circle. Find the percentage of the cost of goods sold, selling expenses, general and administrative expenses, and net profit from operations in relation to net sales.

2. Multiply the percentages by 360 degrees to find the number of degrees that should represent each portion of the circle.

3. Measure the portion of the circle for each classification of expense and profit. The figures on the outer edge, or circumference, of the circle will serve as a guide in measuring the circle in case you do not have a protractor.

4. Draw lines from the center point to the edge of the circle.

5. In each portion of the circle, insert an explanation of what it contains and the percentage of the whole.

Chapter **13**

ASSISTING IN MEETING AND CONFERENCE PREPARATION

The ability to relieve the executive of time-consuming responsibilities and knowing when to do so are important aspects of an efficient secretary's work. One way in which you can save your employer's time is to accept the responsibility for planning meetings and conferences. You will need to know how meetings are conducted, how minutes are prepared, and how conferences are planned. The type of meeting or conference you plan will, of course, vary according to the company in which you are employed. For example, you may be responsible for planning the following:

1. Meetings within the company, such as meetings of executives or department heads, sales meetings, meetings of office personnel, and possibly meetings of the board of directors
2. Conferences outside the company
3. Meetings of groups in which you participate as an active member

Although, at first, it is unlikely that you will attend meetings of the nature listed in 1 and 2 above, you are quite likely to be closely involved in their planning and in the preparation of the subsequent minutes. Your guidelines in these functions will probably be notes given to you by your employer. As you become more experienced in your secretarial duties and more familiar with the operation of the company, you may be expected to attend the meetings and to take an active part. It is advisable that you prepare yourself adequately.

General Objectives

Your general objectives for Chapter 13 are to:

1. *Identify the responsibilities of a secretary in planning meetings and conferences*
2. *Prepare notices for meetings*
3. *Type an agenda*
4. *Prepare minutes*
5. *Become familiar with the importance of parliamentary procedure in conducting a meeting*
6. *Identify the responsibilities of a secretary after meetings and conferences*
7. *Understand how teleconferencing is used*

INFORMAL MEETINGS OR OFFICE CONFERENCES

Many company meetings in which you will be involved will be informal. Many office conferences are informal discussions where ideas are exchanged, conclusions are reached, and recommendations are made. For example, you may be asked to set up a meeting for the next day or the next week with several managers in the company. If the meeting is the next day, the most efficient method of notifying the participants is by telephone. If the meeting is the next week, you should send a memorandum to the participants since it will serve as a written reminder of the meeting. In either case, you need to have certain information about the meeting before making any contacts. You must know where the meeting will be held, when it will start, approximately how long it will last, and the purpose. The participants must be prepared with the necessary materials or information; and, unless they know the purpose of the meeting, they cannot come prepared. If your employer does not give you the information, be certain to ask him or her before you start your calls or write the memorandum.

Your responsibilities do not end with informing the necessary participants about the meeting. You need to be sure that the room is prepared. If the meeting is held in your employer's office, see that

Illus. 13-1

© Billy E. Barnes

Many office conferences are informal discussions where ideas are exchanged and recommendations are made.

enough chairs are available. Check with your employer to make sure that all the required materials for the meeting have been assembled. It is also a courteous gesture to offer coffee or tea to the participants at the meeting. You will want to make sure that you have a coffee and/or hot water dispenser, adequate cups (most offices use disposable cups), spoons, sweetener, and cream available. You may be asked to take notes of the meeting. After the meeting, your responsibility is to type a summary of the meeting and distribute it to the participants. If procedures requiring special action have been agreed upon in the meeting, you should note these actions in your summary, specifying the individual responsible for taking the particular action.

FORMAL MEETINGS

In addition to informal meetings, executives are often responsible for various types of formal meetings. Formal meetings usually follow a definite order of business that specifies the general topics to be covered during the meeting. Every formal meeting should follow an agenda if considerable business is to be transacted or if a number of matters are to be discussed.

© Billy E. Barnes

Illus. 13-2
Formal meetings usually follow a definite order of business.

As a secretary, you will probably be of assistance in several formal meetings each year. Your responsibilities for arranging formal meetings are much broader than for informal meetings. In addition to preparing the agenda, taking minutes, and performing follow-up activities, numerous details must be worked out and taken care of before the meeting, during the meeting, and after the meeting.

Before the Meeting

The secretary has several responsibilities before the meeting. Meeting rooms must be reserved, participants must be notified, needed equipment must be obtained, and so forth. You can contribute to a company meeting by performing these functions well.

Reserve the Meeting Room. For a company meeting that is held in a conference room, a reservation to use the room should be obtained from the person or department in charge of the room. When you are given the date and time of the meeting, you should immediately check to see that a conference room is available.

If a meeting is to be held at a location outside the company, arrangements should be made well in advance. Make sure that the space reserved for the meeting has adequate facilities; for example,

- Adequate space, lighting, and ventilation
- Comfortable chairs
- Tables
- Speaker's table, lectern, or podium (if needed)
- Public address system (if needed)

Make Calendar Notations. You should mark on your calendar any notations that will assist you in organizing the details of the meeting. For example, if equipment must be obtained for the meeting, make a note on your calendar when to request the equipment so that it will be available at the appropriate time. Also, determine when you should send notices of the meeting. Do not send the notices so early that the meeting is forgotten; however, it is important that the participants receive the notice of the meeting early enough to plan for it. Once you have decided the date that the notices should be sent, make a calendar notation as a reminder. Planning ahead and making calendar notations will help you keep details straight and accomplish your duties in a timely manner.

Notify the Participants. A written notice of a formal meeting should be sent to all participants. Company participants are usually informed of a meeting by interoffice memorandum. Illus. 13-3 is an interoffice memorandum that might be sent to department supervisors announcing an office meeting. Usually the agenda for the meeting is attached to the meeting notice.

BRENTON INDUSTRIES

INTEROFFICE MEMO

TO: All Department Supervisors
FROM: Eleanor Diamond
DATE: March 5, 19--
SUBJECT: Notice of Meeting

There will be a meeting of all department supervisors Thursday, March 12, at 10 a.m. in the first floor conference room. New products will be discussed. An agenda for the meeting is attached.

If for any reason you cannot attend, please let me know as soon as possible.

ms

Illus. 13-3
Interoffice notice of a meeting

In the case of a club meeting or a meeting involving people outside the company, the secretary usually sends a letter or a postcard to each member announcing the meeting. Illus. 13-4 gives an example of a postcard announcement. A double postcard, with one part of the card used for a reply, may also be used in sending

May 15, 19--

Dear Ms. Diamond

The regular monthly meeting of Toastmasters International will be held at the Colony Inn, 620 Reading Road, on Friday, May 22, at 8 p.m.

This meeting is extremely important because of the annual election of officers.

TOASTMASTERS INTERNATIONAL

Carol Trait

Illus. 13-4
Postcard notice of a meeting

announcements of meetings. The recipient merely indicates whether or not he or she will be able to attend the meeting and mails that portion of the postcard back to the secretary. If a letter is used to announce the meeting, a reply card may be enclosed with the letter.

Prepare an Agenda. An *agenda* is an outline of procedures or the order of business to be followed during a meeting. In many companies the agenda for business meetings or meetings of the board of directors is set up in the company bylaws. Usually the participants of the meeting and the secretary have a copy of the agenda to follow during the meeting. The agenda of a meeting should follow this order of business:

1. Call to order
2. Reading of minutes
3. Treasurer's report
4. Committee reports (list committees)
5. Unfinished business (matters to be continued should be itemized)
6. New business (list matters to be considered)
7. Election and appointments of committees (may be omitted at some meetings)
8. Adjournment

Agendas are usually typed, although occasionally they may be handwritten. When typing an agenda, double- or triple-space between headings so that there will be space to insert reminders of matters to be discussed under certain sections. Illus. 13-5 shows a typical agenda.

Arrange for Materials and Equipment. Be sure that all needed materials and equipment are available. If the meeting is in a hotel, there is usually a special department to handle equipment needs. You merely inform the hotel what equipment is needed and when it is needed. The hotel will set up the equipment in the meeting room. If the meeting is in a company conference room, you may be responsible for requesting and setting up the equipment.

In planning for a formal meeting, first determine how the meeting room should be set up—conference style with tables, classroom style, or small group arrangement. Then check to see if any of the following are needed:

1. Notepaper or pencils
2. Badges for identification
3. Bulletin boards; chalkboards; easels; overhead, motion picture, or slide projectors; tape recording equipment
4. Table decorations for luncheons or dinners
5. Ashtrays, glasses, water
6. Arrangements for morning or afternoon coffee
7. Telephone in the room

```
              AGENDA FOR THE BOARD OF DIRECTORS MEETING

                               of the

            ELLIS COUNTY COMMUNITY COLLEGE DISTRICT
                       December 3, 19--

     I.   Call to Order           Michael Masterson, Chairperson

    II.   Reading of the Minutes  Lynn MacKenzie, Secretary

   III.   Treasurer's Report      Evelyn Piercey, Treasurer

    IV.   Unfinished Business

              Report from the District Foundation, Carol Shiplack
              Purchase of Land for the Job Training Center

     V.   New Business

              Acceptance of Contributions
              Purchase of Equipment
              Marketing Plans

    VI.   Adjournment
```

Illus. 13-5
Typical agenda

Prepare the Room. Once the meeting room is set up, check the room prior to the meeting to see that everything is in order. Make sure that the room is clean, that the proper number of tables, chairs, and other supplies are in the room, and that the temperature is comfortable. If you are using audiovisual equipment, such as tape recorders or projectors, be sure that the equipment is in proper working order. Checking the room before the meeting begins avoids the frustrations of improper room arrangement or malfunctioning equipment during the meeting.

During the Meeting

Your responsibility during the meeting may be to take notes or *minutes* of the proceedings. You may wish to use a tape recorder for taking notes on particular items such as the name and title of a speaker or person making a motion. You may also have other responsibilities during the meeting. For example, if a piece of equipment malfunctions, you may be responsible for obtaining a replacement; if additional information is needed, you may be responsible for getting that information.

Minutes of the Meeting. Minutes should contain a record of all important matters that are presented in the meeting. It is usually to the secretary's advantage to record all information presented at the meeting. This does not mean that you must take the minutes verbatim; you should, however, record all pertinent information. It is much easier to eliminate information that is not essential when typing the minutes than it is to try to remember information that was not recorded. Generally these items should be included in all minutes:

1. The date, time, and place of the meeting
2. The individual presiding at the meeting
3. The members present and absent
4. Approval or correction of the minutes from the previous meeting (if these minutes are read)
5. Reports of committees, officers, or individuals
6. Motions made
7. Appointment of committees
8. Items on which action needs to be taken and the person(s) responsible for taking the action
9. Adjournment of the meeting

Special Problems. Special problems sometimes occur during meetings. For example, you may have difficulty hearing or understanding a speaker. If the meeting is large, it is a good idea to prearrange some type of signal with the person presiding in case you need to have something repeated. If the meeting is small, you can verbally inform the speaker that you are unable to hear. If a motion is made and you are unsure of the person making the motion, immediately ask for the person's name. It is better to interrupt at this point than to try to find out after the meeting. People will usually not remember.

Interruptions may also occur during meetings. If the meeting is at the company, the room may not have a telephone. There are times, however, when an emergency message must be delivered to someone in the meeting. If it is your responsibility to deliver the message, do so as unobtrusively as possible. Get up quietly, answer the door, and deliver the message to the recipient. If you do not know the recipient, give the message to the person presiding. If you have several responsibilities during the meeting (such as taking notes, delivering messages, etc.), it may be necessary for you to have another office support employee from your company assist you.

Parliamentary Procedure. A knowledge of parliamentary procedure will help you in both your job and your professional activities. If you understand parliamentary procedure, you can better report a business meeting. And, as a professional secretary, you will probably become a member of a secretarial organization such as Professional Secretaries International (PSI). By understanding parliamentary law, you can assist the organization in conducting its meetings in an organized manner.

Parliamentary law has been defined as "common sense used in a gracious manner." Its purpose is to arrive at a group decision in an efficient and orderly manner. Parliamentary procedure is based on four principles:

1. Courtesy and justice must be accorded to all.
2. Only one topic is considered at one time.
3. The minority must be heard.
4. The majority must prevail.[1]

After the Meeting

Once the meeting is over, the secretary's responsibilities do not end. You must see that the minutes are prepared and distributed and that all routine follow-up duties are handled.

Prepare Minutes. Most companies have a minutes book in which the minutes of meetings are filed. It is always a good idea for the secretary to prepare a rough draft of the minutes before placing them in the minutes book. Corrections to the final draft of the minutes from the previous meeting when read before the participants should be made in red ink; changes or amendments can be written on a separate page. These changes should be initialed by the signers of the minutes. It is not necessary to file special reports originating from

[1]Estelle L. Popham et al., *Secretarial Procedures and Administration* (8th ed.; Cincinnati: South-Western Publishing Co., 1983), p. 416.

MINUTES--BOARD OF DIRECTORS MEETING
ADMINISTRATIVE MANAGEMENT SOCIETY
San Francisco Chapter
September 8, 19--

TIME AND PLACE OF MEETING

The regular monthly meeting of the AMS San Francisco Chapter Board of Directors was held on Tuesday, September 8, in the main parlor of the Regent Hotel at 6 p.m. The meeting was called to order by the President, Ronald Anderson. All fifteen members were present.

READING OF THE MINUTES

The minutes of the July meeting were approved without reading since each member had received a copy prior to this meeting. (There was no August meeting.)

TREASURER'S REPORT

The treasurer's report (copy attached), showing a balance of $1,623 as of September 1, was read, received, and filed.

UNFINISHED BUSINESS

Ronald Anderson reported that he has received acceptance from H. R. Princeton to speak at the October meeting and that all pictures and publicity items had been turned over to the Publicity Committee.

NEW BUSINESS

Application of T. A. Alexander. The application of T. A. Alexander, substituting for Harold Georgia, Jr., of the Ramsey Business Equipment Company, was unanimously approved.

Chapter Merit Award Qualifications. It was suggested that the merit award qualifications be included in the Chapter bulletin for the first week of October.

Education Teachers' Information Booklet. Copies of the education teachers' booklet, prepared by Cindy Taylor, were distributed to the Board of Directors. Many favorable comments were made about the contents of the booklet and appreciation was expressed to Cindy and to the Brown Life Insurance Company for printing the booklet.

Board of Directors Meeting   2   September 8, 19--

Speakers Bureau. Silas Stehr, chairperson of the Speakers Bureau, said that he and the Bureau are planning to increase the number of speakers at the winter seminar so that the programs can be expanded without placing too heavy a burden on those who are willing to accept speaking assignments.

Information Service Committee. Mildred Gary, chairperson of the Information Service Committee, said that she has written to the national office about the Chapter's willingness to participate in any survey proposed by the national office; so far no request has been received.

Picnic Committee. The Picnic Committee reported that 94 adults and 40 children attended the fall picnic. The cost to the Chapter was $173.85. Several suggestions for next year's outing were included in the report. The Committee will do research on these suggestions.

Publicity Committee. Percy Atwater reported that approval on the solicitation of ads for the roster and the bulletin was received. He explained that the format of the bulletin would have to be changed to accommodate the inclusion of the ads. The Board of Directors approved this action.

In Percy's complete report, which is attached to these minutes, he outlined plans to establish a business education week in November to coincide with our regular education night meeting. Also, it was suggested that a committee be appointed to take care of seminars, special study groups, etc.

ADJOURNMENT

As there was no further business, the meeting was adjourned.

Arthur M. Grant
Arthur M. Grant, Secretary-Treasurer

Illus. 13-6
Minutes of a meeting

meetings with the minutes. The reports can be filed in a special file kept by the secretary of the company.

In some instances, especially meetings of board of directors, the minutes may be duplicated and copies sent to all officers and directors.

Illus. 13–6 shows the minutes for a meeting of the Administrative Management Society. Notice how these minutes are arranged. There are other acceptable formats, however. If you are preparing minutes for a company or organization for the first time, be sure to check the minutes of previous meetings to see which format has been used. The following are general suggestions in preparing minutes.

1. Minutes may be double- or single-spaced. Margins should be at least 1 inch. If the minutes are to be placed in a bound book, the left margin should be 1 1/2 inches.
2. Capitalize and center the heading that designates the official title of the group.
3. Use subject captions for ease in locating various sections of the minutes.
4. Capitalize such words as Board of Directors, Company, Corporation, and Committee in the minutes when they refer to the group conducting the meeting.
5. At the end of the minutes provide a signature line for the secretary of the organization or the presiding officer.
6. In composing the minutes, be sure to give the following information:
   a. Include the day, date, hour, place of meeting, and name of the presiding officer in the first paragraph of the minutes.
   b. Indicate whether a quorum was present. It may be necessary to provide a list of those present and absent.
   c. Record the actions taken at the meeting. Do not include personal opinion or interpretations.
   d. Give a succinct summary of the important points on each area of discussion.
7. Strive to complete the minutes in final form within twenty-four hours after the meeting.

Perform Routine Follow-Up Duties. Although the meeting is over, your secretarial responsibilities do not end. Some of the duties you need to perform after the meeting are listed here.

1. Check the meeting room to see that it is left in good order. All equipment should be returned; ashtrays, coffee cups, etc., should be removed; tables and chairs should be restored to normal room arrangement.
2. If the room needs to be cleaned, you should notify the cleaning staff.
3. Any officers who were not present but who were given duties or assignments at the meeting should be notified.
4. Copies of the minutes should be sent out promptly.

5. Items that require future attention by you or your employer should be written on your calendar.
6. Make sure that all necessary forms are completed by participants who have incurred reimbursable expenses.
7. Letters of congratulations may be sent to newly elected officers.
8. Thank you letters should be written to speakers.
9. Any items that need to be considered at the next meeting as a result of the proceedings of this meeting should be noted for placement on the next meeting's agenda.

CORPORATION MINUTES

The conduct of a corporate meeting, a meeting of the board of directors of a corporation, or a meeting of the stockholders usually follows the form outlined in the bylaws of the corporation. Generally the recording of minutes for a corporation meeting is not greatly different from the recording of minutes previously outlined in this chapter. In preparing minutes of a corporation meeting, side headings should be used to indicate the subjects discussed. One of the duties of the secretary at a corporate meeting of stockholders is to keep a record of the proxies that are sent by stockholders who are unable to be present. In addition to copies of correspondence, two minutes books (one for stockholders' meetings and one for board of directors' meetings), and other supplies ordinarily needed by the secretary in a meeting, the following material usually is needed at a corporation meeting:

1. A copy of the corporation laws of the state in which the company is organized
2. The charter or certificate of incorporation
3. A copy of the bylaws
4. The corporation seal
5. Envelopes and stationery for any special messages that must be sent immediately

Corporate minutes may differ from minutes of rather informal groups in the following respects:

1. A detailed record of those persons present may be necessary.
2. The minutes usually give specific information about the exact time and place of the meeting, and whether it is a regular meeting or a special meeting. If it is the latter, the purpose of the meeting is also given.
3. An accurate record of those making the motions and seconding the motions must be kept.
4. Laws of the state in which the corporation is organized must be followed in conducting corporate meetings.

5. In many corporations, corrections to the minutes of the preceding meeting cannot be inserted in the original minutes but must be prepared separately and appended to the minutes.
6. Although the secretary of a corporation is responsible for keeping the minutes, his or her personal secretary may actually type the minutes and keep them so that they are available when needed.

CONFERENCES AND CONVENTIONS

A conference or convention is usually much larger in scope and number of participants than a formal meeting. For example, if a company has offices in several locations in the United States, a conference may include executives from all offices, with topics of discussion encompassing the numerous operations of the company. Many executives belong to professional organizations such as the American Management Association or Administrative Management Society. These organizations usually hold at least one convention a year that is three to five days long. At conventions a variety of programs and speakers present topics of general interest. Most companies encourage their executives to participate in conferences or conventions since they are a form of professional development. Conferences and conventions allow executives to broaden their knowledge in various fields and to learn from colleagues in other companies as well.

As a secretary to an executive, you may be involved in helping to plan a conference or convention. If so, your duties are usually varied and time-consuming. Planning a national convention, for example, takes months of work. Of course, you will not have the total responsibility for planning this type of function; but you will be involved in a number of tasks that may take many hours to complete.

Before the Conference

The planning that you do before a conference is extremely important. Good planning will assure a smooth flowing, successful conference, whereas poor planning will result in a disorganized, ineffective conference. As a secretary, you should know your role in conference planning and consider all the details carefully.

Meeting Facilities. In planning the arrangements for the meeting facility, it is important to know how many people are expected for the conference and how many people are anticipated at each session. For a large conference, it may be necessary to reserve all the meeting rooms of a hotel. Often keynote speakers at the conference draw the entire conference attendance for their presentations. You will need to know the sessions which the most conference participants are expected to attend so that a room large enough for the expected audience will be provided. Other sessions of the conference may be run *concurrently* (at the same time) with a limited number of participants expected at each session. It is your responsibility to know how many participants are expected at these sessions, too.

Your next responsibility is to determine what equipment is needed for the presentations. A large room usually requires the speaker to use a microphone. The microphone may be attached to a podium, or a lapel microphone may be worn by the speaker if he or she plans to move around during the presentation. If the presentation is a panel discussion, it may be necessary to set up a table at the front of the room with microphones for each panelist.

Other equipment needed may include a tape recorder, flip charts, a chalkboard, an overhead projector, a slide projector, movie projector and screen, and so forth. After you determine what equipment is needed for each speaker and session, you should check the following details:

1. Location and spacing of electrical outlets
2. Distance from outlet to equipment in case an extension cord is needed
3. Spare parts for audiovisual equipment in case of failure; for example, replacement bulbs for overhead projectors
4. Availability of equipment operators
5. Audience position for viewing screens, flip charts, or chalkboards
6. Markers, chalk, and/or pointers for use with overhead projectors, flip charts, and chalkboards

Outside Speakers. If someone from outside the company is to speak at the conference, you will probably be asked to assist in making the arrangements. Since some speakers are booked months in advance, you should engage speakers as early as possible. When you engage a speaker, obtain from him or her any special room arrangements and/or equipment that will be needed for the presentation. Be sure to give the speaker the following details:

1. Date, time, and location of the conference
2. General information about the organization
3. Nature of the audience
4. Purpose of the conference
5. Number of people expected to attend
6. Type of presentation that the speaker should give
7. The amount of money the speaker will receive (If the speaker has a set fee for speaking engagements, find out the amount of this fee.)
8. The expenses that will be paid (hotel, meals, transportation, etc.)

Hotel and Travel Reservations. When out-of-town speakers come to a conference, you will probably be expected to make their hotel and travel reservations. You may also be responsible for making hotel and travel reservations for company employees or guests who attend the conference. You should determine the type of accommodations required—price, room arrangements (single, double, private, or shared room); method of travel (air, bus, car, train); class of travel (first class or coach on flights); arrival and departure times; and so forth. Written confirmations should be obtained from the hotel; the receipt of tickets will serve as confirmation of travel arrangements. If an individual is expected to arrive late at a hotel (usually after 6 p.m.), the hotel should be notified to hold the reservation for late arrival. You should also determine if someone from the company will pick up guests when they arrive in town. If so, the designated person should be given the guests' names, times of arrival, flight numbers, hotel accommodations, and any other necessary information.

Illus. 13-7
A secretary may be responsible for making hotel reservations for out-of-town guests who attend the conference.

Pre-registration. Usually there is a pre-registration period which offers a reduction in cost of the conference if payment is received approximately two weeks before the meeting. If pre-registration is possible, you should keep a record of all participants who pre-register. You might prepare a card file from which name tags can be prepared in advance and from which folders or envelopes containing program schedules, tickets for special events, and other literature such as information about the city can be assembled.

Registration. Registration of participants at the conference requires careful planning several months in advance. Generally you will not be in charge of the total registration process, but you may be asked to assist. Persons to staff the registration tables should be selected prior to the conference and their duties explained in detail. A list should be made of all supplies needed at the registration table; for example, pens, pencils, registration packets, typewriters, name tags, and so forth. Signs should be made directing the participants to the registration desk. If the conference is large, the registration packets should be divided into separate alphabetic sections with each registration assistant responsible for a certain section of the alphabet. Signs should be made to indicate the location of each alphabetic section.

During the Conference

Your responsibilities during the conference may include running errands, assisting in getting messages to participants, and being on hand to help solve any problems that may occur. During a presentation, for example, a speaker may have trouble with an overhead projector or other piece of audiovisual equipment. You may be responsi-

Illus. 13-8

© Billy E. Barnes

Good planning will assure a smooth flowing, successful conference.

ble for seeing that replacement equipment is readily available and setting it up for the speaker. If the conference is large, messages will probably have to be delivered to participants during the various sessions. You may be responsible for devising and carrying out a message delivery system. If so, adhere to the suggestion made earlier in this chapter; that is, deliver messages as unobtrusively as possible.

You may also be responsible for having ice water at the speaker's podium, checking the number of chairs on the platform, checking the seating capacity of the room, escorting the speakers to the appropriate room, checking with the hotel on meal arrangements, seeing that tape recorders are set up to record the proceedings, and so forth. At a conference you are a representative of the company for which you work; thus, you should present an outstanding public relations image at all times. Keep a smile on your face and handle even the most difficult situations with poise and confidence.

After the Conference

After the conference your basic duties involve responsibility for cleanup and follow-up. You may need to see that all equipment is returned to the proper location, out-of-town guests and speakers are assisted with transportation to the airport, letters of appreciation are sent to the speakers, and expense reports are submitted by conference participants. Illus. 13–9 shows a sample letter of appreciation to a speaker.

You may also be responsible for seeing that the proceedings of the conference are published and mailed to the participants. Generally you will not be responsible for the actual writing of the conference proceedings, but you may be called upon to work with the conference reporters in producing a comprehensive report based on the taped conference sessions. Participants are usually charged a fee for a copy of the conference proceedings. This fee may be included in the general registration fee or the participants may pay only if they wish to receive a copy of the proceedings. In either case, you may be responsible for mailing the proceedings, keeping a record of the money collected, and maintaining a mailing list of all participants interested in receiving the proceedings. If papers are read at a conference, each speaker is usually asked prior to the conference to submit the paper which is then printed and distributed to participants before the meeting. Your responsibility may include obtaining copies of the speakers' papers and having them printed.

As a final responsibility, you may be asked to keep a record of problems that occurred and make recommendations for future conferences. Detailed records that are kept at a conference are helpful in planning subsequent conferences.

                    ─────**AMERICAN**
                         MERCHANTS
                         ASSOCIATION─────

                    February 13, 19--

                    Mr. Eduardo Martinez
                    Dallas Enterprises
                    1834 Elm Drive
                    Dallas, TX 75112-7110

                    Dear Mr. Martinez

                    Thank you for speaking at the AMA Conference
                    last Thursday. Your topic, "Management in the
                    80s," was timely and well received by the
                    audience. I heard numerous comments that the
                    suggestions you offered for increasing mana-
                    gerial effectiveness were practical.

                    The conference was one of the best we have
                    had, and your presentation helped make it
                    successful.

                    Sincerely

                    Eric Johnson

                    Eric Johnson
                    Program Chairperson

Illus. 13-9
Letter of appreciation to a speaker

TELECONFERENCING

In this chapter you learned that meetings and conferences are an important part of the business world. They provide a communication link for executives within a company or between companies; they also broaden executives' knowledge about relevant topics. Research has shown that the average business executive spends at least four hours a day in meetings. These meetings are both time-consuming and costly.

As a method of reducing the time and money spent on meetings and conferences, teleconferencing is frequently used.

Teleconferencing means interactive group communication through an electronic medium. It allows individuals at different locations to see and hear each other without leaving their offices. In addition, it also permits the simultaneous exchange of printed information, including graphics. Teleconferencing requires two or more conference rooms equipped with microphones, speakers, TV cameras, monitors, and visual aid equipment.

Teleconferencing facilities can be on the user's premises or located on the premises of a common carrier—a company that provides public communications facilities, such as a telephone or telegraph company. For example, a company may permanently establish a teleconferencing system between offices in New York, California, and Texas, if its communication needs merit the installation of such equipment. With such a system, executives may choose to hold a teleconference each week to discuss major issues of the company. Or a company may choose to use the premises of a common carrier, such as American Telephone and Telegraph Company, for a teleconference if communication needs are infrequent.

The first international teleconferencing service was made available to the public in 1982. The system linked users in New York City to users in London, England, by the use of satellite signals. The costs of international teleconferencing range from $1,500 to $2,000 an hour depending on the special effects desired (from black and white projec-

Intelnet
Videoconferencing Service

Illus. 13-10
Teleconferencing allows individuals at different locations to see and hear each other without leaving their offices.

tion of charts to a full motion video with television quality color transmission). Compared with the cost of travel from New York to London for a number of individuals, these costs are not extravagant.

It has been estimated that travel expenses can be reduced by at least 50 percent in the future with the use of teleconferencing. In addition to the reduction in cost and time of travel, companies that are presently using teleconferencing have cited more efficient decision making and increased input into the decision-making process as benefits. More will be said about teleconferencing in Chapter 19.

PROFESSIONAL POINTERS

Here are some suggestions to help you in planning meetings and conferences.

1. Plan the meeting or conference in advance. A meeting may be planned only a few days or a week in advance; however, several months are usually necessary to plan a conference.

2. Make a checklist of all tasks to be accomplished before, during, and after the meeting or conference. By keeping a checklist you will be organized and able to carry out your duties effectively. Leave a space on the checklist by each item for the date you complete each task.

3. Ask yourself these questions as you plan a meeting or conference:
   a. What should I do first in getting organized?
   b. Which tasks should I complete before the meeting or conference?
   c. When should each task be completed?
   d. Who will be responsible for each specific activity?
   e. Who is participating in the meeting or conference?
   f. Who are the speakers? What equipment or materials will they need?

FOR YOUR REVIEW

1. What responsibilities does the secretary have prior to a formal meeting?

2. What are the secretary's responsibilities during a formal meeting?

3. Explain the importance of understanding the basic rules of parliamentary procedure.

4. How should the minutes of a meeting be typed?

5. List five follow-up duties after a formal meeting.

6. Identify five responsibilities that a secretary may have at a conference or convention.

7. What is teleconferencing? How is it used?

CASE PROBLEM

Beth Mathews has been working for Coosey Frank Associates for six months. On several occasions during this time, Beth has been asked to set up meetings for her employer with two or three company employees. She merely called the employees, giving them the date, time, and place of the meeting. No other arrangements were required. Last week Beth's employer, Marvin Sheen, asked her to set up a meeting with five executives at Coosey Frank and three executives from BPR Engineering.

This was the first formal meeting that Beth had the responsibility for planning. She arranged for the meeting room and called the executives to give them the date, time, and place of the meeting. She made no other arrangements. During the meeting Mr. Sheen called and told Beth (rather irritably) to come to the conference room and record the proceedings of the meeting. When the meeting was over, Beth transcribed the proceedings which she gave to Mr. Sheen. He asked if she had sent copies to the other executives. When Beth said no, Mr. Sheen told her that she would have to do better at handling meetings. He also told her that he was disappointed that she had not arranged to have coffee available at the meeting.

1. What should Beth do to learn the correct procedures for handling meetings?

2. Should she talk with Mr. Sheen about the situation?

3. Did Mr. Sheen make any errors in handling the situation?

4. What steps would you have taken in handling the meeting?

PRODUCTION PROJECTS

PP 13-1

(Objective 1)

Dr. Jackson of the University of Arkansas will conduct a seminar with your employer, Ms. Monique Raphel, and 12 engineering staff members on Tuesday and Wednesday (March 23 and 24) from 10 a.m. to 3 p.m. The seminar on new processes of miniaturization of electronic circuits will be held in the company's Conference Room C on the third floor. Dr. Jackson will arrive at 7 p.m. on Monday and will stay until Wednesday afternoon. An overhead projector and a slide projector will be needed for the presentation.

Prepare a list of your responsibilities in planning this meeting. Title the list *Preparation for Meeting, March 23 and 24.*

PP 13-2

(Objective 2)

Prepare a notice for the meeting discussed in PP 13-1. Type an original and one carbon copy of the notice. Use plain paper and prepare the notice in the form of a memorandum.

PP 13-3

(Objective 6)

You have been asked to take notes at the meeting on March 23 and 24. In addition to taking notes, you are responsible for transcribing the notes at the end of the meeting and performing all other necessary follow-up activities. Make a list of follow-up duties to perform after the meeting. List the items in the order that you will perform them.

PP 13-4

(Objective 4)

Ms. Raphel gives you the notes (in your Supplies Inventory) pertaining to the February 12 AMS (Administrative Management Society) board of directors meeting. Use the notes to type the minutes of the meeting in final form. Use the format discussed in the text. Make an original and a carbon copy of the minutes on plain paper.

PP 13-5

(Objective 3)

After typing the minutes in PP 13-4, prepare an agenda for the next meeting of the AMS board of directors on March 12. List under unfinished business any matters that should be brought up according to the minutes of the February meeting. Ms. Raphel also asks you to include in the March agenda (1) the April election of officers and directors, (2) the national conference in May, (3) the inspection trip to General Supply Corporation, and (4) the summer picnic for families of members.

PP 13-6

(Objectives 1 and 6)

Your employer, who is a member of AMA (American Management Association), has been asked to chair the committee in charge of the annual AMA conference. The hotel has been selected. Your responsibilities include making the necessary plans before the conference, performing any miscellaneous duties during the conference, and handling the follow-up tasks after the conference. Prepare a list of your duties, and explain how you would go about performing them.

PP 13-7

(Objective 5)

Read a recent source on the following points of parliamentary procedure:

a. Making a motion   c. Point of order
b. Amending a motion   d. Suspension of rules

Two possible sources are:

Robert, Sarah Corbin. *The Scott, Foresman Robert's Rules of Order Newly Revised.* Glenview, Ill: Scott, Foresman and Company, 1981.

Bank, Dena Citron. *How Things Get Done: The Nitty-Gritty of Parliamentary Procedures.* Columbia: University of South Carolina Press, 1979.

Summarize your findings on how to handle each point in a short paper entitled, *Rules of Parliamentary Procedure.*

PP 13-8

(Objective 7)

Read two recent articles on how teleconferencing is used in business. Prepare a summary of these articles using plain paper, and note the sources that you used.

Chapter 14

PROVIDING FINANCIAL ASSISTANCE

The secretary's responsibilities in providing financial assistance vary depending on the scope of the job and the size of the company. All companies keep banking, accounting, payroll, investment, and insurance records. Many times the secretary's financial responsibilities are limited. However, a general knowledge of financial transactions will be helpful to you in understanding the operations of a company. If you understand the various financial services available, financial statements, payroll records and deductions from paychecks, types of insurance available, and investment terminology, you will be a knowledgeable and valuable employee.

General Objectives

Your general objectives for Chapter 14 are to:

1. *Write checks*
2. *Make out deposit slips*
3. *Reconcile a bank statement*
4. *Learn about special banking services*
5. *Explain the impact of electronic technology on the banking industry*
6. *Record petty cash transactions*
7. *Interpret and analyze financial statements*
8. *Become familiar with various payroll deductions*
9. *Understand investment terminology*
10. *Become familiar with various types of insurance*

BANKING RECORDS AND PROCEDURES

Banking transactions of importance to you include writing checks, endorsing checks, making deposits, and reconciling the bank balance and checkbook balance.

Writing Checks

A check represents an order by the depositor directing the bank to pay money to a designated person or firm. The person who orders the bank to pay cash from the depositor's account is the *drawer*. The person to whom a check is made payable is the *payee*.

In many companies employees' checks are computer originated. For example, payroll information concerning the number of hours per week an employee has worked, the rate of pay, the deductions to be withheld, and so forth, are fed into a computer. The computer then computes the amount to be paid and prints the check. Companies may still prepare some checks manually, however, and you should know the correct procedures for writing checks. Follow these steps:

1. The check voucher, stub, or register should be filled out first with the date, amount, and purpose of the check. Most companies use a *voucher check* which has a detachable slip on which the information is recorded. (See Illus. 14-1.) A *check stub* is a short leaf of paper attached to the spine of the checkbook after the check has been detached. (See Illus. 14-2.) A *check register* is a separate form for recording the checks written as well as the deposits made. (See Illus. 14-3.) The check stub and check register are used more frequently for personal transactions, whereas the voucher check is the principal type of check used for business related transactions.
2. The date should be entered in the space provided on the check.
3. The name of the payee should be written in full and as far as possible to the left in the space provided.

EASTERN PRODUCTS CORPORATION
511 PACIFIC ROAD
DALLAS, TEXAS 75201-7255

NO. 2071   32-56 / 3110

DATE ___August 7,___ 19 __

PAY ___Three hundred forty-seven and 90/100--------___ DOLLARS $ ___347.90___

TO THE ORDER OF   Topcraft Equipment Company
5909 East Colfax Drive
Denver, Colorado 80220-8120

SPECIMEN

EASTERN PRODUCTS CORPORATION

Russell B. Jones

NATIONAL SAVINGS BANK
DALLAS, TEXAS 75211-7201

⑆311000561⑆ 137⑈10162⑈

- -

EASTERN PRODUCTS CORPORATION
511 PACIFIC ROAD
DALLAS, TEXAS 75201-7255

DETACH AND RETAIN THIS STATEMENT
THE ATTACHED CHECK IS IN PAYMENT OF ITEMS DESCRIBED BELOW

DATE	DESCRIPTION	GROSS AMOUNT	DEDUCTIONS	NET AMOUNT	
7/3/--	Invoice #4608	86.97		86.97	
7/18/--	Invoice #5087	265.14	4.21	260.93	
				347.90	

Illus. 14-1
Voucher check

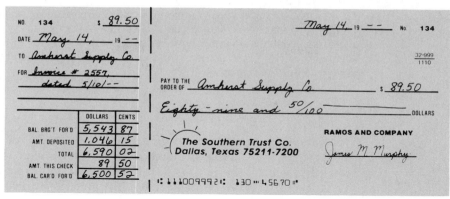

Illus. 14-2
Check with attached stub

4. The amount of the check must be written twice. It is first written in figures after the dollar sign. The figures should be placed as close as possible to the printed dollar sign so that no additional figures can be inserted. The amount of the check is then written on the following line with words for the dollar amount and figures for the cents. Express cents in fractions of 100. The words should be started as far as possible to the left. If the written amount does not fill the entire space, draw a line through the excess space.

CHECK NO.	DATE	CHECK ISSUED TO	BAL. BRG'T. FOR'D.		225	00
396	5/4/--	TO *Carmen Fields*	AMOUNT OF CHECK OR DEPOSIT		19	86
		FOR *Dress Alterations*	BALANCE		205	14
397	5/13/--	TO *Edwards Supply Co.*	AMOUNT OF CHECK OR DEPOSIT		56	25
		FOR *Stationery*	BALANCE		148	89

Illus. 14-3
Check with separate register

5. If you are writing a check for less than $1, circle the amount written in figures; write *Only* before the spelled-out amount.
6. Erasures or changes should be avoided in writing checks. If a mistake is made, write *Void* across the face of the check and the check voucher, stub, or register.

Endorsing Checks

An *endorsement* is a written signature by the holder of a check for the purpose of transferring ownership. The endorsement is usually written on the back of the check. A rubber stamp endorsement may be used if the check is to be deposited only and not transferred to someone else. The common types of endorsements, as shown in Illus. 14-4, are: (1) blank endorsement, (2) endorsement in full, and (3) restrictive endorsement.

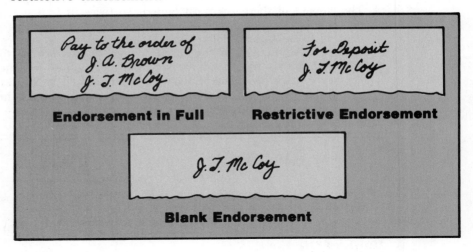

Illus. 14-4
Endorsements

A *blank endorsement* requires only the signature of the payee and makes the check payable to any holder. If a check is endorsed in this manner, it should not be sent through the mail since anyone can cash it. An *endorsement in full* transfers ownership to a person or firm. The name of the person to whom the check is to be transferred is written before the endorser's signature. When a check is endorsed in this manner, it cannot be cashed without the specified payee's signature. A *restrictive endorsement* transfers ownership for a specific purpose. If you are sending a check through the mail for deposit, a restrictive endorsement should be used.

Making Deposits

You may frequently make deposits to the personal account of your employer or to the company's account. The bank provides deposit slips on which you record the date of the deposit and the items to be deposited. Each check should be listed on the deposit slip according to the American Bankers Association (ABA) transit number. The ABA transit number is printed in fraction form in the upper right-hand portion of the check. A transit number also appears on the deposit slip to identify the bank receiving the deposit. For example, Illus. 14-5, 32 indicates the city or state, and 999 indicates the specific bank within that area. The number 1110 below the line is a Federal Reserve number that is used by banks in sorting checks. The Federal Reserve number is not used in listing the checks on the deposit slip.

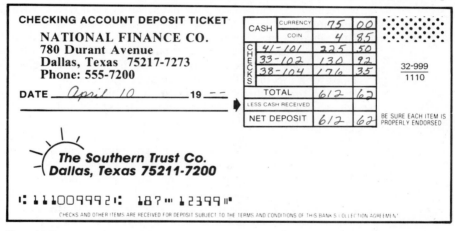

Illus. 14-5
Deposit slip

Make sure that the name of the payee is written on all checks being deposited. If it is not on the check, write it or use a stamp (many business firms have stamps with the company name). Also, make sure that the checks are endorsed properly. Again, a stamped or handwritten endorsement may be made.

Checks and deposit slips are deposited electronically. In order to aid in this electronic processing, the bank's transit number and the depositor's account number are preprinted in magnetic ink characters in a uniform position at the bottom of the checks and deposit slips. Notice the characters on the deposit ticket in Illus. 14-5. When a check or deposit slip is received at the bank, the amount, the date, and other information are also recorded in magnetic ink. Optical character recognition (OCR) equipment sorts the checks and deposit slips and posts to the depositor's account.

Reconciling the Bank Balance

Each month banks usually send depositors a statement showing deposits, withdrawals, and charges in connection with their checking accounts. Since the bank statement balance and the checkbook balance are not equal, a reconciliation is made to account for the difference and to correct any errors.

Follow these procedures in reconciling the bank statement:

1. Look at the check stubs to see that all check amounts have been deducted from the preceding balances and that all deposit amounts have been entered and added to the balances.
2. Sort in numerical order the canceled checks that have been returned by the bank. Usually a statement is accompanied with the checks that have been paid by the bank.[1]
3. If checks are returned by your bank, verify each check with the corresponding check stub. Place a check mark on the stub.
4. On a separate sheet of paper, list the numbers and the amounts of the checks that are outstanding. An outstanding check is an issued check that has not yet been cashed by the bank nor deducted from the depositor's account. Total the outstanding checks.
5. Add the total unlisted deposits to the bank balance.
6. Add to the checkbook balance any interest earned on the checking account. (Banks today offer interest-bearing checking accounts in which interest is paid on the average daily balance of the account.)
7. Deduct the total amount of the outstanding checks from the balance shown on the bank statement.
8. Deduct from the checkbook balance any service charges or special fees. If there are any charges, they will be shown as separate deductions on the bank statement. The checkbook balance and the balance on the bank statement should now agree.
9. If the reconciliation does not balance after a careful verification, the discrepancy should be brought to the attention of the bank. Errors are seldom traced to faulty bookkeeping by the bank, however.

To reconcile the bank balance and the checkbook balance, follow this example:

Bank statement balance	$2,002
Add: late deposits	+500
Subtotal	$2,502
Subtract: outstanding checks	−180
Adjusted bank balance	$2,322

---

[1] Some banks use *check truncation* (also referred to as *check retention* or *check safekeeping*). With this process, the bank keeps your checks rather than returning them to you. You get a monthly statement listing the number and amount of each check that has been cashed. You may request a copy of a check you need (sometimes a fee is charged for this service) or you may get a special checkbook in which you automatically make copies of each check that you write.

Checkbook balance... $1,800
    Add: credit memos (such as the collection of notes made by
        bank).. +540
        accumulated interest.................................. 2
            Subtotal.. $2,342
    Subtract: service charge .... −20
Adjusted checkbook balance $2,322

Using Special Bank Services

Banks offer numerous special services that you may find beneficial. These services include special types of checks and safe-deposit
boxes.

Certified Check. A *certified check* is a personal or company
check that is guaranteed by the bank on which it is drawn. To certify
a check, follow these procedures:

1. Prepare a company or personal check in the usual manner.
2. Take the check to the bank on which it is drawn, and present it to the
   bank official responsible for certifying checks. The bank official will
   then investigate the drawer's account to see if there are sufficient
   funds to cover the check.
3. After it is determined that there are sufficient funds in the account to
   pay the check, the word *CERTIFIED* is stamped on the face of the
   check and an official signature is added.
4. The account is immediately charged with the amount of the check,
   and the money is transferred by the bank to a special account on its
   books. A small fee is usually charged to certify a check. Illus. 14-6
   shows a certified check.

Illus. 14-6
Certified check

Cashier's Check. Another means of payment frequently used when a personal or company check is not acceptable is a *cashier's check*. This check is issued by the cashier of a bank and is drawn on the bank's own funds. For a small fee, a cashier's check can be purchased by giving the bank cash or a check for the amount of money desired. Recommended practice is to have the cashier's check made payable to the purchaser of the check; the purchaser then endorses it to the person to whom payment is to be made. The canceled check then becomes proof of payment.

No. 59314

The Southern Trust Co.
Dallas, Texas 75211-7200   June 16, ____ 19 —— $\frac{32\text{-}999}{1110}$

PAY TO THE
ORDER OF _____ Danielle Freeman _____ $ 11.50

The sum of $11 and 50 cts _____ DOLLARS

CASHIER'S CHECK   *Pat McKnight*   VICE PRESIDENT - CASHIER

⑈ ⑈⑈⑈⑆⑆⑅⑅⑅⑈⑈ ⑆⑈⑆ ⑅⑆⑆⑆⑈⑈⑆

Illus. 14-7
Cashier's check

Bank Draft. A *bank draft* is a check written by the bank on its account in another bank. The difference between a cashier's check and a bank draft is that the cashier's check is written on funds in the cashier's own bank while the bank draft is written on funds in another bank. The bank draft is used mainly for the transfer of large sums from one city to another city. For example, if a company buys property in another city, the seller may ask the company to pay for the purchase with a bank draft. This procedure ensures the seller that the money is in the bank.

Bank Money Order. A *bank money order* is sold by the bank and states that a certain amount of money is to be paid to the person named on the money order. Normally cashable at any bank in the United States or abroad, the money order is negotiable and can be transferred by endorsement. The maximum amount for which a money order can be made differs depending on the bank where you buy the money order. If you want to send an amount larger than the maximum, any number of money orders may be purchased and then issued to the same payee. A person who does not have a checking account and who wants to send a small payment through the mail usually purchases a money order.

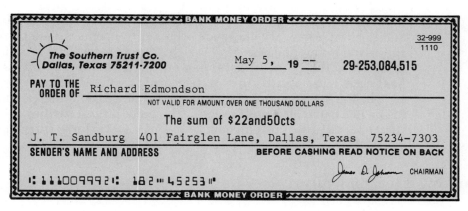

Illus. 14-8
Bank money order

Traveler's Check. The American Express Company and most banks and travel agencies issue a special type of check called a *traveler's check*, which facilitates paying for expenses when traveling. Traveler's checks are sold in various denominations. A small fee is charged, depending on the amount purchased. When traveler's checks are purchased, each check must be signed by the purchaser. When cashed, each traveler's check must be countersigned by the purchaser in the presence of the person who cashes the check.

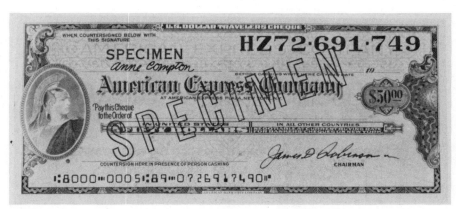

American Express Company

Illus. 14-9
Traveler's check

Safe-Deposit Boxes. Most banks have large vaults that contain boxes known as *safe-deposit boxes*. These boxes are available for persons and companies wishing to store valuable items or important business documents for safekeeping. There is a rental charge to use the boxes.

When a safe-deposit box is rented, the renter signs a special form and is given a key. Two keys are required to open a safe-deposit box—the renter's key and the key used by the bank official who lets the person into the vault. If more than one person is to have access to the box, each must register his or her signature at the time the box is rented. Each time access to the box is requested, the renter must sign his or her name on a special card. The bank official verifies the signature and records the date and time of the renter's entry into the vault.

Banking Electronically

The most important change in the banking industry in the last few years has been in the use of electronic technology. Today numerous banking transactions can be performed electronically; customers can obtain money, transfer funds from one account to another, deposit money, and pay bills without the use of checks and the services of bank personnel. These services are performed through electronic fund transfers (EFTs). Simply stated, with the use of computers, money can be moved from one account to another electronically—without the need for a written form of payment. Some services that are examples of electronic fund transfers are automated teller machines, direct payroll depositing, automatic bill payments, point-of-sale transfers, and pay-by-phone systems.

Automated Teller Machines (ATMs). Automated teller machines allow a customer to obtain cash, make deposits, transfer funds, or even borrow a limited amount of money without writing a check or going to a bank. Shopping malls and supermarkets are popular locations for ATMs.

NCR Corporation

Illus. 14-10
Automated teller machines

To use an ATM, you insert an EFT card (a magnetically encoded plastic card similar to a credit card) into the terminal, enter your secret password or your personal identification number (PIN), and make the desired transaction. The terminal, which is connected to a computer at another location, may serve a bank that is across the street or miles away.

Direct Payroll Depositing. Some companies provide direct depositing of an employee's paycheck. The employee's net pay is deposited directly into the employee's bank account and is automatically withdrawn from the bank account of the company paying the employee. Direct payroll depositing eliminates the writing of paychecks, relieves the employee of the inconvenience of having to go to the bank, and decreases the possible loss or theft of paychecks. In some areas of the country, the federal government deposits social security payments directly to the recipient's bank account rather than writing and mailing a check.

Automatic Bill Payments. It is also possible in some areas of the country to pay utility bills, mortgage installments, and insurance premiums automatically. For example, when a utility bill is due, the bank deducts the amount of the bill from the customer's account and adds the same amount to the account of the utility company. The customer receives a copy of the utility bill for his or her records.

Point-of-Sale (POS) Transfers. Point-of-sale (POS) systems allow the electronic transfer of money from a purchaser's bank account to a store's bank account. In one such system, a cashier or salesperson can pass a customer's bank issued card (called a *debit card*) through a reader attached to a POS terminal that functions as a cash register and enter the amount of the purchase on the keyboard. The customer then punches in his or her personal identification number and the amount of the bill is instantly deducted from the customer's checking account and added to the store's account.

The ability to facilitate the transfer of funds at the moment of purchase is one of the major reasons for merchants to install POS systems. Funds available to a merchant at the moment of purchase increase the merchant's cash flow and reduce the number of bad checks and fraudulent charges, both of which are costly to banks and merchants.

Pay-by-Phone Systems. From the comfort of your home or the convenience of your office, pay-by-phone systems permit you to telephone your bank (or other financial institution) and instruct it to pay certain bills or to transfer funds between accounts. You can also learn your checking, savings, and credit balances through the use of such systems. There are three things you need in order to use the system:

1. Access to a Touch-Tone telephone
2. Your EFT card number
3. Your password or personal identification number (PIN)

ACCOUNTING RECORDS AND STATEMENTS

As a secretary, you will not be expected to have an extensive knowledge of accounting, but you should be familiar with certain accounting records and statements. You may also be expected to keep simple accounting records such as a petty cash account.

Petty Cash

Companies usually make immediate payments for small items, such as delivery charges, postage due, and emergency office supplies. These small expenses are paid in cash from a *petty cash fund*. This petty cash fund is established with a specified amount, such as $50. A check is written for the initial amount, cashed, and placed in a petty cash box. Each time a payment is made from the petty cash fund, a voucher or a receipt similar to the one in Illus. 14-11 is prepared.

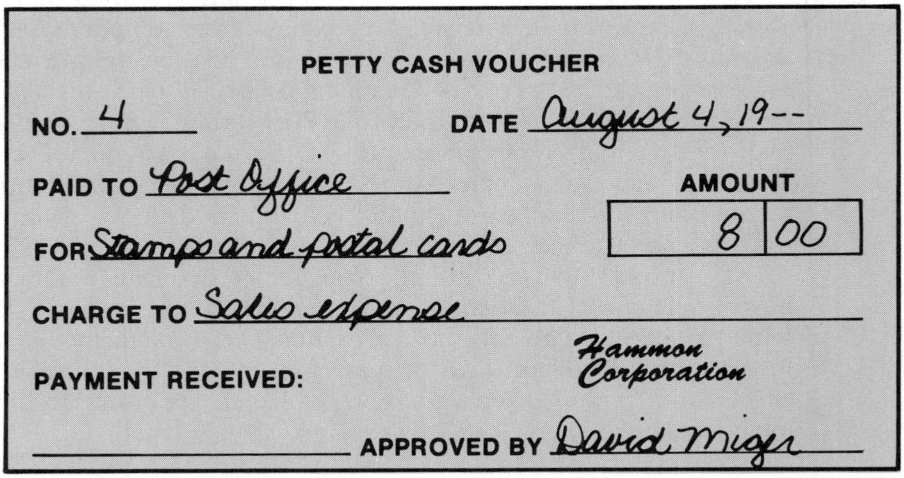

PETTY CASH VOUCHER

NO. *4*   DATE *August 4, 19--*

PAID TO *Post Office*   **AMOUNT**

FOR *Stamps and postal cards*   *8 | 00*

CHARGE TO *Sales expense*

PAYMENT RECEIVED: *Hammon Corporation*

APPROVED BY *David Miger*

Illus. 14-11
A petty cash voucher should show the date, the person or firm to whom the payment is to be made, and the purpose of the payment. The voucher should be signed, numbered, and kept in the petty cash box.

When the money in the petty cash fund gets low, a check is written to replenish the fund. The steps to replenish the fund are as follows:

1. Total the amount used according to the vouchers and any other receipts.
2. Count the cash on hand.
3. Add the cash amount to the total amount used. The combined figure should equal the original amount of the fund.
4. Prepare or request a check for replenishing the fund. The amount of the check will equal the expenditures.
5. Cash the check and add the money to the petty cash fund.

Financial Statements

Managers, owners, and creditors of a company are naturally concerned with the financial health of the company. The statements that are commonly used to report financial health are the balance sheet and the income statement.

Balance Sheet. The balance sheet shows the financial condition of the company on a certain date—how much it owns and how much it owes. In order to interpret a balance sheet, you must have an understanding of its major sections. Notice that the balance sheet in Illus. 14-12 contains three major sections—assets, liabilities, and stockholders' equity.

The *assets* of a company are the properties or economic resources owned by the company. There are two major classifications of assets—current assets and plant and equipment. *Current assets* consist of cash and assets that are expected to be turned into cash, sold, or consumed within a short period, usually one year. *Plant and equipment* assets are relatively long-lived assets that are used in the operation of the company.

Another asset category that may be included on the balance sheet is *long-term investments*. Stocks, bonds, and promissory notes that will be held for more than one year appear under this classification.

Liabilities are the debts of the company. *Current liabilities* are debts that must be paid within one year. *Long-term liabilities* are debts that are not due for a comparatively long period, usually more than one year. Common long-term liability items are mortgages payable, bonds payable, and notes payable.

The *stockholders' equity* section of the balance sheet shows the interest of the owner or owners of a company in its assets. The equity of the owner or owners represents the excess of assets over liabilities.

```
                        BAUGHMAN'S SUPPLY COMPANY
                             Balance Sheet
                           December 31, 19--

                                 Assets

Current assets
  Cash                                              $ 22,240
  Accounts receivable                    $ 41,500
    Less allowance for bad debts            2,500     39,000
  Merchandise inventory                              105,725
  Supplies                                             4,000
  Prepaid insurance                                    2,900
    Total current assets                                        $173,865
Plant and equipment
  Office equipment                       $ 18,000
    Less accumulated depreciation           8,100   $  9,900
  Factory equipment                      $276,000
    Less accumulated depreciation         163,500    112,500
  Buildings                              $125,000
    Less accumulated depreciation          20,000    105,000
  Land                                                35,000
    Total plant and equipment                                  $262,400
Total assets                                                   $436,265


                               Liabilities

Current liabilities
  Accounts payable                       $ 38,600
  Estimated income tax payable             15,100
  Salaries and wages payable               1,965
  Interest payable                         1,250
    Total current liabilities                       $ 56,915
Long-term liabilities
  Mortgage payable                       $ 50,000
  Notes payable, due December 31, 2000     22,500
    Total long-term liabilities                       72,500
Total liabilities                                              $129,415


                           Stockholders' Equity

Common stock                                        $150,000
Retained earnings                                    156,850
  Total stockholders' equity                                   $306,850

Total liabilities and stockholders' equity                     $436,265
```

Illus. 14-12
Balance sheet

Income Statement. Another financial statement that reflects the financial health of the company is the income statement. The income statement covers the results of the operation of a company for a certain period of time. It shows the total amount of money earned and the total amount of the expenses involved in earning the money. Illus. 14-13 shows an income statement.

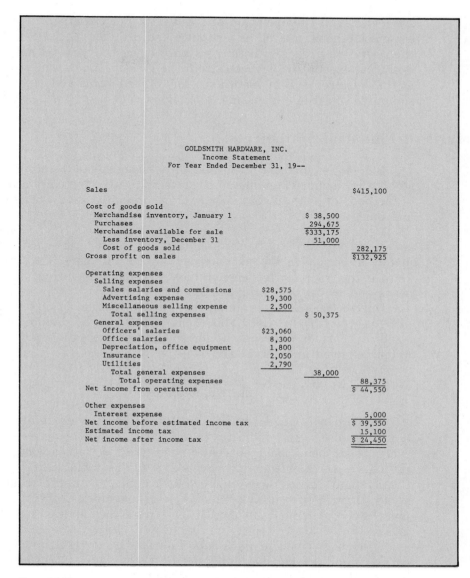

```
                        GOLDSMITH HARDWARE, INC.
                            Income Statement
                    For Year Ended December 31, 19--


Sales                                                         $415,100

Cost of goods sold
   Merchandise inventory, January 1            $ 38,500
   Purchases                                    294,675
   Merchandise available for sale              $333,175
     Less inventory, December 31                 51,000
        Cost of goods sold                                     282,175
Gross profit on sales                                         $132,925

Operating expenses
   Selling expenses
     Sales salaries and commissions   $28,575
     Advertising expense               19,300
     Miscellaneous selling expense      2,500
        Total selling expenses                 $ 50,375
   General expenses
     Officers' salaries               $23,060
     Office salaries                    8,300
     Depreciation, office equipment     1,800
     Insurance                          2,050
     Utilities                          2,790
        Total general expenses                   38,000
           Total operating expenses                            88,375
Net income from operations                                   $ 44,550

Other expenses
   Interest expense                                             5,000
Net income before estimated income tax                       $ 39,550
Estimated income tax                                           15,100
Net income after income tax                                  $ 24,450
```

Illus. 14-13
Income statement

The first section of the income statement is the income section. This section shows the total amount of sales the company has made and the cost of the merchandise that was sold. The difference between these two items is the gross profit on sales. If there were no other expenses in connection with the sales, the gross profit would become the net income earned by the business. However, additional expenses are incurred in the operation of a business. For example, the employees must be paid as well as insurance and utilities. Notice that under the operating expenses these costs are itemized. The total amount of operating expenses is deducted from the gross profit on sales to arrive at the net income from operations. Any other income and expenses are computed and the net income is obtained.

Analysis of Financial Statements

Before the financial condition of a business can be truly understood, the financial statements must be analyzed. There are a number of methods of analysis, but only two are presented here—current ratio and quick ratio.

Current Ratio. Bankers and other short-term creditors are mainly interested in the current position of a company. They want to know if the company has enough money to meet its current operating needs and to pay its current debts.

One method of determining the current position of a company is to figure the *current ratio*. This figure is obtained by dividing current assets by current liabilities. Refer to the current assets and current liabilities given in Illus. 14-12.

$$\text{Current ratio} = \frac{\text{current assets (\$173,865)}}{\text{current liabilities (\$56,915)}} = 3.05{:}1$$

A company's current ratio indicates its debt-paying ability. A current ratio of 3.05 to 1 indicates that $3.05 in cash is being received for every dollar being paid out within the year. A satisfactory current ratio for a merchandising business is 2 to 1. This ratio will be higher if the company carries merchandise that is subject to abrupt changes in styles. But a public utility, which has no inventories other than supplies, is considered solvent even if its current ratio is less than 1 to 1.

Quick Ratio. The *quick ratio* indicates the extent to which total current liabilities can be liquidated on short notice. It measures the instant debt-paying ability of a company. Cash, notes receivable, accounts receivable, interest receivable, and marketable securities are considered quick assets. Inventories and prepaid expenses are not considered since they are further removed from conversion into cash than other current assets. The quick ratio is determined by dividing quick assets by current liabilities. The quick assets in Illus. 14-12 total $61,240.

$$\text{Quick ratio} = \frac{\text{quick assets (\$61,240)}}{\text{current liabilities (\$56,915)}} = 1.08{:}1$$

The 1.08 to 1 ratio indicates that $1.08 in cash can be quickly received for every dollar to be paid out within the year. This ratio is adequate since a ratio of 1 to 1 is usually considered satisfactory.

PAYROLL LAWS AND DEDUCTIONS

If you work in a payroll department, you will probably have certain payroll responsibilities, such as computing wages and salaries for each pay period and keeping a record of employees' working time. But, even if you never work in a payroll department, you should be familiar with payroll laws and records in order to understand the deductions that are taken from your gross earnings.

Fair Labor Standards Act

The Fair Labor Standards Act of 1938, better known as the Wage and Hour Act, requires that companies in interstate commerce keep a record of hours worked and pay a minimum hourly wage. In addition, the law requires that certain employees be paid at a rate at least one and a half times the regular hourly rate for all work in excess of 40 hours during a workweek. Persons in administrative or executive positions are not governed by the law, however. While the Wage and Hour Act does not require that any reports showing hours worked be filed, company records must be kept on file for three years. Government examiners may inspect the records at any time to determine whether the employer is meeting the requirements of the act.

Social Security

The social security tax (FICA—Federal Insurance Contribution Act) provides retirement income, survivor benefits, and hospital and medical insurance benefits for the aged and disabled. Both the employee and the employer contribute an equal amount to the federal government each pay period.

The amount of money which you and your employer pay is based on a percentage of your salary. This percentage has risen steadily for the last several years. Illus. 14-14 shows the percentage increases for a five-year period. The maximum earnings base on which the tax is levied also increases. For example, in 1983 the tax was levied on a base of $35,700. If you made $26,000 a year, you paid social security on your total earnings. However, if you made $45,000 in 1983, you paid social security taxes on only $35,700, the base for 1983.

FICA TAX RATES

Year	Employer	Employee	Base	
1983	6.70 percent	6.70 percent	$35,700	
1984	7.00 percent	6.70 percent	37,800	
1985	7.05 percent	7.05 percent	39,300	(Estimated)
1986	7.15 percent	7.15 percent	42,000	(Estimated)
1987	7.15 percent	7.15 percent	45,000	(Estimated)

Illus. 14-14
FICA tax rates for a five-year period

All employees who work in occupations covered by the provisions of the Social Security Act must have a social security number for government identification. To obtain a social security number, you must file an application with your local social security office. You will receive a card printed with your social security number. If you lose your card, you may apply for a duplicate. Employers must also obtain an identification number.

Federal Income Tax

The amount deducted from your earnings for federal income tax depends on your earnings and the number of dependents you claim. Each employee must fill out a Form W-4 (Employee's Withholding Allowance Certificate), which is shown in Illus. 14-15. The amount of income tax withheld by employers is paid quarterly or monthly to the

---

Form **W-4**	Department of the Treasury—Internal Revenue Service	OMB No. 1545-0010
(Rev. January 1982)	**Employee's Withholding Allowance Certificate**	Expires 4-30-83

1 Type or print your full name

Robert Henry Gausnell

2 Your social security number

_310 - 48 - 8293_

Home address (number and street or rural route)

7448 Chesterfield Avenue

3 Marital Status

☐ Single ☒ Married
☐ Married, but withhold at higher Single rate

Note: If married, but legally separated, or spouse is a nonresident alien, check the Single box.

City or town, State, and ZIP code

Boise, Idaho 83709-8282

4 Total number of allowances you are claiming (from line F of the worksheet on page 2) . . . .   _2_

5 Additional amount, if any, you want deducted from each pay . . . . $

6 I claim exemption from withholding because (see instructions and check boxes below that apply):

   a ☐ Last year I did not owe any Federal income tax and had a right to a full refund of **ALL** income tax withheld, **AND**

   b ☐ This year I do not expect to owe any Federal income tax and expect to have a right to a full refund of **ALL** income tax withheld. If both a and b apply, enter "EXEMPT" here . . . . ▶

   c If you entered "EXEMPT" on line 6b, are you a full-time student? . . . .   ☐ Yes ☐ No

Under the penalties of perjury, I certify that I am entitled to the number of withholding allowances claimed on this certificate, or if claiming exemption from withholding, that I am entitled to claim the exempt status.

Employee's signature ▶ _Robert Henry Gausnell_   Date ▶ _March 5_   19

7 Employer's name and address (including ZIP code) (FOR EMPLOYER'S USE ONLY)

8 Office code

9 Employer identification number

-------- Detach along this line --------

Illus. 14-15
Form W-4 (Employee's Withholding Allowance Certificate)

district office of the Internal Revenue Service. Some states and cities also tax a person's income. These deductions are withheld in much the same way as the federal income tax.

Unemployment Compensation Tax

This tax provides some relief to those who become unemployed as a result of economic forces outside their control. To finance the program, all employers covered by the law are subject to a federal and state tax. The state employment rate and the wage base subject to the tax vary from state to state. Provision is made for employers with a favorable record of employment to pay a lower rate than employers with an unfavorable record of employment. The federal portion of the tax (as of 1984) paid by employers is uniformly calculated at a rate of 0.8 percent (.008) on a base of $7,000 of wages paid to each employee in a calendar year.

Other Deductions

There are many other deductions that may be made from your earnings. Common examples are local or state payroll or income taxes, union dues, charitable contributions, savings bond purchases, group insurance, and hospitalization. Illus. 14-16 shows an example of a payroll check with a list of the deductions.

Stan Pat, Inc.
2400 Fargo Lane
Dallas, Texas 75228-7280

324
32-56
3110

February 15, 19 --

PAY TO THE ORDER OF Joann D. Boyd $ 464.08

Four hundred sixty-four and 08/100--DOLLARS

NATIONAL SAVINGS BANK
DALLAS, TEXAS 75211-7201

⑈ 311000561⑈ 333 ⑈ 60459 ⑈

STATEMENT OF EMPLOYEE EARNINGS AND PAYROLL DEDUCTIONS

TWO-WEEK PERIOD ENDING	HOURS	EARNINGS		TOTAL EARNINGS	FEDERAL INCOME TAX	FICA TAX	HOSP INS	OTHER	TOTAL DEDUC-TIONS	NET PAY
		REGULAR	OVERTIME							
2/15/--	90½	484.00	95.29	579.29	59.40	38.81	12.00	5.00	115.21	464.08
YEAR TO DATE TOTALS		1,452.00	95.29	1,547.29	150.60	103.67	36.00	15.00	305.27	1,242.02

Illus. 14-16
Payroll check

TAX RETURNS

As a secretary, you are not expected to be a tax expert. Usually a certified public accountant (CPA) is employed to prepare the tax return. However, you may be responsible for keeping certain records and furnishing information to the CPA.

Record of Income

For income tax purposes, it is required by law that all income be accounted for and reported. In addition to business profits, sources of income include dividends from investments, interest on savings or bonds, interest on personal loans that have been made to others, rent income from property owned less expenses on such property, and income which represents gain from the sale or exchange of property.

In preparing a tax return for an individual who receives a salary, it is usually not necessary to keep a detailed record of the weekly or monthly income. At the end of the year, the employer gives each employee two copies of the Form W-2 which shows total earnings and the amount of FICA and income taxes withheld during the year. One copy of this form is attached to the income tax return when it is filed.

Record of Deductions

A record of expenses and other deductions is just as important as a record of income in preparing a tax return. Tax regulations are very strict when it comes to accounting for business expenses. Those business expenses for which a person is not reimbursed are deductible on the personal income tax return. However, proof that such expenses were incurred and are legitimate deductions is the responsibility of the taxpayer. Similarly, records must be kept of contributions to charitable and religious organizations, medical and dental expenses, taxes that are paid during the year, losses from various causes if not covered by insurance, interest paid, and debts that have been proven uncollectible.

Other Tax Records

While federal social security taxes, federal income taxes, and state and local income taxes require most of the record keeping for tax purposes, records must also be kept for other taxes imposed on businesses. These taxes vary depending on the location of the business, the type of business, the number of branches and subsidiaries, and other factors. The following are some of the most common types of other taxes that are levied on business enterprises:

1. Property taxes
2. Sales taxes
3. Excise taxes
4. License taxes

Property Taxes. Most property taxes are levied by state and local governments for the purpose of maintaining local governments and schools. A portion is also generally used to pay the expenses of state government. The taxes are usually classified as (1) real property tax, (2) personal property tax, and (3) intangible property tax.

A *real property tax* is levied on land, buildings, and other permanent improvements on land. The value of the real estate is determined by periodic appraisal, and the tax is levied as a certain amount on each $100 or $1,000 of appraised value. A *personal property tax* is levied on furniture and equipment, automobiles, and machinery. An *intangible property tax* is a tax on assets, such as money in banks or other savings institutions, stocks, bonds, and other securities. In a business, accurately kept records of the assets, including property, equipment, and securities, will help your employer to prepare the returns and reports for these kinds of properties.

Sales Taxes. Most states and some cities levy a *sales tax* on retail sales. The tax is collected at the time of a sale. Detailed records must be kept of collections so that amounts may be remitted periodically to the taxing agency. In some states the sales tax may take the form of a gross receipts tax with the business paying a certain percentage of the sales during a year. In either case the tax laws require that certain records of collections be kept and reports filed periodically, either monthly, quarterly, or annually.

Excise Taxes. An *excise tax* is a tax that is levied on manufactured products and on services. The tax is levied on the manufacturer or producer and passed on to the consumer in the form of higher prices.

License Taxes. Probably the most common *license tax* with which you are acquainted is the automobile license tax which is levied by your state for the privilege of operating an automobile. There are, however, many other kinds of federal, state, and local license taxes. Restaurants frequently must purchase several licenses in order to operate. You will see the license certificates posted in most restaurants. Food stores and nearly all kinds of retail outlets require licenses to operate. Professionals, such as doctors and lawyers, must have a license to practice. A license indicates that permission to operate or conduct a business has been granted by the proper authorities.

Tax Information

The following references may prove helpful to you in keeping tax records. These references are published each year with the latest tax information.

- James B. Bower and Harold Q. Langenderfer, *Income Tax Procedure* (Cincinnati: South-Western Publishing Co.).
- J. K. Lasser, *J. K. Lasser's Your Income Tax* (New York: Simon and Schuster, Inc.).

Tax Return Typing

Even though your employer may have the assistance of an accountant or a lawyer in gathering final figures for tax returns, you may be responsible for typing the final copies of the tax returns. The following suggestions will help you in typing tax returns.

1. Be sure to include all necessary information.
2. Check all figures carefully after typing them and verify any calculations.
3. Include any supplementary reports required with the typewritten forms.
4. See that the reports are properly signed.
5. Make at least one extra copy of tax reports for future reference.
6. Do not rely on the company mail room to mail tax returns. Prepare the material for mailing yourself and be sure that all necessary enclosures and remittances are in the envelope.

INVESTMENT TERMINOLOGY

As you assume more responsibility in secretarial work, your employer may entrust you with knowledge about certain investments. These investments may include stocks, bonds, and money market funds. A knowledge of the terminology and the procedures in buying and selling securities will help you understand and handle some of the details relating to investments.

Stocks

Stocks represent shares of ownership in a company. Stockholders invest in a company by buying shares of stock. They are issued stock certificates which show the number of shares owned.

Kinds of Stock. Stock in a company can be classified as either *common stock* or *preferred stock*. Common stockholders usually have the right to vote at periodic stockholders' meetings. Common stockholders do not receive a fixed dividend. A *dividend* is a distribution paid to stockholders by the corporation. Dividends are declared or voted by the board of directors of the corporation. Dividends may be distributed in cash, other assets, or in the corporation's own stock. If dividends are distributed in cash (which is the most common method of distribution), the earnings of the corporation determine the dollar amount of dividends paid per share of stock.

Preferred stockholders have preference over common stockholders because dividends are paid on preferred stock before they are paid on common stock. When dividends are declared, preferred stockholders must be paid in full before common stockholders can be paid any dividends. The preferred stockholders are paid at a set dividend rate. For example, a share of preferred stock with a par value of $200 and a stated 8 percent dividend rate would entitle the owner to $16 yearly. *Par value* is an arbitrary amount assigned to the stock when issued that has no relationship to the actual market value of the stock. In rare instances, preferred stock is issued without a stated par value. Such no-par stock has a stated dollar dividend amount instead of a dividend rate.

There are several classes of both common and preferred stocks that give stockholders various rights or privileges. Generally the income on preferred stock is more certain than that on common stock. The market value of common stock may fluctuate more than the market value of preferred stock due to the uncertain amount of dividends on common stock. In periods of high earnings and expansion of a corporation, common stockholders ordinarily receive a much larger share of the increased earnings than preferred stockholders since the income on preferred stock is fixed. Some companies have *participating preferred stock* which allows stockholders to receive extra dividends over and above the fixed amount after the common stockholders have received a certain income on their holdings.

Stock Exchanges. The marketplace where some stocks and other types of securities such as bonds are traded is called the *stock exchange*. The two national stock exchanges are the New York Stock Exchange and the American Stock Exchange. In addition to these stock exchanges, there are various regional and foreign exchanges. In order to transact business on an exchange, an individual broker or brokerage firm must be a member. This membership, called a *seat on the exchange*, allows the person or firm to trade stocks with others on the exchange. The number of seats on the New York Stock Exchange is fixed at 1,366. To become a member, a prospective trader must purchase the seat of a current member.

An individual investor does not buy and sell securities on a stock exchange. Instead, the investor deals with a broker who handles the transaction and charges a fee for the service. When stocks are bought or sold in lots of less than 100 shares, a fee, called an *odd-lot fee,* is charged. Stocks are not transferred directly from seller to buyer; they are exchanged through a transfer agent who cancels the old stock of the seller and issues new stock in the name of the buyer.

Over-the-Counter Market. The New York Stock Exchange is the largest stock exchange, but only a portion of the stocks traded are listed on this exchange. Many stocks are *unlisted* and are traded on the over-the-counter market (OTC). The OTC permits the buying and selling of stocks that are not listed on a stock exchange. Face-to-face bargaining does not take place at a centralized location, such as the New York Stock Exchange. Instead, brokers scattered throughout the country buy and sell stocks over the telephone or by telegram. Stocks traded on the OTC are reported in newspapers at *bid* and *ask* prices which represent the approximate buying and selling prices of stock sold over-the-counter. To buy stock over-the-counter, an individual investor must contact a broker.

Illus. 14-17
You can keep up to date on the details relating to investments by reading a daily newspaper.

Stock Quotations. Most daily newspapers in large cities carry financial sections that report stock transactions over-the-counter and on the major stock exchanges. Illus. 14-18 shows a partial list of stock quotations on the New York Stock Exchange. Notice ACF (ACF

52-week High	52-week Low	Stock	Div.	Yld.	PE	Sales 100s	High	Low	Last	Chg.
				– A–A–A –						
17 3/4	8 5/8	AAR	.44	2.6	21	183	17 1/2	17 1/8	17 1/4	....
52 3/8	30 1/2	ACF	1.40	2.8	238	354	50	49 1/8	50	+ 3/4
22	18 1/4	AMCA	n	..	..	1	21 5/8	21 5/8	21 5/8	+ 1/8
18 7/8	14 3/4	AMF	.50	3.1	..	714	16 1/8	16	16	– 1/4
39 1/8	18 1/2	AMR Cp		..	16	3985	36 1/8	35 1/2	36 1/8	+ 3/4
19 1/2	15	AMR	pf 2.18	11.	..	123	u19 3/4	19	19 3/4	+ 3/4

Illus. 14-18
Stock quotations

Industries Incorporated) which is circled. The first column gives the highest price paid for the stock so far this year (52 3/8 or $52.375), and the second column gives the lowest price paid for the stock so far this year (30 1/2 or $30.50). Next the name of the stock is given, followed by the annual dividend the corporation is currently paying per share ($1.40). The Yld. column gives the yield (as a percentage) and the PE column states the price-earnings ratio. The Sales column reports the number of shares (in hundreds) traded on a single day. The High column represents the highest price paid for a share during the day's trading session (50 or $50.00), and the Low column denotes the low price of the stock for the day (49 1/8 or $49.125). The Last column gives the final (closing) price of the stock on that day. The Chg. column (net change) reveals the change in the price of the stock from the close of business one day to the next.

Bonds

A *bond* is a certificate that promises to pay a definite sum of money at a specified time with interest payable periodically to the holder of the bond. Thus, bonds do not represent a share of ownership in a company but are evidence of a debt owed by the firm. A *bondholder* lends money to a company and in return receives a bond which is a preferred lien against the company. Bonds of corporations are considered among the safest kinds of investments since the interest on bonds must be paid before the stockholders may share in the earnings of the company. Although bonds are considered safer investments than stocks, the interest that the bondholder receives may not be as much as the dividends paid a stockholder with the same amount of investment.

Bonds are usually of two classes: registered bonds and coupon bonds. The owner of a *registered bond* receives interest by check from the company issuing the bonds. Interest on a *coupon bond* is payable to the holder of the bond; if the bond or coupon is stolen or lost, it may be cashed by someone else. If your responsibilities include the safekeeping of stocks or bonds, it is extremely important that such investments be kept in a safe-deposit box.

The Money Market

Funds deposited in banks, savings and loan associations, and brokerage firms are commonly invested in money markets. A distinction is made between capital markets, in which ownership shares (stocks) and long-term debt obligations (bonds) are bought and sold, and money markets, in which short-term debt obligations (such as Treasury bills and notes) are traded. Financial institutions offer various money market plans based on the amount of money you wish to invest and how long you wish to keep your money in the market. In this section, three types of money market plans—money market mutual funds, money market deposit accounts, and money market certificates of deposit—will be examined.

Money Market Mutual Funds. A *mutual fund* is a company that combines the investment funds of many people and in turn invests their funds in a variety of securities. (*Securities* is used here in its broadest sense to include debt obligations that mature within a relatively short term—frequently one year or less.) More specifically, mutual funds sell shares of stock to investors. They then take the money received from the sale of shares and invest in various types of short-term securities. They distribute earnings realized from investing in securities as dividends to their investors or reinvest the dividends in additional fund shares. These funds will sell shares of stock at any time and in any quantity. They are also ready at any time to redeem or buy back shares at the request of the investor.

Money market mutual funds typically invest in United States government securities such as Treasury bills and notes or in commercial paper of large corporations. *Commercial papers* are short-term (up to 270 days), unsecured promissory notes issued by a corporation to raise money. The rate of return on money invested in a mutual fund varies daily. These funds are not insured; so it is conceivable that you could lose money as a result of fraud, mismanagement, or an economic calamity. No penalty is paid for withdrawing your money from a mutual fund.

Money Market Deposit Accounts. On December 14, 1982, banks and savings and loan associations began offering a new type of account designed to compete directly with money market mutual funds. Financial institutions can guarantee the rates on these accounts for up to one month; on the other hand, money market fund rates are not guaranteed and vary daily. The $2,500 minimum opening deposit for this account will drop to $1,000 on January 1, 1985, and will be eliminated altogether on January 1, 1986. Depositors can withdraw from a money market account at any time, but they can write only three checks a month on the account and arrange a total of only six transfers from the account (including the checks) in one month. This type of account has one major advantage over a money market fund—deposits are insured.

Money Market Certificates of Deposit. Commercial banks, mutual savings banks, and savings and loan associations are authorized to issue money market certificates of deposit. The names of these certificates vary depending on where they are purchased. These certificates are bought for a fixed period of time, and the interest rate is usually a fixed percentage. For example, you may buy a 26-week certificate requiring a $500 deposit and paying 8 percent interest. Or you may buy a three and one-half year certificate of deposit for $500 with an interest rate of 10 percent. Certificates of deposit are less liquid than money market mutual funds. You cannot sell the certificates on the open market; and, if you wish to cash them in before maturity, you must pay a substantial withdrawal penalty. Certificates in depository institutions are usually insured, however, which makes them as safe as any investment can be.

Record of Investments

One of your responsibilities as secretary may be to work with your employer in keeping a record of investments and the income

SECURITY RECORD

Property of	Peter G. McDonald			Name of Corporation	Consolidated Products	
Registered in name of	Peter G. McDonald			Address of Corporation	New York, NY 10021-0011	
Where deposited	National Savings Bank			Description of Issue	Common Stock 3/16, 6/16	
				Interest or Dividend Rate .825 quar. Dates	9/16, 12/16	

NO. SHARES	DATE BOUGHT	PRICE	COST	DATE SOLD	PRICE	PROCEEDS	PROFIT OR (LOSS)
50	7/6/80	76 1/4	$3,844.60 (includes odd-lot fee, $32.10)				

DIVIDEND OR INTEREST RECORD

YEAR	JAN./FEB./MAR.			APR./MAY/JUNE			JULY/AUG./SEPT.			OCT./NOV./DEC.			ANNUAL TOTAL	YIELD
	DATE	PER SH.	AMT.	DATE	PER SH.	AMT.	DATE	PER SH.	AMT.	DATE	PER SH.	AMT.		
1980							9/18	.75	37.50	12/17	.75	37.50	75.00	3.90
1981	3/17	.75	37.50	6/17	.825	41.25	9/18	.825	41.25	12/17	.825	41.25	161.25	4.19
1982	3/17	.825	41.25	6/17	.825	41.25	9/18	.825	41.25	12/17	.825	41.25	165.00	4.29

Illus. 14-19
Record of investments

from them. A separate card should be kept for each lot of securities purchased, and information regarding where the securities are kept may be placed on the back of the card. Such a record is needed as a matter of general information and also for tax purposes. All income from investments (except tax free securities) must be reported on the federal income tax return. Likewise, any profit or loss from the sale of securities or other investments must be reported on the income tax return. Illus. 14-19 is typical of a record that might be kept to show details about the purchase and sale of stocks and the income from investments.

TYPES OF INSURANCE

Your work as a secretary may involve a knowledge of several kinds of insurance. You may be responsible for handling some of the insurance records of the company for which you work. The types of insurance carried by most companies are so varied and so numerous that it would be impossible to list them all in this textbook; however, insurance commonly carried by most companies is presented here.

Merchandise and Inventory Insurance

Most companies that buy and sell merchandise, supplies, or equipment carry insurance on all inventories to protect the business from loss by fire or other causes. Although the total amount of inventories may not be covered by insurance, the amount of insurance carried is usually sufficient to cover any loss incurred.

Equipment Insurance

Most companies carry insurance on desks, tables, chairs, filing cabinets, typewriters, and other office equipment. This insurance is a means of protecting the business from loss in case equipment is destroyed or damaged by fire or other causes. Some records must be available to show the value of various pieces of equipment so that this information can be used as a guide in determining the amount of insurance that should be carried.

Illus. 14-20 shows one type of record recommended in determining the value of equipment. Although you may not be required to keep the equipment record, you should know whether such a record is maintained because of the close relationship between this record and the amount of insurance required for adequate coverage.

PERPETUAL RECORD OF EQUIPMENT								
Description	Calculator				Account	Office Equipment		
Age when acquired	New		Estimated life 5 years			Annual depreciation	20%	

COST				DEPRECIATION RECORD				
Date Purchased	Description		Amount		Year	Rate	Amount	Total to Date
July 1 82	1 Victor 850,		167	65	82	20%	16 77	16 77
	12-digit electronic				83	20%	33 53	50 30
	print/display							
	calculator, #8530,							
	Taylor Equipment							
	Company, Chicago,							
	Illinois 60601-6450							

SOLD, EXCHANGED, OR DISCARDED					
Date	Explanation	Amount Realized	MORE THAN / LESS THAN	BOOK VALUE	Debit Reserve

Illus. 14-20
Record of equipment

Business Property Insurance

Usually when a company owns the building or buildings in which it operates, insurance is carried on the property. Most policies of this nature are purchased as fire insurance policies; but they usually carry special features that take care of losses caused by windstorms, riots, and other causes.

Automobile Insurance

You should know about the various kinds of automobile insurance because you may be responsible for handling some of the details in purchasing automobile insurance as well as details that may arise in handling claims.

Since laws vary among the states, be sure that you are familiar with the laws of your particular state and that you are aware of any changes.

Liability Insurance. The owner or operator of a motor vehicle may obtain liability insurance as protection against claims made by third persons for damages resulting from an automobile accident. If you have an automobile accident in which you are at fault, your liability insurance will pay the claims made by the other party in the accident. Liability insurance also protects you from debts when your automobile is operated by a family member or a person who has your permission.

Collision Insurance. Liability insurance protects the insured against claims made by a third person, whereas collision insurance protects the insured from loss or damage to his or her own car when involved in a collision of any kind. With collision insurance there may be a deductible clause that limits payment on claims. For example, a policy with a $100 deductible clause pays damages only above $100, and the policyholder pays all damages up to $100 for each claim.

Uninsured Motorists. You can obtain uninsured motorist insurance which will protect you if you are injured in an accident with a person who does not have liability insurance. The other person must be proven negligent in the accident, however, before you will be covered by the uninsured motorist clause.

Comprehensive Insurance. Comprehensive insurance protects the insured from virtually all risks except collision. Protection is provided against losses resulting from theft or pilferage, fire, tornadoes, windstorms, glass breakage, and similar causes.

Record of Insurance

Since most companies have numerous types of insurance, it is important to maintain a record showing the types of policies, amount of insurance, distribution of insurance premium payments, and so forth. Illus. 14-21 shows one way in which such a record may be set up.

INSURANCE POLICY REGISTER 19_ _					
COMPANY AND POLICY NO.	TYPE OF POLICY	AMOUNT	PREMIUM AMOUNT	PAYABLE	PAYMENT DATES
Capital Insurance # 3711962	Building	$500,000	$800	Semiannually	1/4, 7/4
Kelley Mutual # AE 8210R	Furniture	$250,000	$400	Quarterly	2/6, 5/6, 8/6, 11/6
Nation Insurance Co. # 67853XL	Merchandise	$100,000	$150	Annually	6/6
Fidelity Central # 107091	Office Equipment	$60,000	$90	Annually	10/8

Illus. 14-21
Record of insurance

PROFESSIONAL POINTERS

Here are some tips to help you as you work with financial records.

1. Double-check figures on all forms that you handle.

2. When you type figures, proofread by doing the following:
   a. Have someone else read the figures to you.
   b. Add all columns of figures that have a total.

3. When you handwrite figures, be certain that you take the time to make the figures legible.

4. Keep current on all laws that affect any financial records you might be handling.

5. If you work for a financial organization such as a bank, insurance company, or brokerage firm, increase your knowledge of the specialized financial records they maintain. To do so, read company literature, attend company seminars, take courses from a local college, or read any pertinent literature which may be available at your local library.

6. Be knowledgeable of the terminology used in your company. Many financial terms are technical in nature. If you don't know what a term means, ask someone in the company to explain it to you.

7. Keep up to date on how electronic technology is affecting your organization. For example, if you work in a bank, discover how electronic technology has and will impact the way banking transactions are handled. Keep current by observing what is happening in your bank and by reading any material on the subject that may be available.

FOR YOUR REVIEW

1. What steps should you follow in writing a check?

2. Identify and explain the types of endorsements.

3. Identify and explain three types of special bank services.

4. How has electronic technology influenced the banking world?

5. Name the two major financial statements of a company. What do these statements tell a company?

6. How do the social security tax and the Fair Labor Standards Act affect the amount of money a person earns?

7. Explain the difference between a stock and a bond.

8. How are stocks traded?

9. What are money market mutual funds and money market certificates of deposit?

10. Explain three types of automobile insurance.

CASE PROBLEM

Martin Mahomes has been working as a secretary for Gettinger Stores for the past three years. Two months ago, he was promoted to the accounting department which is managed by Ms. Delphene Woods. Ms. Woods is a brilliant person, but Martin has been having trouble working for her. She never admits that she is wrong. Instead, she accuses Martin of making the mistake.

Martin types a number of statistical reports. He adds the figures on the calculator to be certain that the totals are correct and always gets someone to proofread the reports with him. Last month Ms. Woods's boss brought back three reports containing errors—cash was not included in the current assets. Each time Ms. Woods replied, "I included the figures. I guess Martin overlooked the cash amounts when he typed the reports." However, the cash amounts were not listed on the rough drafts.

Another incident involved a phone call from a customer who requested that Ms. Woods return the call. Martin left the message on Ms. Woods's desk, but she did not call the customer. When the angry customer finally reached her, she said, "I didn't return your call because my secretary didn't give me the message."

Martin is concerned that other employees in the company will begin to question his efficiency as a secretary if these kinds of activities continue.

1. What appears to be the problem in the case?

2. Should Martin take any action? Explain your response.

PRODUCTION PROJECTS

PP 14-1

(Objectives 1, 2, and 3)

Your employer, Benji Yoshino, is secretary-treasurer of the local AMA (American Management Association) chapter. He asks that you assist him in making out deposit slips, writing checks, and reconciling a bank statement. The forms that you will need for this project are in your Supplies Inventory.

1. Mr. Yoshino gives you the following to be deposited to the AMA account on April 15.

Currency $215.00
Coins 5.75
Checks 21-52 .... 25.00
       23-54 .... 25.00
       23-34 .... 52.00

2. Write checks for the following, and date them April 15. The balance brought forward which should be posted on the first check stub is $895.43.

   a. Check 1001, Peck's Office Supply, $25.16, office supplies

   b. Check 1002, Ambassador Inn, $234.75, luncheon

   c. Check 1003, Ruth Shaw, $100, honorarium

   d. Check 1004, Eckert Printing Co., $150, printing of newsletters

3. On April 30 you make the following deposit to the AMA account.

Currency .... $ 58.00
Coins 15.25
Checks 21-58 .... 137.00

4. The April bank statement for the local AMA chapter is given in your Supplies Inventory. After verifying the canceled checks with your check stubs, you find that Check 1002 for $234.75 and Check 1004 for $150 are outstanding. In the space below the bank statement, reconcile the bank balance with the check stub balance of $918.52. Notice that there was a charge of $3.75 (check printing) against the account, interest added of $1.36, a service charge of $2.35, and that the deposit made on April 30 did not reach the bank in time to be recorded on the bank statement.

PP 14-2

(Objective 4)

Explain what bank service you would use in each of the following situations. Type your answers on plain paper.

1. AMH Equipment is buying goods from your company in the amount of $12,000. AMH Equipment is located out of town and has no line of credit established with you. You need guaranteed payment. What type of service would you request that AMH Equipment use?

2. LaBarba Manufacturing is buying goods from your company in the amount of $5,525. LaBarba is located in the same city as your company. You have not done business with them before, and they have no line of credit established with your company. Which type of service should LaBarba Manufacturing use?

3. Your employer is planning a business trip to England. He needs $1,500 in cash. Which type of service would you use?

4. You work for a small company that began business only two months ago. There are already several valuable papers that the company needs to be sure are in a safe place. Which type of service would you suggest?

PP 14-3

(Objective 5)

Read two current articles on electronic banking. Sources you might use include *Money, Forbes, Business Week, United States Banker,* and *Bankers Monthly.* As you read the articles, ask this question: What impact has electronic technology made on the banking industry? Summarize the articles on plain paper, and give the sources of the articles. After you have summarized the articles, answer the question concerning the impact of electronic technology on banking.

PP 14-4

(Objective 6)

Your employer gives you the responsibility for keeping the petty cash record for the AMA chapter. Instead of writing checks for small expenditures, a petty cash fund is used. On the petty cash record in your Supplies Inventory, enter the petty cash transactions listed at the bottom of the form.

PP 14-5

(Objective 7)

The annual report for your company was recently published. In reading it, you find that you are unable to understand much of the financial terminology. In order to learn more about financial statements, do the following:

1. Read and study the information on financial statements in an accounting text, or talk with a CPA or an accounting instructor concerning the interpretation of financial statements.

2. From the information that you have obtained, define the following terms:

   a. Current assets
   b. Accounts receivable
   c. Accounts payable
   d. Profit and loss statement
   e. Stockholders' equity

   f. Retained earnings
   g. Fiscal year
   h. Net income
   i. Operating expenses
   j. Cash

PP 14-6

(Objective 7)

Using the balance sheet in your Supplies Inventory, compute the totals, type the balance sheet, and figure the current ratio and quick ratio. Type the current and quick ratio information on a separate sheet of paper.

PP 14-7

(Objective 8)

In your Supplies Inventory is a payroll register for several employees. The rate of pay and the total hours worked are given for each employee. All employees are paid one and a half times their regular rate for time worked over 40 hours per week. Figure the FICA tax at 6.7%. The amount withheld for income tax purposes and the deduction for hospitalization have been inserted for each employee. Fill out the form, showing the regular earnings, overtime earnings, total earnings, FICA tax, and the net earnings. Total all columns.

PP 14-8

(Objective 9)

To help you become familiar with investment terms, define the following terms. Recent general business or finance textbooks are excellent reference sources for this activity.

   a. Bull market
   b. Bear market
   c. Blue chip stocks
   d. Price-earnings ratio
   e. Dow Jones Averages

   f. Registered bond
   g. Stock split
   h. Bond discount
   i. Bond premium

PP 14-9

(Objective 10)

To learn more about insurance, do *one* of the following:

1. Investigate the insurance plan for employees at a local company and prepare a short report on this plan. Type the report in proper form.

2. Call a local insurance company and get information on different types of life insurance and car insurance. Prepare a short report on your findings. Present your report to the class.

3. Do library research on the various types of insurance. Prepare a report on your findings. Type the report in proper form, and indicate the sources that you used.

Chapter 15

MAKING TRAVEL ARRANGEMENTS

Travel in today's fast-moving, constantly expanding business world is an integral part of many executives' work. Even with sophisticated telecommunications systems which transmit information quickly from one distant location to another, it is essential that executives communicate face-to-face with associates in negotiating business deals and in learning new techniques. Travel to meetings, conferences, and conventions averages one to two days a week and is commonplace for many executives.

Generally large companies have a travel department that handles arrangements for executive trips. Small companies may rely on travel agencies to make arrangements for executives. Still other companies may expect executives to be responsible for making their own travel arrangements. In such situations, the secretary usually obtains all the necessary information and confirms arrangements for a trip. Company policy notwithstanding, you should be aware of company procedures concerning travel and your employer's preferences regarding airlines, hotels, rental cars, and other travel related matters. You also need to keep current on the travel services available.

General Objectives

Your general objectives for Chapter 15 are to:

1. *Understand how to make travel arrangements*
2. *Prepare an itinerary*
3. *Know which duties should be performed while the executive is away*
4. *Know which duties should be performed when the executive returns*
5. *Prepare an expense report*

METHODS OF TRAVEL

Since time is so important to the busy executive, practically all travel today is by air. As a secretary, you may rarely make arrangements for your employer to travel by train or bus. If your employer plans to travel by train, however, you may obtain information through the Amtrak WATS number (a toll free number listed in your local directory) or in the *Official Railway Guide*, published by the National Railway Publication Company, 424 West 33rd Street, New York, NY 10001. Information concerning bus travel may be obtained from your local bus lines.

The basic travel duties, such as making reservations, preparing the itinerary and other materials for your employer's trip, understanding which duties should be performed during or after your employer's trip, and making out an expense report, are the same regardless of which method of travel is used. Since bus and train travel are used so infrequently, the concentration in this chapter is on air travel.

TRAVEL ARRANGEMENTS

Company policies on making travel arrangements vary. Therefore, it is important to find out the procedures the company follows regarding travel arrangements. Does the company have a travel department? use a travel agency? Or is the secretary responsible for making all arrangements?

Travel Department

If you work for a large company, there may be a separate travel department in the company which handles all travel arrangements. When your employer plans a trip, you call the travel department and give the following information:

1. Employer's name, title, department
2. The cities to be visited along with the dates and times of expected arrivals and departures
3. Preferences as to motel or hotel (type of accommodation, price range)
4. Rental car, if desired
5. Advance expense money requested

The travel department maintains up-to-date airline schedules. Many companies subscribe to the *Official Airline Guide,* which is published twice monthly by Official Airline Guides, Inc., 2000 Clearwater Drive, Oak Brook, IL 60521. This guide provides information on fares, schedules, types of aircraft, and food service. Travel departments may also maintain copies of the *Hotel and Motel Red Book* which provides information about hotel and motel accommodations. It is published by the American Hotel Association Directory Corporation, 888 Seventh Avenue, New York, NY 10019.

Travel Agencies

Travel agencies now handle many of the travel arrangements for business executives. In fact, some agencies serve business firms exclusively. A travel agency does not charge the customer a fee; the transportation companies that book the customer pay the fee.

When travel arrangements are made through a travel agency, it is necessary to supply basic information such as the employer's name, the cities to be visited along with the dates and times of expected arrivals and departures, preferences as to motel or hotel (type of accommodation and price range), and rental car services. You should also give the agency the office and home telephone numbers of the executive and any cost limitations. The agency makes all travel arrangements—obtains tickets, makes hotel and motel reservations, and arranges car rental. The agency will also provide a complete itinerary which gives flight numbers, arrival and departure times, and so forth.

Arrangements by the Secretary

If the company provides neither the services of a travel department nor a travel agency, it is the responsibility of the secretary to make all travel arrangements. The secretary works directly with airlines, hotels or motels, and car rental agencies by calling them and getting the needed information. It is usually a good idea to call several airlines to get the best flight accommodations as to arrival and departure times, flight connections, and prices. Follow this procedure in making hotel or motel reservations, too. If the executive is attending a conference or convention, the hotel or motel hosting the function may offer rooms at a reduced rate for the event. At any rate, as an efficient secretary, you should be aware of your employer's preferences regarding travel services and make travel arrangements accordingly.

Traveler's Rights and Responsibilities

When you purchase an airline ticket, you enter into a contract with the airline. Your rights and responsibilities in this contract as well as the airline's rights and responsibilities are made available through information on the ticket and through additional printed materials that you may obtain at the airport or ticket office. Information of which you should be aware when traveling by air includes such items as fare changes, responsibility for schedules and operations, baggage requirements and liabilities, check-in requirements, refunds, and claims. All travelers should be aware of the conditions of this contract by obtaining and reading the appropriate information.

DOMESTIC AIR TRAVEL

When you make arrangements for domestic air travel, you need to be familiar with the classes of flights available, methods of making flight reservations, airport services provided, hotel reservation services, and car rental services.

Flight Classifications

When you make flight reservations, you need to know your company's policy regarding the classes of air travel. Airlines have basically two classes of flight available: first class and coach. Since first class is more expensive than coach, most companies have a policy that only chief executives travel first class. Usually the chief executives of a company include the chairman of the board, the president, and sometimes the executive vice-president.

Radio Shack, a Division
of Tandy Corporation

Illus. 15-1
Most executives traveling on business prefer to fly, especially on long trips, because they save time.

First-class accommodations are more luxurious than coach. The seats are wider, farther apart, and provide more legroom than those in the coach section. Several flight attendants are available to take care of your needs. Elegant meals and generous refreshments, including alcoholic beverages, are served free of charge.

Coach accommodations provide snacks, soft drinks, tea or coffee, and meals free of charge. However, seats are closer together, more people use the coach section, and fewer attendants are available; in short, the atmosphere is not as luxurious nor is the service as attentive as that in first class.

Some airlines now offer another flight accommodation called business class. This class is not provided on all planes nor on all routes. For example, it is usually provided only on large planes such as 747s or 767s on long distance routes, say from New York to the West Coast. Business class is slightly more expensive than coach. The business class section on a plane is located directly behind first class and in front of coach. Accommodations include more spacious seating than coach, complimentary alcoholic beverages, headsets for listening to music, and special meals if requested when making reservations.

Air Fares

The airlines business is very competitive, and air fares are constantly changing. When making airline reservations, it is wise to check several airlines for price and flight information. If it is convenient for your employer to travel at night or on weekends, special prices usually are available which are lower than weekday flight rates. Also, if you know about your employer's travel needs several weeks in advance, you may be able to take advantage of special offers. Some airlines offer discount rates on tickets to certain locations for a limited number of days.

Flight Reservations

If you are responsible for making flight reservations for your employer, call the airline's reservation number listed in your local directory. You should supply the agent with the necessary information: destination, date and approximate time of departure, date and approximate time of return, and class of service desired. The agent then checks the availability of the flight and confirms your reservation while you are still on the phone. Confirmation is a rapid process since airlines use computers to check seat availability. If no space is available, the agent will check other airlines. If all space is reserved, your employer's name can be placed on a waiting list.

A ticket can be picked up at the airport, mailed, or sent by private courier service (for a fee). Payment can be made by cash, by check with a valid driver's license and a major credit card for identification, or with an approved credit card (one accepted by the airline). If your employer picks up the ticket at the airport, he or she should arrive at least thirty minutes before the flight departure. If tickets are sent by mail, you may give the reservations agent a credit card number and the tickets will be charged to your account; or you may choose to send the airlines a check for the tickets.

When reservations are made through a travel agency, the company is usually billed for the tickets. The company may have an arrangement whereby it is billed monthly for all travel arrangements made through the agency. In any case, if you work for a large company, the invoice will be sent to the accounting department for payment; and you will not be involved in handling it. If you work for a small company, you may receive the invoice directly and be responsible for seeing that the amount is paid.

Limousine Service

Limousine service is available at most airports. This service is provided to and from the airport and major hotels. Limousine companies usually charge a lower rate than taxi drivers. There are designated locations outside airports and at hotels where passengers are picked up and dropped off for limousine service.

Hotel Reservations

You may make hotel or motel reservations by any of the following means:

1. Telephoning the hotel or motel
2. Sending a Mailgram or telegram to the hotel or motel
3. Calling a central reservations number, which is listed in the telephone directory, for major hotel and motel chains (This number is usually toll free.)
4. Writing a letter to the hotel or motel

In making room reservations, you should specify the kind of accommodation desired (single or double room), preferred room rate, number of persons registering, date and approximate time of arrival, and length of stay. You should also request a confirmation. Most hotels and motels will confirm your reservation over the telephone by giving you a confirmation number in exchange for your supplying them with a major credit card number. Hotels and motels will also send a written confirmation, and it is wise to ask for this written confirmation.

Car Rental

Many times an executive travels by air and rents a car for convenience in keeping business appointments at his or her destination. Reservations for cars can be made through the airlines or by calling a car rental agency. Toll free numbers for car rental agencies are listed in the telephone directory. When renting a car, specify the make and model of car preferred and the date and time the car will be picked up and returned.

Upon arriving at the destination airport, an executive will go to the car rental desk (usually located close to the baggage pickup area), present his or her driver's license, and make financial arrangements for renting the car. Car rental agencies will accept cash, a check when backed by a driver's license and a major credit card, or an approved credit card (one accepted by the car rental agency). When the rental car is returned, the total amount of the bill is figured. The agencies have two methods for determining the cost of a rental car: (1) a flat daily rate plus an amount for each mile driven or (2) a flat daily rate with unlimited mileage.

Most car rental agencies will provide maps of the area and assist in planning the best travel route. They will also supply information about hotels and restaurants in the area and information identifying historical sites and tourist attractions of interest in the area.

INTERNATIONAL TRAVEL

Today, with many companies having divisions in Europe, Japan, and other overseas locations, it is not uncommon for executives to make business trips abroad. As a secretary, you need to know how to make arrangements for an overseas trip.

Travel Agency Services

Travel departments or travel agencies are essential in planning trips abroad. If your company does not have a travel department, a travel agency will be extremely valuable to you in planning the trip. The agency can assist you with the numerous, necessary details. Because these agencies frequently work with foreign travelers, it is their business to have a great deal of information about travel to various countries. Some of the services of travel agencies are listed below.

- Prepare trip itineraries
- Purchase tickets
- Make hotel reservations

- Make car rental reservations
- Give currency information
- Obtain necessary insurance
- Provide passport applications
- Get visas
- Explain baggage restrictions
- Identify the travel documents required and how to obtain them

Passports

A *passport* is an official government document that certifies the identity and citizenship of an individual and grants the person permission to travel abroad. A passport is required in all countries outside the United States with the exception of Canada, Mexico, Bermuda, the West Indies, and Central American countries. A visitor to Mexico who plans to stay longer than three days must obtain a travel permit at the port of entry.

Passport application forms can be obtained from a travel agency or a passport office. You can find your local passport office telephone number by looking under "United States Government, Passport Information," in your local telephone directory. In order to obtain a passport for the first time, the individual must appear in person before an agent of the passport office or a clerk of a federal court or a state court. The applicant must present the following items:

1. A completed application
2. Proof of United States citizenship through a certified copy of a birth certificate, baptismal certificate, or certificate of naturalization (If such proof is not available, the applicant must submit a notice that no birth record exists and secondary evidence such as census records, family Bibles, school records, or affidavits of persons with personal knowledge of the applicant's birth.)
3. Proof of identification through such documents as a driver's license
4. Two signed duplicate photographs taken by a photographer within the past six months
5. The passport fee

A passport is valid for ten years from the date of issue. As soon as the passport is received, it should be signed and the information requested on the inside cover filled in. While traveling abroad, the passport should always be carried by the traveler; it should never be left in a hotel room.

Visas

A *visa* is a document granted by a foreign government which permits a traveler to enter and travel within a particular country. A visa usually appears as a stamped notation on a passport indicating that the bearer may enter the country for a certain purpose and period of time. If you have any doubt as to whether or not a visa is needed, you should contact the consulate for the particular country.

Flights

International air travel is basically the same as domestic air travel. Classes of flight are the same—first class and coach. (Coach is also referred to as tourist or economy class.) Weight and size restrictions for luggage vary slightly from one airline to another, with the following example being typical of weight and size requirements. First-class passengers are allowed to carry on one piece of luggage which measures no more than 45 inches in either direction and weighs no more than 70 pounds. First-class passengers may check two pieces of luggage with neither piece measuring more than 62 inches in either direction and weighing more than 70 pounds. Coach passengers may also carry on one piece of luggage of the same size and weight as first-class passengers. They may also check two pieces of luggage with each piece weighing no more than 70 pounds and measuring no more than 62 inches. Both pieces may measure no more than 106 inches, however. Fares vary with the season.

Hotel Reservations

Hotel reservations can be made either through a travel agent or through an airline. A continental breakfast is often included in the hotel charge. If secretarial assistance or a meeting room is needed at the hotel abroad, a travel agent can also arrange for these services.

Car Rental

Rental cars are usually readily available in foreign countries, and a travel agency can arrange for the rental. In most countries a United States driver's license is sufficient. To ensure that everything is in order, however, a traveler may obtain an American International Driving Permit from the American Automobile Association either here or in Europe for a small fee.

SECRETARIAL RESPONSIBILITIES BEFORE THE TRIP

A secretary usually becomes deeply involved in helping an executive plan the trip, making the appropriate reservations, and preparing the necessary materials for the trip. These responsibilities are extremely important and must be done carefully. One incorrect flight time or the wrong accommodations at a hotel can cost an executive considerable time and contribute to a high level of stress.

Plan the Trip

Your major planning responsibilities include getting accurate information for your employer concerning flights, hotels and motels, and car rentals. If you work with a travel department in the company, you should give the department the approximate times that the executive wishes to travel and the types of accommodations preferred. Then the travel department will check out the options available and inform you of the various flight possibilities, hotel accommodations, and car rentals, giving you the cost of all services. If you work with a travel agency, you should give the travel agent the same information. If you make all reservations yourself, you should call several airlines or review various flight schedules, determine the type of hotel or motel accommodations needed, verify hotel or motel prices, and determine prices from one or two car rental agencies.

Once you receive the travel options available from the travel department or travel agency or have gathered the travel information yourself, you should arrange it for your employer in an easy-to-read format. Then present the information to your employer, who will decide which options best fit his or her needs.

Make Reservations

Once your employer has determined the appropriate arrangements, you are responsible for either making the reservations or seeing that they are made. If you work with a travel department or travel agency, give the personnel the necessary information. If you make the reservations yourself, contact the airlines, hotel or motel, and car rental agency. Be certain that you give the person contacted all the necessary information. Request written confirmation whenever possible.

Prepare an Itinerary

The *itinerary,* a detailed outline of the trip, is a must for you and your employer. If you work with a travel agency, the agency will prepare a brief itinerary which covers such items as the flight number and departure and arrival times. This itinerary is helpful; but a comprehensive itinerary which includes appointments, hotel and motel reservations, and helpful reminders, along with the flight information, is invaluable. Illus. 15-2 shows a clear, concise itinerary set up in an easy-to-read format. Notice that it includes various time zones since the traveler is going from one time zone to another. If your employer is traveling in only one time zone, you do not need to include the time zones. When he or she is traveling from one time zone to another, however, an indication of the time change is helpful.

```
                      ITINERARY FOR PAUL FORREST
                           March 5-6, 19--
                          Trip to San Francisco

     MONDAY, MARCH 5 (DALLAS TO SAN FRANCISCO)
         9:30 a.m. CST      Leave Dallas--DFW Regional Airport on American
                            Flight 55 (pick up ticket at airport).

        10:30 a.m. PST      Arrive San Francisco--San Francisco Interna-
                            tional Airport (pick up rental car at airport;
                            hotel reservation at Hilton, 300 Airport
                            Freeway, telephone:  772-3100).

         2:00 p.m. PST      Appointment with Peter Nelson of Nelson & Nelson
                            in his office, 1214 Harwood Avenue, telephone:
                            772-5418 (correspondence file in briefcase).


     TUESDAY, MARCH 6 (SAN FRANCISCO TO DALLAS)
        10:00 a.m. PST      Appointment with Roger Hall of San Francisco
                            office (reports in briefcase).

         2:00 p.m. PST      Appointment with Carla Hampton of San Francisco
                            office (reports in briefcase).

         5:00 p.m. PST      Leave San Francisco International Airport on
                            American Flight 43.

        10:00 p.m. CST      Arrive Dallas--DFW Regional Airport.
```

Illus. 15-2
Itinerary

As you begin planning a trip, it is a good idea to set up a travel folder for the trip. Place all information that you receive concerning the trip in the folder. When you are ready to prepare the itinerary, you will have all the necessary information in one location. In addition to the itinerary, some executives prefer to have a separate appointment schedule which isolates the appointments on one form. An appointment schedule, as shown in Illus. 15-3, provides a quick and easy reference for the executive.

APPOINTMENT SCHEDULE

City	Date/Time	With	Telephone	Location	Remarks
Chicago	Thursday, April 13, 10:00 a.m.	Max Goldberg	555-5620	Room 212 Oil & Gas Building	Blue folder contains papers for meeting.
Chicago	Friday, April 14, 8:30 a.m.	Betty Martin	555-8900	To be arranged	Call Betty Martin Thursday afternoon to determine meeting location.

Illus. 15-3
Appointment schedule

Obtain Travel Funds

The executive may receive money in advance from the company for the trip or may use personal funds and be reimbursed by the company at the conclusion of the trip. Whatever the procedure, you may be responsible for helping the executive arrange for traveler's checks or money orders.

In Chapter 14 you learned about traveler's checks and bank money orders. Traveler's checks must be purchased by the person who will use them since they must be signed at the time of purchase. Traveler's checks are available from the American Express Company and most banks and travel agencies. The secretary may obtain money orders for the executive. Money orders may be purchased at a bank or from the American Express Company. If the executive is stranded without funds, he or she can call or wire the secretary to send a money order by telegraph.

Many executives prefer to use either personal credit cards or company credit cards while traveling. These cards, such as VISA, American Express, and MasterCard, are accepted by most businesses in the United States or abroad. Your secretarial responsibility here may be requesting new credit cards when they expire and in keeping a record of the credit card numbers. If a credit card is lost or stolen, it is important that the company be notified immediately. To do so, you need to have the credit card number readily available.

Illus. 15-4
You may be responsible for helping the executive obtain travel funds for domestic as well as international travel.

Prepare Materials for the Trip

Your employer may need to take business correspondence on a trip. If so, it is a good idea to supply just the necessary copies rather than the entire file folder. By making copies of the correspondence, you retain the original files in the office in case they are needed in your employer's absence.

If a presentation is planned, your duties may include typing the presentation or researching the topic. Be sure to find out your employer's preference as to format before typing the presentation—small cards may be preferable to regular typing paper since they are easier to handle when making a presentation.

Check the Calendar

Check your employer's calendar and your desk calendar to see if appointments have been scheduled for the period in which your employer will be gone. If so, find out if they are to be canceled or if someone else in the company will handle them. Then notify the people involved.

Illus. 15-5
When planning a trip, check your employer's calendar and your desk calendar for appointments that may be scheduled while your employer is away.

Know How Matters Are to Be Handled

Find out who is to be in charge during your employer's absence. Check to see if your employer is expecting any important papers that should be forwarded. Be sure you understand how to handle all the incoming mail and other daily duties.

Confirm Appointments for the Trip

Either write or call persons whom your employer plans to see during the trip to confirm the appointments. It is wise to do this before preparing the itinerary.

Assemble Items for the Trip

Various items are needed for a trip. A representative list includes the following:

- Plane tickets (may be picked up at the airport)
- Copy of itinerary

- Travel money, credit cards
- Hotel confirmations
- Copies of correspondence, speeches, etc., needed for the trip
- Information on companies that will be visited
- Reading materials

RESPONSIBILITIES WHILE EMPLOYER IS AWAY

You have worked hard and efficiently to facilitate your employer's departure. What happens now? Is it playtime for you? Not quite. Your pace may moderate slightly while your employer is out of the office, or it may even accelerate. Your responsibility is to handle the office routine smoothly and efficiently during your employer's absence.

Handle Correspondence

There may be correspondence that you will need to forward to your employer. It is a good idea to send copies of the correspondence rather than the original; keep the original in your files.

Answer any routine mail that you can. If you receive mail that needs immediate attention but that you are unable to handle, you can usually refer it to someone else in the office who has been designated by your employer. This person should furnish you with a file copy of the correspondence so that your employer will be informed as to how the matter was handled.

Make Decisions

You have the responsibility of making wise decisions during your employer's absence. You should know which matters to refer to someone else in the company and which matters to refer directly to your employer through a telephone call or telegram. Certainly you do not want to place excessive calls to your employer while he or she is away. But there may be matters that your employer must be informed of immediately. Your responsibility is to make the correct decisions.

Keep a Record of Mail

Keep a record of all the mail that comes in while your employer is away. Include in the record the sender's name, the date, and a brief summary of the contents. Illus. 15-6 shows a record of incoming mail.

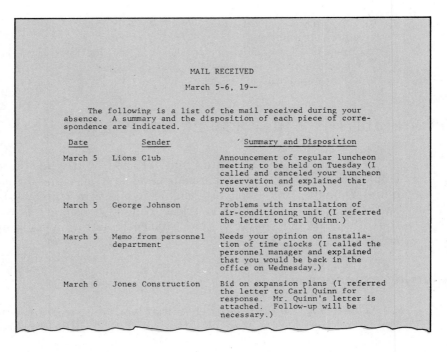

```
                              MAIL RECEIVED
                             March 5-6, 19--

            The following is a list of the mail received during your
        absence.  A summary and the disposition of each piece of corre-
        spondence are indicated.

           Date            Sender              Summary and Disposition

        March 5     Lions Club           Announcement of regular luncheon
                                         meeting to be held on Tuesday (I
                                         called and canceled your luncheon
                                         reservation and explained that
                                         you were out of town.)

        March 5     George Johnson       Problems with installation of
                                         air-conditioning unit (I referred
                                         the letter to Carl Quinn.)

        March 5     Memo from personnel  Needs your opinion on installa-
                    department           tion of time clocks (I called the
                                         personnel manager and explained
                                         that you would be back in the
                                         office on Wednesday.)

        March 6     Jones Construction   Bid on expansion plans (I referred
                                         the letter to Carl Quinn for
                                         response.  Mr. Quinn's letter is
                                         attached.  Follow-up will be
                                         necessary.)
```

Illus. 15-6
Record of incoming mail

This itemized list can help your employer increase his or her effectiveness. By scanning this list, your employer can make a quick check of the incoming correspondence and pick out the most important items first.

Keep a Record of Visitors and Telephone Calls

It is important to keep a log of all office visits and telephone calls while your employer is away. When your employer comes back to the office, you do not have to relay all the information verbally—you can merely have the log available for review. An example of such a log is shown in Illus. 15-7.

Set Up Appointments

While your employer is away, you will probably need to set up appointments for persons who want to see your employer after the trip. Remember, when you are setting up the appointments, your employer will probably already have a full day of work in the office to handle on the first day back. Thus, it is not a good idea to schedule appointments for this day. If you must do so, however, remember to

```
                    VISITORS AND TELEPHONE CALLS
                          March 5-6, 19--

        Date/                                  Reason
        Time          Visitor      Telephone   for Call      Action

      March 5      Reese Vaughn                 Personal    Told him
      8:45 a.m.    Maxwell & Co.                            you would
                                                            be back
                                                            Wednesday
                                                            and sug-
                                                            gested he
                                                            call you
                                                            Friday

      March 5                      Martin Steel Expansion   Will call
      9:00 a.m.                    555-5118     plans       Friday

      March 5      Clara Campbell               Insurance   Will tele-
      9:30 a.m.    Allhome Insurance            policy      phone for
                                                            appointment
                                                            on Thursday

      March 5                      Connie Novak Marketing   Referred
      9:42 a.m.                    Ext. 345     report      her to
                                                            Carl Quinn
```

Illus. 15-7
Visitors' and telephone log

schedule as few appointments as possible and to keep the timing convenient for your employer.

Use Time Wisely

Assume that you have handled all routine correspondence and all special matters. Your workday is from 8 a.m. to 5 p.m., and it is now 2 p.m. What should you do? There are many things that you can catch up on while your employer is away—filing, transferring inactive files, replacing file folders, or a number of other tasks.

What about your employer's desk? Do things need to be straightened? Don't indiscriminately throw things in the trash though. The key is to straighten the desk—not to clean out and discard everything in sight.

Do you know what is happening in the company? Now is a good time to read company publications to learn your company's diversification plans, to acquaint yourself with any new products, any newly acquired subsidiaries, and so on. You can use this time to review general business and economic conditions in magazines like *Forbes, Business Week,* or *Fortune.*

An efficient, worth-your-weight-in-gold secretary does not waste time. Every minute is utilized. There is always something you can do to increase your own personal knowledge and efficiency.

SECRETARIAL DUTIES WHEN THE EXECUTIVE RETURNS

Once your employer returns from a trip, there are a number of tasks that must be done. An expense report of the trip is filled out first. Also, there will be numerous pieces of correspondence to handle. You can assist your employer in going through the correspondence that has accumulated by sorting it in labeled folders. One method is to sort the correspondence in folders labeled: (1) urgent correspondence, (2) memorandums, (3) internal reports, and (4) magazines and periodicals.

In addition to helping your employer fill out an expense report and handle the accumulated correspondence, you should also provide assistance in writing thank you or follow-up letters and returning materials to the files.

Expense Reports

Regardless of whether your employer received funds in advance from the company or used personal funds for which he or she will be reimbursed, careful records must be kept of all expenses. Most compa-

ENTER ONLY ONE AMOUNT PER LINE, PER DAY.

Raython, Incorporated   WEEKLY EXPENSE REPORT

		SAVE NO.	ENDING SPEEDOMETER				CHANGED DRIVER'S LICENSE NO.	TR. NO.
NAME Ruth McConley								S

WEEK ENDING	SATURDAY May 12	SUNDAY	MONDAY	TUESDAY	WEDNESDAY	THURSDAY	FRIDAY	SATURDAY	TOTALS
PERSONAL									
MOTEL OR HOTEL	Hollaran Inn								
CITY	Chicago								
STATE	Illinois								
ROOM CHARGE (ATTACH RECEIPT)	11		85 00	85 00					170 00
BREAKFAST			5 00	4 00	5 25				
LUNCH			6 25	4 50	8 75				
DINNER			12 00	10 00	13 00				
TOTAL MEALS	12		23 25	18 50	27 00				68 75
OTHER PERSONAL	13								
COMPANY OWNED AUTOMOBILE	14								
GAS—OIL									
OTHER OPERATING (INCLUDE PARKING, TOLLS, TAXES, AND FEES)	15		8 00	6 00					14 00
PARTS AND REPAIRS	16								
MISCELLANEOUS ENTERTAINMENT (EXPLAIN—ATTACH RECEIPT IF OVER $25.00)	17								
OTHER TRANSPORTATION (INCLUDE USE OF PERSONAL CAR)	18								
MISC. OTHER (EXPLAIN—ATTACH RECEIPT IF OVER $25.00)	19								
TOTAL FOR DAY			116 25	109 50	27 00				WEEK'S EXPENSES 252 75

EXPLANATION OF ENTERTAINMENT AND MISCELLANEOUS:			INCREASE MY ADVANCE	21	
			DECREASE MY ADVANCE	22	
			ISSUE CHECK	23	252 75

PLEASE SIGN *Ruth McConley*

Illus. 15-8
Expense report

nies require receipts for hotels, registration fees, car rental, plane tickets, and other major expenses. The traveler's word is usually taken for meals, taxi fares, and tips.

Expense forms are provided by the company and should be filled in correctly with the amounts totaled. An example of an expense report is shown in Illus. 15-8. You should type carefully the expense report, double-checking all figures and totals. You should also be sure that the necessary receipts are attached and that the figures on the expense report match the figures on the receipts.

Correspondence

Your employer will probably need to write several thank you and follow-up letters as a result of contacts made on the trip. These letters may be dictated to you, or you may have the responsibility of composing some of the letters with your employer indicating to you what should be said.

You may also have the responsibility of unpacking your employer's briefcase. Reports and materials taken from the files before the trip need to be returned to the files. Any duplicate material should be destroyed.

PROFESSIONAL POINTERS

Answer these questions when preparing for your employer's trip.

1. What is the location of the trip?

2. What are the dates and approximate times for which reservations are needed?

3. Must any appointments be scheduled? If so, when, where, and with whom?

4. Are special services such as rental cars needed?

5. Is it necessary to get funds in advance from the company?

6. Are traveler's checks or money orders needed?

7. Must any special materials be prepared for the trip?

8. What hotel accommodations should be made?

9. Who is in charge while my employer is away?

10. Who needs copies of the itinerary?

FOR YOUR REVIEW

1. List and explain the differences between the two classes of domestic flights.

2. How are flight reservations made?

3. What services does a travel agency provide for both domestic and international travel?

4. How may a passport be obtained?

5. What is a visa?

6. Explain the differences between domestic flights and international flights.

7. Name five secretarial responsibilities that must be handled before a trip.

8. What is an itinerary? What should it include?

9. Describe the secretary's responsibilities while the employer is away.

10. Explain the secretary's responsibilities when the employer returns.

CASE PROBLEM

Jeanice Landlow recently accepted her first secretarial position; she has been working for two months. Last week her employer, Gerald Kerr, asked her to make arrangements for him to go to New York. Jeanice received the necessary travel information from him and made the flight reservations. Mr. Kerr told her that he wanted a rental car for three days while in New York. He also told her that he had three appointments in New York and gave her the names of the people he was seeing and the times of the appointments.

On the day of Mr. Kerr's trip, Jeanice typed his itinerary, including the flight numbers, times, and dates of the departure and return flights. Mr. Kerr took one look at the itinerary and asked why she had not listed the appointments. Jeanice looked perplexed and replied that she didn't know she should have included the appointments. When Mr. Kerr arrived at the airport in New York, he called Jeanice and told her that his rental car was not ready. He asked if she had made the reservations. Jeanice was afraid to tell him that she had forgotten to make them; so she let him believe that the car rental agency had made the mistake.

While Mr. Kerr was gone, Jeanice didn't have anything to do; so she read a book most of the time. Several of the office employees remarked about her not working, but Jeanice just told them that she was all caught up on her work. When Mr. Kerr returned from New York, he discovered that Jeanice had not sorted his correspondence nor kept a record of visitors. He told Jeanice that if her work didn't improve, she would be fired.

1. How should Jeanice have prepared for Mr. Kerr's trip?

2. What should she have done while Mr. Kerr was gone?

3. What would you have done?

PRODUCTION PROJECTS

PP 15-1
(Objective 1)

What offices, agencies, or organizations in your community could provide you with information on the following?

a. Passports
b. Immunization records
c. Visas

d. Car rental information
e. Flight information
f. Currency exchange

PP 15-2
(Objective 1)

Call a local travel agency and find out what services are offered in planning a trip. Write your findings in a short report.

PP 15-3
(Objective 2)

Miss Delana Boudreaux, your employer, leaves a note for you in her out basket. After reading the note, which is in your Supplies Inventory, type an itinerary for her trip. Use the flight information in your Supplies Inventory to choose the appropriate flights for Miss Boudreaux.

PP 15-4
(Objectives 3 and 4)

Read two secretarial procedures books (in addition to your text) on the duties of a secretary while the employer is traveling and when the employer returns. Determine the priority in which these duties should be performed. Summarize your findings and the priorities in a report that lists your reference sources.

PP 15-5

(Objective 5)

When Miss Boudreaux returns from her trip, she gives you the receipts (in your Supplies Inventory). Prepare an expense report, using the form in your Supplies Inventory. In addition to these receipts, Miss Boudreaux spent $580.25 on air fare and the following amounts on meals and taxi service:

Monday
Lunch 6.25
Dinner 18.00
Taxi 25.00

Tuesday
Breakfast 6.00
Lunch 7.50
Dinner 17.75
Taxi 25.00

Wednesday
Breakfast 5.00
Lunch 6.25
Dinner 25.00

Thursday
Breakfast 5.00
Lunch 7.00

Friday
Breakfast 6.00
Lunch 8.00

PART 5
The Office Today and Tomorrow—Where Are We Headed?

Chapter 16   Exploring Data Processing
Chapter 17   Analyzing Word Processing
Chapter 18   Understanding Office Reprographics
Chapter 19   Knowing about Telecommunications

Chapter **16**

EXPLORING DATA PROCESSING

Business today is highly competitive, and managers must be able to make quick, intelligent decisions. Because of the tremendous amount of data available, it has become essential for managers, with the assistance of secretaries, to depend on the fantastic powers of the computer.

The computer and the data processing systems that make it work have created America's fastest growing industry—the information industry. Because American business is becoming more and more dependent on computer produced information, it is imperative that you know what data processing is all about.

General Objectives

Your general objectives for Chapter 16 are to:

1. *Become familiar with data processing terminology*
2. *Identify the six functions in the processing of data*
3. *Explain the use of various input/output media and hardware in an electronic computer system*
4. *Explain the classifications of computer systems*
5. *Discuss the effect of data processing on the secretarial profession*

THE FRAMEWORK OF DATA PROCESSING

The introduction of computers into American business in the early 1950s began a massive, irreversible transformation of society. Today almost every aspect of our lives is enhanced because of computers. In medicine, doctors can use computer produced "maps" of the human body to aid in the early detection and diagnosis of disease; in transportation, computers schedule airline reservations, operate rapid transit systems, load container ships, and monitor automobile fluid levels; and, in the office, computers reduce the amount of paperwork as well as paper costs by handling bookkeeping, record keeping, and document transmission. These examples are only a fraction of the many applications of computers.

© Don Carroll

Illus. 16-1
Computer produced map of the human body

Data Processing Defined

Simply defined, *data processing* is the manipulation of unorganized facts, or data, into coordinated information. Computers are the tools for processing data and for handling and producing information. There are three basic operations that a computer can perform: (1) arithmetic computations (add, subtract, multiply, and divide); (2) comparisons of items (greater than, less than, or equal to); and (3) storage and retrieval of information.

Computers can do no more than humans instruct them to do. They have no intelligence, and they can't think. Computers, however, can carry out instructions given them by people. What makes computers unique in comparison to humans is their speed, accuracy, and ability to store vast amounts of information. Computers are needed to handle the increasing volume of information created in the modern world.

Data Processing Systems

There are several methods of manipulating data to produce usable information. Suppose, for a moment, that you are the owner of a business. How are you going to pay your employees; that is, how will you take the raw facts (the number of hours each person worked) and turn them into organized information (a paycheck)? You could take paper and pencil, do all the computations by hand (manually), and write the check by hand. This method is called a *manual data processing system.*

If your company is too large for a manual system, you could choose a specialized piece of electromechanical equipment to do much of the arithmetic for you. Such systems, called *automatic data processing* (ADP) *systems*, are rarely used today. Punched cards are used for recording data and for operating electromechanical equipment. When cards are accumulated, they are processed by machines that record or print the information.

A third possibility is to put the data into a computer which performs all the computations and prints the employee's paycheck with no human intervention. Most medium and large companies today use this method known as an *electronic data processing* (EDP) *system.*

Each company must choose the system which is appropriate for its type of business. The choice should be based on cost, availability of personnel, and current and future needs.

Data Input, Processing, and Output

Regardless of the type of system chosen, all data processing systems—manual, ADP, or EDP—consist of the same three fundamental operations: input, processing, and output. *Input* is the act of preparing data to be processed. *Processing* involves the manipulation of data to produce results. *Output* is the result of data that has been processed into organized and usable information.

Data Processing Functions

Data processing includes one or more of the following functions: recording, classifying, sorting, calculating, summarizing, and reporting. All data processing includes at least one of these functions. The number and order of these functions depend on the problem being solved.

Recording. *Recording* is the transfer of the data to a permanent medium. This medium must be compatible with the equipment that is used to process the data. For example, a punched card or magnetic tape or disk is an acceptable medium for either an automatic data processing system or an electronic data processing system.

Classifying. *Classifying* (sometimes called *coding*) speeds up processing by assigning symbols, letters, or words to data. In a personnel system, for example, employees may be classified according to the department in which they work; for example, *1* is used to stand for sales, *2* for accounting, *3* for purchasing, *4* for payroll, and so forth.

Sorting. Another data processing function consists of arranging data into a particular sequence based on a common characteristic. *Sorting* involves arranging or separating information into similar groups. The telephone directory is an example of information that has been sorted into alphabetic sequence.

Calculating. *Calculating* is the process of computing in order to arrive at a mathematical result. Common calculations are addition, subtraction, multiplication, and division. A profit-and-loss system, for example, may involve adding all sales and subtracting all costs to yield gross profit.

Summarizing. *Summarizing* is concerned with consolidating results into a concise, organized form. A grade report, for example, is a summary of all tests and quizzes used to measure the performance of a student during a term. All printed reports are summaries.

Reporting. Information that remains in the computer is not particularly useful. Summarized results are of value when they are reported and communicated to others. *Reporting* consists of transmitting information to the appropriate persons.

COMPUTER SYSTEMS

Computer systems consist of (1) equipment, or *hardware*, which is the actual machinery and (2) programs, generally referred to as *software*, which direct the computer. The cycle common to all computer systems involves the entry of data (input), the processing of data, and the delivery of information (output).

Entering Data

Data processing begins when unorganized facts, or *source data*, are converted into machine readable form from a source not acceptable to the computer; for example, sales receipts or invoices. This conversion process is referred to as *data entry*. There are several different materials, or *media*, available for data entry. The media used depend on the nature of the hardware or physical equipment available.

Input Media. Input media refer to any materials used to capture data to be entered into a computer. Included as input media are punched cards, magnetic tape, disk packs, and diskettes.

Punched Cards. The earliest input medium used for data processing was the punched card. The idea for using holes punched in paper was borrowed from a French textile weaver named Joseph Jacquard who had used strips of paper with a series of holes to control the action of the looms.

Jacquard's idea was adapted by a statistician with the United States Bureau of the Census named Herman Hollerith. It was around 1880 that Hollerith invented not only the code used for punching data into cards but also a machine for punching the holes, a machine for sorting the punched cards, and a machine for accumulating and printing totals. The coding mechanism that Hollerith developed for punching the holes in cards is used even in today's data processing systems.

The Bettmann Archive, Inc.

Illus. 16-2
Hollerith machines

The card, often referred to as the *standard* punched card, is a rectangular piece of thin cardboard measuring 7 3/8 by 3 1/4 inches. The card, which is shown in Illus. 16-3, is divided into 80 vertical columns that are numbered 1 to 80 from left to right. Each column is capable of recording one character of information. A character may be either a letter of the alphabet (called an *alphabetic character*), a digit (called a *numeric character*), or a special symbol (called a *special character*) such as a comma, plus symbol, or dollar sign.

Data are usually punched into cards as groups of information. These groups, which may consist of one vertical column or several

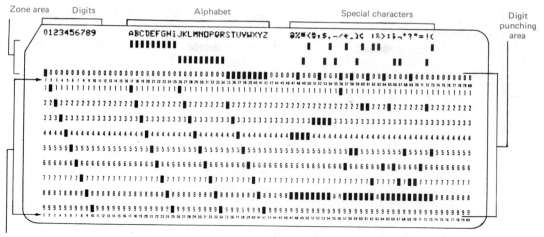

Illus. 16-3
This 80-column punched card represents all the digits, all the letters of the alphabet, and some special characters.

consecutive vertical columns, are called *fields*. Fields of information are limited on the 80-column card. It may be necessary to use several cards to record one group or field of information.

Punched cards have lost popularity in recent years to faster, more efficient media. Other media in widespread use today include magnetic tape, rigid disk packs, and diskettes (better known as *floppy disks*).

Magnetic Tape. The magnetic tape used with computers is similar to the tape used for recording music. Magnetic tape is of considerably higher quality, however. It is composed of a long strip of plastic, approximately one-half inch wide, which has been coated with a magnetically sensitive substance. The data are recorded on the tape as

Illus. 16-4
Three reels of magnetic tape

magnetized spots that create electronic impulses which the computer can read.

A reel of magnetic tape can hold data equal to that held by several thousand punched cards. Also, the tape is more compact and easier to handle. The tape is contained in a plastic case that may be as small as a cassette or as large as a dinner plate. Recording data on magnetic tape is faster than recording data in punched cards. Magnetic tape, like cards, has one major disadvantage: in order to reach a group of related data (called a *record*), an operator must process all the records that occur preceding the record, or information, needed. This is known as *sequential access*; that is, records must be processed in the same sequence as they appear on a reel of magnetic tape. Such a system can be quite time-consuming if the information needed is scattered throughout a tape.

Disk Packs and Diskettes. The ability to get to the desired record without having to process all the stored information preceding it is called *direct* or *random access*. The two most common direct access media are the disk pack (Illus. 16-5) and the diskette or floppy disk (Illus. 16-6). The disk pack may contain one large disk, or there may be several disks in a single pack. The disks are rigid and resemble a stack of phonograph records. The diskette is a small, flexible disk. It is light, compact, and can be easily stored. Both the disk pack and the diskette are thin circular plates coated on both sides with a magnetic material. The data are recorded on these media similar to the way that they are recorded on the magnetic tape.

Illus. 16-5
Disk pack

Illus. 16-6
Floppy disks

Input Devices. Input devices read the input media into the computer. Input devices include the card reader, tape and disk drives, and terminals. Many of the input devices can also be used for output. For example, video display terminals and tape and disk drives perform both functions.

Punched Card Input Devices. As you learned earlier in this chapter, the 80-column card is used for encoding data into machine readable format for computer input. Holes are produced in punched cards through the use of a *keypunch machine* such as the one shown in Illus. 16-7. These cards are then read into the computer using a *card reader*, which translates the punched holes into electrical signals that are transmitted to the computer.

Photo courtesy of
IBM Corporation

Illus. 16-7
Keypunch machine

Card readers may use one of two methods for sensing the holes: a brush or a photoelectric cell. In brush card readers, holes are sensed when a metal brush falls through the hole and makes contact with a metal roller beneath the card, thus completing an electrical circuit (Illus. 16-8A). In photoelectric card readers, holes are sensed when light (which cannot pass through the cardboard) passes through a hole and strikes the photosensitive plate beneath the card, completing the circuit (Illus. 16-8B). In both cases, the completion of the circuit results in the generation of an electrical signal to the computer.

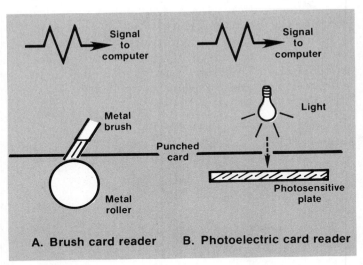

Illus. 16-8
Brush card reader and photoelectric card reader

Key Station Input Devices. An important computer input device that utilizes magnetic tape and disks is the key station input system. There are two major types of key station input systems: key-to-tape devices and key-to-disk devices.

Key-to-tape devices are used for the conversion of source data onto magnetic tape. These machines have a typewriter-like keyboard. Data are keyed as digits, letters, or special characters (symbols) and recorded on the tape as magnetized spots. Some key-to-tape devices have a television-like screen (cathode-ray tube or CRT). A widely used device for entering the data into computers is the tape drive. A *tape drive* is an input/output device that is used for processing magnetic tape records. This device reads data into the computer from the magnetic tape. A detailed explanation of a tape drive is beyond the scope of this chapter.

Key-to-disk devices are similar to key-to-tape devices except that the data are recorded onto magnetic disks. Key-to-disk devices have a television-like screen as well as a keyboard. Some key-to-disk devices display the entire transaction being entered on the screen; data keyed onto some key-to-tape devices can also be displayed in the same way. Thus, the data can be checked for accuracy and corrected if necessary before recording. The keystrokes of several operators using different keyboards (called *stations*) can be entered onto a single disk pack. The output of the operators is merged onto the disk pack for later use by the computer. Data can be entered from disk packs into computers at extremely high speeds through the use of a *disk drive*, an input/output device on which a disk pack is mounted. This device reads data from magnetic disks. The details of the operation of disk drives are beyond the scope of this chapter. Disk drives are also available for inputting/outputting data from a floppy disk. (The floppy disk is most often used with minicomputers and microcomputers.)

Input from Terminals. Data can be entered directly into a computer through a terminal. Terminals that have keyboards and television-like screens are called *video display terminals* (VDTs). As each key is pressed, the corresponding character is displayed on the screen and temporarily stored in the terminal's *buffer* which holds the data temporarily. The data displayed on the screen can be checked for errors before the operator presses the key to transmit the data to the computer. Some systems require that data be transmitted at the end of each line, while others allow a full screen of data to be entered before processing by the computer.

Source Data Automation. Some methods of data entry eliminate the need for transferring data to media such as a punched card or a magnetic disk. With these methods, source data can be recorded directly on a medium acceptable to the computer. Such input methods are referred to as *source data automation.*

Optical recognition systems are an example of source data automation. In optical recognition, an electronic scanning device reads and converts the data into electrical signals for processing by the computer. These systems are designed to recognize bar codes, marks, handwritten or special characters, and magnetic ink characters.

Optical mark recognition (OMR), also known as mark sensing, is one type of optical recognition system. It may be familiar to many students as a technique used in standardized testing. With this

Illus. 16-9
Optical mark recognition

NCR Corporation

method, input data are recorded with a pencil mark in a specified area of a form designated for responses. These marks are sensed with a light beam and converted to electrical signals which are then transmitted to the computer. Optical recognition is also used to read bar codes like the "zebra-striped" Universal Product Code that appears on supermarket products. The bars, represented by an assigned pattern, designate a product's identification number. The Postal Service also uses bar codes to automate the sorting of mail. The bars at the bottom of an envelope contain the ZIP Code and certain letters and numbers from the street address, city, and state.

Optical character recognition (OCR) is perhaps the most common type of optical recognition system. In many cases, the source data is typed using a special OCR font and read using an OCR scanner which uses a light source to recognize the characters. OCR scanners can also read handwritten and typewritten characters as well as tape generated from an adding machine or cash register.

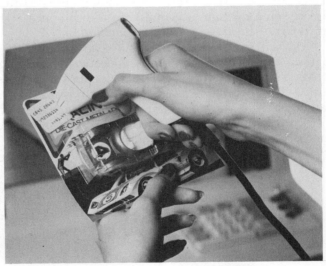

Photo courtesy of
Recognition Equipment, Inc.

Illus. 16-10
OCR scanner

Magnetic ink character recognition (MICR) equipment is designed to read characters printed with magnetic ink. MICR equipment reads the characters and converts them into a machine readable code. An example of this type of optical recognition system is the code printed on the bottom of checks. The code, or set of characters, is printed with magnetic ink so that checks can be processed quickly. As many as 1,500 checks a minute can be processed by MICR.

Processing Data Internally

As you know, data stored on media such as punched cards, magnetic tape, and magnetic disks are read into the computer by such devices as card readers, tape drives, and disk drives. Data may also be entered into a computer through the use of terminals and source data automation. Once data are entered into the memory of the computer, processing takes place under the control of a program which is also in the computer memory. A *program* is a series of instructions directing the computer to perform a sequence of operations. The program tells the computer what to do with the data, step by step. The step-by-step operations are accomplished by the electronic circuitry in the central processing unit of the computer. The *central processing unit* (CPU) is the heart of any computer system; it accepts the data from the input device, processes the data according to the program, and delivers the results. The CPU, as shown in Illus. 16-11, consists of (1) a memory unit, (2) an arithmetic/logic unit, and (3) a control unit.

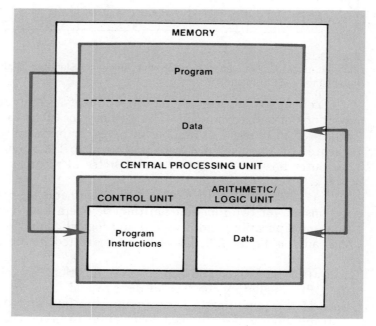

Illus. 16-11
The central processing unit is the heart of a computer system.

Memory Unit. Memory, or primary storage, is used to hold the data and the instructions (program) for manipulating that data. This storage unit has sections or memory locations in which the data and instructions are stored. These locations differ in size according to the kind of computer. In other words, not all computers have the same size memory locations.

Data within a memory location are represented in the form of a code utilizing a *1* or a *0*. These *1*'s or *0*'s are called *binary digits* or *bits*. A bit is the smallest element of data. Data are stored as bits because computers have electronic circuitry that can be turned on and off. The digits *1* and *0* represent the presence or absence of electric current. As a memory device, the computer has *on* or *off* memory states or *1* or *0*.

Combinations of bits are put together to form a *byte*, the smallest unit of storage. A byte represents a character (such as a letter of the alphabet, a number, or a special symbol) in computer memory. Currently the size of most bytes is either six or eight bits. For example, the letter *A* in an eight-bit code would be represented by eight adjacent bits made up of *0*'s and *1*'s (current off and current on signals). Illus. 16-12 depicts the letter *A* in an eight-bit code.

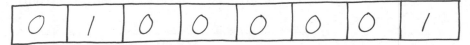

Illus. 16-12
Eight-bit code for the letter *A* using the American Standard Code for Information Interchange (ASCII) method.

You will recall that the storage unit of a computer has memory locations of a fixed amount. The memory locations for computers are expressed in bytes. The number of bytes, or memory locations, is represented by the symbol *K*, which is equal to 1,024 bytes. Thus, a 16K computer has 16 × 1,024 or 16,384 bytes of memory location.

Arithmetic/Logic Unit. The arithmetic/logic unit (ALU) is responsible for two functions: arithmetic operations (addition, subtraction, multiplication, and division) and logical comparisons (Is figure *A* the same as figure *B*?). Data are never stored in the ALU.

Control Unit. The control unit functions as the traffic cop of the CPU, regulating the flow of data to and from the different operations of the computer. All instructions are interpreted here. The control unit determines the next instruction to be executed by the computer. The input and output devices connected to the computer are also under the direction of the control unit.

Delivering Data

As long as processed data remains in memory, it is not particularly useful. Output is the delivery of the results of computer processing. Output may take many forms, including printed or microfilmed pages, a display on the screen of a terminal, or voice response.

Printers. The printer is the most frequently used output device, and by far the most common output medium is the printed page. The term *hard copy* is often used in reference to output from a printer. Printers are classified as either impact or nonimpact.

Illus. 16-13
The most common output medium is the printed page.

An *impact printer* is either a serial printer or a line printer. *Serial printers* have a printing device or element that prints a character at a time. Serial printing devices come in four styles: ball shaped, daisy wheel, thimble, or dot matrix. The ball shaped element is a sphere the size of a golf ball that moves on its own carrier from left to right across the page. A daisy wheel (print wheel) looks like a wheel with 96 spokes each having its own character. Although shaped differently, the thimble is similar to the daisy wheel. It has 64 spokes each with two characters, for a total of 128 different characters. (See Illus. 16-14 for a comparison of the daisy wheel and the thimble.) Dot matrix printing devices strike the paper with different combinations of metal pins. These metal pins create dots in patterns that approximate the shape of characters. Line printers print a line at a time. Just picture a long chain of characters which continually rotates at high speed in front of the paper. When each character is in its proper place, a hammer strikes the chain and the line of characters hits the paper, printing the entire line at once.

NEC Information Systems, Inc.

Illus. 16-14
Daisy wheel and thimble printing devices

Nonimpact printers do not have any mechanical parts that strike the paper. Nonimpact printers have fewer moving parts; they are generally cleaner, faster, and more reliable than impact printers. Characters are printed by methods such as laser, electrothermal (heat), ink jet, or ion disposition to form an image on paper. The disadvantages are high cost and loss of letter quality print with some nonimpact printers.

Computer Output Microfilm (COM). To alleviate the paper glut, many large organizations have begun storing important information on a more compact medium called *computer output microfilm* (COM). With COM, standard printed computer output is photographed and stored as images on a roll of film or a flat piece of film about the size of an index card. Approximately 200 pages of computer printout can be stored on one of these 6-by-4-inch cards, called a *microfiche* (pronounced MI-KRO-FEESH).

Illus. 16-15
Microfiche with equivalent amount of paper

To appreciate the impact of this medium, consider the case of a company that maintains one page of information on each of its 100,000 customers. If the information is stored on paper, it will occupy more than 100 cubic feet of space. Stored on microfiche, the same information will occupy less than one tenth of a cubic foot. Another significant advantage of the microfiche includes the cost savings in distribution and handling.

Video Display Terminals. For special applications, video display terminals are preferred. Video display terminals are capable of displaying results either as words and numbers (alphanumeric terminals) or as pictures (graphics display terminals). The graphics display terminals are used mostly in sophisticated technical situations where extremely accurate design is required. Video display terminals are also called CRTs (cathode-ray tubes) because of their television-like screens. Most terminals can also input data, and virtually all terminals can output data from computers.

Video display terminals output *soft copy*; that is, information is produced on a screen, not on a printed page. Soft copy is more quickly obtainable than hard copy.

Voice Response. Voice response is a small but growing form of computer communication. An output device converts data in the main computer storage into vocal responses understandable by humans.

Applications of voice response include the announcement of departure times at airline and bus terminals, replies to teller inquiries regarding customer bank balances, reading machines for the blind, and certain educational toys.

Magnetic Media. In many computer applications, output data are stored on magnetic media for use at a later time. The data can be recorded onto magnetic media using tape or disk drives. Data stored on tape or disk can be stored indefinitely and can be replaced with new data easily.

COMPUTERS CLASSIFIED BY SIZE

Computers are classified by the amount of storage capacity they contain and their speed. Large, medium, and small computers are grouped in categories and are referred to as mainframes, minicomputers, and microcomputers.

Mainframes

Very large computer systems can process and store tremendous amounts of data. Large computers which are capable of processing large amounts of data at very fast speeds are referred to as *mainframes* because of the CPU's main role in running the computer system.

Mainframes can support many auxiliary storage devices. Hundreds of terminals, printers, disk drives, tape drives, and other input and output equipment can be connected to mainframes.

In large installations the computer system is usually centrally located. All data processing functions occur from one location. There is a trend away from centralized systems because the cost of such systems is extremely high, and they are not as flexible as small systems.

Minicomputers

Because of the high cost of large computer systems, the demand for smaller, less expensive computers led to the development of minicomputers in the early 1960s. *Minicomputers* have the same components as larger mainframes but have reduced memory and slower processing speeds. Minicomputers were made possible through the technology that transferred the thousands of transistors in early generation computers to small circuit boards.

Microcomputers

A *microcomputer* is a miniature information-processing device. Advances in technology in the 1970s permitted the recording of data on silicon chips as small as a fingernail. A microcomputer consists of memory chips together with a *microprocessor*—a chip capable of performing the functions of the CPU—in special housing. The housing contains a power supply and electronic circuitry for communication with outside devices such as the keyboard and floppy disk drive.

Courtesy of Bell Laboratories

Illus. 16-16
This dime size chip is a full 32-bit microprocessor.

Microcomputers, also known as personal computers, are purchased for a variety of purposes that range from office use to use in the home, such as helping a family determine a budget or quizzing children in math or spelling. Software for microcomputers is relatively inexpensive; however, all software cannot be used interchangeably on various makes of microcomputers. Before purchasing software it is necessary to determine its compatibility with the equipment on which it will be used. Until recently computer manufacturers have tended to develop *proprietary systems*; that is, hardware that accepts only the software of the proprietor, or manufacturer, of the computer. If the microcomputer industry is to survive, however, it will have to establish standards that will enable software to be used interchangeably.

Since the first microcomputer appeared on the market in 1975, the number of users in the United States has grown to approximately two million. It is estimated that by the end of this decade one in every four households will have a personal computer. Personal computers will be used for educating, organizing, and entertaining their owners.

Illus. 16-17
The use of microcomputers in school is increasing.

THE IMPACT OF COMPUTERS ON THE OFFICE AND THE SECRETARY

The secretarial profession is very much affected by the technological advances in data processing. Secretarial positions are becoming more and more computer oriented. Many secretaries use video display terminals routinely. Source documents used for updating or changing information in a computer are often originated by secretaries. Secretaries assist in analyzing computer generated reports and distribute these and other forms of output both in and outside the organization.

It is vital, therefore, that you learn data processing terminology and functions so that you can perform effectively as a secretary. The key to becoming a valuable and productive employee is knowing how computers affect office work. Chapters 17, 18, and 19 discuss other technological advances affecting the office. An understanding of basic data processing is fundamental, however, to the comprehension of the capabilities of other systems to be described.

PROFESSIONAL POINTERS

Growth in the use of computers, especially microcomputers, will continue at a rapid pace for many years. More and more people will be required to operate computers. Computer operation is a responsibility that secretaries should expect to have as a part of their jobs. Keep these suggestions in mind when using a computer.

1. Become knowledgeable about data processing so that you will not be intimidated by the equipment.

2. Obtain brochures and manuals from manufacturers that describe how the equipment should be operated. Manufacturing representatives are helpful in assisting new operators and solving problems. Don't be afraid to ask for help.

3. Learn the basic operations of small office computers. You must be able to communicate with the computer. You tell the computer what to do through simple commands. If the computer does not understand your commands, it will ask questions or request that you try again.

4. A computer is a tool, just like a typewriter or a calculator, designed to help you do your job better and faster.

5. Make notes about how you should handle special tasks involving a computer. Then you can refer to your notes the next time you do the task.

6. When you begin to use a computer, keep an accurate log of everything you do on the machine. Record your commands. Then, if something goes wrong, it will be much easier to retrace your steps to determine the nature of the problem.

7. Don't be too quick to discard reports, control sheets, and data listings. They may be useful in tracing an error.

FOR YOUR REVIEW

1. Define the term *data processing*.

2. List three data processing systems.

3. What are the three fundamental operations in any data processing system?

4. List and explain the six functions of data processing.

5. Name four media used for entering data into a computer.

6. Name five devices used to enter data into a computer.

7. What function does the central processing unit serve in a data processing system?

8. Name the types of media that can be used to deliver processed data (output).

9. What are the three size classifications of computers?

10. Describe the impact of computers on secretarial work.

CASE PROBLEM

Patricia Kelley is secretary to the branch manager for Lifetime Insurance Company in Trenton, New Jersey. Not only is she a valuable assistant to the branch manager, but she has the opportunity to work with many people from different departments. Patricia sees much of the work that is done, and she tries to keep up with what is going on in most of the departments.

Patricia maintains high standards of quality and takes on new responsibilities whenever she can. For example, a few months ago a new data processing system was installed by the company, and each branch of Lifetime Insurance Company received a computer terminal. Even though Patricia did not attend the training seminar that was held for the branch managers, she expressed an interest in learning how to use the computer terminal. Of course, the manager was delighted.

In just a matter of weeks, Patricia acquired a working knowledge of the applications for which the terminal was purchased. Because of the valuable experience she has obtained through self-training, the branch manager now includes Patricia in meetings that she had not before been asked to attend. Her responsibilities include preparing reports that give her insights into the business that she might otherwise not have received. Patricia feels a sense of accomplishment in what she has done, and she looks forward to new challenges as she progresses with Lifetime Insurance Company.

1. What has Patricia done differently from a secretary who may not be interested in advancement?

2. Patricia accepted new equipment as a challenge. How do some people feel when faced with new tools that are supposed to make their jobs more productive?

3. How has Patricia become a more valuable employee to Lifetime Insurance Company?

PRODUCTION PROJECTS

PP 16-1

(Objective 1)

It is important for you to be familiar with data processing terminology and to know generally what the terms mean. Refer to the form in your Supplies Inventory and match the data processing terms given to their appropriate meanings.

PP 16-2

(Objective 2)

Choose one of the following projects, and write a report on your findings.

1. Interview a member of your school's administration or data processing department. Determine from the interview the data processing functions that occur in handling student records at your school.

2. Interview an individual responsible for handling the computerized processing of payroll checks for employees in a company in your area. Determine the data processing functions that occur in producing an employee's payroll check.

PP 16-3

(Objective 3)

Collect as many items as you can find that represent input and output materials used in a data processing system. You should be able to explain the role of each item in a computer system. Refer to the chapter if you need to review the forms of entering (inputting) and delivering (outputting) data.

PP 16-4

(Objective 4)

Survey local businesses to find out the size (microcomputer, minicomputer, mainframe) and type of computer used for the processing of data. As part of your survey, discover a local business that does not process its data by computer. Describe the business and the system it uses to process data. If the business should install a computer, what size computer would you recommend be installed? Report your findings to the class.

PP 16-5

(Objective 5)

Assume that you are responsible for addressing approximately 800 envelopes for a major mailing every four months. You now type the envelopes. Find out how this job can be made faster with a computer. You may choose to ask someone in your school's data processing department or a computer vendor. Write a report on your findings.

Chapter 17

ANALYZING WORD PROCESSING

Computers handle data (unorganized facts) according to a set of instructions (the program). When working with text (words, sentences, and paragraphs), however, logical instructions do not work. Instead, the handling of text, known as *text editing*, requires human interpretation and manipulation. *Word processing*, a system of text editing, requires a direct, ongoing interaction between a human and a machine. In contrast, data processing operates under the control of a program stored in the CPU of the computer, with only monitoring required by a human.

You will need to understand word processing as an office system designed to improve the efficiency of business communications. Word processing systems utilize automated equipment along with special work procedures and trained personnel to produce office documents such as letters, memos, and reports. The job tasks of secretaries are greatly affected by the system chosen to aid in the preparation of typed documents within the office. In this chapter you will learn how word processing originated, the effect of word processing on the secretarial profession, the features of word processing systems, the classifications of word processing equipment, and the integration of word processing and data processing.

General Objectives

Your general objectives for Chapter 17 are to:

1. *Define word processing*
2. *Discuss the evolution of word processing*
3. *Describe the effect of word processing on the organization of the office and office personnel*
4. *Identify the basic components of a word processing system*
5. *Describe the equipment used in word processing*
6. *Discuss the integration of word processing and data processing*

WORD PROCESSING AS A CONCEPT

Simply stated, word processing is the transfer of verbal or recorded ideas into typewritten or printed form. Word processing in this context has taken place for centuries. Word processing has hence evolved into a system that consists of specific procedures and sophisticated equipment used by specially trained personnel to produce correspondence. The integration of sophisticated equipment into word processing allows thoughts to be transferred to paper faster, more accurately, and more economically than ever before.

In summary, word processing involves people, automated equipment, and specific procedures. Word processing systems coordinate these elements to transform ideas into written communication.

Preparation of Written Communication

In considering the preparation of written communication, compare the traditional office (one employer to one secretary) to a word processing operation. In a traditional office setting, the employer creates correspondence by dictating directly to a secretary or to a dictating machine; the secretary transcribes the correspondence and returns it to the employer for signature. If the document requires revision, it is returned to the secretary who retypes it. This process of revising and retyping continues until the document is approved and signed.

In a word processing setting, the person who creates correspondence is called a *word originator, user,* or *principal.* The word originator dictates to a recording or dictating machine. After dictation, the document is typed and recorded on magnetic media. When the document is returned to the word originator for revision, a final copy can be produced without the secretary retyping the entire document. With word processing equipment, an entire letter or report is typed only once. Portions of the material can be revised on a screen. Then the equipment automatically plays back the revised, error free final document. The tedious, time-consuming process of retyping a document several times before the copy is approved by the word originator is eliminated.

Evolution of Automated Typewriting Equipment

Word processing systems evolved after the introduction of automated typewriters to the office. The first automated typewriter, the Hooven, was introduced during World War I. The recording medium was an embossed cylinder. (*Medium* refers to the materials or devices used to capture keystrokes.) During the 1930s, the American Automatic Typewriter Company developed the Auto-Typist. This typewriter used a paper roll that resembled a roll used on a player piano as the recommended medium. Later punched paper tape was introduced as a recording medium. Automatic paper tape typewriters were used mainly for the repetitive typing of form letters.

Between World War II and the early 1960s, there were few dramatic advancements in automated typewriter technology. In 1961 IBM introduced the Selectric typewriter with a ball shaped typing element and a stationary carriage. The IBM Selectric was the foundation for the development of word processing equipment. In 1964 a technological advancement occurred that had a great impact on word processing: IBM introduced the Magnetic Tape Selectric Typewriter (MT/ST). Like the automatic paper tape typewriters, the MT/ST captured every keystroke made by a typist on a recording medium. But the recording medium used by the MT/ST was magnetic tape.

Photo courtesy of
IBM Corporation

Illus. 17-1
Magnetic Tape Selectric Typewriter

In the late 1960s IBM introduced the Magnetic Card Selectric Typewriter (MC/ST) which used magnetic cards to capture information. These machines are commonly referred to as Mag Card typewriters. Approximately fifty lines of information can be recorded on one card. Dual sided magnetic cards allow the user to record on both sides of the card, doubling the potential storage capacity. The advantage of magnetic cards over magnetic tape is their ability to advance to the point of a correction or a revision without playing out the entire document first.

The most recent automated word processing equipment uses a screen that visually displays what is being typed. The screen, which makes it possible to visualize a document without the use of paper, is called a *cathode-ray tube* (CRT). Today the term *video display terminal* (VDT) is more commonly used to describe the unit that shows what has been keyboarded (inputted).

A VDT allows an operator to see corrections and changes to the copy as they are made. When copy on a screen is error free, it is stored on magnetic media for playback at a later time. A VDT eliminates the need for a rough draft of typed work. One disadvantage of VDTs is that they often cause eye strain and fatigue through constant exposure or poorly designed display screens.

Photograph courtesy of
Dictaphone Corporation

Illus. 17-2
A VDT allows an operator to see changes to the copy as they are made.

Currently there is a tremendous amount of competition among manufacturers of word processing equipment. Vendors promote such features as the length of the lines or the number of lines that can be displayed on a screen and the quietness of the keystrokes. The results of this competition are improvements in the equipment and a corresponding decrease in cost. Cost reductions have made the purchase of word processing equipment feasible for just about any office today.

WORD PROCESSING AND THE SECRETARY

Word processing permits specialization in the secretarial field. Some persons enjoy typing tasks almost exclusively; others do not. The latter prefer administrative support activities; for example, receptionist duties, filing, communications, researching information, and other secretarial services.

The Distribution of Job Tasks

In many large companies secretarial tasks are often divided between correspondence tasks and administrative tasks. The person who performs the typing and transcribing functions frequently is called a *correspondence secretary*. Other titles for the person who performs these tasks are word processing operator, word processing specialist, correspondence or document specialist, word processor, word processing secretary, or transcription specialist. Secretaries who give nontyping support to their principals are usually identified as *administrative secretaries*. Other titles for these secretaries are administrative specialist, administrative support specialist, or administrative support secretary.

Correspondence Secretaries. Correspondence secretaries are responsible for typing documents. Correspondence secretaries must be able to work with machines and must be familiar with the operative parts of machines. They must like to type and must be able to proofread and edit copy to ensure accuracy. Correspondence secretaries spend much of their time transcribing machine dictation; so they must have excellent listening, spelling, grammar, and punctuation skills.

Correspondence secretaries must also have full knowledge of document formatting—that is, setting up various styles of letters, memorandums, and reports; computing and setting tabulations for statistical typing or indented material; and determining margins. Correspondence secretaries must be able to work on their own, keep accurate records, and handle peak office work loads.

Administrative Secretaries. Secretaries who perform administrative support duties in an office are responsible for all the nontyping tasks. Administrative secretaries answer the telephone, greet callers, file documents, duplicate originals, keep records, handle mail, and perform other secretarial services. Administrative secretaries may also dictate routine documents for typing by correspondence secretaries.

Career Paths

In most offices, a secretary's opportunity for advancement often depends on the employer's advancement potential or the secretary's desire to seek additional responsibility. The advent of word processing has offered secretaries a path for career advancement. Study the diagram in Illus. 17-3 which shows the relationships between correspondence and administrative positions and the various levels of advancement that can be attained. The career paths are usually horizontally structured; that is, the positions have similar status beginning at the entry level.

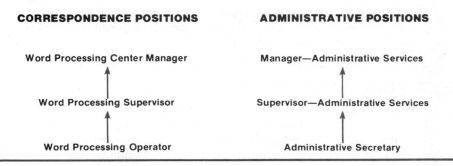

Illus. 17-3
Career opportunities in correspondence and administrative positions

Job responsibilities for each position vary from one organization to another. A general description of the correspondence and administrative positions in Illus. 17-3 is given here.

- *Word Processing Operator:* Must possess good typing and proofreading skills. Knowledge of grammar, punctuation, and spelling necessary. Has ability to operate word processing equipment and machine transcribing units. Has ability to format, input, and revise complicated or specialized documents. Must meet certain productivity standards.
- *Word Processing Supervisor:* Possesses work experience as a word processing operator. Has a thorough knowledge of company procedures and interacts with principals inputting work for word processing. Assigns work to operators and is responsible for accuracy and quality of material produced by personnel. May train new operators or existing staff on new equipment.
- *Word Processing Center Manager:* A management position within the organization. Manager possesses experience in word processing and communications. Recommends staff and equipment changes and sets productivity standards. Manages budget, equipment, and personnel for word processing.

- *Administrative Secretary:* Receives and assists visitors and telephone callers and refers them to appropriate people within company. Maintains filing and records management systems. Operates copying machines. Sorts, reads, and annotates incoming mail. Handles the preparation of outgoing mail. Composes and dictates routine correspondence for own or executive's signature. Makes arrangements for and coordinates conferences and meetings. Maintains financial records. Researches and abstracts information for meetings, special projects, and reports.
- *Supervisor—Administrative Services:* Possesses work experience as an administrative secretary. Responsible for scheduling work flow and quality of work produced by personnel. Trains new personnel or existing staff in new procedures.
- *Manager—Administrative Services:* A management position within the organization. Controls budget and is responsible for all services under administrative support area.

THE ENVIRONMENT FOR WORD PROCESSING

Word processing operations require more than automated equipment and trained individuals. The environment of word processing has a definite effect on the quantity and quality of work produced as well as on the morale of employees. There are four basic designs for a word processing system. Of course, there can be many variations of these four designs because all organizations are different in size, goals, number of employees, and operating budgets. One design cannot be judged better than another because organizational needs are different.

Totally Centralized Word Processing Structure

When word processing systems were first created, the emphasis was on totally centralized services. Thus, most word processing administrative support (nontyping) tasks and correspondence (typing) tasks were grouped together in one area called a *word processing center.* The correspondence and administrative support groups were supervised by a manager who coordinated the work load, determined priorities, and developed efficient procedures. The emphasis was on producing large volumes of correspondence, such as memos, letters, forms, or reports.

This structure was more cost effective than the traditional one-executive-one-secretary arrangement. A secretary was no longer idle because the executive was out of the office. Office tasks were performed quickly and without interruption by any available secretary in the center. Total centralization, however, did not work for some offices; so several alternative structures were developed.

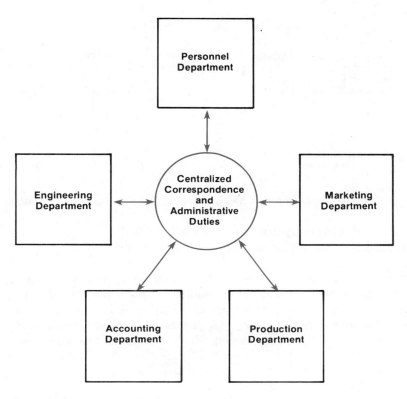

Illus. 17-4
Totally centralized word processing structure

Centralized Correspondence/Decentralized Administrative Word Processing Structure

In an attempt to alleviate some of the problems of the totally centralized word processing structure, some companies created a centralized correspondence center but left the administrative secretaries decentralized. This structure best suits an office in which long or repetitive documents are typed frequently.

A law firm is an example of this structure. All legal documents to be typed are sent to a correspondence center where the documents can be typed, stored, and revised, when required. The correspondence related activities are the centralized portion of the structure. In the decentralized portion of the structure, lawyers' secretaries perform all the administrative functions. These secretaries may still be responsible for some light typing of nonroutine correspondence but are relieved of the time-consuming task of typing long legal documents. Illus. 17-5 shows an example of this type structure.

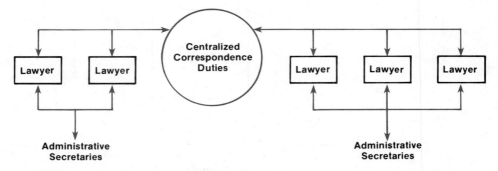

Illus. 17-5
Centralized correspondence/decentralized administrative word processing structure

Decentralized Correspondence/Centralized Administrative Word Processing Structure

This structure is best applied in large companies composed of many departments that require a large volume of typed correspondence. An example is a manufacturing firm that has separate departments for research and development, sales and marketing, accounting, personnel, and production. Each department is large enough and has

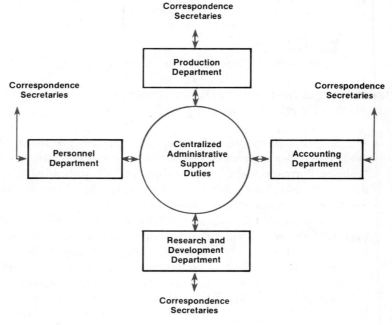

Illus. 17-6
Decentralized correspondence/centralized administrative word processing structure

the specialized correspondence needs to justify its own satellite correspondence center; however, the administrative support services are organized centrally. Therefore, many routine tasks such as filing and handling mail can be performed by a small group of administrative support secretaries in a centralized location.

Totally Decentralized Word Processing Structure

Of the four basic structures, a totally decentralized word processing system is the most inefficient. Simply stated, this is the traditional one-executive-one-secretary arrangement with each secretary having word processing equipment and a desk located near the executive's office. Although word processing equipment certainly improves the quality of a secretary's work, the cost involved in providing equipment for each secretary makes this structure expensive. At the same time, the secretary still has to cope with interruptions, uneven work loads, and inadequate supervision by the executive. This structure is found most often in small offices.

Work Groups

Work groups, sometimes called work clusters, have recently evolved in offices as a support group to existing word processing centers. They usually consist of secretaries who perform both correspondence and administrative activities. In departments where the work load is heavy, it sometimes becomes necessary to develop a small group to absorb the extra work of the center. Work groups are also used for the production of specialized projects or technical documents that would interfere with the regular work load of the word processing center.

COMPONENTS OF WORD PROCESSING SYSTEMS

There are basic components to all word processing systems. These components generally reflect the flow of work within an organization. The basic components of a word processing system are the following:

1. Input—creating correspondence
2. Processing—typing, revising, and playing back correspondence
3. Output—distributing and/or communicating the final document

The next sections will consider each component and how it contributes to the success of an effective word processing system.

Input

Input includes all communication originated or created by a principal. Four common methods of inputting information to a word processing system are longhand, shorthand dictation, machine dictation, and optical character recognition (OCR).

Longhand. Longhand is a basic form of input that involves the use of a pen or pencil and paper. Much input from a principal is in longhand. Handwriting is slow; the average person can compose approximately 10 words a minute. People feel more comfortable organizing their thoughts on paper; however, deciphering the handwriting of principals is one of the major problems with this method.

Shorthand Dictation. Shorthand dictation may also be used by the principal as a method of creating correspondence. Shorthand dictation, however, ties up the time of two people: the principal who dictates and the secretary who takes the shorthand notes. Often a dictator is interrupted by a telephone call or important message, and the secretary must wait until dictation resumes. Shorthand dictation can only be given at times when the secretary is available. Also, most secretaries who take shorthand dislike having to transcribe cold notes. Unless shorthand notes are transcribed immediately, they often are difficult to read. Shorthand is convenient for writing down instructions, recording telephone messages, or taking minutes of a meeting. Although shorthand dictation is much faster than "translating" handwriting, it is still slower than machine dictation.

Machine Dictation. Machine dictation is a fast, efficient method of input. The use of dictation equipment involves only one person at a time. Thus, the principal can dictate when it is convenient, and the dictation can then be given to any trained correspondence secretary to be transcribed. Transcription from the spoken word is usually easier than transcription from handwriting or shorthand notes. Problems do exist, however, with machine dictation. Word originators must be trained to dictate and to use the equipment correctly. Transcribing poorly articulated dictation can be just as frustrating as trying to read illegible handwriting or incorrectly written shorthand notes.

Dictation equipment allows a principal to dictate, to rewind and review what has been said, to make corrections, to indicate the end of dictation, and to give the transcriber instructions. You may recall from Chapter 10 that there are three kinds of dictation equipment: portable units, desktop units, and centralized dictation systems.

Optical Character Recognition (OCR). OCR is becoming an increasingly popular method of input. As you learned in Chapter 16, OCR equipment has the ability to read printed, typewritten, or sometimes handwritten characters from a source document. In a word processing system optical page readers are most often used to transfer the characters onto a magnetic medium. Then the recorded material can be read and processed by word processing equipment.

Inputting information is time-consuming. The use of OCR equipment helps expedite the processing of information since optical page readers convert a document for entry into the word processing system. The converted document is then stored and revised, if necessary.

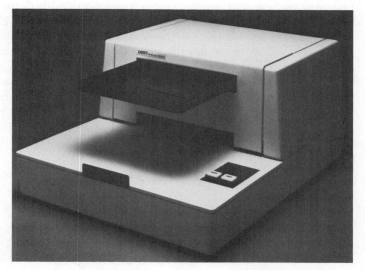

DEST Corporation's
Model 203 Turbofont page reader

Illus. 17-7
DEST Corporation's Model 203 Turbofont page reader, a high-performance member of the WorkLess Station family of OCR desktop scanners, is capable of reading up to 250 pages per hour.

OCR based word processing systems require that all the typewritten material use the same style element. Documents typed for input to OCR equipment must be typed with carbon ribbon and should be in 10-pitch (pica) type. Secretaries should be trained to prepare documents correctly for input to OCR equipment. Paper should be inserted in the typewriter so that the characters appear in a straight line across the page. If paper is not inserted properly, some OCR readers may not pick up the typed information.

Processing

Processing involves making changes to input that result in a final document. Processing of information occurs on automated equipment called *word processors*. Word processing equipment can be categorized or grouped into electronic typewriters, standalone word processors, and multistation systems.

Electronic Typewriters. Most electronic typewriters resemble electric typewriters. Electronic typewriters, however, have automated many of the manual features of electric typewriters, thus increasing the secretary's efficiency in processing documents. These automated features include automatic error correction, automatic centering and underlining, and simple formatting. The features of electronic typewriters vary according to the manufacturer and model. Electronic typewriters (like those discussed in Chapter 8) are affordable for most offices, but they are not practical for large volume typing.

Electronic typewriters usually have a limited amount of memory capability. Information entered on the keyboard can be placed in memory for automatic playback at a later time. But most electronic typewriters are *volatile*, meaning that when the power switch or electricity is turned off all memory is lost.

Standalone Word Processors. Standalone word processors consist of a single station operated by one person. Standalone word processors are self-contained; in other words, they are used alone or

Illus. 17-8
Standalone word processor

independently of other equipment or devices, such as the processing unit of a computer. A standalone word processor consists of a display screen, keyboard, intelligence unit, storage device, and printer.

Standard Parts. Standalone word processors vary greatly, and some are much more complex than others. The following descriptions will give you a basic understanding of the components that all standalone word processors have in common.

A display screen allows the operator to verify text content and format. The operator can make changes or corrections while the text is displayed on the screen. Screens can often be adjusted or tilted for visual satisfaction. You can control the brightness of the words on the screen much like adjusting a television screen. Operators have found that soft colors, such as green or orange, on a black background cause the least amount of eye fatigue. Screens may display a full page of typed material or a limited number of lines.

The keyboard of a standalone word processor looks much like the standard typewriter keyboard except for the addition of some special keys. These special keys permit the operator to perform automatically many tasks that would be time-consuming on a regular typewriter.

The intelligence unit of a standalone consists of a microprocessor—a computer on a chip. The intelligence unit receives instructions through the keyboard and relays instructions to other parts of the word processor. For example, the intelligence unit can instruct the printer to center the title of a document over a certain line.

The storage device holds the storage media (magnetic card, tape, or floppy disk) on which a document is recorded. Today floppy disks are the most popular medium for storing information. Once keyboarded, the document is recorded on magnetic media for future use. If the document needs to be revised, the operator retrieves it from storage, revises the document using the display screen, and then sends the revised document back to storage. Most standalone word processors have a temporary storage feature (known as *buffer storage*) as part of the intelligence unit. Permanent storage requires the recording of a document on magnetic media.

Printers, as discussed in Chapter 16, can be impact or nonimpact devices. Most standalone word processors use impact printers. An impact printer using a daisy wheel mechanism, for example, can print approximately 500 words a minute. A nonimpact printer using laser technology can print up to 36 pages a minute. At present, laser printers are very expensive and can only be justified in a company that has a tremendous volume of printed output.

Special Features. Although not all special features are included on all models, some of the most common are listed here.

- *List/Merge.* A form letter with one or more variables can be stored on magnetic media. *Variables* are items of information that may change from one letter to another, such as the letter address, salutation, account number, or amount of credit being given each customer. The form letter will be on one disk and the variables will be on another disk. The word processor will then merge the information as it is played back and produce the letters as hard copy on a printer.
- *Global Search (Search and Replace).* A single word that is contained in a lengthy document can be found by the word processor, deleted, and replaced by a different word automatically.
- *Wrap Around.* A word at the end of a line can be moved or "wrapped around" to the next line when it would extend beyond the right margin.
- *Right Margin Justification.* This feature allows the right margin of a document to be perfectly even when it is played back. The machine automatically makes allowances for extra spaces between words so that all the lines align at the right margin.
- *Hyphenation.* The machine automatically hyphenates words at the right margin according to a set of rules for hyphenation.

Applications. Software can be used to control the functions of standalone word processors. Machines that use software (and most do) are said to be *programmable.* Floppy disks, which most up-to-date word processors use, contain the software applications.

Multistation Systems. Multistation systems allow several word processors to operate by sharing devices. Some multistation systems share common devices such as a printer, storage units, or a computer. For example, three or four word processors may share one printer. Or

Illus. 17-9
Multistation system

several word processors may share the master file (information about customers, products, employees, and the like) contained on medium within a storage device. By sharing the intelligence (CPU) of a computer, certain mathematical calculations can be done by the arithmetic section of the CPU and added to a report being prepared on a word processor.

Because certain functions are shared, the cost of a multistation system is less than that of a standalone system. Each station does not require all the parts of a standalone word processor. But what happens if a shared part of the system breaks down and several stations are dependent on it? Usually, if one part of the system is out of order, the other parts that depend on it are unable to function.

Output

After information is processed—edited, revised, or manipulated—it is delivered in final form. Word processing output is usually obtained through printers that produce the document on paper. Output takes the form of a printed page most of the time. Output can also be stored on magnetic media for future reference without being printed.

Output can also be received from a visual display screen of a terminal. Information can be entered, stored, and then transmitted from one screen to another. Companies may use visual output to send information or messages internally.

THE INTEGRATION OF WORD AND DATA PROCESSING

Today's office automation is marked by a trend toward integrated data and word processing functions. Data processing equipment has taken on word processing capabilities and vice versa. Integrated systems are being introduced to facilitate the substitution of screen images for paper. Integrated systems lower the cost of processing information by reducing dependency on the printed page. They also expedite the flow of information so that managers can be more responsive to rapidly changing business conditions. In a larger sense, integrated systems expand the potential of the work force by making timely information available in a better organized, more usable form.

The merging or integrating of these two technologies is rapidly occurring because of the capabilities of mini- and microcomputers in handling word processing applications. Word processing packages (software) are being marketed by manufacturers of mini- and microcomputers and software vendors. The functions of data processing and word processing, always separated in the past, are merging because of advances in telecommunications. The technologies are now interconnected through telecommunications networks. Telecommunications gives word processors the capability of acting as terminals that access a computer. Telecommunications networks will be explained in Chapter 19.

PROFESSIONAL POINTERS

As a secretary, you may share responsibility for studying the word processing needs of your company. Do not commit yourself to even consider a word processing system until you know exactly what is needed to accomplish the paperwork in your office. In cooperation with others, survey your needs carefully to determine the following information:

1. What the company plans to accomplish through the use of word processing

2. The type of equipment that will be the most beneficial for the company

3. The cost of the system

4. What type of reorganization will be necessary

5. How the system will be implemented (both personnel and physical facilities involved)

6. The advantages of the word processing system over the system that is presently being used

Such a study will point out the need for word processing in your office and exactly what equipment should be used. Without the knowledge of your company's needs for handling paperwork efficiently, you cannot make a wise decision about the effect of a word processing system in your office. Analyzing the characteristics of your company's word-handling system is a major step toward the successful implementation of word processing.

FOR YOUR REVIEW

1. Which three elements does word processing involve?

2. Which three terms can be used to describe the person who creates documents?

3. In a word processing system, secretarial tasks are often grouped into two categories. Name them.

4. Name the four organizational structures for a word processing system.

5. List and explain the three basic components of a word processing system.

6. Name four methods of originating communication in a word processing system.

7. What are the three categories of word processing equipment?

8. Explain the standard parts of a standalone word processor.

9. What are two factors resulting in the integration of word and data processing?

CASE PROBLEM

The office personnel of Stenbeck Distributing Company work in a traditional office. Most of the correspondence that is generated by the managers and sales representatives consists of form letters to customers. The sales representatives must occasionally submit sales proposals to potential customers. These proposals are usually quite lengthy.

The secretaries are frequently interrupted by telephone calls, clients arriving for appointments, and the general confusion of the many sales representatives checking in at the office or preparing to go out on calls. The quality of the typewritten documents is not good, and many of the managers and sales representatives think that they are spending too much time doing detail work that the secretaries should be doing. The secretaries have more than they can handle—a large volume of typing, filing, mail handling, and copying. As a result, the officers of Stenbeck Distributing Company are considering the implementation of a word processing system.

1. How would word processing benefit the company?

2. How would word processing benefit the secretaries?

3. How would word processing benefit the managers and representatives?

PRODUCTION PROJECTS

PP 17-1

(Objective 1)

Use three different reference sources to obtain definitions of word processing. Write the definitions, and identify your sources on plain paper. Below the definitions, write in your own words what you understand word processing to mean.

PP 17-2
(Objective 2)

Use the library to research how word processing began, and how it has evolved into what it is today. Write a report on your findings. Type a rough draft of your report, and use this copy to make corrections or revisions. Type a final copy of your report, double-space, and use one-inch side margins. Submit the rough draft and final copy to your instructor.

PP 17-3
(Objective 3)

Locate an office in your community that uses a word processing system. Determine whether the structure is centralized or decentralized and how office procedures are governed by word processing. Analyze the assignment of responsibilities within the office by determining who is in charge of which word processing functions. Write a report about your findings. Include a chart that illustrates the system used.

PP 17-4
(Objective 4)

In your Supplies Inventory is an article originated in handwriting by Joji Nozaki for the magazine *Word Processing World*. Mr. Nozaki's firm installed a word processing system about six months ago, and the article concerns the firm's experiences with the system. Mr. Nozaki may wish to make changes in the article; so type a rough draft first. If available, use a word processor so that revisions can be made easily. Use a 60-space line, double-space, and use a two-inch top margin for the first page. Also in your Supplies Inventory you will find Mr. Nozaki's revised copy of the article. Look at the revised copy only after you have typed the first draft. Make the necessary revisions and corrections, and produce a final copy of the article. On a separate sheet of paper, describe how the preparation of the article involved each component of a word processing system (input, processing, and output).

PP 17-5
(Objective 5)

In your Supplies Inventory is a letter written by Charlotte Chancelor, a sales representative for HiGrade Products, Inc. The letter needs to be proofread for errors and then set up as a form letter. It will be used to accompany a price schedule when requested by present and potential customers.

Choose any word processing equipment available to you (electronic typewriter, standalone unit, multistation system). Type one copy of the letter in an acceptable style; leave blank spaces for the variables. Be sure to store the letter.

Refer to your Supplies Inventory, and send the form letter to the individuals on the list. Make each letter an original; fill in the variables as required. Type an envelope for mailing, fold each letter properly, and insert the letter in the envelope.

Submit to your instructor the original copy of your form letter along with the three addressed letters and envelopes. On a separate sheet of paper briefly describe the special features of the equipment you used to accomplish the project.

PP 17-6

(Objective 6)

In your Supplies Inventory, you will find terms that are common to both word processing and data processing systems. Research will be necessary in order to determine the meanings of these terms. Type an appropriate definition of each term given.

Chapter 18

UNDERSTANDING OFFICE REPROGRAPHICS

The reproduction of original documents is known as *reprographics*. As a secretary, you will be expected to know the various methods for reproducing documents. Additionally, you will be responsible for selecting the correct reprographics methods based on the number of copies needed, the required quality and appearance, the intended use, the immediacy of the need, and the cost of the copying process.

General Objectives

Your general objectives for Chapter 18 are to:

1. *Explain the major methods of reproducing documents*
2. *Describe the types of copiers available for office use*
3. *Explain briefly copying technology*
4. *Explain basic and special features of copying machines*
5. *Discuss the law regarding the copying of documents*

METHODS OF REPRODUCING COPY

As a secretary you may be responsible for reproducing documents in the office, or you may simply request from a reprographics department the required number of copies. In either case, you should know about methods of reproducing documents. The basic methods of reproducing documents include the following:

1. Carbon copies
2. Spirit and stencil duplicating
3. Offset printing and phototypesetting
4. Photocopying

The Carbon Process

Making carbon copies is one of the oldest methods of producing multiple copies. Carbon copies are made at the same time the original document is produced.

Assembling Carbon Paper. To assemble your carbon set, place a sheet of onionskin paper (or a second sheet) on your desk; place the inked or coated side of carbon paper on top of the onionskin; repeat this step for each copy desired. The top sheet will be the original (letterhead or plain bond paper). Carefully pick up all the sheets and gently tap the sheets on the desk to straighten the pack. Turn the set around so that the original faces away from you and is upside down, and insert the set in the typewriter by holding it firmly with one hand and turning the platen slowly with the other.

In preassembled carbon packs, the carbon paper is discarded after one use. Carbon packs are bound together at one end so that the sheets do not slip. Companies that use multiple copies or preprinted forms frequently order them in carbon packs to save assembly time and effort. A more expensive version of carbon packs contains paper that has been treated with a special chemical. The back of the paper contains an inklike substance that is undetectable to the naked eye. The impact of the typewriter keys transfers the ink to the next sheet; thus, a copy is made without the use of carbon paper. You will remember from Chapter 8 that this treated paper is called NCR paper.

Illus. 18-1
Preassembled carbon pack

Making Quality Carbons. The copy control mechanism on the typewriter should be appropriately set for the thickness of the carbon pack. To print through eight or even ten sheets of paper, for example, the striking force of the print mechanism must be greater than for one or two copies.

Errors on carbon copies must be erased carefully, since the ink from carbon paper smudges easily. Use a soft eraser on carbon copies; a hard eraser may tear the thin sheets used for carbon copies. When erasing an error on an original, place a small card or piece of heavy paper between the original and the dull side of the first sheet of carbon paper. This will protect the carbon paper and prevent smudging the carbon copy. The same procedure should be followed for inserting the small card and correcting each carbon copy, starting with the first carbon copy and progressing to the last.

Word processors make the production of carbon copies much easier. Once information has been keyboarded and stored, it can be edited and revised before a carbon pack is inserted. The original and carbon copies can then be printed error free at a fast speed. Remember, however, that only impact printers can be used to make carbon copies. Nonimpact printers can produce only originals.

The Spirit and Stencil Processes

Duplicating is a means of making copies of an original document from a prepared master. Documents can be duplicated by the spirit (sometimes called fluid) process and the stencil process.

Spirit Duplicating. The spirit duplicator is used with a three-sheet pack called a *master set*. The top sheet of the master set is glossy white paper connected to a bottom sheet of carbon paper coated with a dye. The secretary removes the protective tissue separating the two connected sheets before typing on the top sheet of the master set.

A spirit master is prepared by typing or writing on the top white sheet of paper attached to the carbon coated second sheet. The carbon coated sheet has a thick waxlike dye that transfers typing or writing onto the back of the white sheet. The characters on the back of the white sheet are a reverse or mirror image of the characters typed on the front.

If an error is made when preparing a spirit master, the carbon side must be scraped or brushed free of the waxy dye. The dye can be scraped off with a sharp-edged device such as a razor blade. A specially designed instrument, called a fiberglass eraser, can also be used. It brushes away the dye before the correction is made. When retyping a character or word, remember to place an unused portion of the carbon coated bottom sheet of a master behind the area needing correction in order to replace the used dye.

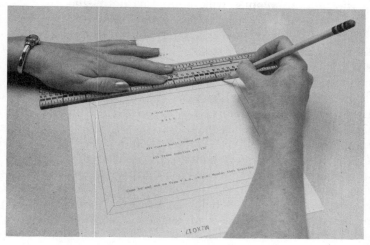

Illus. 18-2
Spirit master

The top white sheet is placed with the carbon side toward the outside on the cylinder of a spirit duplicator. As the cylinder rotates, copy paper moistened with a liquid containing spirits of alcohol comes in contact with the dye on the back of the master which transfers the image onto the copy paper to produce the finished copy. The spirit

Illus. 18-3
Spirit duplicator

Heyer Inc.

process can be used to reproduce as many as 300 copies. Masters have a limited life since the carbon on the master is used up as the master is run, and the copies will become so light that they cannot be read.

Stencil Duplicating. Stencil duplicating requires a different kind of master called a *stencil*. The stencil pack consists of a transparent film, a stencil sheet (a porous sheet of tissue coated with a waxlike substance), a cushion sheet, and a backing sheet.

A stencil must be "cut" by typing on it or drawing on it with a hard pen or a sharp pointed instrument called a *stylus*. In order to cut the stencil properly, a typewriter should be adjusted for a medium to hard impression, and the ribbon should be set on the stencil position. By setting the ribbon control to stencil, the ribbon is disengaged, allowing the element or keys to cut through the stencil without getting any ink from the ribbon on the stencil. A transparent plastic film over the stencil sheet helps protect the stencil from collecting any excess ink from the keys or element. When you type on the stencil sheet, you actually cut into the waxlike coating and create a path through which ink will flow when the stencil is duplicated. Drawing with a stylus or hard pen will produce the same results.

Correcting an error on a stencil is unlike any other kind of correction. Because impressions have actually been cut through the stencil, a special fluid must be applied to restore the thin waxy surface of the stencil sheet. Usually the stencil sheet is burnished (the error is rubbed with a paper clip or other rounded object) before the correction fluid is applied. Stencil correction fluid is applied with a small brush applicator. After the fluid is applied, allow the stencil to dry

Illus. 18-4
In correcting an error on a stencil, the stencil sheet is burnished before correction fluid is applied.

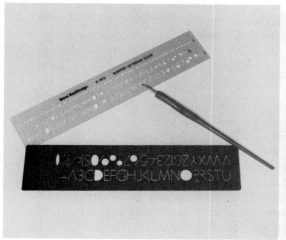

Illus. 18-5
Stylus and letter
guides for drawing
on a stencil,
stencil pack, and
stencil duplicator

Heyer Inc.

thoroughly before recutting the correct characters. The correction
fluid must be applied directly to the stencil and not on the top protective film. It is wise to put a pencil or pen between the backing
sheet and the stencil sheet when applying correction fluid to prevent
the two sheets from sticking together as the fluid dries.

When the stencil is completed, it is placed on the drum of a
duplicator often referred to as a mimeograph machine. The mimeograph process is based on the interaction of the stencil sheet, the
inked cylinder of the mimeograph machine, and the copy paper. When
the stencil is mounted around the cylinder of the machine, ink flows
from the cylinder through the cuts in the stencil where the wax has
been removed by the action of the typewriter keys, leaving a printed
impression on the copy paper. After a run, a properly prepared stencil
can be saved for future use by storing it in a special folder made of

heavy absorbent paper. Copies reproduced by the stencil process are of better quality than those reproduced by the spirit process. Several thousand copies can be reproduced from one stencil.

Offset and Phototypesetting Processes

Because of technological advances in equipment and rising commercial printing costs, many companies now require that volume reproductions be handled in-house. Secretaries, therefore, may be responsible for the layout or design of materials printed in-house. Materials often printed by companies include annual reports, forms, brochures, catalogs, advertising literature, and the like.

Reproducing large quantities of documents can be accomplished by two processes called offset printing and in-house phototypesetting. Both of these methods generally produce high-quality copies.

Offset Printing. A method of printing often used for the reproduction of large quantities of documents is the offset process. Offset printing is a complex procedure frequently used in larger print shops or the reprographics departments of large companies. Secretaries may expect to be more involved in the preparation of offset masters than in operating the equipment. The offset process requires the use of grease based pencils and typewriter ribbons for the preparation of masters.

Typically offset masters are single sheets of specially coated and treated paper, usually a greenish white color. The paper master (also called a *mat*) is prepared by typing, drawing, or writing on the sheet. A carbon (grease based) ribbon must be used when typing a paper master, and a special grease pen or pencil is necessary for handwriting or drawing. Offset presses also use metal masters that have image areas which are receptive to ink and backgrounds which are receptive to water. Offset metal plates are not directly imaged (typed on). They are produced by photographing the image of an original onto the metal plate with a special camera or using a photocopying machine to transfer the image from the original to the metal plate.

A good quality ribbon (carbon or film base) should be used to type directly on a paper offset master. Too heavy an impression should not be made by the typewriter element on the surface of the master. Letters that are pressed into the master (embossed) will reproduce with a hollow appearance. The master should be smooth to the touch as you pass your fingertips across the typed characters.

To draw directly on an offset master, use a black or carbon based pen or pencil. Specially designed writing instruments can be purchased for writing or drawing on offset masters.

Corrections on paper masters should be made by gently erasing the ink from the image area with a very soft eraser. Keep the eraser clean by rubbing it after each correction on an emery board, nail file, or rough piece of paper. Only a slight impression of the character or characters will remain after you have removed all the ink; remaining ghost image will not reproduce. Fingerprints may appear on offset copies if the person handling the master or plate is not careful. The oil from your fingers will show up after processing as smudges; therefore, care must be taken to handle the master or plate by the edges.

The principle behind offset printing is that grease and water do not mix. The master is placed on a cylinder of the offset press. The cylinder comes in contact with rollers that have ink and water on them. The ink adheres to the grease on the master, and the water prevents the ink from adhering to other parts of the master. The image is inked on this master cylinder and then transferred from the master to a blanket or intermediate cylinder. Next, the image is transferred or "offset" from the blanket cylinder to copy paper fed through the machine when an impression roller presses the copy paper against the blanket cylinder.

Reproductions from paper masters may reach 10,000; the number of copies made from a metal plate may be as many as 50,000. Masters can be saved and run again but require special care prior to storage and reproduction.

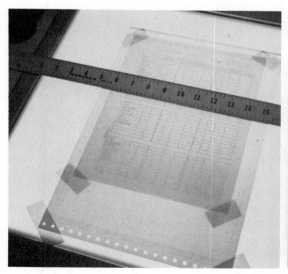 

Illus. 18-6
A paper master is prepared by typing, drawing, or writing on the sheet. The man in the photograph at the right is using an offset press.

Phototypesetting. High-quality printed matter—such as books, brochures, pamphlets, newspapers, and advertisements—is the result of phototypesetting. As shown in Illus. 18-7, a phototypesetter has a

Illus. 18-7
Phototypesetter

video display screen and keyboard that look much like a word processor. The machine is capable of setting type from characters that are entered on the keyboard. In addition to the characters on a standard typewriter keyboard, there are command keys that code in specifications. The codes instruct the phototypesetter by specifying which size and style of type to use, the amount of space to leave between lines, and whether to justify the right margin (make the margin perfectly even).

Phototypesetting is a photographic process. The easiest way to describe a phototypesetter is to compare it to a camera—a camera that takes pictures of keyboarded characters. Once text has been keyboarded, characters are printed optically one at a time at very high speeds on photosensitive material—paper or film. A font containing character images is positioned before the lens, a light flashes, and the image of the character is projected onto photosensitive material. The exposed photosensitive material is taken from the phototypesetter and put into a processing unit. The photosensitive material emerges from the processing unit in the form of *galley* or long pages of text. The galley is cut into manageable pieces and pasted up, producing camera ready copy. This camera ready copy is developed as a photograph onto a master that is used in the printing process. Documents that have been phototypeset are usually reproduced by offset printing.

For years the operator of a phototypesetter had to rekey material that had first been typed. Optical scanners can now convert typed copy into magnetic media for processing by phototypesetting equipment. Copy keyboarded on a word processor can also be captured on magnetic media, such as disks. Magnetic media are the input for the phototypesetter.

Interface devices enable two different pieces of equipment to communicate with each other. In the past, optical scanners and word processors required the use of an interface device which translated text and various codes for the phototypesetter. Today phototypesetters can receive input directly from optical scanners, word processors, and computers. Direct interface greatly reduces keyboarding and proofreading time.

A document that is phototypeset can be condensed to use about 50 percent of the space that it would use if typewritten. Spacing between words and between lines can be adjusted to compress or to expand the material. Many sizes and styles of type help create attractive, easy-to-read information.

The Photocopying Process

Photocopying is a process that has come to replace other methods of reproducing copy. Over 250 billion copies are made by this process each year. Photocopying does not require the preparation of a special master for reproduction. Because any type of document can be reproduced without special preparation, the photocopying process is the most convenient, fastest, and easiest method in use today. You will need to be thoroughly familiar with the equipment and techniques involved in photocopying since it is a major aspect of reprographics.

COPYING MACHINES

Manufacturers have designed copying machines in many different shapes, sizes, and configurations. There are, indeed, copiers available to meet just about every type of copying need. Some copying machines are capable of reproducing copies of an original document so well that it is difficult to distinguish between the copy and the original.

Most machines used today are plain paper copiers. Plain paper copiers produce copies on bond paper. These machines can also make copies on different colored paper, on company stationery, and various kinds of business forms. Some copiers, however, require the use of specially coated, electrostatically charged paper. Many companies use coated paper copiers for reproducing documents for interoffice communication or for files. Coated paper copiers are usually less expensive than plain paper copiers. The main disadvantage of copies on coated paper is their appearance and texture. Plain paper copies look and feel more like the original documents. The number of coated paper copies in use has dwindled steadily with the onslaught of plain paper copiers retailing for lower and lower prices.

Categories of Copiers

Copiers can be classified according to use. The three principal categories of copiers—low-volume, mid- to high-volume, and intelligent copiers/printers—are described and discussed here.

Low-Volume Copiers. Copying machines that are intended for fairly low-volume use are considered convenience or desktop copiers. Not all low-volume copiers sit on a desktop; they may, in fact, be freestanding console units or floor models. Low-volume copiers are usually distributed in heavily trafficked locations for point-of-need copying and can be operated easily.

Illus. 18-8
Low-volume copier

Low-volume copiers generally do not produce copies at fast speeds. Some low-priced machines may make only several copies a minute. Expensive low-volume copiers can produce almost a hundred copies a minute. These machines should be used where the volume of copies produced is less than 20,000 copies each month.

Mid- and High-Volume Copiers. Large volume copying is most efficiently produced on high-speed copiers that are centrally located. Although the initial cost of a floor model copier is usually significant, the price of individual copies is low. A job that may cost 5 cents a copy on a convenience copier will cost 2 or 3 cents a copy on a high-speed unit.

Large volume copying jobs should be done in the copy center, and convenience copiers located throughout a company should be used for small runs. High-volume copiers make from 50 to 90 copies a minute; so they are generally used for volume levels of 50,000 to 100,000 copies a month.

Targeted for monthly levels of 20,000 to 50,000 copies, mid-volume copiers are used in centralized or decentralized office environments. These copiers can be either desktop or floor models.

Illus. 18-9
High-volume copier

Intelligent Copiers/Printers. Some page printers are also called copiers/printers because they combine photocopying and photo-typesetting capabilities. The intelligent copier/printer is essentially a nonimpact printer which accepts input from one or more sources and provides hard copy (printed sheets). Intelligence, which is provided by microprocessor technology, permits the equipment to handle certain information from other sources. For example, the copier/printer can be linked to a word processor, computer, or optical character reader;

therefore, the copier/printer can act as an output device for these pieces of equipment. Data can also be transmitted from one copier/printer to another via telephone lines.

Photocopying Technology

Photocopying involves taking a picture of a document (image) directly from the original itself. Photocopying has virtually replaced traditional methods, such as duplicating or the making of carbon copies, for reproducing documents requiring many copies. Below is a brief discussion of the technology commonly used in office copiers.

Thermography. Thermographic technology is based on the principle that dark colors absorb more heat than light colors. To make use of this principle, thermal (or thermographic) copiers use specially coated, heat sensitive translucent copy paper. The document to be copied and the copy paper are inserted into the copier facing each other. Light passes through the copy paper and is absorbed by the image areas (the printed areas) on the original. Heat is then generated in the image areas and transmitted to the heat sensitive copy paper. The heat that is held in the image area on the original causes the corresponding area on the copy to turn dark, thus forming the copy.

Correction fluid or paper must not be used to correct an original that is to be copied on thermographic equipment. The intense heat burns through the correction device and often reproduces the original image. This equipment makes copies slowly and requires the use of specially coated paper that becomes brittle with age and handling. Today thermal copiers are used infrequently for paper copies.

Thermal copiers are used primarily to make overhead transparencies. Transparency film is placed over the original, and the thermal heat transfers the image from the original onto the film. Transparency films are used on a special projector which magnifies an image onto a screen. Another usage may be for the lamination of an original document with a clear plastic coating.

Thermal copiers can also be used to produce a spirit master or a stencil from an original for duplication. The original document from which a thermal master or stencil is to be made must be very dark and clear. Masters and stencils reproduced by thermography are frequently used by schools and churches.

Xerography. Xerography is the technology that began the copying equipment revolution. Although developed in 1938, xerography was not utilized in copying until 1961. The Xerox Corporation introduced the first copier using xerography. This technology (also called an electrostatic process) dominates the copier field today.

The word *xerography* comes from the Greek words meaning *dry* and *writing*. In xerography an image of the original is transferred to a cylinder or drum which rotates and copies the original on plain paper. Xerography is based on the principle that certain surfaces become better conductors of electrical charges when exposed to a light source.

This method exposes a positively charged drum or cylinder surface within the copier to light reflected through lenses and mirrors from the original document. When light from the white areas of the original strikes the drum, the positive charge disappears. A negatively charged black powder called *toner* adheres to that portion of the drum surface still charged (the image area). The image is immediately transferred from the drum to plain paper where it is permanently affixed by heat.

Fiber Optics. Recently introduced to the reprographics field are copiers that utilize advanced technology. Fiber optics copiers have fewer moving parts and are small and lightweight. Rather than using mirrors and lenses to transfer electrical charges of an image to a drum, optic fibers transmit light from the original to the drum. Optic fibers are made up of rows of tiny glass fibers encased in a thin resin wafer. Each fiber functions as a miniature lens, focusing its tiny segment of the total image on the drum. A unique gripper bar system within the copier guides the paper across the light source assuring 100 percent imaging of the original document. The utilization of fiber optics has occurred mostly in low-volume (convenience) copiers.

Lasers. Many of the intelligent copiers/printers use the xerographic process to produce copies except that laser beams reflect the images. Laser copying uses a stream of red light to transmit the image onto a photosensitive surface. The image is then transferred from the surface to plain paper.

Features of Copying Machines

Today's copiers do more than make the same size copy from an original document. The following features are either designed into the basic copier or are available as add-on accessories.

Basic Features. Most copiers are equipped to handle the two standard paper sizes—8½ by 11 inches and 8½ by 14 inches. In sheet-fed copiers the copy paper comes already cut into standard size sheets and is loaded into the machine's paper tray. The paper tray, which feeds the paper through the machine, may be adjusted for different paper sizes; or there may be separate trays. Machines requiring separate trays use paper cassettes which snap in and out of the copier for loading and unloading paper. Some copiers can be fitted with a roll of continuously fed paper that is cut to specific lengths as it is fed through the machine. Roll-fed machines allow a variety of different size copies to be reproduced. A roll-fed copier is especially suitable in applications where odd size copies are frequently required.

An exposure control allows the operator to instruct the machine to produce lighter or darker copies. This feature is especially helpful when the original document is faint or light.

A copy counter can be preset for the desired number of copies. When the appropriate number of copies has been made, the copier will stop.

New model copiers are equipped with self-diagnostic features that indicate the cause of a machine malfunction. The machine will indicate such things as a paper jam or the lack of toner. Toner, either as liquid ink or dry powder, must be added to the copier by the operator to produce clear, black copies. If a breakdown is too complicated for the operator to handle, some machines will signal the operator to call a service person. A few models are *user friendly*; that is, voice synthesis supports self-diagnoses (the machine responds in a simulated voice to identify a problem).

Special Features. Copiers can be purchased with special features. Technological improvements and innovations have resulted in many convenience copiers that are now equipped with features once found only on high-volume, floor model copiers. Many features can also be added that change the patterns of copier use. Below are features commonly found on high-volume copiers used in the centralized copy centers of companies.

Reduction and Enlargement. Some copiers can reduce the size of the original document in varying degrees usually expressed as percentages. For example, you can reduce an original by 90 percent, 78 percent, or 60 percent. Reduced copies can be made of large documents so that all filed copies are uniform in size. Computer printouts that measure 11 by 17 inches, therefore, could be reduced to fit paper $8\frac{1}{2}$ by 11 inches for easier handling and filing.

An enlargement feature allows an original document to be copied larger than it actually is. Fine details on an original can be made more legible by using the enlargement feature. This is a new feature currently available on convenience copiers. Enlargement may be an attractive option, but the applications may be few.

Duplexing. Copying on both sides of a sheet of paper is known as *duplexing*. This feature saves paper and reduces the number of sheets of paper to be stored in the files. With many high-volume copiers, operators can, by pushing the proper buttons, make two-sided copies of either one- or two-sided originals automatically. When duplexing is a feature of convenience copiers, it is usually necessary to remove the copies from the receiving tray after copying, turn them over, reinsert them into the tray, and make copies on the other side. Unless your copier is designed with the duplexing feature, you should not try duplexing. Otherwise you may get dirty or slightly burnt copies; extensive duplexing may even cause a fire within the copier.

Collating and Stapling. Large copiers permit the collating of multiple page reports. Some machines automatically sort the copies in bins; others collate internally and produce the collated copies in staggered sets. An optional finisher can even staple collated sets of copy.

Touch Control. New copiers use a touch control panel. Dials and buttons are eliminated; the operator simply touches the control panel to instruct the machine which operations to perform. Copiers with a control panel often have the ability to diagnose and display on the panel interruptions or problems that arise in copying.

Job Recovery. A copier with a job recovery feature remembers where it left off and automatically makes the remaining number of copies. It may be necessary for you to interrupt the copying of a large project in order to make a few copies of another document. The job recovery mode stops the copier and remembers how many copies have been made. When you are ready to finish the project, the machine automatically picks up where it left off and makes the required number of copies.

Automatic Document Feed. On some convenience or desktop copiers, you must lift a cover, place the original on a glass surface, and instruct the machine to make the copies. Machines that have a document handler reduce the tedious process of feeding originals into the machine. With semiautomatic document feed (or stream feed), the operator feeds each original into a receiving slot in the machine. With fully automatic document feed (stack feed), the operator may place a stack of originals in the document handler, and each original will be automatically fed into the machine for copying. The operator need only pay occasional attention to the machine while the job is being copied.

Color Reproduction. Most copiers print black and white copies of any color original. A relatively new copier, however, allows the reproduction of the exact colors of the original. The reproduction of copies in color will, no doubt, be especially popular in the future.

Return to Position. This feature clears and returns all controls to the first position within a few seconds after the last copy has been prepared. For example, if the last job required ten copies of each page, the controls would return to *1* so that the next person using the machine does not get ten copies in error.

ANCILLARY REPROGRAPHICS EQUIPMENT

Reprographics is a field that encompasses more than the duplicating and copying equipment described in this chapter. Secretaries should expect to know about or be able to use any of the following pieces of equipment.

Facsimile Machines

A *facsimile device* (also known as FAX) is essentially a type of copier that electronically sends an original document from one location to another. The transmitted document looks exactly like the original, whether it be a photograph, a drawing, or a written document. The document to be transmitted is scanned by a light source (lens, laser, or fiber optics) that converts it into electronic signals. Reproducing documents by facsimile involves the use of telephone communications. A coupler links the telephone to a facsimile machine. Facsimile machines that transmit and receive documents are called *transceivers*. Some FAX machines only transmit; they are called transmitters. Some only receive, they are called receivers. Facsimile devices may also be known as *telecopiers* because they combine telephone and copying technologies.

The facsimile process is also employed to produce offset masters and stencils. The original document to be reproduced is placed on one cylinder of a two-cylinder machine. An electronic (plastic) stencil or offset master is placed on the second cylinder. As the cylinders rotate slowly, a photoelectric eye scans (picks up) the image of the original and transmits it to the other cylinder, where it is reproduced on the master or stencil. A needle on the second cylinder is the device that records the image on the master or stencil.

Lettering Equipment (Headliners)

Preparing material for duplicating or photocopying may involve special lettering on the master or original copy. Often special type styles can be obtained by using certain typewriter elements or fonts. Also, a lettering machine can produce a variety of type styles in different sizes. The print from a lettering machine appears on an adhesive-backed tape that can be positioned on the master or original. See Illus. 18-10 for an example of a lettering machine.

Illus. 18-10
Lettering machine

Collating and Folding Machines

Sorting, collating, and stapling by hand can be a long and tiresome process. Some copying machines collate and staple sets of documents automatically. If a copier does not collate, then an automatic collator may be the answer to the sorting and collating of multipage documents. One manufacturer's collator can collate as many as 1,000 sets of a 10-page document in six minutes. The most common method of holding sets of paper together is by stapling. Electric staplers can staple as rapidly as sets are fed into the unit and should be used for large volume jobs.

A paper folding machine can save hours of tedious folding by hand. Folding machines are practical for large amounts of document folding. Some automatic folding machines can fold 12,000 items an hour.

THE LAW REGARDING COPYING

The Constitution of the United States gives certain rights to authors and inventors. Since 1776, there have been only two major revisions to the copyright law. The first major revision occurred in 1909, and the latest took effect in January, 1978. In a report from a House committee, the following reasons were given for the latest revision to the copyright law.

During the past half century a wide range of new techniques for capturing and communicating printed matter, visual images, and recorded sounds have come into use; and the increasing use of information, storage and retrieval devices, communications satellites, and laser technology promises even greater changes in the near future. The technical advances have generated new industries and new methods for the reproduction and dissemination of copyrighted works, and the business relations between authors and users have evolved new patterns.[1]

You may be responsible for a great deal of copying and duplicating; so you should become informed about this law. Flagrant violation of the copyright law shows a basic disregard for what is fair.

The copyright law is more than 60 pages in length. Here are some of the highlights:

1. Money, postage stamps, United States bonds, Federal Reserve notes, or other securities of the United States *cannot* be reproduced.
2. Birth certificates, passports, draft cards, naturalization and immigration papers *cannot* be reproduced.
3. Driver's licenses, automobile registrations, and certificates of title *cannot* be reproduced.
4. Documents that contain the personal information of an individual are protected by the Right of Privacy Act. They *cannot* be reproduced without the individual's permission.
5. Material that retains a copyright *cannot* be reproduced without the owner's permission. The fair use provision allows some exception to this provision.

The fair use clause means that individuals do have the right to reproduce copyrighted materials without permission under certain fair and reasonable circumstances. In determining whether the use of a work in any particular situation is fair, the following factors should be considered:

1. The purpose and character of the use, including whether such use is of a commercial nature or is for nonprofit educational purposes
2. The nature of the copyrighted work
3. The amount and substantiality of the portion used in relation to the copyrighted work as a whole
4. The effect of the use upon the potential market for or value of the copyrighted work

The four statutory criteria are relevant in determining whether fair use applies to a particular instance of copying. Whether the copying to be done falls within the fair use provision must be decided on an individual basis, however.

The laws regarding copying will, no doubt, change even more in the future. Technological capabilities are increasing faster than laws

---

[1] Excerpt from the House Committee Report, P.L. 94-553

can be made to govern the changes. Think about the copying or duplicating of music and other sound recordings. Home video cassette recorders make it possible to "copy" television programs and other broadcasts that are supposedly protected by certain rights. The reproduction of software packages for computers and word processing equipment is also becoming a serious problem.

Views differ according to the rights of an individual to copy for personal use. Congress is studying not only these rights but also the means of enforcing laws to protect them. Because the issue of copying has certain unresolved questions, it would be wise for any person or organization that makes copies in any manner to seek the counsel of an individual knowledgeable in the law.

PROFESSIONAL POINTERS

Remember that it is illegal to quote or copy the work of another individual without giving proper credit for the material. Apply the following tips when you are typing or reproducing copyrighted material.

1. A direct quotation of four or more typed lines should be single-spaced and indented five spaces from the right and left margins. Quotation marks are not required when using this format.

2. A direct quotation of less than four typed lines should follow the established line length. Quotation marks should be used at the beginning of quoted material and at the conclusion.

3. If you must photocopy a long report, table, or other material for distribution to others, be sure to credit the original source of the material. You should review the copyright law so that you will know what constitutes fair use of someone else's work.

4. *Plagiarism* is the act of using another person's writing as your own. Ideas expressed in copyrighted material of another author must be properly credited when used. Quotation marks are not necessary if you paraphrase someone's writing; however, a footnote reference should appear with any expression of ideas not your own.

FOR YOUR REVIEW

1. Define the term *reprographics*.

2. Name and explain the four major methods of reproducing materials.

3. List and explain the three categories into which copying machines may be grouped.

4. What is meant by *xerography*? How does this copying process work?

5. List at least two basic features and three special features of copying machines.

6. What is a facsimile machine?

7. Discuss the effect of the copyright law on secretarial responsibilities.

8. Name ten items that cannot be reproduced under the terms of the copyright law.

CASE PROBLEM

Benchmark Systems Corporation has recently experienced a problem with the security of information for its new products. The local competitor seems to be obtaining information about the new products before they are put on the market.

When a new product is about to be introduced, copies of a work sheet describing the product are distributed to all department managers. Approximately six weeks after the managers are notified, the product is announced to the market.

As a secretary to one of the department managers, you have made these observations: (1) reproduction of the work sheets takes place in the central copy center and (2) since the copier has been jamming frequently, some copies of the work sheets have been pulled out of the feeding path of the machine and discarded.

1. With only this much information, what is your assessment of the situation?

2. How can this problem be prevented in the future?

3. Would you share your assessment of the situation with anyone? If so, with whom and how?

PRODUCTION PROJECTS

PP 18-1

(Objective 1)

Study the situations given below, and determine which method you would use for each situation: carbon paper, spirit duplicator, stencil duplicator, offset press, high-volume copier, convenience copier. Type your answers on a separate sheet of paper.

1. Type an original and make three copies of a letter to a client.

2. Type and make enough copies to distribute an announcement (for 75 bulletin boards) about the new coffee machine.

3. Type a revised price list and make 6,000 copies.

4. Make 15 copies of a map of the office complex.

5. Type and make 500 copies of a form to be used internally for ordering supplies from the warehouse.

PP 18-2

(Objective 1)

The memorandum in your Supplies Inventory must be typed and reproduced. It will be distributed to 12 departments and circulated among the employees in those departments. Determine from your instructor which methods for reproducing the memo are available to you. Choose an appropriate method, and reproduce 12 copies of your typed memo.

PP 18-3

(Objectives 2, 3, 4)

Choose one of the following assignments:

1. Visit an office equipment distributor in your area, and learn which types of reprographics equipment is sold. Obtain brochures of the different machines. Prepare to give an oral or written report on your findings.

2. Visit a printing shop and observe the different types of reprographics equipment used. Determine if any ancillary equipment is used and for what purpose. Collect samples of the printing, if possible. Present your findings in an oral report to the class.

3. Arrange to visit the copy center of a large company in your area. Answer the following questions and write a report on your findings.
   a. Is the copy center open for use by all employees?
   b. Are records kept of the number of copies made by each individual?
   c. Are all originals sent to the center for copying? Are there any special requirements for the appearance of originals?

d. What copying equipment is used?

e. Describe any special features of the equipment.

f. Are satellite or convenience copiers located in other areas of the company?

PP 18-4

(Objective 4)

Assume that you have been working on a task force to develop an office procedures manual. The manual is almost complete, and you have been chosen to design a cover. The manual will be reproduced on a high-volume copier.

First, make a list of the machine features that would be advantageous in producing several hundred copies of the manual. Second, design the cover for the manual. Include the name of the document (Office Procedures Manual) and the company (Benchmark Systems Corporation). You may cut and paste on your original, and be sure that what you type and/or write is dark enough to be copied clearly. You are encouraged to use different type styles, artwork, or whatever you think will make the cover attractive. The manual will be bound on the left.

PP 18-5

(Objective 5)

Research the 1978 copyright law. Write a paper on the legality of (1) copying the names and addresses of employees in your office to give to a friend who is selling encyclopedias, (2) making five copies of a piece of sheet music to share with your friends at work, and (3) making one copy of a page of secretarial tips from your friend's copy of *The Secretary*. Cite references for your information, and write a report to submit to your instructor.

Chapter 19

KNOWING ABOUT TELECOMMUNICATIONS

The term *telecommunications* is often used today to describe the electronic transmission of information. Telecommunications involves the transmission of text, data, voice, and graphics electronically. Telecommunications results in the accurate and quick exchange of information between two or more points. In this chapter you will learn how information is transmitted electronically, the nature of telecommunications equipment and services, and the impact of telecommunications on society.

General Objectives

Your general objectives for Chapter 19 are to:

1. *Define telecommunications*
2. *Explain how information is transmitted through networks*
3. *Identify telecommunications equipment and services*
4. *Discuss the impact of telecommunications on office work and certain consumer services*

COMMUNICATIONS YESTERDAY AND TODAY

Ways to communicate information take many different forms. Think back to the days of the Pony Express when transmitting messages from one part of our country to another required a determined individual and a surefooted horse galloping over miles of rugged terrain. As our country grew, faster methods of communication were developed.

The first method of transmitting ideas by other than written message was through a universal code of signals. These signals, comprised of dots and dashes, represented words. Known as the Morse Code, these signals were transmitted over wire lines that were strung from one location to another.

The first telephone conversation, or direct voice communication, was made possible over similar wire lines. On July 1, 1881, Alexander

Graham Bell, who was in Boston, Massachusetts, had the first telephone conversation with Thomas Watson a few miles away in Cambridge, Massachusetts. Today you can use the telephone to communicate directly with another individual anywhere in the world.

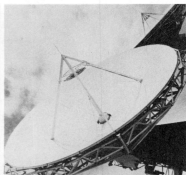

Reproduced with
permission of AT&T

Western Union Corporation

Illus. 19-1
Communicating information takes many different forms.

For the delivery of messages requiring fast transmission and a written record, Western Union introduced teletypewriters in the 1950s. A message is typed on the keyboard of a special typewriter. As the message is typed, it is output onto a tape. Paper tapes are saved for a period of time in case a message must be resent. Through the use of

Illus. 19-2
Teletypewriter

Western Union Corporation

telephone lines, a teletypewriter sends or receives messages; and messages may even be received when the machine is unattended.

Today faster methods of transmitting information are available. Developments in telecommunications have permitted the interconnection of information-processing machines such as computers, word processors, and intelligent copiers. Secretaries are able to make use of the telecommunications services available to them through the interconnection of office equipment.

INFORMATION TRANSMISSION

Two types of signals are available for transmitting information—analog and digital. Analog signals can be heard by the human ear, but digital signals cannot be heard. Analog signals—continuous and wavelike—transmit the human voice. Digital signals transmit data messages by coded characters such as numbers, letters, and symbols. Most equipment used to process information sends and receives digital signals. Most telecommunications media are designed to carry analog signals, however. Therefore, a device must be used to represent a digital signal on an analog channel. This device (called a *modem*) converts a digital signal to analog form. The process of modifying the analog signal to transmit digital information is called *modulation*. When the transmitted signal is received, the information must be reconverted into a digital signal. This process is called *demodulation*. *Modem* is an acronym for *mo*dulator and *dem*odulator. Modems are available in various speeds (measured in bits per second). The higher the modem speed, the faster the information can move through channels, thus saving communication time and cost.

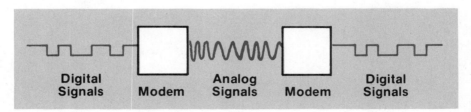

Illus. 19-3
Information transmission

Media

Channels provide the link between two or more pieces of equipment. Information transmitted through channels is carried by certain media. There are four major classifications of transmission media: twisted-pair wire, coaxial cable, fiber optics, and microwaves.

Twisted-Pair Wire. One of the original wire types used in telephone communications, twisted-pair wire, still remains the main form of media for the transmission of information. Typical telephone lines consist of pairs of copper wire twisted together to minimize electrical interference. Twisted-pair wire carries analog signals and is currently the most common form of transmission media.

Coaxial Cable. Telephone companies, particularly for long-distance calls, use coaxial cable installed underground or beneath the ocean. Cable reduces the need for thousands of individual wires strung overland on telephone poles. Cable also offers high transmission speeds with good immunity to electrical interference. Coaxial cable consists of an insulated wire conductor surrounded by fine copper wire mesh and/or an extruded aluminum sleeve.

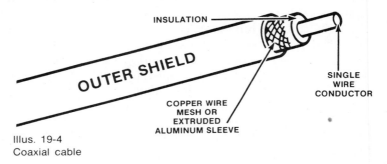

Illus. 19-4
Coaxial cable

Fiber Optics Tubing. Signals can be transmitted in the form of rapid pulses of light through strands of very pure glass contained within a tubing. The light impulses that travel down the fibers are

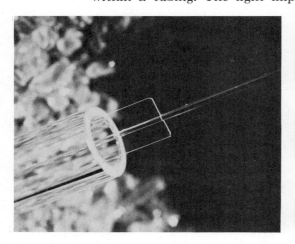

Photos courtesy of Bell Laboratories

Illus. 19-5
Components of a single glass fiber magnified and glass fibers within a tubing

tiny lasers. Digital signals from information-processing equipment can be transmitted optically without conversion to analog signals, giving fiber optics tubing a distinct advantage over twisted-pair wire and coaxial cable. Fiber optics transmissions are not affected by electrical interference. The small size and flexibility of fiber optics tubing allows for the easy installation of this media. Fiber optics tubing is rapidly declining in cost and is expected eventually to become a primary means of telecommunications.

Microwaves. Analog signals can be sent through the air as microwaves. Microwaves must be transmitted in a straight line between two points. Microwave transmission uses line-of-sight towers for the land based transfer of information. A good deal of the analog signals that we receive daily (for example, television and radio) are broadcast through the atmosphere as microwaves. On a worldwide basis, satellites are used for microwave transmission.

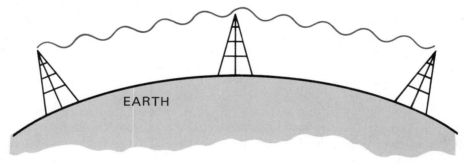

Illus. 19-6
Microwave transmission

Networks

How can a word processor link to another word processor or to a computer? How can word processors connect to other types of information-processing machines such as OCR scanners, phototypesetters, or facsimile units? How can all types of information-processing machines be linked so that any one can talk to any other?

The linkage of information-processing machines is possible through *networks*—systems for connecting pieces of equipment by means of telecommunications channels. The philosophy behind networks is that all types of input/output devices—whether they are computer terminals, facsimile machines, intelligent copiers, and the like—can be connected to one universal system for sharing and exchanging information. Networks allow office personnel to send messages electronically, access common data bases (records on particular subjects), manipulate data and generate reports, share programs, and share expensive storage devices (disk drives, for example) and output devices (copiers, printers, or facsimile machines).

Local Area Networks (LAN). A local area network links various types of equipment used within a building or several buildings within the same geographic area. Links may also be established through the public telephone system (AT&T, for example) between independent local area networks separated by great distances.

A local area network consists of some form of transmission media (quite often coaxial cable) to transmit the information, plus interface units to link the various pieces of equipment to the media. An interface unit converts or translates the language of one type of machine to the language of another (i.e., word processor to intelligent copier). This unit also helps similar machines produced by different manufacturers talk to each other (i.e., an IBM word processor with a Wang word processor).

There are various configurations and media used in local area networks. A discussion of the various arrangements for organizing a network (also known as configurations) are beyond the scope of this chapter. The media used to interconnect pieces of equipment within a network are telephone wires, coaxial cable, and fiber optics tubing.

Large Networks. Local networks can be expanded into extensive networks that enable companies to send information from city to city, across the nation, and to other countries throughout the world. These large telecommunications networks make use of combinations of telephone lines, microwave towers, and satellites to send information.

TELECOMMUNICATIONS EQUIPMENT AND SYSTEMS

The major communications requirement of an office is the timely movement of information to the ultimate user. The ability to provide the proper information to allow for a timely decision will govern the success or failure of a company. The following sections will discuss some commonly used electronic means of distributing information.

The Telephone

Because of rapid changes in electronic technology, telephone equipment has undergone numerous changes in the past several years. It is anticipated that this equipment will continue to be improved as advancements are made in the electronics field. Listed here are several types of telephone equipment representing the broad diversity of equipment that is available.

Single Line Telephones. Single line telephones are used in homes and small offices. As the name implies, these telephones have only a single line available. It is not possible for two or more people to place calls on separate lines as can be done with multiline equipment. These single line telephones are operated by either a rotary dial or push buttons. Push-button telephones are rapidly replacing rotary dial equipment. Both rotary dial and push-button telephones are available in standard table models, wall models, or models with the dial in the handset.

Multiline Telephones. Multiline telephones, or key telephones as they are sometimes called, allow one person to handle several telephone lines. These telephones may be equipped with up to 30 buttons that are placed above, below, or beside the dial. Desk model telephones are available in 6-, 10-, or 20-button sets, with 6- and 10-button sets available in wall models.

Reproduced with
permission of AT&T

Illus. 19-7
Multiline telephone

To place an outside call on a multiline telephone, the caller pushes an unlighted line button and dials the number. To answer an incoming call, an individual pushes the flashing button and picks up the receiver. If a call comes in on one line while an individual is talking on another line, the hold button on the telephone can be utilized by using the following procedure:

1. Ask the caller if he or she is willing to hold; the individual may prefer to call back or have you call back.
2. If the caller is willing to be placed on hold, depress the hold key.

3. Answer the call on the incoming line. If the call becomes longer than 30 or 40 seconds, return to the caller on hold and ask if he or she wants to continue to hold. Do not ever allow a caller to remain on hold for a long period of time without checking back with the caller.

Switching Systems. Calls are routed to and from the public lines of the telephone company to the private lines within an organization through switching systems. These systems include key systems, PBX (private branch exchange) systems, and Centrex.

Key Systems. The key system is used primarily by small companies. The system offers economy and efficiency. With a key system, telephones have lighted buttons (showing which lines are presently engaged) that give employees access to all or many outside lines and usually one or more intercom lines. No full-time attendant is needed.

Key systems are small desktop switchboard systems. These systems can handle up to 21 lines and 52 stations, with adjunct units available if more lines are needed. Incoming calls ring at a central location; however, calls can be answered at any telephone. Conference arrangements are available so that a third party can be added to a call. Outside or intercom calls can be announced by a special tone or voice signal. Calls on hold can be connected to background music. A paging system, linked to speakers throughout the business office, can be used to notify employees of calls.

Reproduced with
permission of AT&T

Illus. 19-8
Key telephone system

PBX Systems. The PBX switchboard system is used by large companies. This system normally channels calls through a central switchboard. A PBX requires a full-time attendant who handles calls coming into the company and connects them with company extensions. While an attendant may have to connect incoming calls to extensions, internal calls are usually made without attendant assistance. Outgoing calls can be made directly by employees dialing 9 to make the connection to an outside line. Today's switchboards are sophisticated electronic consoles of varying sizes and capabilities.

Advanced switching systems operate under the control of a computer. Computerized systems are able to perform functions such as the following:

1. Handling multiple calls by holding one or more calls while one person is talking to another
2. Teleconferencing where several people are allowed to hold meetings without leaving their offices
3. Redialing busy lines automatically
4. Informing an employee that a call is waiting
5. Routing calls automatically from one line to another
6. Allowing an employee to answer any telephone within a certain work area

Reproduced with
permission of AT&T

Illus. 19-9
PBX switchboard system

Centrex. Centrex, or central exchange, allows a call from the outside or a call from one extension to another to be made without the intervention of an attendant. Centrex provides direct inward dialing, in which all calls go directly to the number dialed without use of a switchboard. Every telephone extension in the system has its own number devised by modifying the last four digits of the company number. If a caller does not know a particular Centrex extension number, he or she can dial the company's principal number and ask the attendant to make the connection.

Cellular Technology. Mobile telephones were introduced by AT&T in 1964, but they have never produced quality communications. Each cordless or mobile telephone uses one of only five radio frequencies assigned by the FCC (Federal Communications Commission). If two nearby users have the same frequency, they may pick up each other's calls. This problem can be easily remedied by having a cordless telephone switched to another frequency. A recent FCC proposal to double the number of frequencies should make this interference problem less common.

Cordless telephones are bound to improve as the technology improves. Cellular service will make mobile telephones truly portable. In a cellular system, for example, there may be 50 or more stations, with each station serving one transmitting "cell" (area) from two to ten miles wide. When a customer places a call from a mobile unit, the nearest cell or transmitting station relays it to a central computer which, in turn, patches the call into the local telephone system. When a customer leaves one cell area and enters another, the computer automatically switches the transmission to the next nearest cell. The quality of the transmission never lessens with distance, which is a problem with conventional mobile phones that use radio frequencies.

Electronic Mail

Electronic mail can be defined as an electronic means for communicating textual information. Electronic mail allows messages to be transmitted and received almost instantaneously. Information that is delivered by electronic mail can also be sent by conventional means. Any of the following means can be used instead of electronic mail:

1. U. S. Postal Service. Mail has traditionally been delivered by mail carriers. Mail sent through the U. S. Postal Service can be delivered in as little as one day to as much as a week or more.
2. Interoffice Mail. Memos and other messages are frequently distributed within an organization. Sometimes days pass before interoffice mail is circulated; and once the message has been received, the recipient often does not look at it immediately.
3. Courier Services. Some services such as Federal Express or Purolator guarantee overnight delivery of important documents and packages. A combination of vans, trucks, and airplanes are used for the swift delivery of documents from city to city. While these services are reliable and speedy, they are costly and cannot usually provide anything better than overnight delivery in most situations.
4. Telephones. A telephone conversation is less precise than a written message. Telephone conversations are often not very concrete; follow-

up written work is necessary to confirm information given over the telephone. When messages are given over the telephone, only brief messages are easily recorded.

Conventional, nonelectronic mail services will continue to serve the needs of the business community; however, if time is crucial, electronic mail should be used for sending messages. A discussion of the most used electronic mail systems found in business follows.

Telegrams/Mailgrams. The telegram has traditionally been used by businesses to send an urgent but brief message. Today the telegram has been superseded by the Mailgram, a message transmitted electronically to a designated post office for delivery to the addressee by the U. S. Postal Service. Chapter 11 gives additional information about Mailgrams.

TWX/Telex. There are two networks, Telex and TWX (both operated by Western Union), that can be interconnected through the use of a teletypewriter. The teletypewriter combines the immediacy of the telephone with the documentation provided by a letter. Teletypewriters receive and send messages 24 hours a day, 7 days a week. Telex is commonly used in the international business community because the system features a hard copy of printed information and also allows conversational communications in hard copy form.

A message store-and-forward computer switching system called *InfoMaster* is used in conjunction with Telex/TWX. Through InfoMaster, a subscriber to TWX/Telex may transmit a message to another subscriber even when the teletypewriter at the destination is busy. The message is stored and then forwarded as soon as the teletypewriter at the destination is available.

Facsimile. Transmitting a copy of an original document by electronic means is called *facsimile*. A special copying machine, called a facsimile unit or copier, sends the images of a document over telephone lines to a similar copying machine in another location. Virtually any document (for example, graphs, tables, or correspondence) can be telecopied within a matter of several minutes. Telecopying by facsimile is considered electronic mail because facsimile equipment provides an alternative to putting priority documents in envelopes and sending them through the Postal Service or a courier service.

Communicating Word Processors. Mail can be sent electronically within a network by means of word processors that are interconnected. A message can be keyed in at one word processor and sent to another word processor. The message, whether a memorandum, letter, report, or informal message, is printed immediately at the receiving point and stored on magnetic media for future use. Communicating word processors can usually be used as a link or entry point into an electronic mail system and still maintain their uniqueness as text-editing devices for word processing. Some word processors can also communicate with teletypewriters, offering special options to companies utilizing the Telex network.

Remote Computer Services. If an office does not have its own computer on which to transmit mail electronically, it can share the use of an off-site computer to take advantage of specific information-processing functions. By installing a terminal (an input/output device consisting of a typewriter-like keyboard and sometimes a display screen), an office can communicate over telephone lines to a powerful computer located nearby or hundreds of miles away. Remote computer service is also known as *time-sharing* because a host computer is shared by different users.

Texas Instruments Incorporated

Illus. 19-10
This portable terminal can be used as an input station for sending messages as well as an output station for receiving messages.

Intelligent Copiers. Intelligent copiers/printers can be used to produce hard copy of data, text, and graphics. Information can be transmitted to the copier's storage unit and held until a hard copy is requested. Intelligent copiers are essentially nonimpact printers capable of translating digital information into characters (letters, numbers, and symbols). The hard copy output of an intelligent copier has excellent image quality. An intelligent copier can be connected to terminals by cable or fiber optics tubing in a local area network or linked by telephone lines in a large network.

Voice Mail

Since about one of every three calls doesn't get through on the first attempt, voice messaging has become an efficient way of giving or seeking information with just one call. Voice mail, or voice messaging, is a relatively new technology. The first commercial voice-messaging system was installed in 1980. Voice mail is intended to automate the delivery of brief messages through a telephone network. Voice messaging is used for one-way communicating. Anyone with a telephone on the network can have access to voice mail.

Voice messaging can be provided either as a remotely accessed service or as an on-site installed system. As a remotely accessed service, a central computer is used on a time-sharing basis. As an on-site installed system, a computerized telephone switching system is used. Sending a message by voice mail requires the use of the keys on a push-button telephone. Through the use of a push-button telephone, the user initiates the request for a voice mail transaction, identifies the code number of the recipient's telephone, and designates any time priorities for delivering the message. The user then relays the message over the telephone to the computer, which digitizes the analog (spoken) message, forwards the message to the receiver, and converts the message back to analog form so that the message can be understood by the recipient. If the recipient's line is busy, the computer will store and then forward the message at a later time.

A message can be received at any time convenient for the recipient. By using a push-button telephone, the recipient can key a special code for access to stored messages. The recipient can listen to entire messages, scan others, route certain messages to other individuals, save information for future use, and then delete messages no longer needed.

Voice mail should not be confused with voice recognition systems, which are still in their infancy. Such systems recognize the human voice as input to a computer and thus bypass the need to keyboard information at a terminal for transmission to a computer. To use a voice recognition system, a person simply places a call on a telephone network. The call is transmitted to the voice recognition device, at which point the voice message is converted to the digital code required for computer processing.

The Teleconference

In Chapter 13 you learned about a telecommunications service called a teleconference. Telephone companies for some years have provided a conference call service whereby several individuals can be connected for a conversation. Only in recent years have teleconferences allowed a group of people to see each other as they exchange ideas over communication lines.

Teleconferencing is a general term applied to a variety of technology assisted, two-way (interactive) communications via telephone lines or microwaves. A number of options are available; but the teleconference can be broken down into four general categories—audio conference, audio-plus-graphics conference, video conference, and computer conference.

Audio Conference. An audio conference uses a voice transmission unit (telephone) to connect two or more conversations. This type of teleconference is little more than a group telephone call. A speakerphone is often used for audio conferences. With a speakerphone, a person is not tied to the telephone receiver or a telephone cord. A speakerphone allows a person to take notes with ease, walk around the room, or consult files during the conference.

Audio-Plus-Graphics Conference. An audio-plus-graphics conference involves the transmission of a variety of graphics during an audio conference. The transmission of graphic materials such as illustrations, charts, or tables may be accomplished through the use of facsimile equipment or an electronic blackboard. Telephone lines are used to connect electronic blackboards at the sending and receiving locations. An electronic blackboard can be used just as any other blackboard; in other words, chalk strokes are made on the blackboard. These chalk strokes are converted to digital signals for transmission

Courtesy of Bell Laboratories

Illus. 19-11
Electronic blackboard

over telephone lines. The material placed on an electronic blackboard at the sending location is transmitted to a standard television monitor at the receiving location. The graphics transmitted to the receiving location are clearly displayed on the monitor through the use of one telephone line, while the audio is carried simultaneously on a second telephone line. If one blackboard is not sufficient for a presentation, up to three blackboards can be connected using the same telephone line. When copies of the information presented on the blackboard are required, a copier may be connected to the television monitor to provide hard copy.

Video Conference. There are two types of video conferences—live (also called continuous motion) and freeze frame. With continuous motion, the picture changes 33 times a second to create the impression of a continuously moving picture. With a freeze frame or slow scan, the picture changes only once every few seconds to create a slide show effect. Freeze frame is more economical because it uses conventional telephone lines; on the other hand, live transmission requires the use of microwave channels to achieve the illusion of motion.

Computer Conference. In a computer conference, a number of individuals use computer terminals and telephone lines to access a host computer in order to communicate with one another. All participants do not have to be gathered at telephones or in conference rooms at the same time. A person who arrives at 8 a.m. can see what another did at 1 p.m. the previous day. The participants can transmit their comments to the computer at their convenience, as long as the comments are given prior to the deadline established by the conference manager. The primary advantage of a computer conference is that all participants can review and comment on any material filed in the host computer on their own schedules, in their own offices.

TELECOMMUNICATIONS AND SOCIETY

The structure of society will eventually be changed by telecommunications. The uses of telecommunications have already influenced work patterns, banking procedures, shopping habits, education, and many other areas. A discussion of a few areas affected by electronic communications follows.

Work at Home

For sometime work at home has been forecast; today telecommunications networks make this concept a reality. The office can be wherever you can tie into a network. An alternate work location can benefit the employee and the employer. The employee benefits by not having to spend valuable time and money commuting to work. Employees may produce more because they are allowed to work at times convenient to them.

Work at home may occur gradually rather than rapidly. Here are several problems that must be addressed before this work concept will be widely accepted.

1. Will local zoning ordinances have to be changed in order for people to use their homes for business purposes? Who will pay insurance for the worker, the office at home, and the equipment that will be used?
2. How will workers be supervised when they work at home? What about projects that require considerable interaction with co-workers or management? How will these projects best be accomplished?
3. What about other family members that may be at home? How difficult will it be to establish working hours with family members at home?

Courtesy Mohawk Data
Sciences Corp.

Illus. 19-12
Today telecommunications makes it possible to work at home.

Videotex/Teletext

Videotex and teletext are rapidly emerging as important forces in communications. These technologies, provided through cable television networks, may drastically affect the way corporations communicate—

both internally and with customers. The initial growth for videotex/teletext services has been in electronic banking, catalog shopping, and education.

Teletext is a one-way transmission system for sending—via television channels—a stream of pages containing encoded information. This information is retrieved and decoded by a customer's personal computer or an interface device connected to a television. *Videotex* is similar, but it is a two-way transmission system that enables a customer to respond to the information on the television screen—to make an airline reservation, for example.

Banking. The banking industry is moving into an area of significant change because of electronic technology. Customers in some regions of the country can make deposits or withdrawals, make mortgage payments, or transfer funds from one account to another through the use of their television and interface units. Telebanking will continue to expand and have a profound impact on the way people handle their banking transactions.

Shopping. Teleshopping is the term used for the ability to shop using the information provided by the connection of an interface device and a television. For example, customers will be able to order from catalogs that can be accessed on the television screen. You may be able to locate the most convenient store for buying sportswear by "scrolling" the Yellow Pages of the telephone directory on your screen. Weekly specials at local grocery stores can be checked by tuning into the televised food sections of your newspaper.

Education. The costs of education, including tuition at both private and public institutions, will force consumers to look for alternative methods of learning. Some large universities and colleges already offer courses over local television channels. Teletraining will allow students to interact with teachers from their own homes. Tests can be taken at home rather than at the school's location by the entry of answers on a special keyboard. Vendors of corporate training programs can provide video training sessions through a communications network.

PROFESSIONAL POINTERS

The goal of business organizations is to maximize the benefits and minimize the costs of using telephones. As a secretary, you may be asked to assist your employer in developing some guidelines for cutting telephone costs. Here are some recommendations to be considered.

1. Review telephone statements every month. Spot-check telephone bills for personal long-distance calls. Inform employees that excessive personal calls are grounds for disciplinary action.

2. Issue memos that company telephones are for company use. Stress the fact that employees who abuse personal telephone use cost a company more than the cost of a call. There is a loss of worker productivity, and the company runs the risk of lost business due to tied up telephone lines.

3. Allow only certain employees free access to the telephones. Systems can be established whereby employees receive only certain types of service. For example, certain employees could only receive calls, some could call out only to certain area codes, and others who make many business related calls would have unlimited access.

4. Cut costs of long-distance calls by (a) dialing direct or using the services of private carriers (MCI, for example); (b) using conference calls which interconnect several parties; (c) informing the person called in a diplomatic way that the call is long-distance; and (d) leaving a telephone number if the person called is not immediately available.

5. Consider updating your telephone system for the latest technology. For example, least cost routing is a money-saving feature available on most computerized switchboard systems. With this function, a telephone system can be programmed by the telephone company to complete all outgoing calls through the least expensive route.

6. Evaluate WATS (Wide Area Telecommunications Service) for long-distance incoming (Inward WATS number is 800) or outgoing calls. Companies that make a substantial number of incoming and outgoing calls should investigate the use of WATS.

7. Ask employees for input as to whether the present telephone system is adequate or properly equipped to handle present and projected needs.

8. Above all, determine if the call is necessary. Many business matters can be handled just as well by less expensive means such as a Mailgram, Express Mail, or even first-class mail.

FOR YOUR REVIEW

1. Define the term *telecommunications*.

2. Explain the difference between analog signals and digital signals for the transmission of information.

3. Briefly describe the media used to transmit information.

4. What are local area networks?

5. Explain each of the telephone switching systems—key system, PBX system, and Centrex.

6. List two methods of transmitting mail electronically.

7. What is voice mail?

8. What is the advantage of computer conferences?

9. Identify some of the problems associated with the work-at-home concept as permitted through telecommunications.

10. Explain the difference between videotex and teletext.

CASE PROBLEM

As office manager to the firm of Winston, Heidlberg and Associates, you have been asked to take charge of a study to improve your company's present telephone system. At the recent board of directors meeting the motion was approved that a private consultant who is a specialist in telecommunications conduct the research for the study. Mr. Phillip Hughes, the consultant, will be calling you soon to set up the first meeting. Before you meet with Mr. Hughes, you will need to organize your thoughts and prepare yourself for your responsibilities in this study.

1. How can you assist Mr. Hughes in this study?

2. Outline the information you will need to provide Mr. Hughes in order to assist him in conducting this study.

PRODUCTION PROJECTS

PP 19-1

(Objective 1)

In your Supplies Inventory you will find a list of terms often associated with telecommunications. Research will be necessary in order to determine the meanings of these terms. Write the definition of each term in the space given.

PP 19-2

(Objective 2)

Submit a two- or three-page report on local area networks covering the following points:

1. The need for integrated local communications

2. Ways to design local area networks to meet the communication needs of an organization

3. Recent developments in local area networking

Present your research to your instructor as an unbound report.

PP 19-3

(Objective 3)

Determine the long-distance telecommunications services that are available in your area. You may use the Yellow Pages of your local telephone directory to locate carriers. Conduct a telephone survey of at least two carriers to determine which telephone services they offer. Compare the costs of the carriers in terms of installation charges, monthly subscription charges, minimum usage charges, and billing increments (usually in seconds). The long-distance carriers to consider are AT&T, MCI, Sprint, Allnet-Combined Network, Call U.S., U.S. Telephone, Metrophone, Skyline, ITT. Submit the information to your instructor on a plain sheet of paper.

PP 19-4

(Objective 4)

Read at least two articles in current office procedures magazines on trends in telecommunications. The magazines you choose should not have been published longer than six months ago. Summarize each article on a separate sheet of paper; be sure to include your reference sources. Some suggested magazines are *Modern Office Technology*, *Datamation*, and *Words*.

PART 6
Records Management— How Do You File and Find Information?

Chapter 20   Managing Records Effectively
Chapter 21   Understanding the Technology of Records Management

Chapter 20

MANAGING RECORDS EFFECTIVELY

Business records are kept so that they may be found and used when needed. "Get me the Jones file" is a frequent request heard by the secretary. The secretary is expected to be an expert in filing materials in the appropriate place and retrieving them quickly when needed. In addition to filing and finding materials, the secretary is expected to be familiar with the basic filing methods, to be able to determine the most appropriate filing method for the employer's needs, and to know how to charge out, transfer, and dispose of records.

Records management concerns what happens to records from the time of receipt to the time of disposal. As a secretary, you may not make the initial decisions concerning the organization and control of records; but, since you will be using the system, you should be thoroughly familiar with its various parts. Mismanagement of records can cost a company thousands of dollars.

General Objectives

Your general objectives for Chapter 20 are to:

1. *Become familiar with the basic filing methods*
2. *Follow the proper filing steps*
3. *Learn and use the basic filing rules*
4. *Identify and use charge-out and follow-up procedures*
5. *Become familiar with methods of retention, transfer, and disposal of records*

NEED FOR RECORDS MANAGEMENT

We live in an age that has been referred to as the information society. More information is generated today than ever before; this is due to the explosion of knowledge and technology that has occurred in recent years.

This increase in knowledge is due to the tremendous advances in sophisticated research tools. Computers are now able to provide in seconds information that formerly took hours, days, or weeks to produce manually. And the growth of computer technology is increasing rapidly. Today business takes computers for granted, and increasing numbers of people have computers in their homes. It is expected that by the year 2000 the computer will be as common as the telephone is today.

The technological explosion has allowed companies to use and rely on various computer generated reports. For example, a sales department can now produce reports that give company sales figures by product, salesperson, and location for the past five or ten years and projected sales for the next five or ten years. Marketing firms can generate reports that accurately estimate the market demand for particular products, the sales of those products in selected locations, and the impact of televised commercials on consumers. Such information is widely used to increase markets for products and to anticipate new markets.

What does this increase in the amount of information generated in the office mean to you as a prospective secretary? It means that you will be handling more records than ever before. And it means that you need to have a thorough knowledge of how to maintain records so that they can be found and used efficiently. The records may or may not be in paper form. For the last few years the term *paperless office* has become popular in business journals; we do indeed have the capability for evolving into paperless office systems and are moving steadily in that direction. With the advent of such technological advances as electronic mail and electronic filing, information can be transferred

Illus. 20-1
A secretary must be able to retrieve materials from the files quickly when needed.

from one location to another by word processors, computers, and copiers without ever appearing in paper form. This information transmitted through electronic means may be stored on media such as microfilm, microfiche, magnetic tapes, and diskettes. Regardless of whether this information is stored on microfilm or on paper, it is imperative that it be filed properly. An effective records management system will ensure that information is found quickly when needed.

RECORDS MANAGEMENT CAREERS

As a secretary, you will be responsible for limited records management tasks each day. It is possible to pursue a career in records management, however. If you are interested in such a career, you might begin as a records center clerk and advance through the ranks to the position of records manager. The following sections describe three positions in records management. Descriptions of other positions in records management can be found in the *Dictionary of Occupational Titles.*

Records Center Clerk

The typical responsibilities of a records center clerk include receiving records, preliminary sorting, filing and finding, microfilming, and performing related reference services. The clerk may also be responsible for other clerical tasks such as printing, duplicating, and handling mail.

Records Management Analyst

The responsibilities of a records management analyst may include the following:

1. Examines and evaluates records management systems to develop new or improve existing methods for efficient handling, protecting, and disposing of records
2. Reviews records and reports to ascertain media (paper, microfilm, or computer tape) to use, and reproduction process or electronic data processing involved
3. Reviews records retention schedules and governmental recordkeeping requirements to determine timetables for transferring active records to inactive or archival storage, for converting paper records to micrographic form, or for destroying obsolete or unnecessary records
4. Evaluates findings and recommends changes or modifications in procedures, utilizing knowledge of functions of operating units, coding systems, and filing methods

Records Center Supervisor

The records center supervisor manages and coordinates the activities of employees engaged in maintaining the central records files. He or she directs and assists clerks in searching for and retrieving lost or missing records; routes incorrectly pulled files to clerks for refiling; and directs and assists employees in the periodic disposal of obsolete files, according to company policy and governmental regulations. The supervisor also directs and participates in records management studies and may recommend work procedures to improve the efficiency of the records center.

Illus. 20-2
This employee works in the central records center of a company.

BASIC FILING METHODS

Records managers do not always agree on the classification of filing methods. Some managers categorize the filing methods into two systems—alphabetic and numeric; other managers add a third method called the alpha-numeric; still others consider four or even five filing methods. All five methods will be described in this chapter: alphabetic, numeric, subject, geographic, and chronologic. Each method, with the exception of the chronologic method, uses alphabetic concepts somewhere in its implementation.

Alphabetic Method

The alphabetic method uses letters of the alphabet to determine the order in which the names of people and companies are filed. This method is one of the most common methods used and is found in one form or other in almost every office. With the alphabetic method, the name of the company, the person, or the organization addressed determines the filing order of outgoing correspondence. The name of the company, the individual, or the organization writing the letter determines the filing order of incoming correspondence. Illus. 20-3 shows an alphabetic file. Correspondence is filed according to the basic alphabetic filing rules which will be studied later in this chapter.

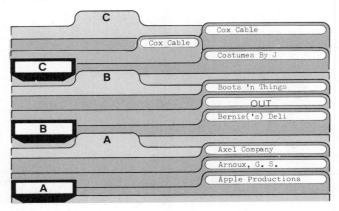

Illus. 20-3
Alphabetic file

The alphabetic method has the following advantages:

1. It is a direct system. There is no need to refer to anything except the file itself to find the name.
2. The dictionary order of arrangement is simple to understand.
3. Misfiling is easily checked by alphabetic sequence.
4. It is less costly to operate than other filing methods.
5. Only one sorting is required.
6. Papers relating to one correspondent are filed in the same location.

Some disadvantages of the alphabetic method are as follows:

1. Misfiling may result when rules are not followed.
2. Similarly spelled names may cause confusion when filed under the alphabetic method.
3. Related records may be filed in more than one place.
4. Expansion may create problems, especially if the expansion takes place in one section of the file where there is no room remaining in that particular section for the insertion of more guides and folders.

5. Excessive cross-referencing can congest the files.
6. Confidentiality of the files cannot be maintained since the file folders bearing names are instantly seen by anyone who happens to glance at a folder.

Numeric Method

Under the numeric method of filing, file cards and folders are given numbers and are arranged in numeric sequence. This method of filing is particularly useful to insurance companies that keep records according to policy numbers, social welfare agencies that maintain records according to case numbers, law firms that assign a case number to each client, warehouses that stock by parts numbers, and real estate agencies that list properties by code numbers.

Basic Parts. The numeric file has four basic parts: (1) numeric guides and folders, (2) alphabetic miscellaneous file, (3) card file, and (4) an accession book.

Numeric Guides and Folders. The numeric file houses the correspondence. It contains a main guide with a number; behind the guide are individual folders with numbered captions. Illus. 20-4 shows the arrangement of a numeric file drawer.

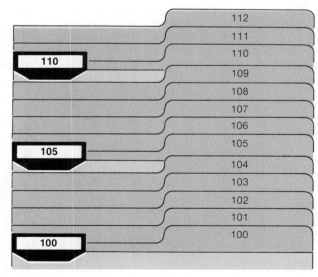

Illus. 20-4
Numeric file

Alphabetic Miscellaneous File. Miscellaneous correspondence is usually arranged alphabetically and filed in the miscellaneous file. The miscellaneous file contains a main guide labeled *Miscellaneous* and individual folders labeled with letters of the alphabet as shown in Illus. 20-5.

Illus. 20-5
Alphabetic miscellaneous file

Card File. After a number is assigned to an item, an index card is prepared, showing the name of the correspondent and the assigned number. This card is placed alphabetically in the card file. The card

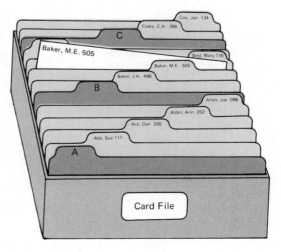

Illus. 20-6
Card file

file is an essential part of a numeric file since it is impossib[le to] remember the names and numbers that have been assigned; it serv[es] as the memory for the numeric file.

Accession Book. The accession book is a record of the numbers which have been assigned. This book shows the next number available for assignment and prevents a secretary from assigning one number to two different names. Illus. 20-7 shows an accession book.

Number	Name	Page 105 Date
504	Travel World	3/16/--
505	M. E. Baker	3/16/--
506	Browning Supply Co.	3/17/--
507	Jan Chinook	3/17/--
508		

Illus. 20-7
Page from an accession book

Filing Procedure. The basic filing procedure in a numeric system follows:

1. A piece of correspondence is received for filing.
2. The card file is consulted to see if the correspondent or subject has been assigned a number.
3. No number is assigned when there is only one piece of correspondence for a company or subject. The name or subject is typed on a card with the letter *M* (miscellaneous) typed in the upper right-hand corner. The card is placed in alphabetic order in the card file, and the piece of correspondence is placed in the miscellaneous file in the appropriate alphabetic folder. When several pieces of correspondence from the same source have been accumulated, the following steps are taken:
   a. The correspondence is removed from the miscellaneous file for placement in the main numeric file.
   b. The accession book is consulted to determine the next number to be assigned. The name of the correspondent is written in the accession book beside the assigned number.
   c. The *M* on the index card is crossed out and the number written on the card.
4. A file label is typed with the assigned number on it, and the correspondence is placed in the file folder.
5. The numbered folder is then placed in correct numeric order in the file drawer.

ric method has the following advantages:

on is unlimited.

nfidential; a card file must be consulted before files on impor-
apers can be located.

an index card is prepared and a number is assigned to a piece of
spondence, filing by number is quicker than filing alphabetically.
filed folders are easily located because numbers out of place are
ier to locate than misfiled alphabetic records.
l cross-references appear in the card file and do not congest the file
olders or drawers.
6. A complete list of the names and addresses of correspondents is
instantly available from the alphabetic card file.
7. In an office using the numeric method, orders, invoices, ledger
accounts, and correspondence of one customer all bear the same
number, making reference to them easy.

Some disadvantages of the numeric method are as follows:

1. It is an indirect method. The card file must be consulted before a
paper can be filed.
2. More equipment is necessary; therefore, the cost is higher.
3. Numbers may be transposed without being detected.
4. Since two methods of filing are involved—alphabetic and numeric—the
disadvantages of the alphabetic method are also disadvantages of the
numeric method.
5. If the card file and the accession book are not kept carefully, one correspondent's papers might be assigned several numbers and filed in
several folders.
6. As the numbers used become larger, it is harder to remember them
and misfiling can easily result.

Variations of the Numeric Method. There are several variations of the basic numeric filing method. Three of these variations will
be described in this chapter—terminal digit filing, middle digit filing,
and skip numbering.

Terminal Digit Filing. In the basic numeric method, as the files
increase, the numbers assigned become higher. When the numbers
become several digits long, it becomes difficult to file items correctly.
Terminal digit filing, which is designed to remedy this problem, is
organized by the final digits of the number. The digits are usually
separated into groups of two or three. For example, assume you have
a file with the number 450763. The last, or terminal, digits (63) identify the file drawer number. The second two digits (07) indicate the
number of the file guide, and the first two digits (45) give the number
of the file folder behind the file guide.

In large organizations where numeric filing is used extensively,
terminal digit filing can save up to 40 percent of the filing costs by

assuring a uniform work load among office workers, fewer misfiled papers, and unlimited expansion. Illus. 20-8 shows a terminal digit file.

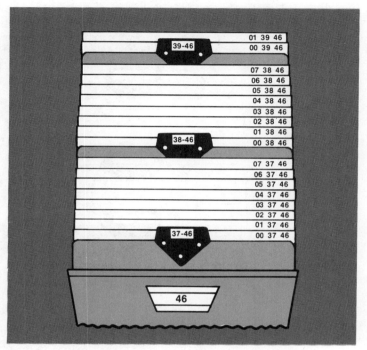

Illus. 20-8
Terminal digit file

Terminal digit filing has the following advantages:

1. Fewer errors may occur with this system than with the basic numeric method because the numbers on the folders are divided into groups of two or three digits, and the file clerk is concerned with only two or three numbers at one time.
2. Transpositions and misreading of numbers are less likely to occur with shorter groups of numbers than with one long number.
3. Folders are distributed throughout the entire file as new ones are added.
4. Several persons can be filing or retrieving folders at the same time without congestion since the folders are distributed throughout the files.

Some disadvantages of terminal digit filing are as follows:

1. Training of file clerks may take longer since the training requires that the numbers be read from right to left.
2. When several folders are requested at the same time, the file clerk must go to several locations to retrieve the folders.

Middle Digit Filing. Another variation of the basic numeric method is middle digit filing, which is similar to terminal digit filing except that the two middle digits identify the file drawer. The first two digits identify the guide number in the drawer; the final two digits identify the file folder. Illus. 20-9 shows a middle digit file.

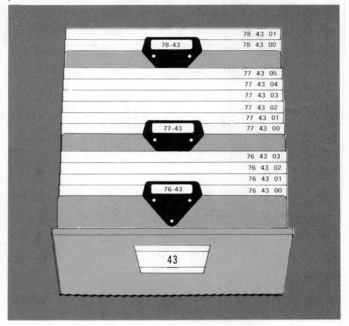

Illus. 20-9
Middle digit file

Middle digit filing has the following advantages:

1. It is easier to convert from the basic numeric method to middle digit filing than to convert from the basic numeric method to terminal digit filing. For example, folders numbered 542400 to 542499 in the basic numeric method would be in the same sequence in the middle digit filing; whereas in terminal digit filing, each folder would be in a different section of the files according to the last two digits.
2. The sorting operation for middle digit filing is reduced to two sorts—by primary and by secondary numbers.

Some disadvantages of middle digit filing are as follows:

1. Retraining of file clerks is necessary.
2. When several folders are requested at the same time, the file clerk must go to several locations to retrieve the folders.

Skip Numbering. A third variation of the basic numeric method is skip numbering. When expansion in a file is anticipated and an alphabetic sequence is desired in the permanent file as well as in the card file, the numbers assigned to names may be spaced quite far apart from each other. An alphabetic group of names may be assigned numbers with skips of 100 or more between the names. For example, all names beginning with *A* may be assigned 100 sequence numbers, and all names beginning with *B* may be assigned 200 sequence numbers. As new names are filed, they are assigned numbers between those originally assigned, again leaving intervals between the numbers. For example, assume Abell was assigned the number 100, Alford the number 150, and Arrington the number 175. Then, a new name of Adams might be assigned the number 125.

A large expansion of names in one section of the file can cause difficulty in maintaining the absolute alphabetic sequence. In this event, alternatives are to (1) accept less than strict alphabetic sequence by assigning a number out of order; (2) renumber all names, allowing more unassigned numbers between names; or (3) add another digit at the end of each already assigned number so that nine new numbers are provided between names.

Skip numbering has the following advantages:

1. If great expansion of a file is not anticipated, skip numbering can be an excellent method for maintaining both alphabetic and numeric sequence.
2. Renumbering by adding a zero at the end of existing numbers is a relatively easy method of securing additional numbers for use.

Some disadvantages of skip numbering are as follows:

1. Unexpected expansion of the file can cause renumbering, which is very time-consuming.
2. The file can become cumbersome as more and more numbers are added.
3. If extreme care and attention to detail are not practiced, misfiling can result.

Subject Method

In a subject file, correspondence is filed according to the subject of the material. Subject filing is used to some extent in all offices. The majority of offices use an alphabetic system as the basic method of filing; subject files may be found in offices or departments where the concern is with a topic. For example, assume a research department is working on a project on microprocessors. By filing the correspondence by subject, all material concerning this research project will be pulled together in one folder.

Although subject filing is useful and necessary in certain situations, it is the most difficult and costly method of filing. Each paper must be read completely to determine the subject. And it is a difficult method to control since one person may read a piece of correspondence and determine that the subject is one thing, and another person may read it and decide that the subject is something entirely different.

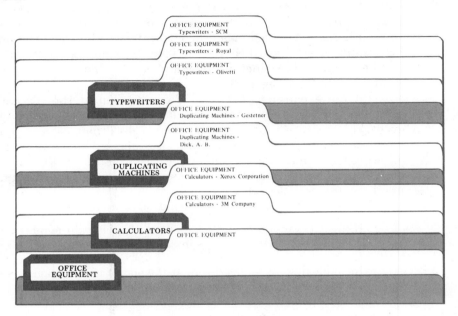

Illus. 20-10
Subject file

A necessary part of a subject file is an index. The index is a list of all subjects under which a piece of correspondence may be filed. Without an index, it is almost impossible for the subject filing method to function satisfactorily. The list should be kept up to date as new subjects are added and old ones eliminated. When new subjects are added, the index provides guidance to avoid the duplication of subjects. The index may be kept on standard sheets of paper and filed in a notebook or on index cards and filed in a card file box. A subject list kept on sheets of paper provides an easier way to see at a glance which subjects exist in the file than does a card index. When subjects are added to the list, however, the sheets must be reworked and updated. With a card index, a card indicating the new subject is simply inserted in the index. Whichever method is used to maintain the index, the important point is that it be kept up to date at all times.

The subject method has the following advantages:

1. Correspondence about one subject is grouped together.
2. The system can be expanded easily by adding subdivisions.

Some disadvantages of the subject method are as follows:

1. It is difficult to classify records by subject.
2. Liberal cross-referencing is necessary since one piece of correspondence may contain several subjects.
3. The system does not satisfactorily provide for miscellaneous records.
4. It is necessary to keep an index of subject headings contained in the file.
5. It is the most expensive method to maintain since it requires very experienced file clerks.
6. Preparation of materials for the subject file takes longer than any other method since each piece of correspondence must be thoroughly and carefully read.

Geographic Method

When the files of correspondents are requested by location rather than by name, geographic filing is advantageous. This method is based first on the location of the correspondents and second on their names.

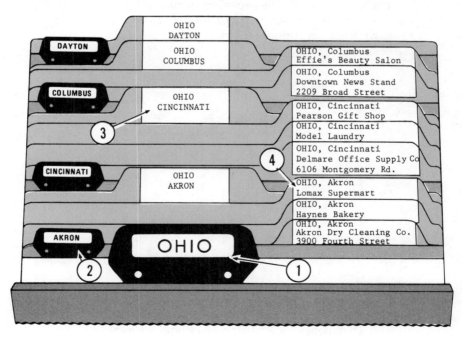

Illus. 20-11
In this geographic file papers are filed alphabetically by the geographic areas indicated by the guides and folders (see No. 1 and No. 2). In the miscellaneous folder for each city (see No. 3), the papers are filed alphabetically by the names of the correspondents. Individual folders are used for correspondents who have enough communications to warrant a separate folder (see No. 4).

It is particularly useful for utility companies where street names and numbers are of primary importance in troubleshooting, real estate firms that have listings according to land areas, sales organizations that are concerned with the geographic location of their customers, and government agencies that file records by state, county, or other geographic division.

In geographic filing, the main divisions may be states, counties, cities, sales territories, and so forth. The breakdown into geographic divisions and subdivisions must fit the type of business, its organization, and its need for specific kinds of information.

In a geographic file by state and city, for example, file guides are used to indicate the state and city. The file folders are arranged alphabetically behind the guides by company or individual. Illus. 20-11 shows a geographic filing arrangement.

An alphabetic card file is an essential element of a geographic filing method. Correspondence may be requested by the name of a correspondent rather than by the address. A file consisting of cards with the names of correspondents in alphabetic order and their complete addresses gives all the necessary information when the file clerk must locate correspondence without knowing the location. Illus. 20-12 shows a card from an alphabetic card file.

```
Erickson, Thomas B.


183 Jungle Avenue
Duncanville, Texas   75116-7606
```

Illus. 20-12
Card from an alphabetic card file

The geographic method has the following advantages:

1. It provides for grouping of records by location.
2. The volume of correspondence within any given geographic area can be seen by glancing at the files.
3. It allows for direct filing if the location is known.
4. All the advantages of alphabetic filing are inherent in this method since it is basically an alphabetic arrangement.

Some disadvantages of the geographic method are as follows:

1. Multiple sorting increases the possibility of error and is time-consuming.
2. The complex arrangement of guides and folders makes filing more difficult.
3. Reference to the card file is necessary if the location is not known.
4. The geographic method takes longer to set up than does the alphabetic method.

Chronologic Method

Chronologic means to arrange in order of time. A chronologic file is simply an arrangement of documents by date. This method may be used for filing daily reports, statements, deposit tickets, order sheets, and freight bills, which may best be stored by date.

A chronologic file may also be used as a supplement to alphabetic, numeric, geographic, or subject files. For example, you may keep a chronologic reading file and an alphabetic correspondence file. Two file copies of all correspondence are made—one is placed in the reading file in date order, and the other is filed under the proper alphabetic caption in the correspondence file. The chronologic reading file is usually kept in a folder on the secretary's desk.

The chronologic reading file is especially helpful when used as an addition to the subject system. It allows you to find correspondence with limited information. Assume your employer asks you to locate a piece of correspondence addressed to L. A. Meador, dated December 11. With a subject system, it would be very difficult to locate the correspondence given this information—you would need the subject of the correspondence. By maintaining a chronologic reading file, however, you could quickly find the correspondence requested.

Another form of chronologic file is the tickler file. The basic arrangement of a tickler file is chronologic in nature: a series of 12 guides with the names of the months printed on the tabs and 31 guides with the numbers 1 through 31 printed on the tabs. The tickler file is generally kept on the secretary's desk. When something must be taken care of on a certain date, a card is prepared with the necessary information and placed behind the appropriate month and date. The file is checked each morning to see what must be done that day. Refer to Chapter 3, page 50, for an example of a tickler file.

The chronologic principle is followed in all methods of filing as papers are placed in their folders. The top of each paper is at the left of the folder, and the paper with the most recent date is on top of each name group so that anyone who opens a folder can see immediately the latest piece of correspondence.

FILING TECHNIQUES

Before material can be filed, the proper filing method must be selected and then appropriate equipment and supplies determined. Once these steps have been taken, certain other steps should be followed which include determining when a piece of correspondence is ready to be filed; deciding under what name, subject, or geographic location the item should be filed; determining whether cross-referencing is necessary; and storing the material in the appropriate file.

Select the Correct Method

You have just learned the basic methods of filing correspondence and the advantages and disadvantages of each method. If you are setting up a new filing system in an office, you should be familiar with these methods and be able to recommend the system most appropriate for the needs of the company. If you are working with already established files, you may be able to recommend a more efficient method of filing based on your knowledge of the basic methods.

Select the Correct Equipment and Supplies

Various types of filing equipment are available: vertical, lateral, rotary, wheel, and magnetized files and micrographics equipment such as readers, printers, and computers. This wide and versatile range of equipment is a radical change from the days when four-drawer steel cabinets were the ultimate assurance of efficiency in a well-equipped office. Today sophisticated micrographics equipment is available. Information is stored on microfilm and retrieved via a computer. Although you may have little to do with the selection of filing equipment, you should keep as current as possible on innovations and changing technology so that you can recommend the latest equipment if given the opportunity.

In addition to selecting and using up-to-date equipment, you need to select the right filing supplies; for example, guides, folders, labels, sorters, and other miscellaneous items. As a secretary, you will usually be responsible for ordering filing supplies; therefore, you need to know what is available. You will learn more about filing equipment and supplies in Chapter 21.

Follow the Proper Filing Steps

Before records can be stored in a folder, they must be prepared for filing. Records must be inspected, indexed, coded, cross-referenced, if necessary, and sorted before they can be filed. These steps are explained in more detail in the following paragraphs.

Inspecting. Incoming correspondence must never be filed until its contents have been read by your employer. Therefore, before filing any incoming correspondence, be sure to inspect the correspondence for a release mark. This release mark may be in the form of initials, a stamp, a check mark, or other filing notation. Sometimes correspondence will be placed in the out basket by mistake. If there is no release mark, be sure to check with your employer to see if he or she has read that particular correspondence.

Outgoing correspondence does not need a release mark since you will be filing the carbon copy. Do not file a carbon copy until it has been signed by your employer since changes may have been made in the original.

Indexing. The process of determining where a piece of correspondence is to be filed is called *indexing*. In alphabetic filing, indexing means determining the name that is to be used. On incoming correspondence, the most likely name to use is in the letterhead. On outgoing correspondence (carbon copies), the most likely name to use is in the letter address.

In subject filing, indexing means determining the most important subject discussed in the correspondence. If there are two subjects, the correspondence should be filed under one subject and cross-referenced under the other. In geographic filing, the location to be used must be determined. In numeric filing, the name and number to be used must be determined.

Coding. Coding is the marking of the correspondence by the name, subject, location, or number that was determined in the process of indexing. The correspondence may be marked by underlining, circling, or checking. Coding is important since it saves time in the refiling process. When a paper has been removed from the files and must be refiled, the secretary does not have to reread the correspondence if it has been coded.

Cross-Referencing. There are occasions when correspondence may be filed under two or more names. For example, assume AWB Corporation is owned by Rose Cuffee. Correspondence may be asked for under the name of Rose Cuffee or AWB Corporation. In this case, the main file would be AWB Corporation with a cross-reference under Rose Cuffee. Cross-reference cards or sheets may be purchased from a commercial company, or you may make your own forms. An example of a cross-reference sheet is shown in Illus. 20-13. Notice that the notation on the sheet indicates where the original correspondence is filed.

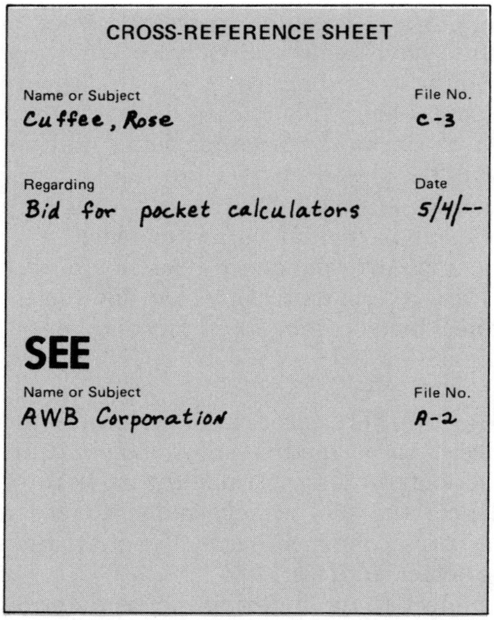

CROSS-REFERENCE SHEET

Name or Subject   File No.
Cuffee, Rose   C-3

Regarding   Date
Bid for pocket calculators   5/4/--

SEE

Name or Subject   File No.
AWB Corporation   A-2

Illus. 20-13
Cross-reference sheet

Sorting. *Sorting* is the arrangement of documents in the order in which they are to be filed. The documents should first be sorted into a few groups, then into the final arrangement. The first sorting is called *rough sorting*. For example, items may be arranged into groups of A to C, D to H, I to M, N to S, and T to Z. The last sorting, or *fine sorting*, consists of arranging the items in exact alphabetic order. When the fine sorting is completed, the materials are ready to be filed.

Sometimes coding and sorting are done in sequence. As the coding is finished, the items are immediately sorted into alphabetic groups. Coordination of inspecting, indexing, coding, and sorting means handling each record only once. A delay in sorting until all records have been coded means handling each record twice; therefore, more time and energy are consumed.

To assist you in efficiently sorting materials, a sorter may be used. Illus. 20-14 shows a sorter. Notice that the guides on each flap of the sorter carry an alphabetic designation. If you do not immediately file materials, it is helpful to have the materials in a sorter at your desk so that they may be located quickly without having to shuffle through a pile of papers.

Illus. 20-14
This employee is using a sorter to arrange materials alphabetically before filing them.

Filing. Filing is the actual process of placing the correspondence in the file folder and the file drawer. Rather than file one piece of correspondence at a time (since this is extremely time-consuming), accumulate several pieces of correspondence before going to the file drawer. As you are accumulating enough papers to file, you should keep these papers in order at your desk in case someone needs to refer to a piece of correspondence. This can be done by placing the papers in alphabetical order within a file sorter. When you are ready to file, take the sorter to the file drawer. Each paper goes into the folder with its top to the left. The most recent paper is always placed on top, which means that the oldest piece of correspondence is always at the back of the folder.

FILING RULES

The foundation of efficient filing is an understanding of the basic alphabetic filing rules and an ability to apply these rules in the day-to-day filing operations of an office. On the following pages twenty-eight rules for alphabetic filing are presented along with illustrative examples.[1]

---

[1]Mina M. Johnson and Norman F. Kallaus, *Records Management* (3d ed.; Cincinnati: South-Western Publishing Co., 1982), pp. 71-103.

Rules for Names of Persons

The following rules explain the way in which the names of people are filed.

1. Order of Units

a. Each part of a person's name is considered to be a separate unit.
b. A person's name is transposed so that the last name is shown as the key unit, the given name or initial as the second unit, and the middle name or initial as the third unit.
c. When the last names of two or more people are alike, filing order is determined by the second units in the names if they are different; if the second as well as the first units are alike, filing order is determined by the third or succeeding units.
d. In all cases, *nothing goes before something*. An initial, therefore, is a unit by itself and precedes a name that begins with the same letter.

		Indexed as		
Names	Units:	Key (1)	2	3
L. M. Conrad		Conrad	L.	M.
Leslie Conrad		Conrad	Leslie	
A. L. Conradt		Conradt	A.	L.
Marshall H. Consolver		Consolver	Marshall	H.

2. Identical Names of Persons

If all units in the names of two or more persons are identical, filing order is determined by addresses, which are used as units. The order of units in an address is (1) city name; (2) state name if the city names are identical; (3) street name, including designations such as *Avenue, Street,* and *Drive,* with directions such as *East* and *West* transposed; and (4) house and building numbers, with the lowest number first.

		Indexed as						
Names	Units:	Key (1)	2	3	4	5	6	7
Cecil Duncan Jacksonville, Florida		Duncan	Cecil	Jacksonville	Florida			
Cecil Duncan 812 East Main Street Jacksonville, Texas		Duncan	Cecil	Jacksonville	Texas	Main	Street	East 812
Cecil Duncan 915 East Main Street Jacksonville, Texas		Duncan	Cecil	Jacksonville	Texas	Main	Street	East 915

3. Hyphenated and Compound Persons' Names

Each part of a hyphenated name or a compound name, whether a given name or a last name, is considered to be a separate unit. The hyphen is disregarded. In a last name containing either the word *Saint* (or its variations *San* and *Santa*) or the abbreviation *St.*, the word or the abbreviation in spelled-out form is considered to be the key unit; the word after *Saint* is considered to be the second unit.

| | | Indexed as | | |
Names	Units:	Key (1)	2	3
Pamela Loaring-Clark		Loaring-	Clark	Pamela
Paul Saint Clair		Saint	Clair	Paul
William St. Jean		Saint	Jean	William
Edward San Verde		San	Verde	Edward

4. Prefixes

A prefix (or particle) in a last name or a given name is considered to be part of the name, not a separate unit. The application of this rule is not affected by spacing between the prefix and the rest of the surname or the given name or by the capitalization or lack of capitalization of the first letter of the prefix.

| | | Indexed as | | |
Names	Units:	Key (1)	2	3
Joseph D'Agostino		D'Agostino	Joseph	
Jack E. LaFaver		LaFaver	Jack	E.
Beatrice La Strapes		LaStrapes	Beatrice	
Katherine von Hass		vonHass	Katherine	

5. Abbreviations

Abbreviated given names are considered as if written in full. But, when a brief form of a given name (such as Bill, Pat, Don) is used by a person in a signature and is in a typed signature or on a letterhead, the brief form is considered as it is spelled.

| | | Indexed as | | |
Names	Units:	Key (1)	2	3
Thos. Collins		Collins	Thomas	
Wm. W. Epperson		Epperson	William	W.
Bill W. Jones		Jones	Bill	W.
Don R. Parks		Parks	Don	R.
Liz L. Roper		Roper	Liz	L.
Jas. Seaver		Seaver	James	

6. Seniority Designations

A seniority designation (Jr., Sr., II, and III) is considered to be a unit only if it is needed to distinguish between two otherwise identical names. The designations *Junior* (Jr.) and *Senior* (Sr.) are used in alphabetic sequence; the titles *II* and *III* are used in numeric sequence.

Names	Units:	Key (1)	Indexed as 2	3	4
Edward Lessen, Jr.		Lessen	Edward (Junior)		
Eugene H. Lessen, Jr.		Lessen	Eugene	H.	Junior
Eugene H. Lessen, Sr.		Lessen	Eugene	H.	Senior
Roy S. Letourneau, II		Letourneau	Roy	S.	II
Roy S. Letourneau, III		Letourneau	Roy	S.	III

7. Titles and Degrees

A title is disregarded if it is followed by a complete name (given name and surname). The title is placed in parentheses after the name so that it will not be omitted from the record. When a title is followed by only the surname or by only a given and a middle name, the title is considered to be the key unit. A degree is disregarded but is placed in parentheses after the name.

Names	Units:	Key (1)	Indexed as 2	3
Brother Roseberry		Brother	Roseberry	
Dr. Donald C. Roseman		Roseman	Donald	C. (Dr.)
Patricia E. Ross, Ph.D.		Ross	Patricia	E. (Ph.D)

8. Unusual and Foreign Names

The last word written in unusual and foreign personal names is considered to be the key unit. These names should usually be cross-referenced.

Names	Units:	Key (1)	Indexed as 2	3
Thao Li Cheng		Cheng	Thao	Li
Tran Cha Ngyen		Ngyen	Tran	Cha

9. Names of Married Women

A married woman's name is filed as she writes it. If an alternative form of her name or if the husband's name is known, a cross-reference should be made to it.

*Cross reference- Filing in 2 or more places.
Make a record of it.*

Names	Units:	Key (1)	Indexed as 2	3
Adriana Romans (Mrs. Kyle C. Romans)		Romans	Adriana	
Mrs. Janet P. Romero		Romero	Janet	P. (Mrs.)
Ms. Joanna Rominger		Rominger	Joanna (Ms.)	

10. A Person's Name Within Another Name

If a person's name appears within a business or other name, the person's name is transposed according to Rule 1.

Names	Units:	Key (1)	Indexed as 2	3	4
Sam Freed Furniture Company		Freed	Sam	Furniture	Company
Jayne Freeman Institutional Foods		Freeman	Jayne	Institutional	Foods
Fred Wilhelm Auto Sales		Wilhelm	Fred	Auto	Sales

Rules for Names of Businesses

The following rules explain the way in which names of businesses are filed.

11. Order of Units

The general rule is that names of businesses, except those containing the full name of a person (as explained in Rule 10), are coded as they are written. A business name consisting of a title followed by a single given name, a last name, or a coined name is considered as it is written. If the title is abbreviated, it is considered as if spelled in full unless the title is *Mr.* or *Mrs.* These two words are not spelled out but are considered alphabetically as they are written.

Names	Units:	Key (1)	Indexed as 2	3	4
Dr. Green Kiddie College		Doctor	Green	Kiddie	College
Donald Foster Real Estate		Foster	Donald	Real	Estate
Dr. Marcia Krantz Management Company		Krantz	Marcia (Dr.)	Management	Company

12. Identical Business Names

If all the units in two or more business names are identical, filing order is determined by addresses, which are considered in the following order: (1) city name; (2) state name if the city names are identical; (3) street name, including such designations as *Avenue, Street,* and *Drive,* with directions such as *East* and *West* transposed; and (4) building numbers with the lowest number filed first. The name of a building is used as a unit only when the street name is not known.

				Indexed as			
Names	Units:	Key (1)	2	3	4	5	6
Dobson Floors 3010 Eastgate Drive Dallas, Texas		Dobson	Floors	Dallas	Texas	Eastgate	Drive 3010
Dobson Floors 6000 Eastgate Drive Dallas, Texas		Dobson	Floors	Dallas	Texas	Eastgate	Drive 6000
Dobson Floors 12300 Inwood Avenue Dallas, Texas		Dobson	Floors	Dallas	Texas	Inwood	Avenue 12300

13. Hyphenated Business Names

When two or more initials, words, names, word substitutes, or coined words in a business name are joined by a hyphen, the hyphen is disregarded and each part of the name is considered a separate unit. When a hyphen joins two parts of a single word, both parts are considered together as one unit. Words of this type often begin with *inter-, non-, trans-,* and so forth.

			Indexed as		
Names	Units:	Key (1)	2	3	4
Co-Operative Management Association		Co-Operative	Management	Association	
Pratt-Lambert Color Service		Pratt-	Lambert	Color	Service
U-Haul Moving Centers		U-	Haul	Moving	Centers

14. Articles, Prepositions, and Conjunctions

English articles, prepositions, and conjunctions that are not joined to other words in business names are generally not considered units. These disregarded words are enclosed in parentheses to set them off from the other units. *The,* when appearing as the first word in a business name, is placed at the end of the name and is enclosed in parentheses. Exception: When a preposition or conjunction is the first word in a business name, the preposition or conjunction is considered the key unit.

Names	Units:	Key (1)	Indexed as 2	Indexed as 3	Indexed as 4
At the Top Cassette Duplicators		At (the)	Top	Cassette	Duplicators
Atlas Sales & Service		Atlas	Sales (&)	Service	
The Down Home Cleaners		Down	Home	Cleaners (The)	

15. Abbreviations

Abbreviations in a business name are considered as if spelled in full.

Names	Units:	Key (1)	Indexed as 2	Indexed as 3	Indexed as 4
TWA, Inc.		Trans	World	Airlines	Incorporated
U.S. Supply Co.		United	States	Supply	Company

16. Single Letters

A single letter (with or without a period) in a business name is considered a separate unit unless that single letter stands for a person's first name. In a business name composed of two or more single letters, each letter is considered a separate unit, whether the letters are written separately or are written together.

Names	Units:	Key (1)	2	Indexed as 3	4
S. Dabney Corporation		Dabney	S.	Corporation	
SBN Construction		S	B	N	Construction
S.C.I. Systems		S.	C.	I.	Systems

17. Numbers and Symbols

Numbers and symbols within a business name are considered as though spelled out. The complete number is considered one word. If the number is accompanied by a symbol, the symbol is considered separately as a spelled-out word. Four-place numbers are expressed in hundreds, not in thousands (resulting in fewer letters to indicate the number).

Names	Units:	Key (1)	Indexed as 2	3	4
4¢ Copy Center		Four	Cents	Copy	Center
4 Seasons Coiffures		Four	Seasons	Coiffures	
The 10-8 Shop		Ten-	Eight	Shop (The)	
1200 Main Place		Twelvehundred	Main	Place	

18. *Possessives*

When a word contains an apostrophe showing possession, the word up to the apostrophe is considered. If an *s* follows the apostrophe, the *s* is disregarded.

			Indexed as	
Names	Units:	Key (1)	2	3
Frank's Private School		Frank('s)	Private	School
Hutchins' Market		Hutchins'	Market	

19. *Words That Can Be Written Singly or Together*

Any word in a business name that may be written as one word is considered one unit, no matter which way the word is written. This rule applies to such words as *airport, cooperative, percent, sometime, northwest,* and so forth.

			Indexed as		
Names	Units:	Key (1)	2	3	4
Good Will Thrift Shop		GoodWill	Thrift	Shop	
North East Texas Land Co.		NorthEast	Texas	Land	Company

20. *Compound Geographic Names*

Each English word in a compound geographic name is considered a separate unit.

			Indexed as		
Names	Units:	Key (1)	2	3	4
Mt. George Center		Mount	George	Center	
St. Louis Skating Rink		Saint	Louis	Skating	Rink

21. *Foreign Business Names*

Each separate word in a foreign business name is considered a separate unit. A foreign prefix or particle is combined with the word following it, and the combination of the two is considered one unit.

			Indexed as	
Names	Units:	Key (1)	2	3
Buenos Aires Fabrics		Buenos	Aires	Fabrics
Los Angeles Lumber Company		LosAngeles	Lumber	Company

Rules for Other Names

The following rules explain how other names are filed.

22. *School Names*

Elementary and secondary school names are considered in the order written, except that a person's name within a school name is transposed. In the case of identically named schools, the city name is considered first followed by the state name if city names are identical.

The name of a college, university, or special school is also considered in the order written except that the words *College, University, and School* are never considered key units. A person's name within a school name is transposed; and with identical names, the city name is considered first followed by the state name.

			Indexed as		
Names	Units:	Key (1)	2	3	4
College of DuPage		DuPage	College (of)		
School of Electronics Technology		Electronics	Technology	School (of)	
Richardson High School		Richardson	High	School	
John Roosevelt Elementary School		Roosevelt	John	Elementary	School

23. *Religious Institutions, Clubs, Lodges, Unions, and Other Privately Owned Groups*

The names of churches, temples, cathedrals, synagogues, and other religious groups are considered by the most clearly identifying word in the name. Words such as *Church, Temple, Cathedral, First,* and *Second* are never the key unit. The denomination, if known, is indexed first.

The names of clubs, lodges, unions, and similar privately owned groups are considered according to the most clearly identifying word in the name. Words such as *Association of, Union of,* and *Brotherhood of* are never the key unit.

			Indexed as		
Names	Units:	Key (1)	2	3	4
Fraternal Order of Eagles		Eagles	Fraternal	Order (of)	
All Saints Episcopal Church		Episcopal	Church	All	Saints
First Church of God		God	First	Church (of)	
American Federation of Musicians		Musicians	American	Federation (of)	
First Unitarian Church		Unitarian	Church	First	

24. *Financial Institutions*

The names of financial institutions are considered by the as-written method. When the names of financial institutions are identical, city and state names are considered. Branch names are considered after the institution, city, and state names. If the name of the institution contains a geographic location, the location is considered only once.

			Indexed as		
Names	Units: Key (1)	2	3	4	5
Bedford Union Trust Bank Bedford, Virginia	Bedford	Union	Trust	Bank	
First National Bank Dallas, Texas	First	National	Bank	Dallas	Texas
First National Bank Duncanville, Texas	First	National	Bank	Duncanville	Texas
First National Bank Durham, North Carolina	First	National	Bank	Durham	North Carolina
Guaranty Savings and Loan Dardanelle, Arkansas	Guaranty	Savings (and)	Loan		

25. Publications: Newspapers, Magazines, and Pamphlets

The names of newspapers, magazines, and pamphlets are considered in the order written. The city of publication of a newspaper is usually the first word in the name of a newspaper; if it is not, a cross-reference should be prepared under the city name.

		Indexed as		
Names	Units: Key (1)	2	3	4
Business Week	Business	Week		
The Dallas Morning News	Dallas	Morning	News (The)	
The Fort Worth Star Telegram	Fort	Worth	Star	Telegram (The)
Modern Office Technology	Modern	Office	Technology	
The Secretary	Secretary (The)			

26. Hotels and Motels

The names of hotels and motels are considered as written except that the words *Hotel* and *Motel* are never the key unit; rather, they are transposed to follow the other words in the name.

		Indexed as	
Names	Units: Key (1)	2	3
Adolphus Hotel	Adolphus	Hotel	
Hotel LeBaron	LeBaron	Hotel	
Lincoln Radisson Motel	Lincoln	Radisson	Motel

27. Radio and Television Stations

The names of radio and television stations may be considered in one of two ways: (1) by call letters, each letter being considered as a separate unit or (2) by the words *Radio* or *Television* considered as the key unit, followed by *Station* as the second unit, and the call letters as the remaining units. Each letter is considered separately.

			Indexed as				
Names	Units:	Key (1)	2	3	4	5	6
KLIF		K	L	I	F		
KTVT		K	T	V	T		
KMEZ Radio Station		Radio	Station	K	M	E	Z
KXAS Television Station		Television	Station	K	X	A	S

28. Government Agencies and Offices

a. United States Government Names. The first three units for any federal government office are *United States Government.* They should be written on any record to which they apply if they do not already appear there. The fourth and succeeding units are the principal words in the name of the department and then the name of the bureau, division, board, or commission. The words *Department of, Bureau of, Division of,* and the like, are transposed; the word *of* is disregarded.

			Indexed as		
Names	Units:	4	5	6	7	8
Office of Civil Rights		Education	Department (of)	Civil	Rights	Office (of)
Internal Revenue Service		Treasury	Department (of the)	Internal	Revenue	Service

b. State, Commonwealth, and Territory Names. The key unit is the name of the state, commonwealth, or territory. It must be written on any record on which it does not already appear. The next unit is the word *State, Commonwealth,* or *Territory.* The succeeding units are the principal words in the name of the bureau, department, board, or office. The words *Department of, Bureau of,* and the like, are transposed; *of* is disregarded.

			Indexed as		
Names	Units:	Key (1)	2	3	4	5
Park and Wildlife Dept., California		California	State (of)	Park (and)	Wildlife	Department
Department of Public Safety, Florida		Florida	State (of)	Public	Safety	Department (of)

c. County, Borough, Parish, and City Names. The key unit is the name of the county, borough, parish, or city. It must be written on any record where it does not already appear. The next unit is the word *County* or *City*. The words *Parish* and *Borough* customarily follow the parish or borough name and are considered in order as written. The succeeding units are the principal words in the name of the department, bureau, board, or office. Such words as *Department of* and *Bureau of* are transposed; the word *of* is always disregarded. If two or more city or county names are identical, state names are considered as units immediately after city or county names. (Alaska is our only state with boroughs; Louisiana is our only state with parishes.)

			Indexed as		
Names	*Units:*	*Key (1)*	*2*	*3*	*4*	*5*
Agricultural Extension Service Boudreaux Parish, Louisiana		Boudreaux	Parish	Agricultural	Extension	Service
Assessor-Collector of Taxes Dallas County, Texas		Dallas	County (of)	Assessor-	Collector (of)	Taxes
Fire Department Mason, Ohio		Mason	City (of)	Fire	Department	
Animal Shelter Richmond, Virginia		Richmond	City (of)	Animal	Shelter	

MANUAL RETRIEVAL OF RECORDS

Once records have been filed, the next step is to be able to find them quickly and efficiently. The manual retrieval of records involves the secretary going into the file drawer and pulling the necessary document from the file folder. This manual method of retrieval was all that was available in years past; however, today we also have electronic systems which allow the retrieval of documents through the use of the computer. You will learn more about this computerized retrieval of records in Chapter 21.

In a manual retrieval system, it is necessary to indicate what was taken from the files if the material is not going to be returned to the files immediately. For example, assume that a secretary from another department asks for some information from the files that you control, stating that the information is needed for approximately three days. If you release the information without making a notation of who has the information and when it will be returned, the likelihood of your forgetting the transaction is great and a valuable piece of correspondence may be lost from the files. There are several standard methods of handling charge-out and follow-up procedures.

Requisition and Charge Out

Requisitions and charge outs are acknowledgments that a borrower has taken a record from the files and intends to return it. The requisition and charge-out procedure may be in the form of a requisition, an out guide, out folder, out card, or out sheet.

Requisition Forms. A requisition form which is usually 5 by 3 inches or 6 by 4 inches in size may be filled out identifying the material borrowed, the name and location of the borrower, the date appearing on the material, the date borrowed, and the date to be returned to the files. This form is usually prepared in duplicate, with one copy kept in a tickler file and the other copy inserted in an out guide or folder. Illus. 20-15 shows a requisition form.

<table>
<tr><td colspan="2" align="center">**REQUISITION FOR MATERIAL FROM FILES**</td></tr>
<tr><td>**Name or subject**</td><td>**Date of material**</td></tr>
<tr><td>Benson Business Machine Co</td><td>11/2/--</td></tr>
<tr><td colspan="2">**Regarding**</td></tr>
<tr><td colspan="2">Sorter Quotations</td></tr>
<tr><td>**Taken by**</td><td>**Date taken**   **Return date**</td></tr>
<tr><td>P. Wilson</td><td>11/17/--   11/24/--</td></tr>
<tr><td>**Signed**</td><td>**Department**</td></tr>
<tr><td>P. Wilson</td><td>Sales</td></tr>
</table>

Illus. 20-15
Requisition form

Out Guide. The out guide is usually a pressboard or plastic guide with the word *OUT* printed on the tab. This guide is used to replace a folder which has been removed from the files. There are two types of out guides as shown in Illus. 20-16. Notice that one guide has lines on which the requisition information is written. The other guide has a pocket to hold the requisition form. The out guide remains in the files until the borrowed folder is returned and refiled.

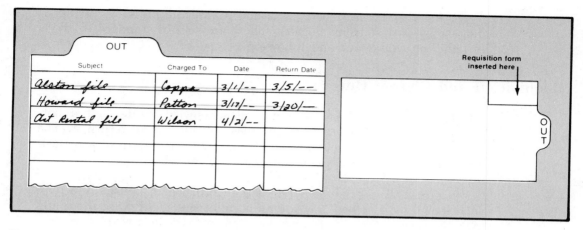

Illus. 20-16
Out guides

Out Folder. When an entire folder is taken from the files, papers for a particular correspondent cannot be filed until the folder has been returned. For continuity in filing, you may choose to use an out folder to take the place of the one borrowed. There are two types of out folders as shown in Illus. 20-17. Notice one folder has lines on it for recording the requisition information. The other folder has a pocket where the requisition form may be inserted.

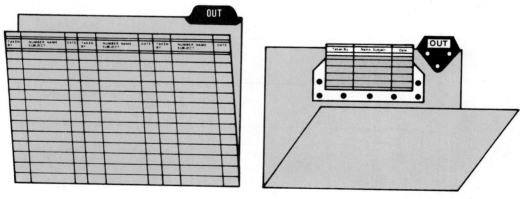

Illus. 20-17
Out folders

Out Card and Out Sheet. An out card or an out sheet is used to replace a single piece of correspondence within a folder. An out card is approximately the size of a guide and has lines on which the requisition information may be written. An out sheet has the same information as the out card but is approximately one half to one third the width of the card. Illus. 20-18 shows both an out card and an out sheet.

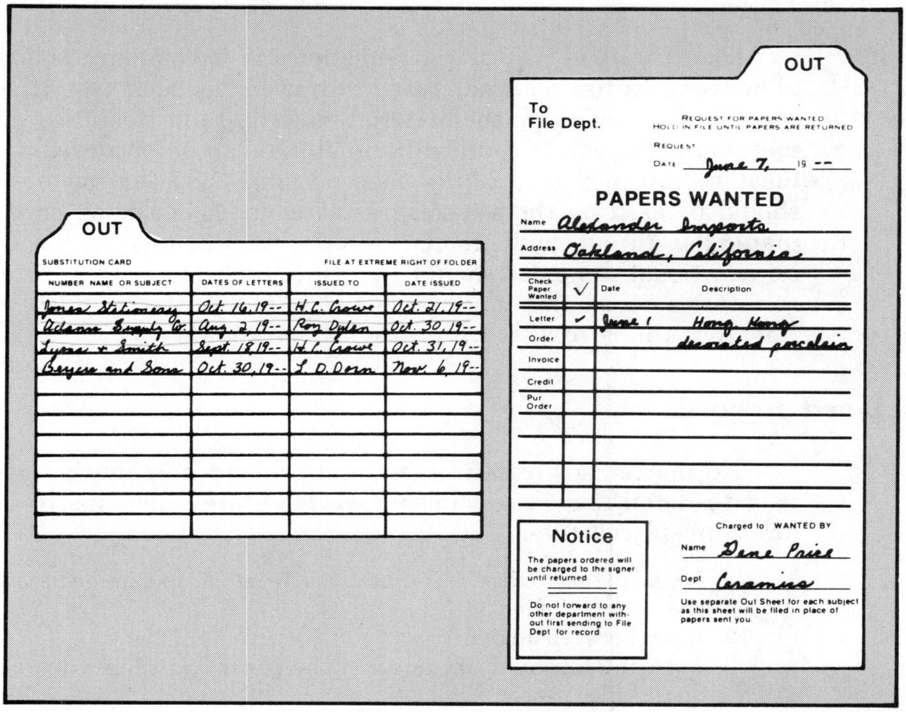

Illus. 20-18
Out card and out sheet

Confidential Records. Most businesses maintain certain records that are considered confidential. It is the responsibility of the secretary to see that these records are not released without proper authority. This authority may be the signature of an officer of the company.

Follow-Up Procedures

Once material has been taken from the files, it is important that it be returned within a reasonable time. Follow-up records must be maintained in case materials are not returned when they should be.

Tickler File. You learned previously that a requisition form may be prepared in duplicate, one copy being placed in the out guide, the other in a tickler file. Such a system provides a quick and efficient method of tracking materials that have not been returned. If requisition forms are not used, then a slip of paper or card may be prepared with the necessary information and placed in the tickler file.

Confidential Material. Sometimes it is company policy not to allow confidential material to be borrowed. In such case, the person interested in reviewing the material must do so in the office where the material is housed. If confidential material can be borrowed, it usually must be returned to the files each evening. A special memory device should be used by the secretary as a reminder of the absence of such materials. An out guide, folder, or sheet may be used in the files. But an additional reminder should be made in the form of a note on the secretary's desk reminding him or her to obtain the confidential material from the borrower before leaving for the day.

Misplaced Records

No matter how careful a secretary is and how much attention is paid to detail, papers get misplaced. Here are some tips to help you locate misplaced files.

1. Look in the folder immediately in front of and immediately behind the correct folder.
2. Look between folders.
3. Push the folders apart to see if the paper has slipped to the bottom of the file drawer.
4. Look in the miscellaneous folder for that particular section.
5. Look for the second, third, or succeeding units of a name rather than for the key unit.
6. Check for misfiling due to misread letters; for example, *C* for *G, K* for *H,* and so forth.
7. Check for alternative spellings of words; for example, *Johnson* or *Johnston.*
8. Look for a double letter instead of a single one.
9. Check for the transposition of numbers.
10. Look in a related subject file.
11. Look in the sorter.
12. Look in the executive's office—on his or her desk and files.

RECORDS TRANSFER AND STORAGE

Not only is it important to file, find, and charge-out materials efficiently but it is also important to know how long to keep papers, when to destroy papers, and when to transfer papers to inactive files.

Retention Control

Retention control involves a set of activities for deciding how long records should be kept and in what locations they should be stored. As the cost of office space continues to rise, the need for retention control becomes more and more important. Filling valuable office space with unnecessary documents and file cabinets is not feasible.

As a secretary, you probably will not make decisions about how long important papers should be kept. The legal counsel for a company is generally consulted as to the length of time that important documents should be retained. If your company is large, it may have developed a retention schedule for various types of papers. If your company does not have a records retention schedule, you should check with your supervisor before making any decisions about how papers should be sorted, transferred, and destroyed. Retention schedules differ depending on the nature and needs of the business. One useful reference on the retention and legality of records is the *Guide to Record Retention Requirements* published annually by the National Archives and Records Service; it is available from the Superintendent of Documents, U.S. Government Printing Office, Washington, DC 20402. To understand more about retention control, consider the following categories into which documents can be classified.

Vital Records. Records that cannot be replaced and should never be destroyed are called *vital records*. These records are essential to the effective, continued operation of the organization and should not be transferred from the active section of the storage area. Some examples of vital records are corporate charters, major contracts, deeds, and tax returns.

Important Records. Records that are necessary to an orderly continuation of the business and are replaceable only with considerable expenditure of time and money are known as *important records*. Such records may be transferred to inactive storage but are not destroyed. Examples of important records are financial statements, operating and statistical records, and sales data.

Useful Records. *Useful records* are those that are useful for the smooth, effective operation of the organization. Such records are replaceable, but their loss involves delay or inconvenience to the organization. Examples include business letters, interoffice memorandums, reports, and bank records.

Nonessential Records. Records that have no future value to the organization are considered *nonessential*. Once the purpose for which they were created has been fulfilled, they may be destroyed.

Transfer Control

Once the secretary understands which records should be retained, then it is possible to set up a transfer control system to determine where records should be stored. In setting up such a system, the degree of records activity should be considered. There are three basic ways of identifying record activity.

1. Active records: Records that are used three or more times a month and that should be kept in an accessible area
2. Semiactive records: Records that are used once or twice a month and that may be stored in less accessible areas than active records
3. Inactive records: Records that are referred to less than 15 times a year and that should be stored in inexpensive storage outside the office area

Transfer Methods. The next consideration in transferring records is to determine the method which best fits the company's needs. Two of the most common methods of transferring records are the perpetual method and the periodic method.

Perpetual Transfer. With the perpetual method, materials are continuously transferred from the active to the inactive files. The advantage of this method is that all files are kept current since any inactive material is immediately transferred to storage. This method can be used fairly successfully in a lawyer's office for transferring the completed case files of clients to storage. The perpetual transfer method is not practical for most offices, however, since it requires the continuous transfer of files. Semiactive records are transferred immediately to storage. For example, if a case of a lawyer needs to be reopened, the file must be retrieved from storage.

Periodic Transfer. When using the periodic transfer method, records may be transferred periodically by the one-period, two-period, or maximum-minimum method. In the one-period method, all correspondence is moved from the active files to the inactive files at least once a year. This system is easy to control, but frequent trips to the inactive files are usually necessary to refer to materials that are only a few months old.

With the two-period method, an inactive file and an active file are maintained side by side. During certain predetermined periods, materials from the inactive files are transferred to the records storage center or destroyed, and materials from the active files are transferred to the inactive files. Then new files are set up in the active file drawers.

The maximum-minimum method is possibly the most useful method. *Maximum* and *minimum* refer to the age of the records at the time of transfer. For example, active materials (six months old or less, or any age determined as active by a company) are kept in the active files. Older materials (all materials for the year preceding the last six months) are transferred to the inactive files in a storage center. If the transfer date is determined to be June 30, all materials dated in the preceding year are transferred on June 30. Thus, transferred material varies in age at the time of transfer from six months (minimum age) to 18 months (maximum age).

Storage Equipment. Efforts should be made to keep the expense of storage center equipment to a minimum. Usually materials are transferred to the storage center in inexpensive cardboard file boxes, and inexpensive shelving is used to house the boxes.

Illus. 20-19
Inexpensive shelving and cardboard file boxes are usually used to store materials in the records storage center.

Disposal Control

Records that no longer have any use should be destroyed. Destroying records may simply mean dropping them into the wastebasket or File 13 as it is sometimes called. Important records should not be destroyed in this manner, however. Here are several suggestions for destroying important records.

1. Use a shredder which cuts the paper into confettilike strips.
2. Use a baler which compacts the records into bundles for easy handling.

3. Deliver the papers to a recycling plant. These plants will usually pick up unwanted papers. Check the Yellow Pages of your local telephone directory under Recycling Centers for information.
4. Burn the records. Stricter laws governing the environment have made this method of record disposal less popular, however.

PROFESSIONAL POINTERS

Here are several tips to help you in filing more efficiently.

1. Determine the best time of the day or week to update your filing. The time you identify should be a period in which there is little activity. It is extremely frustrating and non-productive to attempt to file when the telephones are ringing and there are numerous interruptions.

2. File often. The frequency of filing will differ in every office depending on the volume of paperwork; however, all filing should be kept up to date.

3. Arrange unfiled materials in a sorter. Then, if your employer asks for a piece of correspondence, you can find it quickly without having to rummage through a stack of papers.

4. Fine sort materials before going to the file drawer. Remember that fine sorting means that materials are in exact alphabetic sequence. Have all materials sorted and ready to be placed in the file folders before going to the file drawer.

5. Leave three to four inches of working space in every file drawer.

6. Always close a file drawer before opening the next drawer. It is not safe to have two drawers open at once; the file cabinet may tip over.

7. When a paper is removed from the file, put something in its place—an out sheet, out guide, or a slip of paper—noting what was taken, when, and by whom.

8. Keep an index of file captions when maintaining a subject file so that duplication will not occur.

9. Evaluate the effectiveness of your files.
   a. Do you have adequate guides in your files? If you spend considerable time thumbing through the files, you may not have enough guides.
   b. Do you have too many materials in one file folder? Most file folders will hold approximately three fourths of an inch of material.

      c. Are your folders dog-eared? If so, replace them.

      d. Are labels typed neatly and consistently? For example, are capital letters used consistently?

      e. If you are using color coding, are you consistent in using the appropriate color?

10. Keep a records retention schedule handy at your desk. If your company does not have such a schedule, work with your employer on appropriate transfer and storage requirements for your office.

11. Dispose of useless papers. Do not file useless papers such as advertisements unless your employer asks that you do so.

12. Do not keep records in more than one place. Before filing materials, determine whether they should be maintained in some other office.

FOR YOUR REVIEW

1. Identify and explain three positions available in records management.

2. List two advantages and two disadvantages of the alphabetic, numeric, subject, and geographic filing methods.

3. Identify the four basic parts of the numeric filing method.

4. Explain the difference between terminal and middle digit filing.

5. List and explain the proper steps in filing.

6. What is the purpose of charge-out procedures?

7. How is a tickler file used in the follow-up process?

8. Give five procedures in looking for lost records.

9. Identify four categories of records.

10. Explain the differences between the perpetual and periodic transfer methods.

CASE PROBLEM

Lucinda Lopez has just been promoted to records manager. She has been reviewing the files during the past week and has discovered numerous problems. Some of them are the following:

1. Files are misplaced.
2. Labels are not consistently typed.
3. Color coding is used but not consistently.
4. Folders and file cabinets are overcrowded.
5. Material may remain in a file clerk's in basket for two weeks before being filed.
6. Fine sorting is not done.

There are five file clerks in the center. Lucinda called a meeting to talk with them about the problems she has noted. She explained the problems and told the file clerks that she expected their help in clearing up the situation. Three file clerks immediately became defensive and irate. The other two said nothing. Since it was evident that Lucinda would have trouble getting the file clerks to cooperate, she lost control and told them that she was the boss and they would do as she said. Since the meeting one of the file clerks has turned in a resignation.

1. What should Lucinda do now?

2. What suggestions can you give Lucinda to prevent this situation from recurring?

PRODUCTION PROJECTS

PP 20-1

(Objective 1)

Choose two members of your class to work with you on this project. Visit one or two offices in your area, and get as much information as you can about records management in these offices. Ask the following questions:

1. Which type of filing method is used—alphabetic, geographic, etc.? Is color coding used?

2. What type of equipment is used?

3. How does the records management system work?

4. What are the strengths and weaknesses of the system?

5. What are the charge-out procedures?

6. What are the transfer procedures?

Prepare a report and type it in final form. Present the report orally to the class, or submit your written report to your instructor.

PP 20-2

(Objective 1)

Which filing method would be most efficient in the following departments? Explain why.

1. Research and design department

2. Personnel department

3. Central files department (one copy of all correspondence for the entire company is filed here)

4. Marketing department (salespeople responsible for a particular geographic area work in this department)

5. Case files in a law office

6. Real estate files where a certain location is important

7. Student records at a college

PP 20-3

(Objective 2)

Your employer places the letter in your Supplies Inventory in the out basket. It is ready to be filed. On a plain sheet of paper, explain the steps that you will take to file the letter under the alphabetic method; submit the paper to your instructor.

PP 20-4

(Objective 3)

On index cards or pieces of paper, type the names given in your Supplies Inventory in indexing order; then arrange the cards alphabetically. On a separate sheet of paper, type the names in the order in which you have them alphabetized. As a heading, type "Answer Sheet for PP 20-4," and list the 30 names under the appropriate indexing units. Submit the answer sheet to your instructor, but keep the cards for use in PP 20-7.

PP 20-5

(Objective 3)

Follow the instructions given in PP 20-4 for this list of names in your Supplies Inventory. Entitle this answer sheet "Answer Sheet for PP 20-5." Keep the cards for use in PP 20-7.

PP 20-6

(Objective 3)

Follow the instructions given in PP 20-4 for this list of names in your Supplies Inventory. Entitle this answer sheet "Answer Sheet for PP 20-6." Keep the cards for use in PP 20-7.

PP 20-7

(Objective 3)

Combine the cards from PP 20-4, PP 20-5, and PP 20-6 in alphabetic order. Prepare an answer sheet for this job, entitle it "Answer Sheet for PP 20-7," and submit it to your instructor. You may destroy the cards since they will not be used again.

PP 20-8

(Objectives 1 and 3)

On index cards or pieces of paper, type the names given in your Supplies Inventory in indexing order for a geographic file by city. Arrange the cards alphabetically. On a separate sheet of paper entitled "Answer Sheet for PP 20-8," list the 20 names under the appropriate indexing units. Submit the answer sheet to your instructor; you may destroy the cards.

PP 20-9

(Objective 4)

In your Supplies Inventory are four requisition forms that are to be used in charging out materials. Fill out the forms with a pen or pencil according to the following situations. You are working in the central files department.

1. Letter requested is from A. D. Ford, 3729 Katrine Road, Fort Worth, Texas; requested by John Anders; date of letter, November 24; letter requested on December 2; letter to be returned on December 10.

2. Letter requested is from DeKalb Jewelers dated September 14 concerning price quotation; requested by Kathrine Malcolm on November 15; letter to be returned November 18.

3. Letter requested is from Del Norte Lock Company dated September 12; requested by Edward Robinson on October 1; letter to be returned on October 9.

4. Letter requested is from 4-by-4 Lumber Company dated August 24 concerning a lumber order; requested by Mary Edwards on September 1; letter to be returned on September 5.

PP 20-10

(Objective 5)

You have been asked to set up a retention, transfer, and disposal system for your company, a manufacturing company. Research three sources of current information on records management. Here are some sources you may use.

Textbooks:
> *Information Resource Management* by Dr. Betty Ricks and Dr. Kay Gow, South-Western Publishing Co., 1984
> *Records Management,* Third Edition, by Mina M. Johnson and Norman F. Kallaus, South-Western Publishing Co., 1982

Periodicals:
> *Management World*
> *Modern Office Technology*
> *The Office*
> *Records Management Quarterly*

Based on information from your research and from this textbook, do the following:

1. Put each of these company records into one of the four categories of records: (1) interoffice memorandums, (2) business letters, (3) tax records, (4) personnel records, (5) company policies and procedures, (6) contracts, (7) financial records, (8) invoices and purchase orders, (9) sales reports, and (10) advertising material from vendors.

2. Determine which transfer method should be used by the company.

3. Identify the storage equipment that should be used for records transfer.

4. Determine the process to be used in destroying records that are no longer of use to the company.

5. Write a short summary of what you learned from your research concerning retention, transfer, and disposal. If you discovered any new methods of records control and/or equipment used, identify these methods and equipment. List your research sources.

Chapter 21

UNDERSTANDING THE TECHNOLOGY OF RECORDS MANAGEMENT

The organization of paper files and other records for storage and retrieval by a systematic method is a complex and time-consuming task. Also, paper files are vulnerable to loss resulting from disaster, inadvertent destruction, theft, misfiling, or mishandling. The maintenance of paper records typically requires large numbers of filing cabinets and ever increasing amounts of floor space. Therefore, records managers have been deeply committed to the development of cost effective alternatives to paper records storage systems for many years.

In this chapter you will have an opportunity to look at some of the alternatives to traditional paper filing systems. The chapter will first cover conventional filing equipment and materials. Then computerized filing, micrographics, and the integration of micrographics and computers (electronic filing) will be discussed. At the end of this chapter, you will be given information about records management trends for the future.

General Objectives

Your general objectives for Chapter 21 are to:

1. *Determine the types of filing supplies and manual filing equipment available*
2. *Become familiar with mechanized and computerized storage and retrieval of information*
3. *Understand the use of microforms*
4. *Determine the features of electronic filing systems*
5. *Understand the benefits of electronic filing systems*
6. *Explain the future trends in records management*

BASIC FILING SUPPLIES AND EQUIPMENT

Conventional filing supplies include such items as file folders, suspension folders, file guides, labels, tabs, and other miscellaneous materials. Basic storage equipment consists of manual files. These manual files are available in several styles, sizes, and shapes including vertical, lateral, horizontal, open shelf, wheel, mobile, and visible card files. An explanation of these types of supplies and equipment is given in the following sections.

Filing Supplies

In order to file efficiently, correct supplies must be used. The major filing supplies are discussed and illustrated here.

File Folders. A file folder is a container for correspondence or other materials; a manila folder is most commonly used. The filing designation is typed on a gummed label which is then affixed to the tab (the portion of the folder that extends above the regular height of the folder). Folders are made with tabs of various widths, called *cuts*, such as straight cut, one-half cut, one-third cut, and one-fifth cut. Illus. 21-1 shows folders with tabs of various widths.

In addition to manila folders, color coded folders may also be used. These folders are available in a variety of colors including green, blue, orange, purple, tan, yellow, brown, grey, pink, red, and white.

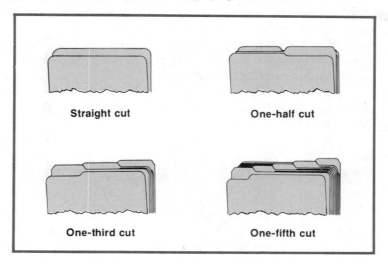

Illus. 21-1
Folder cuts

Suspension Folders. In addition to standard file folders, suspension folders are also available. These folders are sometimes called hanging folders because small metal rods are attached to the folders allowing them to hang on the sides of the file drawer. Illus. 21-2 shows a suspension folder and the plastic tabs and insertable labels that are used with the folders. The tabs are placed in any position (first, second, third, etc.) in the precut slots in the folder. Once the tab is in place, the typed label is inserted.

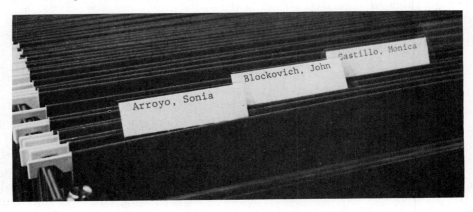

Illus. 21-2
Suspension folders with plastic tabs and insertable labels

File Guides. A file guide is usually made of heavy pressboard and is used to separate the file drawer into various sections. Each guide has a tab on which is printed a name, a number, or a letter representing a section of the file drawer in accordance with the filing system. For example, the letter *B*, the number *200*, or the subject *Applications* may appear on the tab.

Guides with hollow tabs in which labels are inserted are also available. The filing designation is typed on a label and inserted in the tab. Illus. 21-3 shows two types of file guides.

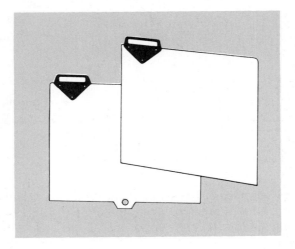

Illus. 21-3
File guides

File Folder Labels. File folder labels may be purchased in a sheet or roll and in various sizes and colors. Different colored labels can speed up the process of filing and finding records and eliminate much misfiling. It is very easy to spot a colored label that has been misfiled since that color stands out from the other colors that surround it.

Colored labels can be used in the following ways in a filing system:

1. To designate a particular subject (For example, green labels may designate budget items, blue labels may designate personnel items, and the like.)
2. To indicate geographic divisions of the country
3. To indicate when a folder should be removed from the files
4. To designate particular sections of the file

Illus. 21-4
File folder labels

Metal Tabs. Metal tabs (tabs that are slipped over the edge of a folder) can be used to indicate different kinds of information, different subjects, and so forth. For example, in a sales manager's office, a blue metal tab on a file folder may indicate that a particular salesperson is ahead of quota, while a red metal tab may indicate that the salesperson has fallen dangerously below quota.

Miscellaneous Supplies. Other supplies that are needed in the filing process include cross-reference sheets, sorters, out guides, out sheets, and out folders which were discussed in Chapter 20. In addition, you may find transparent gummed tape, thumbers (rubber finger guards), colored pencils, and staplers useful in the filing process.

Manual Filing Equipment

Manual filing equipment requires no mechanical or computerized operation but consists merely of a standard file cabinet. You will learn about mechanized and computerized filing equipment later in this chapter. Numerous types of manual filing equipment are available; the major types are described here.

Vertical Files. Vertical files are among the most commonly used manual filing equipment. Papers are placed in the files on the long edge. Vertical files are available in a variety of heights, ranging from cabinets with one drawer to those with six drawers, and widths to accommodate letter size or legal size paper.

Lateral Files. The lateral file is similar to the vertical file except that the drawer rolls out sideways exposing the entire contents of the file drawer at once. Less aisle space is needed for a lateral file than for a vertical file since the depth of the lateral drawer is less than its width. Illus. 21-5 shows a lateral file cabinet.

Illus. 21-5
Lateral file cabinet

Horizontal Files. Documents are stored in a flat position in horizontal files. Horizontal files are most commonly found in engineering or architectural offices where maps and blueprints are filed. A horizontal file is generally much larger in length and width than a vertical file but the height of each drawer is shallow since only a few documents are stored in each drawer.

Open Shelf Files. Open shelf files consist of open shelves arranged horizontally in stationary bookshelf position or in rotary form. Illus. 21-6 shows both types of open shelf files. The advantage of an open shelf file is that records can be easily filed and located. Open files generally do not appear as neat as closed files, however.

Illus. 21-6
Open shelf files in bookshelf and rotary forms

Wheel Files. Wheel files contain cards that are snapped in place over a rod and kept within bounds by the outer rims of the wheel. Wheel files may vary from desktop units approximately eight inches high to large motorized desk-size units. In the case of a large motorized unit, the wheel file would be classified as a mechanized file. Illus. 21-7 shows a small wheel file.

Illus. 21-7
Wheel file

Mobile Files. The purpose of a mobile file is to bring the file unit to the operations area rather than forcing the employee to go to the file. Most mobile files are small single units which have rollers and can be easily pushed like carts.

Visible Card Files. Many types of visible card files are used in business offices. The cards may be arranged in a tray (as shown in Illus. 21-8), in the form of a book, or on a revolving wheel. The cards are arranged so that one card overlaps another with a portion of each card being visible. An entire card can be examined by lifting the cards that overlap it. Visible card files are used for personnel, sales, credit, accounting, purchases, and other departmental records that require quick reference for information and for recording purposes.

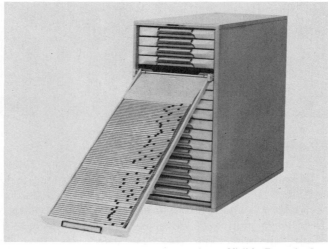

Acme Visible Records, Inc.
Crozet, Virginia

Illus. 21-8
Visible card file

MECHANIZED STORAGE AND RETRIEVAL OF INFORMATION

The manual equipment of which you have just learned is the least expensive and least complex filing equipment available. Mechanized equipment involves the use of machines and is expensive and difficult to set up and operate. Thus, before the records manager or executive determines that a mechanized system should be installed, careful consideration should be given to the needs of the business.

Requirements for Mechanization

Here are some questions that should be asked before mechanized filing equipment is installed.

1. What is the present size of the files?
2. What is the anticipated growth rate of the files?
3. How many employees will be using the system? Where are these employees located?
4. How fast are records needed?
5. What funds are available for purchasing equipment and training personnel?

Obviously business executives are concerned about getting information in a timely and efficient manner. They are also concerned about using personnel and equipment efficiently. Thus, a mechanized storage and retrieval system must be able to process records faster, more accurately, and less expensively than a manual system in order for such a system to be considered cost effective.

Mechanized Equipment

Various types of mechanized equipment are available. Two types are explained here: movable-aisle systems and motorized shelf files.

Movable-Aisle Systems. Movable-aisle systems consist of modular units of regular files mounted on tracks constructed in the floor. Unlike conventional fixed shelf storage, movable storage files are placed directly against each other. Wheels or rails permit the individual units to be moved apart for access. Illus. 21-9 shows a movable file. The movable racks are electrically powered. Some of the features of a movable system are the following:

- *Quick access.* The system allows access into an aisle as soon as sufficient space has opened for entry, which is generally from five to fifteen seconds.
- *General safety.* A few of the safety features available are floor level safety bars that deactivate under pressure to assure safety for operators as well as any forgotten materials left lying on the floor, waist level safety bars, electric eyes, and magnetic limiter switches that prevent aisles from banging against each other.
- *Restricted access.* Some filing systems require that confidential files be stored separately where access is restricted. In some movable-aisle systems a coded, restricted access card can be used to gain entry to confidential files. Thus, confidential files are stored with other files and do not require additional space.

Spacesaver Corporation

Illus. 21-9
Movable-aisle file

Motorized Shelf Files. The storing of a record in a motorized file is manual, but the retrieval of a record is mechanical since the motorized file brings the record to the operator. Here is how a typical motorized shelf file works.

Sperry Univac Office
Equipment Division

Illus. 21-10
Motorized shelf file

1. An index register contains the file numbers of all folders within the system. The operator consults this index register to find the number of the file requested.
2. The operator depresses the file number on the keyboard of the motorized file console.
3. The shelf where the file is stored then rotates to a position in front of the operator.
4. The operator scans the shelf for the appropriate file.

COMPUTERIZED STORAGE AND RETRIEVAL OF INFORMATION

With the increase in records today and the need for fast retrieval, computerized filing systems are being used more and more. It is anticipated that computerized systems, along with electronic filing systems, will be the standard filing systems of the future.

Computer Storage

Information that is filed in a computerized system must be stored on some type of media. The two most common types of storage media used today are magnetic tapes and magnetic disks. Magnetic tape is wound on a reel called a *file reel* or *supply reel* in much the same way that motion picture film is wound on a reel. Generally a reel of magnetic tape is one-half inch wide and 2,400 feet long. A reel of magnetic tape can hold as much data as can be punched into several hundred thousand cards.

The advantages of magnetic tape storage are that the cost of storing records is low and little space is required. However, magnetic tape has a very definite disadvantage as a storage and retrieval mechanism. Retrieval is slower on a tape than on a disk because all records preceding the record needed must be read before access is gained to the particular record. This is called sequential access.

On a magnetic disk records are stored on circular tracks similar to a jukebox arrangement of phonograph records. One advantage of the disk over the tape is that a record can be accessed quicker. A magnetic disk uses random access; that is, the record needed can be obtained without processing all the records preceding it.

Perhaps the most critical disadvantage of the magnetic disk is that it does not usually provide for a backup copy. When data are recorded on a magnetic disk, only one copy is made. In comparison, when data are recorded on a magnetic tape, an extra copy of the tape can be made with relative ease, thus ensuring protection from accidental erasure or destruction. Another disadvantage of magnetic disk storage is that it costs more than magnetic tape storage.

Tape Retrieval Systems

In order to locate material stored on magnetic tape, a search must be made according to a code by which the record has been filed (for example, employee number, part number, social security number, and the like). Tape retrieval involves the following steps:

1. A request is made for a certain record.
2. The appropriate tape is obtained from the tape library and mounted on the tape drive unit.
3. The computer's internally stored program directs the computer to scan the contents of the tape to locate the record. Since the tape is sequential in nature, all records preceding the one needed must be read. For example, assume that you need to read the file of employee No. 1050. If the tape begins with employee No. 1, then the previous 1,049 records must be read before the needed record, No. 1050, is located. When the record is located, the information can be printed out on the computer's printer.

Disk Retrieval Systems

A disk retrieval system permits a metal arm that moves in and out between the disks to locate any track on the rotating disk and read its contents. Each track on the disk has an address that serves as the key for locating a record. This method of retrieval (random access) provides for much quicker access to the records. Once the record is found, it is sent electronically to a printer or to the display screen of a terminal. If it is sent to a display screen of a terminal, a printed copy may or may not be desired. If no printed copy is needed, the individual requesting the information merely reads it from the terminal screen. If a printed copy is desired, then a printer is used to produce the copy.

Computerized Filing Applications

Computerized filing is frequently used in large businesses. To help you understand its use, here are some examples.

1. Banks use computerized filing. One application is through automated teller machines which allow customers to obtain and deposit cash, to transfer money from a checking account to a savings account, and to borrow money without writing a check or going to a bank.

2. Insurance companies use computerized filing to keep track of and update customers' insurance policies. When a new policy is written, the customer's name, address, account number, and any other pertinent information are inputted into the computer files. If the customer adds another policy, that policy is also inputted into the files. Any policy transactions are also recorded; thus, the files constantly reflect a current picture of the customer's insurance record.

3. Airlines use computerized filing systems for handling reservations. Information concerning flight numbers and dates is entered in the files. A record of how many people are on the flight and the space available is maintained on file at all times. If a customer cancels a flight, this information is also fed into the files immediately.

AN INTRODUCTION TO MICROGRAPHICS

With the advent of the computer, it is possible for companies to produce more and more records in less time than has been possible in the past. The growth of these records requires an increase in storage capacity. Thus, records managers have turned to micrographics for reducing paper records to a very small size (*microforms*) and for saving storage space. *Micrographics* refers to the technology by which information can be reduced to a microform, stored conveniently, and then easily retrieved for reference and use.

Types of Microforms

Although microfilm has been known as the most common type of microform, several other types are used extensively today. The main types of microforms, which include microfilm, mocrofiche, ultrafiche, and aperture cards, are described in the following sections.

Microfilm. Microfilm is a roll containing a series of frames or images much like a movie film. Paper records are photographed on film 16, 35, 70, or 105 millimeters (mm) in width. The most widely used widths are 16mm and 35mm. The procedure is to reduce the size of the record to make it fit the film and then magnify it later to read the contents of the film projected on a screen.

Microfilm may be stored on reels or in cartridges, cassettes, or jackets. Microfilm on reels was one of the first microforms. Reels are desirable for storing large volumes of records that do not require frequent changes. For correspondence, checks, and similar information, 16mm reels are often used. For graphics and large documents such as engineering drawings, X rays, newspapers, and maps, 35mm reels are used.

Unlike microfilm on reels which require threading, cartridges are self-threading. Cartridges protect the images on the film from fingerprints and other damage. Thus, microfilm stored in cartridges is convenient and easy to use. Microfilm stored in cassettes is also convenient. Each cassette contains two small film reels, a feed reel and a take-up reel. The cassette operates just like a cassette tape recording.

Still another method of storing microfilm is by cutting it into strips and placing the film in a plastic carrier, or jacket. A 6-by-4-inch jacket will usually contain 5 strips with 12 images in each, or 60 images in all. The jacket storage method allows portions of a file to be updated easily, since a strip of film can be removed and replaced with a new strip. Illus. 21-11 shows microfilm stored on a reel, in a cartridge, in a cassette, and in a jacket.

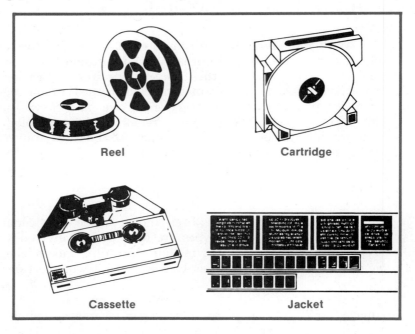

Reel   **Cartridge**

Cassette   **Jacket**

Illus. 21-11
Microfilm packages

Microfiche and Ultrafiche. Microfiche is a sheet of film containing a series of images arranged in rows and columns (grid pattern) on a card. Although it is available in several sizes, the 6-by-4-inch microfiche is considered the standard size sheet.

Ultrafiche is a variation of microfiche. The standard size microfiche contains 98 frames (images); however, one ultrafiche can store thousands of images. Illus. 21-12 shows a microfiche and an ultrafiche.

Courtesy of
Minolta Corporation

Illus. 21-12
Microfiche (top) and ultrafiche (bottom)

Aperture Cards. An aperture card is a standard punched card with a window (aperture) cut in it over which a portion of film is mounted. Aperture cards may contain a single image; however, up to four letter size pages can be included within the frame at a reduction ratio of 16 to 1, and up to 400 pages can be contained in the aperture at a reduction ratio of 160 to 1. A reduction ratio of 16 to 1 simply means that the image on the film is 1/16th the size of the original record, whereas a reduction ratio of 160 to 1 means that the image on the film is 1/160th the size of the original record. This reduction ratio may also be stated as 16X and 160X. Obviously many other reduction ratios are available, ranging from 5X to more than 2400X. These

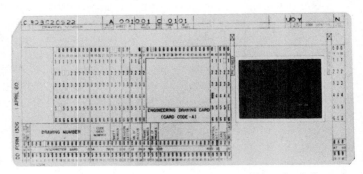

Association for Information
and Image Management

Illus. 21-13
Aperture card

reduction ratios apply not only to aperture cards but also to all other types of microforms. Information is punched into the top of the aperture card and serves as an index for retrieving the card.

Elements of the Micrographics System

In order to produce and use microforms, a micrographics system which encompasses these phases is essential: converting the records to film, processing and duplicating the film, and displaying and reproducing the film. The phases of this system are explained here.

Converting to Film. Several types of cameras can be used in the filming process including a planetary camera, a rotary camera, and a step and repeat camera. When a planetary camera is used, the material to be converted to film is laid on a board with the camera overhead looking down on the board. A rotary camera continuously photographs documents that are fed through a narrow slit while both the film and document are in motion. A rotary camera may photograph either the front of a document only or the front and back of a document at the same time. A planetary camera produces a higher quality image than a rotary camera.

A step and repeat camera is used to film microfiche only. It photographs images onto a 4-inch wide film which is then cut to 6-inch lengths to provide a standard size microfiche of 6 by 4 inches. This film must be developed on a special piece of equipment called a *processor*.

Although some companies photograph records in-house, many others hire service bureaus to assist in the conversion of large quantities of documents. The service bureaus can prove especially useful in the conversion of numerous inactive records.

Processing. The next step in the production of microforms is processing the film. The same processing techniques are used as in developing standard photographs. Although the processing of film is most likely to be handled by a service bureau, some companies prefer to do in-house film processing. Companies considering in-house film processing should realize that more than just purchasing a machine is involved. Special plumbing may be required, and compliance with local waste disposal ordinances is necessary. There is also the continuing need to replenish and refresh processing chemicals and to keep a close check on the quality of the processed images.

Duplicating. Copies of the microforms may be required. For example, a company may have several branches and need the same records at each location. Thus, the microforms must be duplicated. Duplication of microforms usually involves a special film which is made for copying purposes only. Duplication takes place with the original microform in direct physical contact with the copy film. Two types of copy film are *diazo* (developed by ammonia gas) and *vesicular* film (developed by heat). Duplicators are available for every type of microform. For example, there are reel-to-reel duplicators, fiche-to-fiche duplicators, aperture card-to-reel duplicators, and reel-to-aperture card duplicators. These duplicators vary in duplicating volume and in degree of automation, depending on whether they are designed for production or demand duplicating purposes. A demand duplicator is relatively compact and is designed for use in the office environment.

Displaying and Reproducing. To read a microform, you must place it in a projector called a *reader* or *viewer*. A reader displays the microform in an enlarged form on a screen so that it can be read easily. The typical reader is a desktop unit designed to accept a specific microform such as microfiche or microfilm. There are multimedia readers, however, designed to accept two or more different types of microforms. Readers are also available in a variety of magnifications determined by the reduction ratio of the microform and the size of the viewing screen. Many readers have interchanging lenses to satisfy various user requirements.

Portable readers are also available which are lighter in weight and less expensive than desktop readers. Lap readers are often used in cars, at outside job locations, or by an executive on the road. Since these readers are so inexpensive (some costing less than $100), they may be used at home as a supplement to existing office equipment. A desktop reader and a lap reader are shown in Illus. 21-14.

Bell & Howell
Business Equipment Group

Micro Design

Illus. 21-14
Desktop and lap readers

Often a person viewing a microform needs a paper copy of the record. This copy may be obtained through the use of a *reader-printer*. The microform is inserted in the reader-printer and each image is portrayed on the viewing screen. If the viewer desires a hard copy, a button is pushed on the machine and a copy is produced in seconds. The copies range in size from 8 1/2 by 11 inches to as large as 20 by 30 inches, depending on the capabilities of the printer used. Illus. 21-15 shows a reader-printer.

Bell & Howell
Business Equipment Group

Illus. 21-15
Paper copy of a microform record can be
obtained from a reader-printer.

Need for Microforms

Today more and more records are being stored on microforms. Here are the basic reasons for this increase in the use of microforms.

1. Microforms need only a fraction of the storage space occupied by paper records. The original material can be stored or destroyed.
2. Vital records can be protected against loss through disaster, theft, or negligence.
3. Microforms provide an efficient method of storage and retrieval of often used records. Valuable hours once devoted to sorting and filing paper records can be channeled into more productive work.

4. For security purposes, duplicate records can be prepared at nominal cost and kept at other locations for use.

The Law and Microforms

The Uniform Photographic Copies of Business Records Act allows microforms of certain business documents to be admitted as evidence in courts of law. However, records such as accounting journals, government securities, licenses, and passports may not be produced on microforms. For those records that may be microfilmed, the records must be legible and accurately photographed in their entirety. A certificate of authenticity stating that the microform is a true copy of the original document should be on file.

The Use of Microforms

When determining whether to store information on microforms, consider the following points:

1. The length of time the record must be maintained
   a. If records are to be retained for seven years or less, it may be less expensive to keep them in paper form.
   b. If records are to be kept from seven to fifteen years, consideration should be given to placing them on microforms.
   c. Generally permanent records should be converted to microforms.
2. The cost of microforms
   a. Equipment such as cameras to photograph original records and readers to enlarge the records are needed.
   b. Supplies such as film, cards, cassettes, and the like, must be purchased.
   c. Clerical costs for preparing records to be microfilmed and managerial costs for inspecting records and supervising workers are necessary.
3. The legality of microforms
   a. Which records can be legally filmed and which records cannot be filmed must be determined.
   b. The filming of records must occur in the normal operation of a company.

ELECTRONIC FILING SYSTEMS

Electronic filing is an integration of micrographics and computer technology. This combination of micrographics with the computer has made the storage and retrieval of microforms a speedy, inexpensive, and efficient operation.

Computer Output Microfilm (COM)

One of the big problems of processing data by computer is the enormous amount of paper printouts that are created. Such paper must be stored, and storage is expensive. One result of using the computer in conjunction with micrographics is computer output microfilm (COM). With COM, no paper documents are produced; instead, documents are produced on microforms which may be microfiche or microfilm.

Here is how the COM process works. Document information is fed into the computer and stored on a magnetic tape. Then the stored information is translated into readable form and shown on a terminal display screen or CRT (cathode-ray tube). A microfilm camera photographs the displayed information and reduces it to microform size. A processor develops the film. If desired, a duplicator may be used for making additional copies of the film.

Computer Input Microfilm (CIM)

Computer input microfilm is literally COM in reverse. Plain language data on microfilm are converted into computer readable (digital) data for use in a computer. A CIM device functions simply as a converter of information into a form that the computer can read. With CIM, it becomes possible to use microfilm rather than magnetic tape as the long-term retention medium for digital data. Such a storage method is cost effective since the same number of characters that may cost several dollars to store on magnetic tape can be stored on microfilm for a one-time cost of a few cents.

Computer Aided Retrieval (CAR)

Computer aided retrieval systems are designed to solve two common problems encountered in records systems—the high expense and the difficulty of finding documents filed manually. Drawing on a combination of micrographics and computer technology, CAR can result in more effective and economical approaches to document storage and retrieval. With CAR, access to randomly filed documents on microforms are facilitated by the use of the computer.

Here is how CAR works. (This example will discuss the use of microfilm only.) Documents are indexed by the entry of such data as the date, author, and subject into a computer. As data are transmitted to the computer, software establishes and/or updates a series of indexes maintained on-line with a disk drive. *On-line* is a term indicating that a unit of equipment is connected directly to the computer for the storage of document information. In retrieving documents, the user may request all documents written on a particular date, by a particular person, and dealing with a particular subject. The computer then gives the user a report of the number of items requested. The user has the option to narrow, broaden, or otherwise alter the search. The final outcome is the identification of one or more microfilm addresses (reel and frame numbers) containing the desired documents. The user selects the reel (or cartridge or cassette) indicated, mounts it on a reader or reader-printer, and advances the film to the indicated frame position. Or the reader-printer may operate on-line with the computer; in other words, once the appropriate reel (or cartridge or cassette) is mounted, the frame selection is automatic.

Benefits of Electronic Filing Systems

Electronic filing systems allow records to be stored in an effective and efficient manner. Here are some of the benefits of electronic filing.

1. Space savings. By using microforms for document storage, the space required by a paper filing system can be reduced up to 98 percent. This is an important consideration with the continually escalating cost of floor space.
2. Cost savings as compared with a manual system. In a paper based system, it has been estimated that between 125 and 175 documents can be filed manually in an hour. The time typically spent in filing 2,000 documents is more than 11 hours. Whereas, with electronic filing systems, up to 2,000 documents can be filmed and the appropriate index information inputted on a computer in about three hours. This is less than a third of the time generally required to file the same number of documents in a paper based system. Retrieval time is also greatly reduced with electronic filing as compared with a manual system. Still another cost savings results from the elimination of file cabinets and filing supplies.
3. Cost savings as compared with computer storage. Entering information in a computerized filing system can be slow due to the keyboarding time involved. And signatures on documents and graphics usually cannot be captured for storage in the computer. It can cost as much as $1 to store a document on a magnetic disk for a year. In comparison, a document can be stored on a microform for less than a tenth of a cent. Obviously these costs are subject to change, but the percentage of difference between the two will remain relatively constant.
4. Increased productivity. By using electronic filing systems, the laborious and time-consuming tasks involved in manual sorting, filing, retrieving, refiling, updating, and destroying are eliminated. Employees are available to take on productive assignments.
5. Elimination of lost or misfiled papers. It is estimated that typically between 4 and 8 percent of all paper documents in a manual system

are lost. And it costs approximately $60 to recover or reconstruct (if possible) a lost document. With electronic filing systems, problems of lost and misfiled documents are virtually eliminated.

6. A secure and easily duplicated storage medium. Microforms are difficult for an unauthorized person to access. Microforms may also be reproduced easily and inexpensively so that duplicates of important records can be stored off company premises for protection in case of fire or other catastrophe.

TRENDS IN RECORDS MANAGEMENT

As you have learned in this chapter, there have been numerous changes in the records management field mainly due to technological advancements. Here are some trends that you may expect in the future.

1. More versatile equipment. Filing equipment will become increasingly versatile to help companies solve their critical space problems; for example, narrow tiers of filing equipment that stand alone or fit on tracks to maximize the use of wall space, improved use of movable filing equipment, equipment that can hold a variety of media, and extensive use of electronic direct access filing systems that deliver files automatically. Such equipment exists today in limited form, but we can expect to see refinements to the equipment and wider use in offices.

2. Increased productivity. An important consideration in the selection of filing equipment will be the productivity benefits. New products and systems will need to provide real cost savings as well as an increase in the productivity of workers.

3. An increase in the use of electronic systems. One indication of this trend is the development of prepackaged software programs, available through micrographics equipment suppliers, that make micrographics equipment compatible with a variety of computer hardware. It is projected that additional software will be developed. Such developments will make micrographics and computer technology more compatible than they are today and provide users with additional information storage and retrieval flexibility.

4. The use of optical disks. The optical disk is intended as a more efficient substitute for magnetic media in storing and retrieving digital data. Optical disks are used to record and play back individual frames of data. Basically information is captured through physical impressions on a disk (similar to a phonograph record) which can be read and decoded as video (television signals). The storage capacity of optical disks has increased to the point of 54,000 frames per disk. One of the initial applications of this technology is expected to be in the banking industry where the disks will be used to store digitized images of processed checks. A potential advantage of optical disks over other

media for information storage and retrieval is speed of access. It is anticipated that a document can be located and displayed within a fraction of a second.

5. Growth in the use of optical character recognition (OCR) and optical mark recognition (OMR). OCR provides the ability to read document pages character by character automatically and rapidly, converting the characters it reads into electrical signals that computers can store, manipulate, transmit, and reproduce. Today some OCR systems can read a wide range of type styles and even handwritten characters, but these systems are expensive. Projections indicate that they will become less expensive. In addition to OCR, OMR is used today as the product identifying bar codes on packaged goods. With the aid of a relatively simple scanning device, OMR facilitates computer based price reporting and inventory control. In micrographics, bar codes printed on microforms can aid in the sorting, retrieval, duplication, and distribution of records. It is expected that all microforms will ultimately contain identifying bar codes.

PROFESSIONAL POINTERS

Here are several suggestions to help you manage records more efficiently.

1. Determine any problems that your organization has in managing records properly. Some common problems include the following:
   a. Temporary or permanent loss of important records
   b. Limited space to store records
   c. Poor organization of files
   d. Little control over files
   e. Poor work methods of filing personnel
2. Prepare a records management manual. This manual should describe the job responsibilities of records personnel and the equipment and systems used for controlling records.

3. Maintain effective operating procedures. Keep track of who does what and when.

4. Set standards for job performance.
   a. Determine the value of the work performed.
   b. Evaluate the need for improving office records management systems.
   c. Determine the practicality of installing new equipment.

5. Measure efficiency in finding materials.
   a. Determine the number of misfiles.
   b. Determine the number of lost items.
   c. Determine the time required to locate items.

6. Set up efficient files; decide who has access to the files.

7. Train records personnel in good filing and locating techniques.

8. Maintain close contact with representatives of forms and equipment suppliers who can provide advice on handling paperwork efficiently.

9. File only the records that should be filed. One study of filed correspondence showed that over 30 percent of the incoming correspondence was so routine that it could have been thrown away after it was answered.

10. Set up files where they are convenient for all users. Be certain that filing areas are well lit and attractive.

11. Use equipment that saves space; for example, using five-drawer cabinets instead of four-drawer cabinets results in a 25 percent increase in filing space and also saves floor space.

FOR YOUR REVIEW

1. How may colored file folder labels be used in a filing system?

2. What are the major types of manual filing equipment available for office use?

3. What are movable-aisle systems?

4. Explain how material in a motorized shelf file is accessed.

5. What is computerized filing? In what types of businesses is it used?

6. Define the term *micrographics*.

7. List and explain three types of microforms.

8. What are the elements of a micrographics system?

9. What factors should be considered before storing records on microfilm?

10. Define and explain COM, CIM, and CAR.

CASE PROBLEM

Janis, an administrative assistant to the records manager, Mr. Isaac Robard, has been asked to accompany him on a business trip to examine electronic filing systems. Mr. Robard is considering installing a system and wants to examine equipment and techniques. Janis works closely with him, and he will need her assistance in examining the new systems. Janis has never before accompanied him on a trip. They will be gone three days.

Much to Janis's astonishment, she has discovered that word is going around the office that she and Mr. Robard will be engaged in more than just business during the trip. It is a vicious rumor. Janis is happily married and so is Mr. Robard; their business relationship is strictly professional. Janis has considered three courses of action: (1) ignoring the rumor, (2) talking with the parties involved in spreading the rumor, or (3) refusing to go on the trip.

Which course of action would you suggest that Janis take?

PRODUCTION PROJECTS

PP 21-1
(Objective 1)

Complete one of the following activities:

a. With a group of three or four classmates, select one local company to visit and examine the filing system. Pay particular attention to the types of filing supplies and equipment that are used. Present an oral report of your findings to the class.

b. Write a local filing supplies and equipment company for information on the filing products carried by the company. Present your findings to the class.

PP 21-2
(Objective 2)

As a new records manager of a manufacturing firm, you notice that time is wasted by the filing personnel in searching for and storing information in the manual filing system that is used. You believe that a mechanized or computerized filing system would be more appropriate for the company.

1. What factors should you consider before implementing a mechanized or computerized filing system?

2. After researching the types of mechanized and computerized filing systems (in current periodicals and records management publications), determine the type of system you would propose and the reasons for your suggestion.

Write a short report responding to the situation given above. List your references in your report.

PP 21-3
(Objective 3)

Visit your school or public library. Discover which types of information are stored on microforms. Determine also the types of microforms used. Use a reader-printer to make a copy of a record stored on each type of microform. For example, if the library uses microfilm and microfiche, use the reader-printer to obtain copies of a record on microfilm and microfiche. In a short written report, identify the types of microforms used and the reader-printer equipment available.

PP 21-4
(Objectives 1 and 3)

In your Supplies Inventory is a case problem with a list of questions at the end for your response. Work with one of your classmates in determining the solutions for this case. You may wish to research recent office related periodicals before attempting to answer the questions. Present your solutions in a short report to your class.

PP 21-5
(Objectives 4, 5, and 6)

Using recent issues of such periodicals as *Modern Office Technology, The Office,* and *Information Management,* select six articles covering the following topics:

1. Computerized filing

2. Electronic filing

3. Records management trends

Read and summarize these articles in a report, giving the reference sources for the articles. In your report, explain the benefits of both computerized and electronic filing systems.

PP 21-6
(Objectives 3, 4, and 5)

In your Supplies Inventory is a case problem. Read the case and answer the questions at the end of the case. Research your answers in the most recent sources available. Write a short report, citing the sources used.

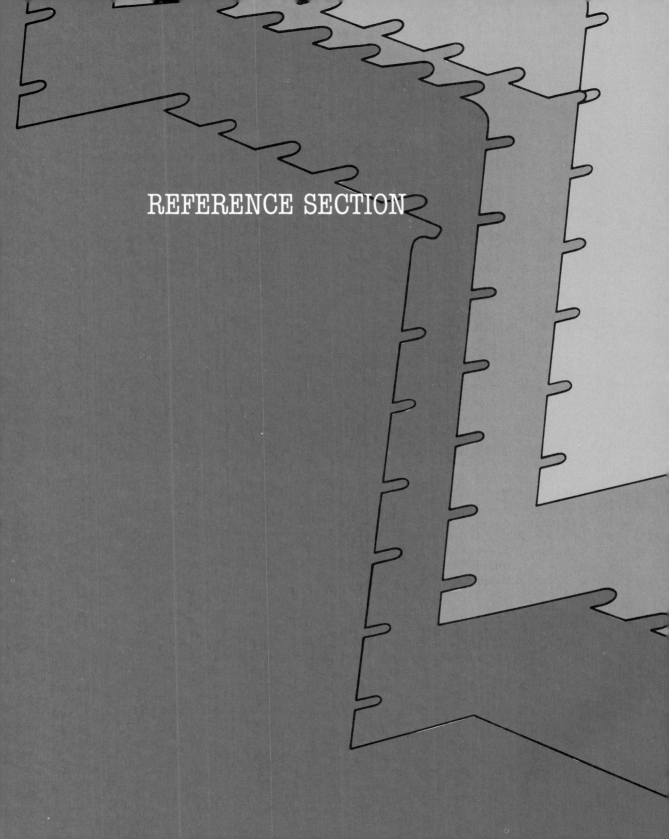

REFERENCE SECTION

REFERENCE SECTION

This section is designed to help you review English fundamentals. It provides a handy reference to grammar and punctuation rules that will help you carry out your secretarial responsibilities with confidence. The nine parts of the Reference Section are as follows:

Abbreviations 540

Capitalization 542

Numbers 545

Often Misused Words and Phrases 548

Plurals and Possessives 551

Proofreaders' Marks 553

Punctuation 554

Spelling 560

Word Division 561

ABBREVIATIONS

1. Academic degrees are generally abbreviated; no space follows the periods in the abbreviation.

Ph.D.	Doctor of Philosophy
B.S.	Bachelor of Science

2. Many companies and professional organizations are known by abbreviated names. These abbreviated names are typed in capital letters with no periods and no spaces between the letters.

IBM	International Business Machines
YMCA	Young Men's Christian Association

3. Certain foreign expressions are abbreviated.

e.g.	*exempli gratia* (for example)
etc.	*et cetera* (and so forth)
i.e.	*id est* (that is)

4. Names of countries should be abbreviated only in tabulations or enumerations and should be written in capital letters; periods may or may not be used in these abbreviations.

U.S.A.	or	USA
U.S.S.R.	or	USSR

5. Abbreviations for government agencies are usually written in capital letters with no periods and no spaces between the letters.

FTC	Federal Trade Commission
CIA	Central Intelligence Agency

6. The personal titles *Mr., Mrs., Ms., Messrs.*, and *Dr.* are abbreviated when written before a name.

Mrs. Ellen Herrera	Messrs. Fleming and Brown
Dr. Joseph Andrano	Ms. Johnson

7. Other personal titles such as *Rev., Hon., Prof., Gen., Col., Capt.*, and *Lieut.* are abbreviated when they precede a surname and a given name. When only the surname is used, these titles should be spelled out.

Prof. Mark Huddleston
Professor Huddleston

8. The titles *Reverend* and *Honorable* are spelled out if preceded by *the*.

the Honorable Marjorie Popham

9. The abbreviations *B.C., A.D., a.m., p.m., No.*, and *$* may be used with numerals.

8:15 a.m.
No. 51345

10. The abbreviations *Bro., Bros., Co., Corp., Inc., Ltd.*, and *&* may be used as part of a company name. It is recommended that the official spelling of the company name be determined and that usage followed.

11. Use only one period if an abbreviation containing a period falls at the end of a sentence. In sentences ending with a question mark or an exclamation mark, place the punctuation mark directly after the period.

The play began at 8:15 p.m.
Does the class start at 9:30 a.m.?

12. Avoid abbreviating the following categories of words unless these words appear in tabulations or enumerations:

a. Names of territories and possessions of the United States, countries, states, and cities

b. Names of months

c. Days of the week

d. Given names, such as *Wm.* for *William*

e. Words such as *avenue, boulevard, court, street, drive, road, building*

f. Parts of geographic names such as *Mt.* (Mountain) and *Ft.* (Fort)

g. Parts of company names, such as *Bro., Bros., Co.,* and *Corp.,* unless they are abbreviated in the official company name

h. Compass directions when they are part of an address (Use *North, South, East, West. NW, NE, SE,* and *SW* may be abbreviated after a street name, however.)

i. The word *number* unless it is followed by a numeral

CAPITALIZATION

1. The first word of a sentence is always capitalized.

   This project is important.

2. Capitalize the titles of specific courses.

   He took Psychology 131 last semester.

Do not capitalize general references to academic subject areas.

   She wants to take a course in government.

3. Capitalize titles that precede a person's name and abbreviations after a name.

   General Rodgers
   Mark Jones, Jr.

Do not capitalize titles when they follow a personal name or are used in place of a personal name. Exceptions are made when high governmental titles such as President, Attorney General, Chief Justice, and so forth, are used in formal acknowledgments and lists.

   Robert A. Fulton, president of Dillon Industries, will speak tonight.
   The treasurer reported the error.
   Ladies and gentlemen, the President of the United States.

4. Specific trade names of products should be capitalized.

> He bought an Apple computer.

5. Capitalize the first word in each line of a poem.

> The doors of the morning must open.
> The keys of the night are not thrown away.
>
> I who have loved morning know its doors.
> I who have loved night know its keys.
>
> Carl Sandburg

6. Capitalize the first word of a direct quotation.

> Michael replied, "The sky is the limit."

7. Compass directions are capitalized when they refer to specific regions or when the direction is part of a specific name. Directions are not capitalized when they indicate a general location or direction.

> Eastern Airlines
> I grew up in the East.
> He lives on the west side of town.

8. The first word and all words except articles, prepositions, and conjunctions in the titles of books, articles, poems, and plays are capitalized.

> *Edge of the Pond*
> *Effective Communication in Business*

9. All words referring to the deity, the Bible, the books of the Bible, and other sacred books should be capitalized.

> the Koran
> our Lord and Savior

10. Capitalize names of organizations, political parties, and religious bodies

> Girl Scouts
> the Presbyterian Church

11. Capitalize names of months, days of the week, holidays, holy days, and periods of history.

> Monday   January
> Christmas   the Middle Ages

12. Capitalize names of geographic sections and places: continents, countries, states, cities, rivers, mountains, lakes, and islands.

> Lake Michigan   Rocky Mountains
> New York   Africa

13. Capitalize names of divisions of a college or university.

> Business Division
> School of Medicine

14. Names of specific historical events, specific laws, treaties, and departments of government are capitalized.

> Viet Nam War
> Department of Defense

15. Capitalize names of streets, avenues, buildings, churches, hotels, parks, and theaters.

> One Main Place
> The Seasons Hotel

16. Capitalize only the parts of a hyphenated word that you would capitalize if the word were not hyphenated.

> mid-July
> President-elect Blackshear

17. Nouns followed by numbers or letters, with the exception of *line, note, page, paragraph, size,* and *verse,* are capitalized.

> Chapter 12
> page 2

18. Names of constellations, planets, and stars should be capitalized.

> Venus
> the North Star

19. Titles of relatives are capitalized when they precede a name or when the title is used as a name. Family titles are not capitalized when they are preceded by possessive pronouns and when they describe a family relationship.

> I telephoned Uncle Ed and Aunt Betty last night.
> Yesterday Mom called me about the tickets.
> My cousin is in town.

20. Every word in the salutation of a letter is capitalized except when *dear* is not the first word. Only the first word in the complimentary close of a letter is capitalized.

> Dear Miss Edwards   Sincerely yours
> My dear Mr. Smith

21. Avoid capitalizing the following:

> a. Names of the seasons of the year unless the season is personified
>
> My favorite season is spring; Spring comes in all her glory.

b. Prefixes to proper names

non-European country

c. Words that were once proper nouns but which through common usage have become common nouns

turkish towel
venetian blinds

NUMBERS

1. The general rule is to spell out numbers one through ten and use figures for numbers over ten. If a sentence contains a series of numbers any of which is over ten, use all figures.

2. Round numbers are spelled out when they can be expressed in one or two words. If the numbers contained in a sentence or paragraph are in different categories, use consistency in treating them in context.

Approximately thirty people attended the party.

3. Always spell out a number that begins a sentence. If the number is large, rearrange the sentence so that the number is not the first word of the sentence.

Five hundred books were ordered.
We had a good year in 1981. *Not:* Nineteen hundred and eighty-one was a good year.

4. Form the plural of figures by adding *s*.

The 1980s are technological years.

5. Hyphenate spelled out numbers from 21 to 99 and any number that is part of a compound adjective.

thirty-four hundred
a two-hundred-mile trip

6. Spell out approximate ages; use figures for exact ages.

She is almost eighteen.
He is 21 today.

7. Use cardinal numbers (1, 2, 3, 4, etc.) to express dates appearing in normal month-day-year order.

June 12, 1983

If the month follows the day or is not stated, use ordinal numbers (1st, 2d, 3d, 4th, etc.).

It happened on the 15th of April.

8. In the United States military and in certain foreign nations, dates are stated in day-month-year sequence. In this format, the day is written in cardinal numbers.

> 28 October 1982

9. In formal documents, dates should be spelled out.

> May tenth
> nineteen hundred and eighty-two

10. Decades and centuries should be spelled out in lowercase letters.

> the twenty-first century

11. House or building numbers are usually written in figures. However, when *One* is used alone, it is spelled out.

> One Patricia Avenue
> 115 Huntington Avenue

12. Spell out numbered street names from one to ten. Otherwise use figures. To avoid confusion, use a hyphen preceded and followed by a space when figures are used for both the house number and the street name. When using ordinals in street names, *2d* and *3d* are preferred to *2nd* and *3rd*.

> 122 Sixth Avenue
> 3456 - 22d Street

13. In legal documents (wills, agreements, etc.) and negotiable instruments (checks, notes, bonds, etc.), numbers are stated in words and figures for clarity and certainty. Legal documents use capitalized words to express sums of money.

> sixteen (16) weeks
> I agree to pay the sum of One Hundred Twenty-Eight Dollars ($128).

14. Specific amounts of money are generally expressed in figures.

> $10 $5.27

15. Indefinite amounts of money should be written in words.

> several hundred dollars

16. Round number amounts of $1 million and more may be written as:

> $5 million $10 billion

17. When writing money amounts in figures, do not use zeros after even amounts.

> $10 $20

Exception: Whole dollar amounts take zeros after the decimal point when they appear in the same context with fractional amounts.

> The book was $15.50, but the store offered a discount of $1.00.

18. Amounts of money less than a dollar are typed in figures with the word *cents* spelled out.

> The small bottle of lotion cost 99 cents.

In formal writing, or in stating an isolated amount in cents, spell out the amount and the word *cents.*

> twenty-five cents

If an amount is less than a dollar but is part of a series in which some amounts are a dollar or more, use *$.00* as the form.

> The prices of the items you want are $1.25, $.85, and $3.50 respectively.

19. In general usage, times of day are written in figures with *a.m.* or *p.m.*

> 12:10 a.m.   3:30 p.m.   8 p.m.

Note: The abbreviations *a.m.* and *p.m.* are typed in small letters without spaces.

20. In formal usage, approximate and on-the-half-hour times are spelled out.

> half past three o'clock   eight o'clock
> half after three o'clock

21. Use *o'clock* with spelled out numbers and *a.m.* or *p.m.* with figures.

> eight o'clock in the morning   8:10 p.m.

22. The times *noon* and *midnight* may be expressed in words alone except when these times are given with other times expressed in figures.

> Busses run on this route from 5 a.m. to 12 midnight.

23. When expressing time without *a.m., p.m.,* or *o'clock,* either spell out the time or use all figures.

> half past eight *or* eight-thirty *or* 8:30

24. In general usage, express percentages in figures; spell out *percent.*

> 10 percent

In formal writing, spell out the amount and *percent.*

> Ninety-eight percent

25. Ratios and proportions are written in figures.

    3 to 1   4:1

26. An isolated simple fraction should be spelled out unless it is part of a mixed number.

    one-half
    3 1/3

27. Use figures with symbols and abbreviations.

    #14   10% $34   18 in.

OFTEN MISUSED WORDS AND PHRASES

1. *A* or *an* before the letter *h*

A is used before all consonant sounds, including *h* when sounded. *An* is used before all vowel sounds, except long *u*.

    a historic event, an honor, a hotel

2. A while, awhile

A while is a noun meaning a short time.

    We plan to go home in a while.

Awhile is an adverb meaning a short time.

    She wrote the poem awhile ago.

3. About, at

Use either *about* or *at*—not both.

    He will leave about noon.
    He will leave at noon.

4. Accept, except

Accept means to receive; it is always a verb.

    I accept the gift.

Except as a preposition means with the exception of.

    Everyone left except him.

Except as a verb means to exclude.

    When the sentence was excepted, the committee approved the report.

5. Addition, edition

Addition is the process of adding.

> They plan to add an addition to the building.

Edition is a particular version of printed material.

> This is the fourth edition of the book.

6. Advice, advise

Advice is a noun meaning a recommendation.

> She did not follow my advice.

Advise is a verb meaning to counsel.

> The counselor will advise you.

7. All, all of

Use *all; of* is redundant. If a pronoun follows *all*, reword the sentence.

> Check all the items.
> They are all going.

8. All right

All right is the only correct usage. *Alright* is incorrect.

9. Among, between

Among is used when referring to three or more persons or things.

> The inheritance was divided among the four relatives.

Between is used when referring to two persons or things.

> The choice is between you and me.

10. Bad, badly

Bad is an adjective and should be used after verbs of sense; *badly* is an adverb.

> He feels bad about losing. She looks bad.
> The football team played badly tonight.

11. Biannual, biennial

Biannual means occurring twice a year.

> The biannual meeting will be held next month.

Biennial means occurring once every two years.

> The biennial evaluation will be done in May.

12. Capital, capitol

Capital is used unless you are referring to the building that houses a government.

> Austin is the capital of Texas.
> We toured the United States Capitol in Washington.

13. Cite, sight, site

Cite means to quote; *sight* means vision; *site* means location.

> She cited the correct reference.
> That is a pleasant sight.
> They sighted a whale.
> The site for the new building will be determined soon.

14. Complement, compliment

Complement means to complete, fill, or make perfect; *compliment* means to praise.

> His thorough report complemented the presentation.
> I complimented Jane on her new dress.

15. Council, counsel

Council is a noun meaning a governing body.

> The council meets today.

Counsel as a noun means advice; it also means a lawyer. *Counsel* as a verb means to advise.

> Dr. Baker's counsel helped Chris overcome her fears.
> Counsel was consulted on the case.
> He is there to counsel you.

16. Farther, further

Farther refers to distance; *further* refers to a greater degree or extent.

> The store is a mile farther down the road.
> We will discuss the matter further tomorrow.

17. Good, well

Both *good* and *well* are adjectives. *Well* is used to mean in fine health; *good* is used to mean pleasant or attractive.

> I feel well.
> She feels good about her job.

18. Its, it's

Its is the possessive form of it.

> The family had its reunion yesterday.

It's is the contraction of it is.

It's probably going to rain.

19. Percent, per cent, percentage

Percent is the correct usage; not *per cent. Percentage* is also one word and should not be used with numbers.

20. Principal, principle

Principal as an adjective means main; as a noun, it means the main person or a capital sum.

The principal actor was outstanding.
The principals in the case are present.

Principle is a noun meaning a rule, guide, truth; it never refers directly to a person.

She held steadfast to her principles.

21. Stationary, stationery

Stationary means stable or fixed; *stationery* is writing paper.

The ladder seems stationary.
Order three boxes of stationery.

22. That, which, who

Who is used to refer to persons; *which* refers to animals and inanimate objects; *that* is used to refer to animals, inanimate objects, or a classification of persons.

Mr. King is a man who has a thorough understanding of the situation.
Which animal do you mean?
The book that I read yesterday was good.

23. Who, whom

Who is used as the subject of a verb; *whom* is used as an object of a verb or preposition.

Send it to the people who asked for it.
Whom shall I ask first?
Whom did they ask to represent the president?
The person to whom I gave the information used it improperly.

PLURALS AND POSSESSIVES

1. When a compound word contains a noun and is hyphenated or made up of two or more words, the principal word takes an *s* to form

the plural. If there is no principal word, add an *s* to the end of the compound word.

> commanders in chief   runners-up
> mothers-in-law   forget-me-nots
> passersby

2. The plural of letters is formed by adding *s* or *'s*. The apostrophe is unnecessary except where confusion might result.

> CPAs
> dotting the *i*'s

3. Singular nouns form the possessive by adding *'s*. If a singular noun has two or more syllables and if the last syllable is not accented and is preceded by a sibilant sound (*s, x, z*), add only the apostrophe for ease of pronunciation.

> the secretary's typewriter   Mrs. Jones's office
> the department's rules   Ulysses' voyage

4. Plural nouns form the possessive by adding an apostrophe if the plural ends in *s* or by adding *'s* when the plural does not end in *s*.

> the boys' grades
> ladies' wear
> the children's bicycles

5. When a verb form ending in *ing* is used as a noun (gerund), a noun or pronoun before it takes the possessive form.

> Mr. Ware's talking was not anticipated.
> Their shouting disturbed me.
> I appreciate your being here today.
> We were surprised at Helen's leaving.

6. To form the possessive of a compound word, add the possessive ending to the last syllable.

> A passerby's scarf blew off.
> Her mother-in-law's gift arrived.
> The record player's needle was new.

7. Joint possession is indicated by adding the possessive ending to the last noun.

> We are near Jan and Mike's store.
> Drs. Edison and Martin's article was published this week.

8. In idiomatic construction, possessive form is often used.

> a day's work   two weeks' vacation
> two dollars' worth this month's pay

9. The possessive form is used in cases where the noun modified is not expressed.

Take it to the plumber's. (shop)
Stop at the Taylors'. (home)

10. The possessive form of personal pronouns is written without an apostrophe.

He has her book.
She will deliver yours tomorrow.
I have his and he has mine.

PROOFREADERS' MARKS

MARK	EXPLANATION	EXAMPLE
¶	Paragraph	¶Start a new paragraph here.
∧	Insert	Insert a letter h⟨e⟩re.
ℛ	Delete	Take out this extra word.
stet or - - - -	Let it stand	stet Do not delete these words.
tr or ∿	Transpose	tr Turn this around sentence.
⊏	Move to the left	⌐Move this copy to the left.
⊐	Move to the right	Move this copy to the right.
◠	Close up	Close up the extra space.
Cap or ≡	Set in capitals	cap Her name is Barbara walters.
lc or /	Set in lowercase	lc These letters Should not be Capitalized.
⊙	Insert a period	Insert a period at this point⊙
⟨"⟩ ⟨"⟩	Quotation marks	Bob said, I think Nadine is sick.
∧	Comma	Yes⟨,⟩place a comma here.
#	Insert space	Space between these two⟨#⟩words.
=/	Hyphen	They will take a three⟨=⟩day trip.
⟨3⟩	Use superior figure	Place a footnote at the end of this sentence.⟨3⟩
[/]	Brackets	[/] John⟨∧⟩the author⟨∧⟩wrote the students a letter.
⟨sp⟩	Spell out	Spell out *cents* in 23¢.
Center or]⊏	Center	CHINN-HARTWELL CORPORATION ⌐Income Statement⌐

PUNCTUATION

The Period

The period indicates a full stop and is used in the following instances:

1. At the end of a complete and declarative or imperative sentence.

2. After abbreviations and after a single or double initial that represents a word

acct.	etc.
U.S.	p.m.
Ph.D.	pp.

Some abbreviations that are made up of several capital letters do not require periods.

AAA (American Automobile Association)
YWCA (Young Women's Christian Association)

3. Between dollars and cents

$42.65 $1.47

4. To indicate a decimal figure

3.5 bushels   12.65 bushels   6.25 feet

The Comma

The comma indicates a partial stop and is used in the following instances:

1. To separate independent clauses that are connected by coordinating conjunctions, such as *and, but, or, for,* and *nor,* unless the clauses are short and closely connected

We have a supply on hand, but I think we should order an additional quantity.
She had to work late, for the auditors were examining the books.

2. To set off a subordinate clause that precedes the main clause

Assuming that there will be no changes, I suggest that you proceed with your instructions.

3. After an introductory phrase containing a verb form or an introductory adverbial phrase or clause

To finish his work, he remained at the office after hours.
After planning the program, she proceeded to put it into effect.
Because of the unusual circumstances, the president of the company addressed the assembled employees.
Although he would have preferred to stay, Peter had to leave the party long before it ended.

4. To set off a nonrestrictive adjectival phrase or clause that follows the noun

The beacon, rising proudly toward the sky, guided the pilots safely home.
Our group, which had never lost a debate, won the grand prize.

5. To separate from the rest of the sentence a word or a group of words that breaks the continuity of the sentence

John, even though his work was completed, was always willing to help others.

6. To separate parenthetical expressions from the rest of the sentence

We have, as you know, two persons who can handle the reorganization.

7. To set off names used in direct address or to set off appositives

I think you, Mr. Bennett, will agree with the statement.
Ms. Linda Tom, our vice-president, will be in your city soon.

8. To separate from the rest of the sentence expressions that, without punctuation, may be interpreted incorrectly

Misleading: Ever since we have filed our reports monthly.
Better: Ever since, we have filed our reports monthly.

9. To separate words or groups of words when they are used in a series of three or more

Most executives agree that dependability, trustworthiness, ambition, and judgment are required of their office workers.

10. To set off short direct quotations from the rest of the sentence

He said, "I shall be there."
"The committees have agreed," he said, "to work together on the project."

11. To separate geographical names and dates

Our southern branch is located in Atlanta, Georgia.
The department was divided on February 15, 1983, into three sections.

12. To separate abbreviations of titles from the name

William R. Warner, Jr.   Ramona Sanchez, Ph.D.

The Semicolon

The semicolon should be used in the following instances:

1. Between independent clauses joined by a coordinating conjunction when either or both contain internal punctuation

> He was outstanding in his knowledge of typing, shorthand, spelling, and related subjects; but he was lacking in many desirable personal qualities.

2. Between two independent, closely related clauses when the coordinating conjunction is omitted

> Many executives would rather dictate to a machine than to a secretary; the machine won't talk back.

3. To precede expressions such as *namely (viz.), for example (e.g.), that is (i.e.),* when used to introduce a clause

> We selected the machine for two reasons; namely, because it is as reasonable in price as any other and because it does better work than others. There are several reasons for changing the routine of handling mail; i.e., to reduce postage, to conserve time, and to place responsibility.

4. To separate items in a series which are long or complex or which have internal punctuation

> When the vote was tabulated, Alvarez won first place; O'Connor, second place; and Schmidt, third place.

The Colon

The colon is recommended in the following instances:

1. After the salutation in a business letter except when open punctuation is used

> Ladies and Gentlemen: Dear Ms. Carroll:

2. Following introductory expressions, such as *the following, as follows,* and other expressions that precede enumerations

> You will need the following:
>   1. A pen or pencil
>   2. An eraser
>   3. A steno pad
> The officers elected were as follows: president, Carol Scott; vice-president, Jim Kinney; and treasurer, Jill Goodman.

3. To separate hours and minutes in indicating time

> 2:10 p.m.   4:45 p.m.   12:15 a.m.

4. To introduce a long quotation

The agreement read: "We the undersigned hereby agree . . . ."

5. To separate two independent clauses or independent sentences when the second explains or expands the statement in the first

We selected the machine for one reason: in competitive tests it surpassed all other machines.

The first word of an independent sentence after a colon is capitalized when it is a long, formal statement, quotation, or a speech in dialogue.

In time, one of her favorite contentions was justified: In the long run people who are conscientious and work diligently will achieve the position for which they are best qualified.

The Question Mark

The question mark should be used in the following instances:

1. After a direct question

When do you expect to arrive in Philadelphia?

An exception to the foregoing is a request, suggestion, or command phrased as a question out of courtesy. Use a period at the end of this kind of sentence since the reader is expected to respond by taking action rather than giving a yes or no answer.

Will you please send us an up-to-date statement of our account.
Will the audience please rise.

2. After each question in a series of questions within one sentence

What is your opinion of the IBM typewriter? the Smith-Corona? the Royal? the Olympia?
Our questions are: When will you arrive? where will you stay? will you have transportation?

The Exclamation Point

The exclamation point is ordinarily used after words or groups of words that express command, strong feeling, emotion, or an exclamation.

Don't waste office supplies!
It can't be done!
Stop!

The Dash

The dash is used in the following instances:

1. To indicate an omission of letters or figures

Dear Mr. —
Date the letter July 16, 19—

2. When strong emphasis is desired

This book is not a revision of an old book—it is a completely new book.
He had spent several hours explaining the operation—an operation that
would, he hoped, put an end to the resistance.

Be careful, however, not to overdo the use of the dash.

3. To separate parenthetical expressions that have internal punctuation or when unusual emphasis on the parenthetical expression is desired

These sales arguments—and every one of them is important—should
result in getting the order.

Quotation Marks

Certain basic rules should be followed in using quotation marks.
These rules are as follows:

1. When quotation marks are used with a comma or a period, the
comma or period should be placed inside the closing quotation mark.

She said, "I plan to complete my program in college before seeking a
position."

2. When quotation marks are used with a semicolon or a colon, the
semicolon or colon should be placed outside the closing quotation
mark.

The treasurer said, "I plan to go by train"; others in the group stated
that they would go by plane.

3. With more than one paragraph of quoted material, quotation
marks should appear at the beginning of each paragraph and at the
end of the last paragraph.

"_____
_____
_____ .

"_____
_____
_____ ."

4. To indicate a quotation within a quotation, use single quotation marks.

> The author states, "Too frequent use of 'very' and 'most' weakens the appeal."

5. Quotation marks are used in the following instances:

    a. Before and after direct quotations

> The author states, "Too frequent use of certain words weakens the appeal."

    b. To indicate the title of a published article, a chapter in a book, and an individual poem, essay, or story in a volume

> Have you read the article, "Automation in the Office"?
> He asked, "Have you read 'Automation in the Office'?"

Omission Marks or Ellipsis

Ellipsis marks (. . .) are frequently used to denote the omission of letters or words in quoted material. If the material omitted comes at the end of a sentence, a period is used along with the ellipsis marks (. . . .).

> He quoted the proverb, "A soft answer turneth away wrath: . . . ."
> She quoted Plato, "Nothing is more unworthy of a wise man . . . than to have allowed more time for trifling, and useless things, then they deserved."

Parentheses

Although parentheses are frequently used as a catchall in writing, they are correctly used in the following instances:

1. When amounts expressed in words are followed by figures

> He agreed to pay twenty-five dollars ($25) as soon as possible.

2. Around words that are used in parenthetical expressions

> Our letter costs (excluding paper and postage) are much too high for this type of business.

3. To indicate technical references

> Sodium chloride (NaCl) is the chemical name for common table salt.

4. When enumerations are included in narrative form

> Here are the reasons for my resignation: (1) advanced age, (2) failing health, and (3) a desire to travel.

SPELLING

1. Put *i* before *e* except after *c* or when sounded like *a* as in *neighbor* or *weigh*.

Exceptions: either, neither, seize, weird, leisure, financier, conscience

2. When a one-syllable word ends in a single consonant and when that final consonant is preceded by a single vowel, double the final consonant before a suffix that begins with a vowel or the suffix *y*.

run	running	drop	dropped
bag	baggage	skin	skinny

3. When a word of more than one syllable ends in a single consonant, when that final consonant is preceded by a single vowel, and when the word is accented on the last syllable, double the final consonant before a suffix that begins with a vowel.

begin	beginning	concur	concurrent

When the accent does not fall on the last syllable, do not double the final consonant before a suffix that begins with a vowel.

travel	traveler	differ	differing

4. When the final consonant in a word of one or more syllables is preceded by another consonant or by two vowels, do not double the final consonant before any suffix.

look	looked	deceit	deceitful
act	acting	warm	warmly

5. Words ending in a silent *e* generally drop the *e* before a suffix that begins with a vowel.

guide	guidance	use	usable

6. Words ending in silent *e* generally retain the *e* before a suffix that begins with a consonant unless another vowel precedes the final *e*.

hate	hateful	due	duly
excite	excitement	argue	argument

7. Words ending in *ie* drop the *e* and change the *i* to *y* before adding *ing*.

lie	lying	die	dying

8. Words ending *ce* or *ge* generally retain the final *e* before the suffixes *-able* and *-ous* but drop the final *e* before the suffixes *-ible* and *-ing*.

    manage   manageable   force   forcible

9. When a word ends in *c*, insert a *k* before adding a suffix beginning with *e*, *i*, or *y*.

    picnic   picnicking

10. Words ending in *y* preceded by a consonant generally change the *y* to *i* before any suffix except one beginning with *i*.

    modify   modifying   modifier   lonely   lonelier

11. Words ending in *o* preceded by a vowel form the plural by adding *s*. Words ending in *o* preceded by a consonant generally form the plural by adding *es*.

    folio   folios   potato   potatoes

12. Words ending in *y* preceded by a vowel form the plural by adding *s*; words ending in *y* preceded by a consonant change the *y* to *i* and add *es* to form the plural.

    attorney   attorneys   lady   ladies

WORD DIVISION

1. Divide words between syllables.

    moun-tain

2. Do not divide words of five or fewer letters (preferably six or fewer).

    apple   among   finger

3. Do not divide one-syllable words.

    helped   eighth

4. If a one-letter syllable falls within a word, divide the word after the one-letter syllable.

    regu-late   sepa-rate

5. If 2 one-letter syllables occur together within a word, divide between the one-letter syllables.

    continu-ation   radi-ator

6. Divide between double consonants that appear within a word. Also, when the final consonant of a base word is doubled to add a suffix, divide between the double consonants.

    neces-sary   omit-ted

7. When a base word ends in a double consonant, divide between the base word and the suffix.

    tell-ing   careless-ness

8. Divide hyphenated compound words at existing hyphens only.

    two-thirds   self-control

9. Avoid dividing a date, personal name, or address. If it is absolutely necessary, maximize readability by doing the following:

    a. Divide a date between the day and the year.

    b. Divide a personal name between the first name and surname.

    c. Divide an address between the city and state.

10. Avoid dividing figures, abbreviations, and symbols.

    $20,000   YMCA   #109

11. Do not divide contractions.

    he'll   wouldn't

12. Divide no more than three or four words on a typewritten page.

13. Avoid dividing words at the end of the first and last lines of a paragraph.

14. Do not divide the last word on a typewritten page.

15. The first part of a divided word must contain at least two letters; the latter part must contain at least three.

    around (not a-round)
    lately (not late-ly)

INDEX

A

ABA (American Bankers Association) transit number, 329
Abstract, defined, 276
Accession book, defined and illustrated, 477
Accountable mail, defined, 251. *See* Mail
Accounting records and statements: financial statements, 337, 340; petty cash, 336
Acute stress, defined, 57
Administrative Management Society (AMS), 3, 314; job titles and secretarial positions, classified by the, 5; *Office Salaries Directory for the United States and Canada, 1983-84,* 16; simplified letter, 205
Administrative secretary, defined, 410
Advertisements, newspaper, signed and blind, illustrated, 23
Affirmative action guidelines, 115
Agenda, defined, 307; illustrated, 308
Allness, defined, 87
Almanacs and yearbooks, as reference sources, 270
Alphabetic filing, advantages and disadvantages of, 474
American Automobile Association, 369
American Express Company, 333; credit card, 372
American Management Association, 314
American Standard Code for Information Interchange (ASCII), 396
American Stock Exchange, 347
AO mail, defined, 257

Aperture card, illustrated, 527
Application for employment, 27, 31, 32
Appointments, canceling, 133; scheduling, 132, 372
Area code map, 141
Ask (price), defined, 348
Assets, defined, 337
Autocratic leadership, defined, 111
Automated typewriter equipment, evolution of, 407-409
Automatic data processing (ADP) system, defined, 386
Automobile insurance: collision and comprehensive, 354; liability, 353; uninsured motorists, 354

B

Balance sheet, illustrated, 338; terms used in the, 337
Bank draft, defined, 332
Bank money order, 332
Banking records and procedures: bank balance, reconciling the, 330; banking electronically, 334; checks, writing, 325; deposits, making, 329; special bank services, using, 331
Bar code sorter (BCS) machine, 245
Bar graph, 291
Bell, Alexander Graham, 449, 450
Bibliography, how to arrange a, 286
Bid (price), defined, 348
Bill of lading, defined, 261
Binary digits (bits), defined, 396
Bits, defined, 396
Blank endorsement, defined, 328
Blind advertisement, defined, 23
Block style letter, 205, 206

Body language, a method of nonverbal communication, 81
Body motions or gestures, communication barriers, 88
Bond, defined, 349
Bondholder, defined, 349
Buffer storage, defined, 419
Buffer (VDT), defined, 393
Bureau of National Affairs, Inc., 273
Business forms, special, 185
Business letter, appearance of, 196; parts of the, 197; styles, 205; *See* Letter parts
Business property insurance, 353
Business Week (magazine), 377
Byte, defined, 396

C

Calculating (data), defined, 387
Carbon film, defined, 184
Carbon process of reproducing copies, 427
Card reader, defined, 391
Career goals, master plan for, 20
Cashier's check, 332
Categorization, defined, 89
Cathode ray tube (CRT), 392, 532; defined, 409
Cellular technology, 458
Central processing unit (CPU), defined and illustrated, 395
Centralized dictation system, 229
Centrex system, defined, 457
Certificate of deposit, 351
Certificate of mailing, 253
Certification program of PSI, 14
Certified check, defined, 331
Certified mail, 252
Certifying Secretaries, Institute for, 14
Character (punched card), defined, 388

Checks, cashier's, 332; certified, 331; depositing, 329; endorsing, 328; writing, 325
Chronic stress, defined, 58
Chronologic method of filing, 458
Circular graph, 293; illustrated, 294
Circumference, defined, 295
Civil Rights Act of 1964, Title VII, 115, 116
Classifying (data), defined, 387
COD mail, 252
Collating and folding machines, 443
Columnar bar graph, illustrated, 292
Combination (dictation) unit, defined, 228
Commerce Clearing House, Inc., 273
Commercial papers, defined, 350
Common carrier, defined, 258; private, 259
Common message, defined, 255
Common stock, defined, 347
Communicate, defined, 74
Communication: effective, in supervision, 162; formal organizational, 109; horizontal, 110; ineffective, a time waster, 47; informal organizational, 110; organizational techniques of, 111-113
Communication barriers: allness, 87; body motions or gestures, 88; categorization, 89; evaluation, 85; inference, 87; language usage, 84; noise, 84; reducing, 89-93
Communication patterns, 77
Communication process, 79-81
Communication techniques, 54; organizational, 111
Component bar graph, illustrated, 293
Composition, a document source, 176
Computer aided retrieval (CAR), defined, 532
Computer input film (CIM), defined, 532
Computer output microfilm (COM), 398, 532

Computer services, remote, 460
Computer systems: delivering data, 396; entering data, 387; processing data internally, 395
Computerized filing systems. See Filing systems, computerized
Computers classified by size: mainframe, 399; microcomputer, 400; minicomputer, 400
Computers, impact on office and on secretary, 401
Conference, before the: meeting facilities, 314; pre-registration, 316; registration, 317; reservations, hotel and travel, 315; speakers, outside, 315; See also Conferences, Convention, Meeting, Meetings, Teleconference
Conference Board, Inc., 273
Conferences, advantages of shorthand record, 217; See Meetings
Convention, after the, 318; before the, 314; during the, 317; See also Conferences
Copying, law regarding, 443
Copying machines: categories of, 436; features of, 439; photocopying technology, 433
Copyright law, highlights of, 444
Cordless telephones, 458
Corporation minutes (of a meeting), 313
Correction tools for typing, 179
Correspondence, composition of: C's of, 194; kinds of, 191; organization of, 192; psychological patterns of, 192-193
Correspondence secretary, defined, 410
Coupon bond, defined, 349
Creativity, defined, 65
Current assets, defined, 337
Current liabilities, defined, 337
Current ratio, defined, 340

D

Daisy wheel, 397, 398

Dartnell Institute of Business Research, 208, 225
Data, delivering: computer output microfilm (COM), 398; magnetic media, 399; printers, 397; video display terminals, 399; voice response, 399
Data, entering: input devices, 390; input media, 388
Data entry, defined, 387
Data processing: defined, 385; functions of, 386; input and output, 386; systems, 385; See Computer systems
Data processing, internal: arithmetic/logic unit, 396; control unit, 396; memory unit, 395
Decision making, approach to, 61; creativity and, 65; steps in, 62
Deductions, miscellaneous payroll, 343
Demodulation, defined, 451
Deposit slip, illustrated, 329
Desktop copiers, 436
Desktop dictation equipment, 228
Diazo film, defined, 529
Dictation: conferences, taking notes at, 217; a document source, 176; preparing for, 215; speed recommended, 219; taking, 217; tips for taking, 220; See also Employer dictation, Machine dictation, Shorthand dictation, Stenographic machines
Dictation equipment: centralized dictation systems, 229; desktop units, 228; portable units, 227; recording media, 226
Dictation supplies: calendar, 219; notebook, 217; paper clips and rubber bands, 218; pens/pencils, 218
Dictionary of Occupational Titles, 472
Diet and exercise, importance of, 59
Direct approach letters, 192
Direct Distance Dialing (DDD), 140
Direct payroll depositing, 335

Discrete media, defined, 226
Discrimination, elimination of, 114-116
Disk drive (defined), 392
Disorganization, a time waster, 47
Distress, defined, 56
Divergent thinking, defined, 65
Dividend, defined, 347
Document sources, 175-177
Domestic air travel: air fares, 365; car rental, 367; flight classifications, 364; flight reservations, 365; hotel reservations, 366; limousine service, 366
Draft, defined, 261
Drawer (check), defined, 326
Drucker, Peter F., 148
Duplexing, defined, 440
Duplicating, defined, 428

E

EEOC. See Equal Employment Opportunity Commission
EFTs (electronic fund transfers), 334
Electric typewriter, 171-174
Electronic banking, 334-336
Electronic computer originated mail, 255
Electronic data processing (EDP) system, defined, 386
Electronic filing systems. See Filing system, electronic
Electronic mail, 254-256, 458-460; defined, 458
Electronic typewriters, 174
Element (typewriter), defined, 171
Elite pitch, defined, 173
Employee's Withholding Allowance Certificate (Form W-4), 342
Employer dictation, 216
Employment agencies, 24
Encoding, defined, 79
Encyclopedia of Associations, 271
Endless loop media, defined, 226
Endorsement, defined, 328; in full, defined, 328

Endorsements, checks, illustrated, 328
Envelopes: address formats, 207; addressed, illustrated, 207; automation requirements for, 244; bar code sorter (BCS) machines for, 245; interoffice, illustrated, 210; letter-sorting machines (LSM), 244; optical character recognition (OCR) equipment for, 245; sizes and shapes, Postal Service requirements, 244; standard sizes, 207; state abbreviations and ZIP Codes for, 246; ZIP Code use on, 244, 246
Environment, importance of, to productivity: physiological factors in, 117-119; safety and health hazard factors, 119
Equal Employment Act of 1972, 115-116
Equal Employment Opportunity Commission (EEOC): racial discrimination guidelines, 115; sexual harassment, criteria for, 114
Equal Pay Act, 1963, 116
Equipment insurance, 352
Equipment record, illustrated, 353
Ergonomics, defined, 117
Etiquette suggestions, 12
Etymologists, defined, 85
Evaluation (judgment), a communication barrier, 85
Evaluation of performance, 157, 158
Excise tax, defined, 345
Exercise and diet, importance of, 59
Expense report, illustrated, 378
Express mail, 249
Express shipments, 259

F

Facsimile, defined, 459
Fair Labor Standards Act, 116, 341

Fair use clause in copyright law, 444
FAX (facsimile device), defined, 442
Federal Communications Commission, 458
Federal Express, overnight service, 259
Federal income tax, 342
Federal Insurance Contribution Act (FICA), 341, 344
Fiber optics copiers, 439
Fiber optics tubing, illustrated, 452
FICA (Federal Insurance Contribution Act), 341, 344
Fields (punched card), defined, 389
File folder cuts, defined and illustrated, 515
File reel, defined, 523
Filing equipment, manual: horizontal files, 518; lateral files, 518; mobile files, 520; open shelf files, 519; vertical files, 518; visible card files, 520; wheel files, 519
Filing equipment, mechanized: motorized shelf files, 522; movable aisle systems, 521
Filing methods, basic: alphabetic, 474; chronologic, 485; geographic, 483; numeric, 475; subject, 481
Filing rules, 489
Filing supplies: folders, 515; guides, 516; labels, 517; metal tabs, 517; miscellaneous, 517; suspension folders, 515
Filing systems, computerized: applications of, 524; disk retrieval, 524; storage, 523; tape retrieval, 524
Filing systems, electronic: benefits of, 533; computer aided retrieval (CAR), 532; computer input microfilm (COM), 532; computer output microfilm (COM), 532
Filing techniques, 486-489
Final copy, a document source, 176
Financial assistance, providing, 325-354

Financial data reference books, 272

Financial statements: analysis of, 340; balance sheet, 337; income statement, 338

Finish (paper), defined, 183

First-class mail, 250

Flexibility, defined, 65

Floppy disks, defined, 389

Footnote on a report, illustrated, 285

Forbes (magazine), 377

Form W-4 (Employee's Withholding Allowance Certificate), 342

Form W-2, Wage and Tax Statement, 344

Formal meetings. *See* Meetings

Formatting, defined, 177

Fortune (magazine), 377

Fourth-class mail, 251

Franked mail, defined, 257

Freight: bills of lading, used in shipping by, 261; defined, 259; methods of shipping by, 260

G

Galley, defined, 434

Geographic method of filing, 483

Girth (mail), defined, 250

Goal, defined, 148

Goals, defining, 103

Government publications, as reference sources, 270

Grapevine, defined, 110

Graphic aids: graphs, 289-294; tables, 287

Greyhound express shipping, 259

Guide to American Directories, 271

Guide to Record Retention Requirements, 505

H

Handicapped, mail for the, 257

Handwritten copy, a document source, 175

Hard copy, defined, 397

Hardware, defined, 387

Hazards, potential office, 120

High-volume copiers, 437

Hollerith, Herman, 388

Horizontal communication, 110

Hotel and Motel Red Book, 362

I

Impact printer, defined, 397

Important records, defined, 505

Income statement defined, 338; illustrated, 339

Income Tax Procedure, 346

Index slip illustrated, 231

Indirect approach letter, 193

Inference, a communication barrier, 87

Informal meetings. *See* Meetings

Information transmission: media, 451; networks, 453

Input (data), defined, 386

Input devices, 390-394

Input media: disk pack, diskettes, 390; magnetic tape, 389; punched cards, 388

Institute for Certifying Secretaries, 14

Insurance, record of, illustrated, 354

Insurance, types of: automobile, 353; business property, 353; equipment, 352; merchandise and inventory, 352; *See also* Automobile insurance

Insured mail, 252

Intangible property tax, defined, 345

Intelligent copiers-printers, 437, 460

Interface (electronic scales and postage meters), defined, 248

International Business Machines Corporation (IBM), 171

International driving permit, 369

International mail, 257

International parcel post, 257

International shipments, freight, documents needed for, 261

International travel: car rental, 369; flights, classes of, 369; hotel reservations, 369; pass-ports, 368; travel agency services, 367; visas, 368

Interoffice envelope, illustrated, 210

Interoffice memorandum, 208, 209

Interruptions, reducing, 54

Interview, the, 33-37

Itinerary, defined, 371; illustrated, 371

Investment terminology: bonds, 349; money market, 350; record of investments, 351; stocks, 346

J

Jacquard, Joseph, 388

Jiffy (mail) bags, 258

J.K. Lasser's Your Income Tax, 346

Job, advancement on the, 39

Job analysis, 150

Job application process: application blank, 30; application letter, 26; company information, 25; interview, the, 33; personal data sheet, 28

Job description, illustrated, 151

Job information, sources of: advertisements, newspaper, 23; employment agencies, 24; friends and relatives, 22; school placement offices and instructions, 22

Job insecurity, a stress factor, 57

Job performance, evaluation of, 37

Justify (typewritten lines), defined, 173

K

Keypunch machine, defined and illustrated, 391

Key system, defined, 456

L

Language usage, a communication barrier, 84

Laser copying, 439

LC mail, defined, 257

Leadership style: questions to ask about, 161; Theory X, 160; Theory Y, 161; Theory Z, 161

Letter: annotated, 241; of application, illustrated, 27; cost of producing, 208, 225; folding a, illustrated, 198, 199; of transmitted (for a report), illustrated, 283

Letter parts: attention line, 200; body, 201; complimentary close, 202; dateline, 197; letter address, 198; notations, 203; reference initials, 203; salutation, 200; second page heading, 201; subject line, 201

Letter styles, 205; illustrated, 206

Letterhead, defined, 183

Lettering (headliner) equipment, 442

Letter-sorting machine (LSM), 244

Liabilities, defined, 337

Library, using the: abstracting articles, 276; card catalog, 274; copying material, 277; information, finding, 274; microfiche catalog, 274; notes, taking, 275; reference cards, compiling, 275

License tax, defined, 345

Log (time) analysis, 49

Long-range planning, defined, 148

Long-term investments, defined, 337

Long-term liabilities, defined, 337

Luggage, weight and size restrictions, for air travel, 369

M

Machine dictation: advantages of, 226; disadvantages of, 226; index slip, illustrated, 231; indexing or queuing feature, 231; kinds of, 226; special instructions, 231; tran-

scribing from, 231; versus shorthand dictation, 225; word processing input, 416; work organization for transcription, 232

Magnetic ink character recognition (MICR), 394

Magnetic Tape Selectric Typewriter, illustrated, 408

Mail bags (Jiffy), 258

Mail, classifications of, 249-251; international, 257; special services, 251-254

Mail, incoming: date and time stamp the, 241; log of incoming, 242; read and annotate the, 242; route the, 242; sorting, 240

Mail log, illustrated, 242

Mail, outgoing: enclosures, check for, 244; envelopes, preparing, 244; postage, determine, 247; presort the, 247; schedule, establish a, 247; See also Envelopes

Mail, special services, 251-254

Mailgrams, 254, 459, 461

Mailing privileges, special, 256

Mainframes (computers), defined, 399

Management, defined, 147

Management by objectives (MBO), defined, 148

Management responsibilities: controlling production, 157; evaluating, 157; planning and organizing operations, 147; recruiting, training, and motivating, 152

Management Review, 163

Management World, 163

Manual data processing, defined, 386

Manual typewriter, 170

Margins, for body of a report, 283; typewriter, determining, 178

Master set (spirit duplicating), defined, 428

MasterCard credit card, 372

Mat (offset), defined, 432

McGregor, Douglas, 160

Media (data), defined, 387

Medium, defined, 407

Meeting, after the: minutes,

preparing the, 310; routine follow-up duties, 312

Meeting, before the: agenda, preparation of, 307; calendar notations, making, 305; materials and equipment, arranging for, 307; notice of, 306; participants, notifying the, 305; room, preparing the, 308; room, reservation for a, 305

Meeting, during the: minutes, 309; parliamentary procedure, 310; problems, special, 309

Meetings, formal, 304; informal, 303

Merchandise and inventory insurance, 352

Merit rating, defined, 37

Method, defined, 157

MICR (magnetic ink character recognition) equipment, 394

Microcomputer, defined, 400

Microfiche, defined, 398; illustrated, 527

Microfilm, computer output (COM), 532

Microfilm packages, illustrated, 526

Microforms: aperture cards, 527; law and, 531; microfiche and ultrafiche, 526; microfilm, 525; need for, 530; use of, 531

Micrographics, defined, 525

Micrographics systems, elements of, 528

Microprocessor, defined, 400

Microwave transmission, illustrated, 453

Military mail, overseas, 256

Minicomputer, defined, 400

Minutes of a meeting, 309; corporation, 313; illustrated, 311

Mnemonic device, defined, 91

Modem, defined, 451

Modern Office Technology (periodical), 51

Modified block letter, illustrated, 205

Modulation, defined, 451

Money market, 350

Money orders, 258

Moody's Investors Service, 272

Morse Code, 449
Motivation, defined, 155
Motivation techniques, 156
Mutual fund, defined, 350

N

National Five Digit ZIP Code and Post Office Directory, 247
National Shorthand Reporters Association, 234
National Trade and Professional Associations of the U.S. and Canada and Labor Unions, 271
NCR paper, defined, 184
Negative stress, defined, 56
Networks, defined, 453
New York Stock Exchange, 347, 348
Noise, a communication barrier, 84, 118; effect on productivity, 118
Nonessential records, defined, 505
Nonimpact printers, defined, 398
Nonverbal communication, 81-84
Numeric filing method: parts of, basic, 475; procedure for, 477; variations of the, 478

O

Objective, defined, 148
Objectives, performance review of, 159
Obligations: employer's to secretary, 106-108; secretary's to employer, 104-106
Occupational Outlook Handbook, 22
Occupational Safety and Health Act, 1970 (OSHA), 119
OCR. *See* Optical character recognition
Odd-lot fee, defined, 348
Office Administration and Automation, 163
Office callers. *See* Visitors

Office correspondence. *See* Correspondence
Office operations, planning and organizing, 147-152
Office team: composition and needs of, 103; developing the, 100; factors contributing to growth of, 120
Office, The (periodical), 51
Official Airline Guide, 362
Official (government) mail, 256
Official Railway Guide, 362
Offset printing, 432
Onionskin (paper), defined, 185
On-line, defined, 532
Optical character recognition (OCR): equipment, sorting checks by, 329; machines, 245; scanner, 394; word processing input, 417
Optical mark recognition (OMR), defined, 393
Order bill of lading, defined, 261
Organization chart, illustrated, 111
Organization of work, 150
Organizing, defined, 147
Ouchi, William G., 161
Outline (of a report), defined and illustrated, 277, 278
Output (data), defined, 386
Overseas military mail, 256
Over-the-counter market (OTC), 348

P

Par value, defined, 347
Paraphrase, defined, 92
Parcel post (international), 257
Parcel post mail, 251
Parliamentary law, defined, 310
Parliamentary procedure, 310; reference sources for, 324
Participating preferred stock, defined, 347
Participative leadership, defined, 111
Passport, defined, 368
Pay-by-phone systems, 335
Payee (check), defined, 326
Payroll deductions, miscellaneous, 343

Payroll laws and deductions: deductions, other, 343; Fair Labor Standards Act, 341; federal income tax, 342; social security (FICA), 341; unemployment compensation tax, 343
PBX system, defined, 457
Penalty mail, defined, 257
Performance evaluation, 37, 157; techniques of, 158
Performance review of objectives, 159
Periodicals recommended, for a secretary, 14
Person-to-person calls, 140
Personal data sheet (résumé), defined, 28; illustrated, 29
Personal problems, a stress factor, 57
Personal property tax, defined, 345
Personalized message, defined, 255
Personnel, training, 154
Petty cash fund, defined, 336
Philatelic (stamp collecting) services, 258
Photocopying process of reproducing copy, 435
Photocopying technology: fiber optics, 439; lasers, 439; thermography, 438; xerography, 438
Phototypesetting, 433-435
Pica pitch, defined, 172
Pie chart, defined, 293; illustrated, 294
PIN (personal identification number), 335
Pitch (typewriter) defined, 172
Planning, defined, 147
Plant and equipment assets, defined, 337
Platen, defined, 172
Plot (figures in a graph), defined, 291
Point-of-sale (POS) transfers, 335
Portable dictation equipment, 227
Postal Service: automation requirements, 244; envelope size requirements, 244; letter-

sorting machine (LSM), use of, 244; optical character recognition (OCR) equipment, 245; two-letter state abbreviations, use of, 245, 246; ZIP Code, use of, 244, 246; ZIP + 4 plan, use of, 247
Postal Service and electronic mail, 254-256
Postal Service mail classifications, 249-251
Postal services, kinds of, 258
Postal union mail, 257
Preassembled carbon pack, illustrated, 427
Preferred stock, defined, 347
Pregnancy Discrimination Act, 1978, 116
Prejudice, defined, 115
Presorting mail, advantages of, 247
Primary needs of the individual, 101
Print wheel, defined, 175, 397, 398
Printer's ream, defined, 183
Priorities, setting, 46, 51
Priority mail, 250, 251
Procedures, defined, 157
Processing (data), defined, 386
Processor, defined, 528
Procrastination, defined, 48
Production, control of, 157
Professional growth, how to acquire, 13
Professional image, importance of a, 10
Professional Secretaries International (PSI), 3, 310; certification program of the, 14; chapters, 14; Code of Ethics of, 6; statement on sexual harassment, 114
Program (computer), defined, 395
Programmable, defined, 420
Proofreading documents, importance of, 177
Proofreading transcription, suggestions for, 224
Property taxes, 345
Proprietary systems, defined, 401
Protractor, defined, 295

Proxemics, defined, 83
Public relations, defined, 125
Public relations responsibilities. See also Appointments, Telephone calls, Telephone techniques, Visitors
Punctuation, mixed and open, in letters, 205; illustrated, 206

Q

Qualities, important personal, 6-8
Quick ratio, defined, 340

R

Racial discrimination, 115, 116
Radius, defined, 295
Rag content (paper), defined, 182
Reader-printer, defined, 530
Real Estate Guide, 273
Real property tax, defined, 345
Recall of mail, 253
Record (input media), defined, 390
Recording (data), defined, 386
Recording dictation equipment, 226
Records management careers: records center clerk, 472; records center supervisor, 473; records management analyst, 472
Records management, need for, 470
Records management, trends in, 534
Records retrieval, manual: follow-up procedures, 503; misplaced records, 504; requisition and charge-out, 501
Records transfer and storage: disposal control, 507; retention control, 505; transfer control, 506
Recruiting employees, 152
Reference cards, compiling, 275
Reference sources: almanacs and yearbooks, 270; atlases,

270; biographic references, 271; dictionaries, 268; directories (city, business, trade and professional), 271; financial data, 272; government publications, 270; guides, 272; indexes, various, 272; secretarial handbooks, 273; subscription information services, 273
Registered bond, defined, 349
Registered mail, 251
Remote computer services, 460
Report, parts of the: bibliography, 286; body, 282; contents, table of, 282; first page of unbound report, illustrated, 284; footnote, illustrated, 285; letter of transmittal, 280; margin settings for body, 283; title page, 279
Reporting (data), defined, 387
Reports, preparing: graphic aids, 286; outline, the, 277; parts of the report, 279; rough draft, 278; tables, 287
Reproducing copy, methods of: carbon process, 427; offset and phototypesetting processes, 432; photocopying process, 435; spirit and stencil processes, 428
Reprographics: ancillary reprographics equipment, 442; copying machines, 435; defined, 426; law regarding copying, 443; reproducing copy, methods of, 434. See also Copying machines; Reproducing copy, methods of; Reprographics equipment
Reprographics equipment: collating and folding machines, 443; facsimile machines, 442; lettering equipment (headliners), 442
Restrictive endorsement, defined, 328
Résumé (personal data sheet), illustrated, 29
Right of Privacy Act, 444
Roget's International Thesaurus, 269

Role ambiguity, a stress factor, 56
Rough draft, a document source, 176; of a report, 278
Routing slip, illustrated, 243

S

Safe-deposit box, defined, 333
Sales tax, defined, 345
Schedule: daily, establishing a, 50; weekly, maintaining a, 51
School placement offices and instructors, sources of job information, 22
Seat on the exchange, defined, 347
Second-class mail, 250
Secretarial duties, summary of, 4
Secretarial duties when employer returns from a trip: correspondence, 379; expense report, 378
Secretarial handbooks, recommended, 273, 274; specialized, for professional offices, 274
Secretarial position, applying for a, 20-37
Secretarial responsibilities for employer's trip: appointment schedule, 372; appointments, confirming for trip, 374; calendar, checking the, 373; items to assemble for trip, 374; itinerary, preparing an, 370; materials, preparing for the trip, 373; matters, handling, during employer's absence, 374; reservations, making, 370; travel funds, obtaining, 372; trip, planning the, 370
Secretarial responsibilities while employer away: appointments, setting up, 376; correspondence, handling, 375; decisions, making, 375; mail, keeping a record of, 375; time, using wisely, 377; visitors and telephone calls, keeping a record of, 376

Secretarial stress. See Stress
Secretarial tasks, distribution of, 410
Secretarial title. See Secretary
Secretary: administrative, defined, 410; correspondence, defined, 410; duties of, 4; employment opportunities for, 2; etiquette suggestions for a professional, 12; job titles and positions, AMS description of, 5; periodicals, recommended, for a, 14; professional growth, need for, 13, 14; professional image, need to project a, 10, 11; qualities, important personal, of a, 6-8; salary information for a, 16; skills needed by a, 8-10; title of, defined, 3; in today's office, 15; word processing, impact on the, 410
Secretary/co-worker relationships, 108
Secretary, The (periodical), 51
Securities, defined, 350
Self-concept: and communication, 74-81; development, 75; strengtheners, 77
Sender's Application for Recall of Mail, 253
Sequential access, defined, 390
Serial printing, defined, 397
Serving Post Offices (SPOs), defined, 255
Sexual harassment, 114, 116
Shipping services, types of: express, 259; freight, 259; international, 261
Sholes, Christopher, 170
Shorthand dictation: advantages of, 226; conferences, 217; disadvantages of, 226; employer, 216; longhand used during, 219; notes and reminders, 217; questions during, 219; speed, 219; telephone messages, 217; tips for taking, 220; as word processing input, 416. See Machine dictation; Shorthand transcription; Stenographic machines, operating

Shorthand notes, suggestions for transcribing, 223
Shorthand transcription: dictation, 222; notes, editing, 221; priorities, set, 221; supplies, preparation of, 221; transcription, proofread, 222; work, submitting completed, 224
Short-range planning, defined, 148
Signed advertisement, defined, 23
Skills, necessary secretarial, 8-10
Social needs of the individual, 101
Social Security Act, 341, 342
Socializing, a time waster, 47
Soft copy, defined, 399
Software, 387, 401
Sorting (data), defined, 387
Source data, defined, 387
Source data automation, defined, 393
Sources of documents. See Document sources
Space, a nonverbal communicator, 80
Span of control, defined, 150
Special delivery mail, 252
Spirit duplicating, 428
Standard and Poor's Corporation, 273; various publications of, 273
Station (key-to-disk device), defined, 392
Station-to-station calls, 140
Stationery, varieties of, 182-185
Stencil (duplicating), defined, 181, 430; illustrated, 430-432
Stenographic machines, 232; certification of proficiency in, 234; fields requiring, 234
Stock, defined, 346; exchanges, 347; kinds of, 347; over-the-counter market, 348; quotations, 348
Stock exchange, defined, 347
Stock quotations, illustrated, 349
Stockholders' equity, defined, 337
Straight bill of lading, defined, 261

Stress: contributing factors to, 56; coping with, 59; cost of, 58; defined, 55; negative, 56; types of, 57

Stylus, defined, 430

Subject method of filing, 481-483

Substance (paper) defined, 183

Summarizing (data), defined, 387

Supervising secretary, qualities of a: communication, effective at, 162; continuous learning, 163; flexibility, 162; leadership styles, knowledge of, 160

Supervision of employees, by high-level secretary, 147-163

Supervisor's control monitor, defined, 230

Supply reel, defined, 523

System, defined, 157

T

Tact, defined, 108

Tape drive (defined), 392

Tax returns: income and deductions, records of, 344; tax information references, 346; tax records, 344-345; typing of, 346

Telecommunications: defined, 449; equipment and systems, 454; historical perspective, 449; information transmission, 451; society, impact on, 463. See also Electronic mail; Information transmission; Teleconference; Telecommunications equipment and systems; Telephone

Telecommunications equipment and systems: electronic mail, 458; teleconference, 461; telephone, 454; voice mail, 461

Teleconference, 319, 462; audio conference, 462; audio-plus-graphics conference, 462; computer conference, 463; defined, 320, 462; video conference, 463

Telecopiers, defined, 442

Telegrams, 459

Telephone, the: cellular technology, 458; multiline, 455; single line, 455; switching systems, 456

Telephone calls: incoming, 138; long-distance, 140; outgoing, 139; time differences, 140

Telephone callers, 133

Telephone messages, 216

Telephone techniques, 134-138

Teletext, defined, 465

Telex/TWX, 459

Territoriality, defined, 83

Text editing, defined, 406

Thank you letter for interview, 38

Theory X, 160

Theory Y, 161

Theory Z, 161

Thermography, 433

Third-class mail, 251

Tickler file, defined and illustrated, 50

Time inventory, 49

Time log preparation, 49

Time management, 44-49; techniques, effective, for, 50-55

Time misconceptions, 45

Time, a nonverbal communicator, 82; unique resource, 45

Time-sharing, defined, 460

Time/stress management, ripple effect of, illustrated, 66

Time wasters, 47

Time zone map, United States, 141

Title VII, Civil Rights Act of 1964, 115, 116

Toner, defined, 439

Training personnel, 154

Transceivers, defined, 442

Transcribing shorthand notes, suggestions for, 223

Transcription. See Shorthand transcription

Travel arrangements: by the secretary, 363; rights and responsibilities of travelers, 363; by travel agencies, 363; by travel department, 362

Travel, methods of, 361. See Domestic air travel, International travel

Traveler's check, defined, 333

Two-letter state abbreviations, 245, 246

Typewriter, evaluation of the: manual, 170; electric, 171; electronic, 174

Typewriting supplies: business forms, 185; correction tools, 179; ribbons, 181; stationery, 182

Typewriting techniques: formatting, 177; machine parts, learning, 177

Typing font, defined, 172

U

Ultrafiche, illustrated, 527

Unemployment compensation tax, 343

Uniform Photographic Copies of Business Records Act, 531

United Parcel Service (UPS), 259

United States Department of Labor, 153

United States Employment Service, 153

Universal Product Code, 394

Unlisted (stocks), defined, 348

Useful records, defined, 505

V

Values: clarification of, 60; defined, 101; importance of, in decision making, 61

Variable message, defined, 255

Vesicular film, defined, 529

Video display terminal (VDT), 393, 399; illustrated, 409

Videotex, defined, 464

Videotex/teletext, 464; use in banking, education, shopping, 465

Visa, defined, 368

VISA credit card, 372

Visitor register, illustrated, 128

Visitors: difficult, 131; employer's preferences regarding, 126; greeting, 126; interruptions, handling, 130; intro-

ductions, 129; receiving, 127; register of, 128; remembering names and faces, 129; waiting, 130
Visualization, defined, 60
Vital records, defined, 505
Voice mail, 461
Voice quality, a form of nonverbal communication, 82
Voice response computer communication, 399
Volatile (in word processing), defined, 418
Voucher checks, defined, 326

W

Wage and Hour Act, 341
Watermark, defined, 182
Webster's New Dictionary of Synonyms, 269
Who's Who in . . ., various biographical reference books, 271, 272

Wide Area Telecommunications Service (WATS), 140
Word and date processing, integration of, 421
Word management, defined, 230
Word originator, user, principal, defined, 407
Word processing: automated typewriting equipment, evolution of, 407; career opportunities in, 111; center, defined, 412; components of WP systems, 415; concept of, 407; defined, 406; environment for, 412; impact on secretary, 410; integration of word and data processing, 421; structures, various, 412-415
Word processing equipment: electronic typewriters, 418; multistation systems, 420; standalone word processors, 418
Word processing systems, components of: input, 416; output, 421; processing 418

Word processor, defined, 418
Word processors, communicating, 459
Work management, advantages of, 66
Work organization, 150
Work periods, defined, 150
Work station, organizing a, 51-54
Work overload, a stress factor, 57
Working conditions and relationships, stress factors, 57

X

Xerography, defined, 439

Z

ZIP Codes, use of, 244, 245, 246
ZIP + 4 plan, 247